PALGRAVE STUDIES IN THEATRE AND PERFORMANCE HISTORY is a series devoted to the best of theatre/performance scholarship currently available, accessible, and free of jargon. It strives to include a wide range of topics, from the more traditional to those performance forms that in recent years have helped broaden the understanding of what theatre as a category might include (from variety forms as diverse as the circus and burlesque to street buskers, stage magic, and musical theatre, among many others). Although historical, critical, or analytical studies are of special interest, more theoretical projects, if not the dominant thrust of a study, but utilized as important underpinning or as a historiographical or analytical method of exploration, are also of interest. Textual studies of drama or other types of less traditional performance texts are also germane to the series if placed in their cultural, historical, social, or political and economic context. There is no geographical focus for this series and works of excellence of a diverse and international nature, including comparative studies, are sought.

The editor of the series is Don B. Wilmeth (EMERITUS, Brown University), PhD, University of Illinois, who brings to the series over a dozen years as editor of a book series on American theatre and drama, in addition to his own extensive experience as an editor of books and journals. He is the author of several award-winning books and has received numerous career achievement awards, including one for sustained excellence in editing from the Association for Theatre in Higher Education.

Also in the series:

The Group Theatre

Passion, Politics, and Performance in the Depression Era

Helen Krich Chinoy

Edited by
Don B. Wilmeth and Milly S. Barranger

palgrave
macmillan

THE GROUP THEATRE
Copyright © Helen Krich Chinoy, 2013.

First published in 2013 by
PALGRAVE MACMILLAN®
in the United States—a division of St. Martin's Press LLC,
175 Fifth Avenue, New York, NY 10010.

Where this book is distributed in the UK, Europe and the rest of the world,
this is by Palgrave Macmillan, a division of Macmillan Publishers Limited,
registered in England, company number 785998, of Houndmills,
Basingstoke, Hampshire RG21 6XS.

Palgrave Macmillan is the global academic imprint of the above companies
and has companies and representatives throughout the world.

Palgrave® and Macmillan® are registered trademarks in the United States,
the United Kingdom, Europe and other countries.

ISBN: 978–1–137–29459–3

Library of Congress Cataloging-in-Publication Data is available from the
Library of Congress.

A catalogue record of the book is available from the British Library.

Design by Newgen Knowledge Works (P) Ltd., Chennai, India.

First edition: October 2013

10 9 8 7 6 5 4 3 2 1

Printed in the United States of America.

*To my children and grandchildren, and
in memory of my husband Ely Chinoy.
Helen Krich Chinoy*

Contents ❧

Illustrations ❧

Cover and Frontispiece. Eight Group Theatre productions found on the program cover for Irwin Shaw's *The Gentle People*, February 6, 1939

Following page 164

THE PLAYBILL

"THE HOUSE OF CONNELLY"
By PAUL GREEN

"SUCCESS STORY"
By JOHN HOWARD LAWSON

"MEN IN WHITE"
By
SIDNEY KINGSLEY

"AWAKE AND SING"
By CLIFFORD ODETS

GROUP THEATRE PRODUCTIONS

"WAITING FOR LEFTY"
By CLIFFORD ODETS

"PARADISE LOST"
By CLIFFORD ODETS

"GOLDEN BOY"
By CLIFFORD ODETS

"JOHNNY JOHNSON"
By PAUL GREEN

BELASCO THEATRE

Eight Group Theatre productions found on the program cover for Irwin Shaw's *The Gentle People*, February 6, 1939. All rights reserved by PLAYBILL, Inc., and used by permission. Photos by Alfredo Valente and used by permission of the Valente estate. From the Program in the collection of Don. B. Wilmeth.

Preface ⟨℘⟩

The late Helen Krich Chinoy (1922–2010), born to Ukrainian immigrants in Newark, NJ, became one of our most distinguished American theater scholars and devoted over three decades to her study of the Group Theatre. This was a natural extension of a number of earlier projects, including the seminal *Actors on Acting* (1949) and *Directors on Directing* (1953), both still in print and coedited with Toby Cole (a theater agent and Helen's sister-in-law), and the pilot project of Group Theatre interviews, which preceded and formed the nucleus of the manuscript she left behind and which forms the heart of her history. These interviews began as a unique feature of the annual meeting of what was then the American Theatre Association on August 12, 1974, in Minneapolis, MN. This session, which featured pioneers Harold Clurman, Morris Carnovsky, and Robert Lewis, was the first step toward a larger reunion of Group members.

For the next two years Helen sought out other Group participants and added their voices to those of the original three contributors in Minneapolis. These theater artists also made available to Helen source material that became part of her version of their story. The edited collection of her interviews first appeared in the *Educational Theatre Journal* (December 1976) as *Reunion: A Self-Portrait of the Group Theatre* and was then reprinted as a special publication with the same title. Both publications included transcripts of key interviews with 14 Group participants, notably Clurman, Stella Adler, Cheryl Crawford, Mordecai Gorelik, Elia Kazan, Bobby Lewis, Clifford Odets, and Lee Strasberg. As a consultant for an American Masters episode on the Group (1989), Helen was involved with additional conversations with Group members.

These various interviews were all key to her strategy for writing what she envisioned as a "collective biography of the Group Theatre." The final result was more than a series of biographies, though whenever possible she tried to tell her version of the Group's history through the words of those who lived its story. Chinoy became so closely identified with this project through her research, lectures, and essays published in various journals that many believed she had been there! As Helen often confessed, she was too young to be a player in that historical moment. She candidly stated on a number of occasions that, like the Federal Theatre Project, she "missed that experience," although "bitten by the theatre bug." She noted that she had "to dip into her 'Golden Box' for an emotional memory to fill out what life was like when the crash came and the Group was founded." She recalled "as a little girl crying in [her] bedroom when I overheard my father worrying about losing his job." "I still remember," she later wrote, "the fear, even though true to the immigrant's American dream, he vowed to go door-to-door selling things to support the family."

Before Helen could complete her Group Theatre narrative, she felt that first she had to complete (with Linda Walsh Jenkins) a new edition of *Women in American Theatre*, the pioneer collection of essays, interviews, and other accounts of women's contributions to our theater as actresses, directors, playwrights, designers, and so forth, originally published in 1981. This new edition appeared in 2005, her final published project—until now. The onset of Alzheimer's prevented her from completing her Group Theatre history, though she did leave drafts of most chapters; those that were missing or incomplete were of peripheral significance (e.g., chapters on the Group's legacy and the careers of Group members in film).

In addition to her scholarship and writing, Chinoy's many contributions included a three-decade teaching career at Smith College (retiring in 1987). Her years in academe were noteworthy for her vigorous efforts on behalf of women (significantly, she includes in her history a chapter on the women in the Group), and, as one colleague stated, her contributions that "stretched the boundaries of theatre to include topics and perspectives previously ignored." With the enthusiastic support of her husband, Ely Chinoy (they married in 1948), a Smith sociologist, Helen worked earnestly on her Group Theatre efforts. Ely died in a tragic automobile accident in 1975. Helen wrote in her introduction to *Reunion* that "working on the Group Theatre and with its members, whose vision we both deeply admired, sustained me in the most difficult year of my life."

She dedicated the reprinted version of *Reunion* to Ely and, as editors of her work, we believe she would have wanted this expanded effort to be also dedicated to his memory—and to her children, Claire and Mike, who first offered us the opportunity to edit Helen's wonderfully sensitive and often evocative prose and then were instrumental in supporting our efforts to see their mother's crowning effort in print.

As friends and professional colleagues of Helen Chinoy, we should confess that there were large challenges in this effort: the manuscript was longer than our publisher's contractual agreement allowed and, as explained in our Note on Sources, Helen did not include with her drafts of chapters details as to sources and documentation. We have attempted to provide some guidance as to both in her text and in a selected bibliography; all sources in parentheses within the text were added by the editors, and information in brackets is provided by us as well. But we have not tried to retrace her extensive research. Similarly, in our deletion of portions of the text (again, because of length) we have tried to be faithful to Helen's objectives and to her masterful telling of the Group Theatre's story.

In a précis to a 1988 talk in Paris on the legacy of the Group Theatre, Chinoy wrote of the experience of those in this collective: "...something uniquely rewarding held them together. Afraid to lie, they created out of their innermost impulses, but the personal was informed by a large idea that was aesthetic, social, and political. It was 'a great life experience,' a 'spiritual home,' a 'close-knit family,' 'an oasis within the city,' a 'utopia.' No wonder the Group Theatre has been called 'the bravest and single most significant experiment in the history of American theatre.'" Chinoy takes us through this experience as only she could with her compelling voice and her vivid reexamination of the Group Theatre's amazing decade.

Acknowledgments ✑

As indicated earlier, this project owes much to the publication by the American Theatre Association in 1976 of *Reunion*. We are happy to acknowledge the editor of that publication, Virginia Scott, also a good friend and supporter of our work on Helen's final manuscript. From that early effort, we are pleased to reiterate the names of those she recognized then as instrumental in obtaining and publishing the interviews: Harold Clurman, Cheryl Crawford, Vera Mowry Roberts, Robert Lewis, Morris Carnovsky, Phoebe Brand, Mordecai Gorelik, Ralph Steiner, Arthur Wagner, Attilio Favorini, George Bogusch, Thomas O'Connell, Sally Donohue, Erica Bianci-Jones, Greg Jones, Toby Cole, Aron Krich (Helen's brother), and her late husband Ely Chinoy. Many of these supporters of Helen's effort are now gone but nonetheless deserve to be remembered.

In the later stages of her effort we would add the following to this list: Marlene Wong and staff at the Werner Josten Library at Smith College; Ellen Kaplan, chair of the theatre department at Smith, and her colleagues (in particular Kiki Smith) who supported the efforts of the editors and helped obtain subvention for photographic and permission costs; Nanci Young of the Smith Archive who made available Helen's relevant files from that repository; Joan Kramer and Joanne Woodward, producer and narrator of "Broadway Dreamers," the 1989 PBS documentary on the Group Theatre, with whom Helen worked as consultant; local friends and colleagues Marcia Burick and Peter and Hedy Rose. We know there were others who read and commented on Helen's work but unfortunately names of these individuals have not been found, but we gratefully acknowledge these anonymous efforts, and all those who over decades encouraged Helen to complete her study of the Group.

For the book's cover we are grateful to PLAYBILL, Inc. for permission to reproduce the Group Theatre program cover for Irwin Shaw's *The Gentle People* in early 1939. Interior photographs were generously made available from the Group Theatre Collection with the assistance of Jeremy Megraw, Photograph Librarian at the New York Public Library for the Performing Arts, Lincoln Center, and Tom Lisanti, permissions director, of the New York Public Library.

The editors are of course indebted to each of the aforementioned. In addition, we would like to single out Helen's son and daughter, Michael and Claire Nicole. Without their support, suggestions, and encouragement we simply could not have completed our task. Thanks to Jennifer Lee of the Columbia University Library. We are also indebted to our press editor at Palgrave Macmillan, Robyn Curtis, who has similarly inspired every step in this process and persuaded superiors at Palgrave to be generous toward our pleas for more words and time to complete our tasks. Our families and friends have likewise unstintingly supported this labor of love.

DBW & MSB

Introduction: A Cautionary Tale ✌

With Elia Kazan and Robert ("Bobby") Lewis looking on, Harold Clurman quietly locked the door of the Group Theatre's office in New York's Sardi Building on Forty-fourth Street for the last time. On this grim day in the spring of 1941, they wondered if anybody cared. The hopes, aspirations, and accomplishments nurtured during the extraordinary Depression decade were laid to waste. They were losing their creative home, their safe haven. (Clurman, "Group Theatre's Future")

Adrift in a world where war was raging in Europe, and, six months later, the disaster would overwhelm the United States at Pearl Harbor, the Group members had to find a new basis for their lives. In later years, many of these talented artists would become big names in the American theater—acting gurus Stella Adler, Sanford Meisner, and Lee Strasberg; producer Cheryl Crawford; directors of stage and screen Elia Kazan, Robert Lewis, Martin Ritt; actors Morris Carnovsky, Lee J. Cobb, Frances Farmer, John Garfield, and the triple-threat director, critic, teacher Harold Clurman—to name only a few of the best known. For all of them, the days of the Group Theatre remained the defining experience of their lives.

In the history of American theater, the Group Theatre holds a special place. Chalk it up in part to Harold Clurman's *The Fervent Years: The Group Theatre and the Thirties*, still in print in a 1983 edition. No company has been more fortunate in having its story told by one of its founders than the Group. Published first in 1945, *The Fervent Years* has taken its place as a seminal account of the life of a theater. Clurman's vivid narrative of young artists determined to change themselves, the theater, and society during the Great Depression is inspirational, although today it may seem a romance of long ago—a paradise of the 1930s. It stirs nostalgia for a time that looks simpler, more unified, more hopeful than the confusion, fragmentation, and impotence sensed at the close of the last millennium.

Yet, more than a sense of romance or nostalgia links us to this theater of the past. Much has gotten in the way of our full appreciation and understanding of the Group and the cultural life of the 1930s, namely, hot and cold wars, congressional investigations and industry blacklists, the prosperity and success of many of the participants. Nevertheless, American theater has deep but often hidden roots in this dynamic decade that rediscovered an idea of theater along with an enlarged sense of political life and a method for sharing a widely held message. Because the Group Theatre was actively engaged in the artistic and political conflicts of a troubled era, its work is often denigrated as limited, dated, relevant only to the 1930s. Yet, it was the belief that engagement with their own time must involve, as Clurman put it, "the discovery of those methods that would most truly convey this life though theatre" that gave the Group its distinction and remains the task for today. "In 1931 we began to ask what is it all about?" Clurman recalled. "Our feeling was let's answer all questions honestly and sincerely in terms of our own life. Let's find out what life's all about. What our art is all about. How does the Stanislavsky method affect us? There's a Depression. How does it affect us? It is important. All the questions were to be answered anew."

Many of the questions about art and society that the Group confronted during the Great Depression challenged us again at the end of the twentieth century with great urgency. Although the varied performances of the company, the intense craft classes, the endless meetings and debates, and manifestoes on art and politics may not have changed the world as they hoped, nevertheless, their successes as well as their disappointments did change forever what theater could mean for members of the Group and for subsequent generations of theater lovers.

The Great Depression was the catalyst for the transformation of our nation in the 1930s. Like the American Civil War, the only comparable crisis, the Depression destroyed the very fabric of public and private life. It seemed necessary to scrutinize oneself and one's society and to join with the rest of suffering humanity to fight for radical change. Realigning the self and society was the "crucial task" of the 1930s, its intellectual historians tell us. For art and artists this break with the past opened up new possibilities. Gertrude Stein's "lost" generation artists of the 1920s returned from exile in Paris to face the breadlines, Hoovervilles (or shanty towns built by the homeless on America's streets and named for then-US president Herbert Hoover), and bank failures that resulted from the stock market crash of 1929. Instead of succumbing to despair, however, many converted themselves into members of the "found" generation as they espoused the need for collective responsibility to replace the ruthless individualism that had been touted as the American way of life. As the Depression shattered the notion that the individual or art could be autonomous, the search for an alternative vision became an exciting challenge. Many groups set forth in a spirit of discovery, rethinking every aspect of art and society. Like Enrico Caruso on the recording that so moved the radical grandfather Jacob in Odets's *Awake and Sing!*, they discerned a new land: "a Utopia…Oh Paradise on earth!"

The founding members of the Group Theatre were uniquely qualified for the adventure. Most of them had started out in those lively theaters of the 1920s—the Provincetown Players, the Theatre Guild, even the "revolting" New Playwrights Theatre—that brought a new sophistication, maturity, and depth to American theater. Nevertheless, they felt that something basic was missing in the "culture of abundance": the Provincetown Players' productions were often badly acted, the Theatre Guild had fine actors and plays but no deep convictions about American life, and the New Playwrights Theatre had convictions but no effective creative process to communicate their vision. (Reinelt, *Crucible of Crisis*, 1–2)

The Group Theatre founders had read the books written in the 1920s that proselytized for a new spirit in drama and art and thrilled to the international performances available on Broadway, especially the magic of Eleonora Duse and the rich reality of the Moscow Art Theatre. Studying with Konstantin Stanislavsky's disciples, Richard Boleslavsky and Maria Ouspenskaya, and reading the new depth psychology of Sigmund Freud had emboldened Lee Strasberg to test a method of acting that would become the basis of all their work, administrative jobs with the Theatre Guild had given Cheryl Crawford organizational know-how, and spokesman Harold Clurman possessed the ideas and passion to bond them together as a group with something to say about the world in which they were living.

When Clurman vehemently declared in the spring of 1931, as he, Strasberg, and Crawford were organizing the Group, that "America has as yet no Theatre," he challenged the theatrical establishment they had known. Although close to two hundred shows were on Broadway's stages that year, including such notable successes as George and Ira Gershwin's *Of Thee I Sing*, the first musical to win a Pulitzer Prize, and Eugene O'Neill's trilogy *Mourning Becomes Electra*, critics complained about untalented playwrights, vain actors, money-grubbing managers who cared little about art and set ticket prices too high. The perceptive young Clurman thought these perennial protests about what's wrong with the fabulous invalid totally beside the point. "Nothing can be wrong with the theatre," he said, "where no Theatre exists" (*Drama*, April 1931).

Today the indictments of a greatly diminished Broadway theater are much the same as the complaints of over 80 years ago, and the brave ventures Off and Off Off Broadway and in the regional theaters have not changed the basic problem. Clurman's rejoinder is more pertinent than ever. We still do not have a theater in our country—certainly not one that corresponds to the utopian project envisioned in the Great Depression. Challenging the American antipathy to ideas, especially in show business, the Group dared to build their theater on an Idea that linked individual and group, art and society.

Long before our current fascination with *performance* as a favored metaphor for the construction of social reality, the Group theorized true theater and good social order as very similar models of human interaction. Clurman liked to elaborate to his cronies the notion that both theater and society are group functions that call for discipline, morality, and leadership based on consent, sacrifice for the common need, and self-realization through the unit of which each one is part. "The theatre with its interrelation of elements," he wrote, "shows us something of what society needs, and a study of society may lead us to see what the theatre needs or...what the theatre can be." In this configuration the actor is not an isolated individual but a member of a group whose experiences and common feelings, shared by the larger society of which they are a part, become the content of theatrical performance. Conceived as a social crucible, their idea of theater embraced more than self-expression, aesthetics, or ideology. They envisioned artists and audiences, together, creating an intensely personal work of art that was at the same time a communal "cultural unit."

Clurman's early ruminations on theater were hardly the usual show-business chatter. No wonder it was rumored that a college-level exam was required to become a member of the Group! But Clurman had an uncanny ability to translate these basic insights into the inspirational "Group Idea" that finally brought their new theater into existence. During some six months of passionate talks in the winter of 1930–31, Clurman managed to elucidate technical points about the individual actor, the ensemble, the director, the playwright, the audience, and the organization

in the light of a vague but all-encompassing vision of a theater reflecting and affect-
ing the life of the time. Together, he, Crawford, and Strasberg identified from
among the many young Broadway professionals who came to listen to him, those
in sympathy with their views and capable of personal and creative development. No
"finished actors" were wanted (*Reunion*, 481). For those who were moved to commit
themselves to Clurman's demanding vision, his talks marked the turning point of
their lives. With their Chosen Ones and their Idea, the Group launched a ten-year
investigation into the nature of theater, the most sustained and all-embracing ever
undertaken in America.

LARGE THEMES

To build a theater rather than just put on shows, Group members subjected every
aspect of their art and society to intense investigation. In their ambitious, self-conscious undertaking, they viewed each choice, each crisis, each opportunity from two
perspectives—*performance* and *politics*.

It is around these two themes that I have structured my book, aware that what
engaged the Group has reemerged as major concerns of theater today. The Group
members endlessly debated the relationship of their art to their idea of theater
and the needs of society. But, unlike the postmodernists, who theorize the total
interdependence of performance and politics in almost every discourse, the Group
compartmentalized the interaction of these often "contested" concepts. There was
performance, their special approach to acting and the stage, and there was politics,
the radical activism that impinged on their creative and organizational choices and
on the larger world beyond their theater. Each activity had a trajectory of its own,
and, during their ten-year history, the members discovered the complex interaction
of politics and performance in their theater.

I explore performance and politics in separate sections of this book in order to
reveal the evolution of the Group's concerns in the rich historical detail of the ongoing life of the company. Although theory may have propelled the Group's overall
direction, the members were not humorless idealists or wild-eyed radicals, as they
were sometimes characterized as being. They were young, talented, ambitious, and
their days and nights were full of music, laughter, sex, and late-night binges or
glasses of tea even while taking their method and their message very seriously. I have
tried to capture, often in their own words, the varied, often clashing strands of their
sometimes "grotesque" but passionate dedication.

What animated the Group actors was a deep desire to grow as serious performers
in ways not possible in the professional theater. Rehearsing with Lee Strasberg in a
totally new process was thrilling even if sometimes painful. This talented gathering
of strangers attempted to forge the ensemble and permanent company that Clurman
envisioned. They had the courage to submit themselves to a collective discipline in
order to gain what actors who risk so much to tell us something about ourselves long
for but almost never achieve: a method of creation, a bit of security, continuity of
work, a shared artistic and social purpose, a family, and a creative home.

The Group's experiment in theater and living became more than a rejection
of Broadway's commercialism. Part of the growing revolt against the chaotic,

individualistic, capitalistic basis of American life that was disintegrating around them was the beginning of a viable alternative approach to theater. Whatever the difficulties the Group members faced in fully carrying out their plans, and however different the 1990s are from the 1930s, their aspirations and practice have contributed significantly to the ongoing pursuit of a meaningful idea of theater in our country. The Group evolved a method of acting that challenged the individualistic, intuitive process that was considered the American approach. Lee Strasberg instructed the actors in a version of the Stanislavsky system modified by Richard Boleslavsky and his own, very 1920s fascination with the newly popular theories of Sigmund Freud. The famous exercises, as taught by Strasberg, were central to an ordered training of imagination, emotion, and inspiration. They were explored in rehearsals, where "taking a minute" to dip into the "Golden Box" of emotional preparation was part of the collective process of the ensemble, and in classes, which Strasberg, ever the teacher, valued even more than productions. He taught them to reject the hegemony of literature in theater, insisting that only what was done on stage was meaningful and that "the manner in which a play is done is in itself a content" (*FY,* 11). Every detail of enactment in the scenic space was significant. In spite of his own intimidating authoritarian style, in this decade of the "little man," Strasberg empowered the actors by making them aware of themselves, of their senses, their minds, their subjectivity.

With the company of actors as the creative core, the Group shifted the basis of production from the text to performance and from the creative power of individual writers and actors to a company of players led by their directors. The willingness of the members to give themselves to the collective journey initiated by the founders is the "subtext," the underpinning of their productions, their personal relationships, and their organizational structure. Admittedly, it was a unique, but not a clearly defined commitment, and, like many others, became an ongoing source of controversy. Were they a family, an ideological collective, or an exploitative business? The obligations of the individual to the group and the group to the individual were often issues of acrimonious debate as was the relationship among the three directors and between the directors and the company.

Although collectivism was a distinguishing mark of this decade that organized workers, tenants, and the unemployed in new unions, put artists on the government's payroll, and introduced social security, the American dream of individual success still exerted a powerful attraction. Theirs was one of many "balancing acts" that distinguished the decade. These talented artists wanted to have all that the Group ideal promised, and, as it became possible, they also wanted commercial success on Broadway and in Hollywood. Clurman called it the American "dementia," or "the tragedy of choice."

The largely middle-class professionals of the Group stood positioned between the Broadway theater where they had made their home and the burgeoning workers' theater movement of the 1930s. The radical activists of the Workers' Drama League, later called the New Theatre League, went further than the Group in abandoning what they considered the bourgeois aesthetic of the literary text with its linear plot, psychological exploration of character, proscenium stage, and business ethic. Nevertheless, their ideological practices and their Marxist theories influenced individual Group members and the organization as a whole more than Clurman's somewhat sanitized narrative in *The Fervent Years* suggests, written as it was in the 1940s at the beginning of the anticommunist crusade. The Group's greatest notoriety would derive from revelations during the investigations of the US House Committee on Un-American Activities (HUAC) in the 1950s that some members comprised a secret Communist Party Unit within the Group Theatre. Party influence intensified the controversies about art and politics, but most of the Group members shared the leftist consensus of the decade, believing that the end of capitalism along with great social change was at hand. In this crisis, art was not neutral. Even when no explicit propaganda was apparent, art was deemed to serve a social and political function.

That the Group's founders and followers thought they could bring some spiritual order to the "anarchy" of Broadway is a striking reminder of the optimistic aspirations of the 1930s. It really seemed a possible dream to transform show business into true theater. This hope was the through-line of the Group's endeavors. Nevertheless, operating on "the great white way" rather than in some workers' hall or Greenwich Village venue or even outside of New York City entangled the Group in the kind of irreconcilable contradictions between their means and ends that destroyed many brave theatrical experiments. Financial, political, and organizational entanglements distorted their play choices, their commitment to pay a company, their casting choices, their interpersonal relations, and the development of an audience truly theirs.

Yet, in defiance of these contradictions and pressures, the Group persevered. They redefined the task of the director to reflect their new found personal, performance, and political values. Lee Strasberg's later Actors Studio fame as an acting teacher has obscured his very important innovations and achievements in his nine Group productions, which ranged from heightened realism to historical saga and epic-style theatricalism. No matter the play, the actors gave performances of psychological complexity and explosive emotional power in productions marked by the Group's positive, activist-1930s point of view. Interested more in the process than the final production, Strasberg turned rehearsals into the actors' disciplined search for personal emotion, for improvisational spontaneity, and for ways to express their collective understanding of the script. It was the beginning of a new American style of acting.

Strasberg trained the company in the early years, but his obsession with emotional-memory exercises as the solution to what he called the "problem of the actor" led to a traumatic confrontation. Stella Adler brought back word from Konstantin Stanislavsky, with whom she studied in Paris in the summer of 1934, that Strasberg's use of the exercise was a misuse of the Russian's system. Many of the actors, released from what they felt was Strasberg's insistent probing, applauded her revelations as they argued the finer points of acting. The duel over the interpretation of the Russian master challenged Strasberg's authority over the company, initiated Stella Adler's career as the teacher of what some of the members considered a healthier method, and led to a schism in American actor training.

When Harold Clurman staged his first production in 1935, he relied on the extraordinary ensemble that Strasberg had developed in the first years of the company, but emphasized different facets of the director's task. Beginning with Clifford Odets's *Awake and Sing!*, his first production directed for the Group, Clurman dedicated himself to realizing the Group's dream that from their ranks would come a playwright trained in their method and able to articulate their message. Clifford Odets was their man! In a unique collaboration, Clurman staged five full-length plays by Odets. Clurman's directorial strength became the interpretation of the script in performance terms. In the convivial atmosphere of rehearsals, the whole company nurtured their playwright, whose work spoke not only for him but also for themselves as they became those vivid ethnic characters Odets had written for their specific talents. With his gutsy but poetic plays, Odets became the dramatist of the 1930s, and the Group took its place as the theater of the decade. Other new writers benefited from Clurman's skills, and other Group directors, including Elia Kazan, Bobby Lewis, Cheryl Crawford, and Stella Adler, staged shows in the Group's unique way.

Nevertheless, finding plays to suit the Group Idea became one of their main problems. In the ten years of their existence, they produced 21 new American plays intended to stir an immediate response to the turmoil of the decade. They provided an incubator for the first plays not only of Clifford Odets but of Sidney Kingsley, Robert Ardrey, Irwin Shaw, William Saroyan, and others—a remarkable record. Just as they sought to elevate the actor from ignominy, the Group wanted to rescue the writer from his isolation. They hoped to collaborate with the playwright in ways that went far deeper than the usual required rewrites. Plays were judged by how well they served the needs of the company and the audience, not by abstract aesthetic values. They would be performed if they gave form to the Group's Idea. That was the theory, at any rate. Some playwrights turned them down, unwilling to be part of the collective process, where scenes were sometimes written out of the actors' improvisations, or revised to agree with the Group's ideology or aesthetic. In the desperate struggle to find material to keep the ensemble working—and therefore paid—they scrounged for scripts, often making decisions to produce out of desperation rather than choice.

AN AMERICAN GALLERY

Despite constraints on their operation with their playwrights and their trained actors, the Group opened up mainstream American theater to new voices and the new physiognomies. Odets called them "an American gallery" peopled with strikers, secretaries, dentists, small-time gangsters, ambitious advertising men, disappointed middle-class dreamers from different ethnic groups, and Jewish characters from his own plays. (Lahr, *The New Yorker*, October 26, 1992) Both actors and audiences were empowered by being represented on the stage. Although women as performers, as characters, and as members of the Group often felt unfulfilled in this male-dominated company, they, too, honored the aspiring Group spirit.

Because they had a method, a message, a point of view, the Group members became our most famous teachers. They felt a mission to spread the word about the work they had carried out in classes, workshops, and studios as well as in productions. Although they were not a school, they believed that "work in the theatre should constitute a schooling" (*FY*, 23). It wasn't only the emotions and the imaginations that were being developed, but the body and the mind. This theater of the "thinking actor" required its members to test themselves in dance classes and attend talks by Clurman, Strasberg, and by the musicians, photographers, writers, and activists who joined the company for their summer gatherings.

This vision and spirit, what Morris Carnovsky in *Theatre Arts Magazine* called a "peculiar elevation of devotion," animated their performances in ways the surviving scripts of their repertory barely suggest. Recalling the stunning impact the Group made on a budding playwright, Arthur Miller captured their special quality.

> I had my brain branded by the kind of beauty of the Group Theatre's productions...and the special kind of hush that surrounded the actors, who seemed both natural and surreal at the same time. To this day I can replay in memory certain big scenes acted by Luther and Stella Adler...Elia Kazan, Bobby Lewis, Sanford Meisner, and the others, and I can place each actor exactly where he was on the stage fifty years ago. This is less a feat of memory than a tribute to the capacity of these actors to concentrate, to *be* on the stage. When I recall them, time is stopped. (*Timebends*, 230)

The dark days of the Depression nurtured bright visions. In the 1930s, I participated in classes and performances organized for children by radical fraternal organizations dedicated to making culture serve the people. Our crude but lively performances were the potent ideological weapon we carried in our touring truck to union halls, picket lines, and club houses in my hometown of Newark, New Jersey, where actors were arrested for staging Odets's *Waiting for Lefty*. We played for our so-called progressive audiences the emerging repertory of anti-Nazi, antiwar, strike dramas, whose formula, we used to quip, was "[i]n the first act, we suffer, in the second act, we give out leaflets, and in the third act, we go on strike."

At the same time we devoured articles on acting, directing, and dramaturgy in the left-wing *New Theatre Magazine* by, among others, Lee Strasberg, Harold Clurman, and Bobby Lewis. The performances we attended had a powerful impact. I can still hear the insistent rhythms of poet Alfred Kreymborg's *America! America!*: "What have you done with all your gold, America, America? What have you bought and calmly sold of human flesh and misery?" I still see vividly in my mind's eye the simple emblematic set of Hallie Flanagan and Margaret Ellen Clifford's *Can You Hear Their Voices?*, based on Whittaker Chambers's story in *New Masses*, with the rich boys and girls on one side of the stage dancing at their debutante party and the drought-stricken farmers' wives (the heart of the story) on the other, arming themselves to wrest milk for their children from the company store. The final cry, originally addressed to a Vassar College audience, still rings in my ears and my conscience: "Can You Hear Their Voices?" (Bentley, *Hallie Flanagan*, 121–22).

There were many popular hits on Broadway just across the Hudson River from Newark, but they were not for us. We had our group, our audience, our plays. We spoke of the issues of the day—of poverty, fascism, war, Spain. We were doing something about them in and out of the theater. The personal was the political and the political was personal and artistic. When the Group Theatre toured Newark with

Odets's *Awake and Sing!*, its highly professional mix of economics, ethnic pungency, personal lyricism, and social hope convinced us that a true theater was possible in our time.

Looking back, I realize how much this youthful exposure to a different idea of theater influenced my later interests—from researching what actors have thought about their craft for *Actors on Acting*; exploring how directors make performance meaningful to audiences for *Directors on Directing* (books written with Toby Cole); redressing the neglect of women's contributions in *Women in American Theatre* with Linda Walsh Jenkins; charting the legacy of the Group Theatre in *Reunion: A Self-Portrait of the Group Theatre*; in *Broadway Dreamers* (1989), a television documentary on the Group Theatre; and in many articles, talks, academic courses, and now in this book.

The theater of our "strenuous decade" had its limitations, and the experience of the 1930s had its share of bitter personal, political, and aesthetic struggles. As I write this from the theoretical posture of the 1990s, it would be easy to put down the Group as a white, sexist, racist theater, trapped in a psychological method and a realistic style that made it complicit with hegemonic Broadway. Such strictures must be addressed but within the context of the pervasive contradictions of the decade that shaped the art and actions of the Group. Their story is *a cautionary tale*. We can learn from their sectarianism, their factionalism, their rigidities, their ambitions, and their delusions to examine our own.

Even as we "re-vision" the 1930s, the heritage of the company remains inspirational. In the lean days of the Great Depression, they sought a new way for themselves and their art. They brought to the task not only the varied talents and temperaments of the individual artists but also the extraordinary range of theatrical, cultural, social, and political experiences and values needed to respond to the unique challenge of their troubled decade. The ten-year struggle to sustain their large vision remains the most important experiment in American theater. The mimetic and the didactic, the personal and the social, the poetic and the political, all became artistic strategies—equipment for living. In making their theater a home for ideas and ideals, the Group hoped to restore American theater to its proper function as a vital public art where we come together to challenge, change, and celebrate our humanity.

Part I   People ✎

1. The Chosen Ones ⤳

On a rainy June 8, 1931, they packed wives, children, friends, Victrolas, and radios into a caravan of cars, and squeezed rotund Bobby Lewis and his cello into the rumble seat of Margaret (nicknamed "Beany") Barker's car. They were the Chosen Ones: the 27 young professional actors that Harold Clurman, Cheryl Crawford, and Lee Strasberg had selected to share a unique destiny. The colorful caravan took off from the front of the Theatre Guild on West 52nd Street in the heart of New York City on a pilgrimage to a barn and some cottages in Brookfield, Connecticut. Here they planned to work on Paul Green's play *The House of Connelly*. During that fateful summer these eager adventurers would become the Group Theatre.

What had brought them together were some wild, utopian ideas elaborated in a series of talks given by Harold Clurman the previous winter and spring. "You would hear people say, 'Come and hear Harold talk,'" the talented Ruth Nelson remembered. "It went all around town. All the youngsters were there" (*Reunion*, 527). Very late Friday nights, after the curtain had fallen on the Broadway shows most of them were playing in, the sessions would begin. Cofounder Lee Strasberg was away much of the time, playing the pedlar in the Theatre Guild production of *Green Grow the Lilacs*, and Cheryl Crawford, the third member of the team, was behind the scenes as an assistant stage manager, but Clurman talked. From November 1930 to May 1931—first in apartments belonging to Clurman, Crawford, and even their photographer friend Ralph Steiner, who one evening rented chairs from an undertaker to accommodate the growing crowd, and then in Steinway Hall on West 57th Street—young professionals listened to Clurman's fervent oratory. Using rhetoric that Crawford once dubbed a combination of Jeremiah and Walt Whitman, Clurman gesticulated wildly, like a juggler. Sometimes he would grab a chair, twisting and turning it, giving it a terrible beating. With the same wild enthusiasm, he was able to beat the rather inchoate, eager desire of his audience into that large vision that was to become the distinguishing mark of the Group Theatre.

The passionate style—unique, explosive, frenetic, humorous—carried a message whose inspirational power was vividly recalled by all those who attended. Although we do not have transcripts of the original talks, these words taken from one of Clurman's later attempts to recapture the initial inspiration of the Group suggest his rousing rhetoric.

> We are people who want to act. It's the essential impulse from which anything we do derives. Why do you want to act? You say, "I want to make money." Well, you can't make any money because there's terrific unemployment prevalent. You might want to act for fame. Your ego needs that. Will you give up acting if you aren't one of the big stars?

Suppose you want to become an actor to show off. That's not a bad thing either. It's part of human nature to take pleasure in a kind of exhibitionism...This makes it necessary for us to question why we want to act, and how we can get ourselves to the point where we are permitted to act. We have to fight for the right of a theatre in which to act.

Clurman's exhortations challenged the American theater of the "roaring twenties." The United States had come of age theatrically with Eugene O'Neill at the head of a long line of exciting new writers: Elmer Rice, Maxwell Anderson, Robert Sherwood, and many more. They had moved American drama out of Puritanism and provincialism onto the international stage. There were important new directors—Arthur Hopkins, Philip Moeller, Rouben Mamoulian—and innovative new designers—Robert Edmond Jones, Lee Simonson, Jo Mielziner. Stars shot across the sky: John Barrymore, Laurette Taylor, Jeanne Eagels, Pauline Lord. Brilliant as they were, they couldn't seem to find personal or professional nurture for their talent. A leading lady like Katharine Cornell, for instance, controlled her destiny by being her own producer, but to many, she seemed more a radiant personality than an important artist. Then there were the run-of-the-mill actors, slick, superficial, cliché-ridden. They filled the stage with "genteel behavior," "crisp diction," "the barest hint of emotion and the mere fig leaf of an idea," in Morris Carnovsky's witty words.

One of the pet grievances of Eugene O'Neill during the 1920s was "the inadequacy of actors." Performers seemed unable to infuse the vivid reality of rough American life with the sense of tragic mystery he wanted to communicate. He blamed theaters and audiences for not helping actors become artists capable of portraying his elevated themes. O'Neill urged his Provincetown Players to develop a plan

that will make young actors want to grow up with it as part of a whole, giving their acting a new clear, fakeless group excellence and group eloquence that will be our unique acting, our own thing, born in our American theatre as not so long ago Irish acting was born in the Irish plays, modern Russian acting in the Moscow Art Theatre, or modern German acting in the Reinhardt group.

He prophesied that the "immediate future of the theatre is in the actor," who must reject "type casting" for "long painful self-training."

Clurman offered his young listeners a view of acting that came close to O'Neill's dream. He placed the actor at the very center of theater. In his marvelously apoplectic way, he would shout:

The impulse, "I want to act," where does it come from? From saying, "I am alive; I experience certain things."...It comes from where you come from, the family that bore you, and those you lived with and loved, from what you read, and so forth. We are really acting out our life in imaginative form.

None of the actors had ever heard anything like this before!

In *The Fervent Years*, Clurman later restated in more subdued prose the essence of these messianic talks. "The theatre begins with the actor and achieves expression through him," he wrote, "but he is not by himself the theatre, for the content of the theatrical performance generally arises from a unifying group experience." He declared that "our interest in the life of our times must lead us to the discovery of those methods that would most truly convey this life through the theatre."

On Broadway, where Clurman and most of his audience worked, there was very little reflection of the life of the times. It was 1930–31, the first years of the Depression, but one would hardly know it from the theater. The Great White Way was still lit up by the sparkle of the usual commercial hits: rowdy and exuberant farces, action-packed suspenseful melodramas, sentimental romances, and titillating comedies. Only a few plays running in 1930 seemed artistic or poetic—Marc Connelly's Pulitzer Prize–winning, if patronizing folk play, *The Green Pastures*; Rudolf Beisier's literary romance, *The Barretts of Wimpole Street*; Maxwell Anderson's pseudo-Shakespearian *Elizabeth the Queen*. In the opinion of the day, these plays were art, but in Clurman's view they had no "blood relationship" to either the players or to the audience.

The harsh reality of the Depression was casting its dark shadow over this theater. With the stock market crash of 1929, the United States collapsed into economic chaos. Industrial output fell, banks defaulted, businesses failed, unemployment soared, and hunger spread. On Broadway, which is as much business as art, 50 fewer shows were produced in 1930 than in 1929. By the end of that year, *Variety* reported that half the legitimate theaters in New York were dark and attendance fell to "a new low for modern times." Destitute actors had to turn to the Stage Relief Fund for a handout.

In his talks, Clurman did not address these social dislocations with any sort of dogmatic program; indeed, he didn't deal directly with economics or politics. His talks concentrated on theater as art. Looking back in *The Fervent Years*, he explained: "From considerations of acting and plays we were plunged into a chaos of life questions . . . From an experiment in theatre, we were in some way impelled to an experiment in living" (*FY*, see chapter 3).

In those hard times Clurman's listeners were led to probe their own motives, asking "Why do I want to act?" He pressed them to calculate the problems and possibilities of theater as never before. In an article in *The Drama* (April 1931) at the time of his talks, he identified the origins of theater in the primitive tribe, tracing its evolution as a form from the interaction of the actor and the community who share a single vision. "We have, on the American stage, all the separate elements for a Theatre, but no Theatre. We have playwrights without their theatre-groups, directors without their actors, actors without plays or directors, scene-designers without anything. Our theatre is an anarchy of individual talents." Only a "conscious approach" to the "Idea of a Theatre" could provide the "starting point" and "basis" for a new unity.

Clurman took what he later called an "almost metaphysical line which . . . emphasized the theatre's reason for being." The Depression intensified his commitment to the composite, collaborative art of theater as a paradigm for a dynamic relationship of individual and society. Indeed, he had come to believe that "laws of the theatre are really the laws of society."

Clurman was articulating for theater the redefinition of basic values taking place across the nation in the 1930s. A reassessment had begun in the late 1920s, when the frenzied roller coaster of the jazz age slowed down. The search for psychological and cultural freedom of the early half of the decade began to be replaced by a new concern for economics and politics. It was a period of transition from the "self-discovery and self-expression" of the early 1920s to the "social discovery and social experience" of the early 1930s. The execution of the anarchists Nicola Sacco and Bartolomeo Vanzetti in 1927, a signal turning point, radicalized many young artists. The pressure to participate in the social conflicts of American society undermined the earlier aloofness, detachment, and aestheticism of the artistic community. As the crisis destroyed confidence in the myth of rugged individualism, it forced a painful recognition of the social determinants of people's lives. Collectivism became the transforming concept for change, and realigning the self and society the crucial task of the decade. The critic Alfred Kazin caught the new spirit when he wrote in his autobiographical *Starting Out in the Thirties* that "there seemed to be no division between my effort at personal liberation and the apparent effort of humanity to deliver itself."

In a similar vein Clurman urged the actors to abandon a life in the theater as conventionally defined, with its illusion of fame and fortune and its reality of lifelong insecurity and isolation. By 1931, the actor's life, precarious even in the 1920s, had become "unspeakable," according to contemporary commentators, who were beginning to realize that without steady work an actor could not learn his or her craft. In the opening days of the 1930s, even the critic Burns Mantle, no radical, noted a characteristic 1930s paradox, namely, that "shaken by the economic element," the theater "might be finding its soul in this widely advertised depression." In contrast to the expansive 1920s, which had the luxury of literary and theatrical growth and experimentation, the lean years of the 1930s identified the neglected actor and his provocative human acts as the essence of theater. The activist idealism of the time inspired the actors to believe that they could change themselves and the theater, and in turn change the world through the collective experience.

In his harangues, Clurman linked the critique of American life with the innovative technique of acting Lee Strasberg was developing from the Stanislavsky system, which embodied the same humanistic principles. Clurman talked of an economically secure, permanent ensemble of professional players trained in a unified way of working, which would allow them to reflect and affect the life around them. With a common approach they would start a theater in which, as he put it, "our philosophy of life might be translated into a philosophy of theatre." He insisted that a true theater depended on "a unity of background, of feeling, of thought, of need, among a group of people" and envisioned an organic community sharing a large unifying purpose.

The first prototype of the Group Theatre took place in 1928. Harold Clurman and Lee Strasberg, then fellow bit players in the Theatre Guild, loved to exchange ideas about theater. Between scenes, on walks, or over salami and eggs, they tore into Broadway and fantasized about "our theatre." They decided to take some steps toward its realization by inviting a few actors—among them Morris Carnovsky, Franchot Tone, and Sanford Meisner—to work on Waldo Frank's *New Year's Eve*. They had no immediate production plans. For some 17 weeks they rehearsed in the Riverside Drive studio of well-to-do real estate broker Sidney Ross, who they hoped would sponsor a theatrical venture. Directed by Strasberg, the text was explored primarily for the actors' personal artistic growth, something almost completely neglected in regular productions even by the Theatre Guild, the most artistic of the Broadway institutions. "The rehearsals themselves would constitute a schooling" was the way Clurman put it. (*Reunion*, 473)

The participants probed the craft of the actor according to the teaching of Richard Boleslavsky and Maria Ouspenskaya at the American Laboratory Theatre, where Strasberg and several others had been studying. Former members of the Moscow Art Theatre, the Russians introduced American students to Konstantin Stanislavsky's systematic analysis of acting and the concept of the theater as a laboratory for an ensemble of players. The training Boleslavsky offered required the actor to go well beyond mere technical improvements to an intimate linking of the self with the inner life of the character, the overall vision projected by the playwright, and the collective spirit of the ensemble. The actor had to be in touch with and make use of his own senses, his feelings, his thoughts, his whole life and society. Only through these means could the actor realize the true purpose of theater, which Stanislavsky defined as "the creation of the inner life of a human spirit, and its expression in an artistic form." Acting became a spiritual exercise involving a disciplined struggle for self-discovery, personal authenticity, and social concern that was capable of transforming both the artist and the audience.

Clurman, Strasberg, and Crawford hoped that, in addition to actors, playwrights, directors, and designers would share this approach to art. Someday, perhaps, they would have their own theater. For the moment an opportunity to practice the new technique of acting was all that was promised. It was what the actors wanted and could not get in the show business production process. They dreamed of working together in the country during the summer as Boleslavsky and Stanislavsky had done, but could not find the necessary backing. Still, a start had been made.

In 1929, some of the same people plus others—Cheryl Crawford, Ruth Nelson, Eunice Stoddard, Luther Adler, William Challee, and a very young Julie (later John) Garfield—were involved in a production of *Red Rust* by V. Kirchon and A. Ouspensky. It was offered as a special event by the Theatre Guild Studio, newly organized on the model of the studios of the Moscow Art Theatre. Only the second Soviet play to be shown on Broadway, *Red Rust* was directed by Herbert Biberman, who with Crawford and Clurman comprised a production committee. Not surprisingly the production stirred considerable political and artistic discussion. Although many negative judgments were leveled, critics, nevertheless, liked the play's documentation of the current lives of students and young Communist Party workers in Moscow. The immediacy of the drama roused the audience. Clurman himself was "startled at the applause when the 'Internationale' was sung before the curtain on opening night." Photographs of the production show future Group members in strong revolutionary stances. Although the production lost some $13,000, it perked up a dull season and the Theatre Guild won praise for allowing the young performers to stage contemporary Soviet life.

Four or five who had been in *Red Rust* continued to meet informally to bridge the isolation each felt in the increasingly chaotic times. Clurman, ever the spokesman for their personal and artistic longings, stigmatized the alienation of American society. "People don't seem to talk to one another enough. We are separate. Our contacts are hasty, utilitarian or escapist." He urged his friends to work together in the theater for their personal and social salvation. "We must get to know ourselves by getting to know one another." This was to become one of the basic themes of the Group Theatre.

Behind these efforts to come together were even earlier experiences. Clurman, Strasberg, and Crawford knew one another from their work at the Theatre Guild. Clurman recalled seeing Strasberg for the first time in a 1925 trial performance by some of the young Theatre Guild actors of Pirandello's *Right You Are, If You Think Are*. This "intense-looking" young man with a "face that expressed keen intelligence, suffering, ascetic control," though well cast for the "typical Pirandello hero," in Clurman's view, "did not seem like an actor." As they came to know each other, he discovered that Strasberg was, indeed, an actor with a difference. Strasberg had already taken courses at the American Laboratory Theatre, to which he introduced Clurman, and had begun to try his hand at using what he was learning by directing amateurs at the Chrystie Street Settlement House on the Lower-East-Side of Manhattan.

Short, shy, and intense, young Strasberg took an indirect route to professional theater. Looking for individuals who shared his interests and also for what he called "female companionship," he had joined the amateur Students of Art and Drama, the SAD's as they called themselves, largely as a social activity. "I had no romantic ideas about myself as an actor and therefore would never have involved myself in any kind of professional activity in the hopes of some ego gratification." The introverted son of immigrant parents with no theater in his background, he was in business as a manufacturer of ladies' hairpieces, "the human hair business," as he dubbed it. He had shown considerable talent playing a few small parts in productions by the Yiddish cultural groups that were an important part of Lower-East-Side community life. Nevertheless, he did not think of himself as an actor. Yet, he was fascinated by the parade of great performers who appeared on a newly sophisticated Broadway in the early 1920s. Recalling in vivid detail the art of Eleonora Duse, Giovanni Grasso, Laurette Taylor, Jacob Ben-Ami, Pauline Lord, Eva Le Gallienne, and Jeanne Eagels, as well as such greats of the Yiddish stage as David Kessler and Jacob Adler, Strasberg felt grateful to have witnessed what he called "a golden age of acting." He also read voraciously the current books that were elaborating a new idea of theater. The volume that had the greatest influence on him, as it did on many others, was Edward Gordon Craig's *On the Art of the Theatre* (1911). Craig was the evangelist of the "New Movement" that defined theater as a synthesis of action, words, line, color, and rhythm created by the director, whom he proclaimed to be "the artist of the theatre." Craig celebrated a popular, sensuous art that would unite the performer and the audience, transcending the individual ego. Strasberg was thrilled.

The spell cast by the Moscow Art Theatre during its performances in New York in 1923, however, had the greatest impact on the thoughtful autodidact. Observing the extraordinary reality of the acting, he noted that all the members of the company were "not equally great, but equally real." The lowest supernumerary had the same reality as the great actors Konstantin Stanislavsky, Vassily Kachlov, and Ivan Moskvin. Always intrigued to analyze the technique of acting, he determined that all the actors were working in the same way, doing something every actor could do no matter his talent. "What was that?" he asked himself. It was the Stanislavsky system. Strasberg sold his business to his partner, enrolled in the Clare Tree Major School of Theatre, but soon left it for the newly organized American Laboratory Theatre. From there he went on to the Theatre Guild, his first professional experience.

The presence of Jacques Copeau in New York in 1927 spurred Strasberg and Clurman to take seriously the idea of starting a theater. Clurman called Copeau the "catalytic agent" (*FY*, 16). His austere, noble dedication to theater art had inspired an earlier generation of theater innovators during the New York performances of his Théâtre du Vieux-Columbier company in 1917. He had returned to direct his dramatization of *The Brothers Karamazov* with Alfred Lunt and Lynn Fontanne for the Theatre Guild. Clurman knew and admired Copeau, whose lectures he had attended in Paris during his years at the Sorbonne writing a thesis on turn-of-the-century French drama. In New York, Clurman followed closely the lectures that Copeau gave at the American Laboratory Theatre and even helped Copeau communicate with the audience. The Theatre Guild allowed him to attend Copeau's rehearsals to facilitate the directing when the Frenchman's "English went dry" and used an article by Clurman for publicity. Clurman invited the French master to a dress rehearsal of Copeau's own play, *The House Into Which We Are Born*, then being staged in his honor by Strasberg at Chrystie Street. Although Strasberg hardly exchanged a word with their distinguished visitor, Copeau's presence and practice heartened the hopes of the two young men that the theater they had been dreaming about might become a reality.

Clurman's experience in practical theater was still fairly limited at that time. He had acquired "a passionate inclination for the theatre" at age six when he was taken to see Jacob Adler, the great Jewish actor, as Uriel Acosta and Shylock. (*FY*, 4) His enthusiasm was nurtured during his early years by frequent visits to this vital Yiddish theater on the Lower-East-Side, where his rather literary father was a doctor. However, his path to theater participation, like Strasberg's, was indirect. After two years at Columbia University, his indulgent father allowed his very intelligent son to go to Paris to study at the Sorbonne. "We were very serious about the arts," he recalled of himself and his roommate, the budding composer Aaron Copland, "but we had a lot of fun too, going around to places like Sylvia Beach's bookstore and catching glimpses of famous writers like Hemingway, Joyce, and Pound, and seeing the composers and poets in the cafés and restaurants." Despite his admiration for the Paris productions of Copeau and Georges Pitoëff, he felt that the theater lacked the "significant contemporaneity" of the other arts he was enjoying.

When he and Copland returned with their European liberal education in 1924, they knew that they wanted to be spokesmen for their generation in American arts. Looking for something to do, the rather bumbling, sometimes tongue-tied Clurman eventually turned to the theater, although his interests, then as later, were not limited to the theater. His first job was as an extra in the Provincetown Playhouse, where the critic Stark Young's play, *The Saint*, was being produced by the newly reorganized triumvirate of designer Robert Edmond Jones, playwright Eugene O'Neill, and critic Kenneth Macgowan. Here, Clurman was moved listening to the spiritual words of Jones, who, with Young, was directing the play, but Clurman felt that the great designer made no real contact with the performers. The Provincetown people called in Boleslavsky, the Russian-trained professional director, to pull the production together, providing Clurman an opportunity to observe the man with whom he would shortly study directing.

After much persistence, Clurman was taken on as an extra by the Theatre Guild. He and Strasberg thus worked in various Guild productions, including the famous Rodgers and Hart musical take-off, *The Garrick Gaieties* of 1925. They had small roles—Strasberg did some singing and dancing—or served as stage managers. This left them time to promote their growing interest in a different idea of theater.

Cheryl Crawford listened with special attention to their speculations. At the Theatre Guild she was then third assistant stage manager on the production of Franz Werfel's *Juarez and Maximilian*, in which Clurman was playing several bits, including a Mexican peon slouching in front of an adobe hut. Although on stage he didn't say much more than "Ugh," off stage he filled Crawford's ears with his ideas for the theater he and Strasberg were dreaming of. "I was very taken with it and overwhelmed by it," she recalled (*Reunion*, 491). She had come to theater through acting, directing, and producing as a student at Smith College. Although no one in what she called her "nice, normal, mid-western family" in Akron, Ohio, had been involved in theater, there was enough theatricality in her childhood to spark her interest. Her mother had gone to the Emerson School of Elocution, her father was given to declaiming Shakespeare at the dinner table, and a stock company in Akron provided some glimpses of popular shows. Her first direct theater experience came when she worked with Professor Samuel Eliot at Smith College. A nephew of the renowned Harvard professor George Pierce Baker, whose Workshop 47 theater course nurtured many playwrights and directors, Eliot had been a member of the innovative Washington Square Players. Crawford's life was transformed by Eliot's wide knowledge of international drama and his almost religious vision of theater. President of the Dramatic Association, the sturdy Crawford played male leads with success in the all-girl casts and astounded audiences by a spectacular staging of the Indian drama *Shakuntala*, replete with a water curtain dug in the Smith president's elegant garden, which served as the stage. Although she was expelled for a time in her senior year—rumors about smoking, drinking, sexual irregularity, and reading Nietzsche to freshmen—President Neilson brought her back to stage a play at Northampton's historic Academy of Music for the fiftieth anniversary of the College. A summer in Provincetown with some of the original Players and then study at the short-lived Theatre Guild School led her to production and management with the Guild. Here, Theresa Helburn, one of the few women producers in New York, helped launch Crawford's career.

Crawford recalled being very happy at the Guild, where she tried her hand as stage manager, assistant to the producers, and even casting director. "But this guy, Harold Clurman, kept picking at me all the time and saying, 'This isn't what you really want to do, is it?' And he finally convinced me that it wasn't." She turned down income and advancement at the Guild because she decided that "Harold was right and Lee was right and the Theatre Guild was not really what I wanted to have in theatre at all" (*Naked Individual*, 51).

With her executive ability and shrewd, practical know-how, Crawford convinced Clurman and Strasberg to move from talk to action. She suggested that they find actors for the permanent company of which they were dreaming. Once people and plans were decided on, she would seek whatever help they needed at the Guild and elsewhere. In his autobiography, Lawrence Langner noted the ambivalence of the Theatre Guild directors toward their rebellious young associates: "The best that the parents of a child can do when that child wants independence is to help it on its way; and this the Guild Board did, even though it was apparent later on that our offspring regarded us as old-fashioned fogies running around the theatre in circles" (250). Clurman undertook to talk to potential members, "excite their enthusiasm, and generate the momentum that would transform what had been a somewhat vague program into a going concern." Thus, the Friday night gatherings began, at which, the actress Aline McMahon supposedly once quipped, Harold Clurman "talked the Group Theatre into existence."

Although Clurman's talks were based on theorizing, they embodied a plan of action. With Crawford and Strasberg, he hoped that among the several hundred who came to listen over the months, a few would be inspired to join them in their experiment. Not everyone who took part in the late night vigils responded; some, bored or confused, left. One bewildered man asked him, "Is it a religion?" Clurman replied, "Yes."

A strikingly beautiful, cultivated young woman named Katharine Hepburn, who had not yet appeared on Broadway, came with her friend Eunice Stoddard. "We sat together," Hepburn recalled,

> and I listened about what a wonderful thing...the Group Theatre was going to be. Everyone was going to play little parts, and they were going to do wonderful plays. And, as I listened to them, I felt they were all going to be quite invisible...except for a few. 'Cause that's inevitable. And there came a pause in the meeting and I got up and said, "I'm going." They said, "You're what?" I said, "I'm leaving. I don't want to be a member of a group. I want to be a great, big star. And I left."

Her friends were outraged. "Why, Katie, how can you even think that way?" Ruth Nelson asked. The young women had gathered at the brownstone home owned by Eunice Stoddard's parents on East 65th Street, where they stretched out before a glowing fire to chat about the new theater. Hepburn said, "I don't know. I just feel that I have to do it alone." She wanted to "paddle her own canoe" (*Reunion*, 527).

Ruth Nelson never forgot that night. She and Eunice Stoddard as well as Stella Adler, Franchot Tone, Margaret Barker, J. Edward Bromberg, Robert Lewis, Sanford Meisner, Clifford Odets, Morris Carnovsky, Phoebe Brand, Tony Kraber, and a number of others wanted to be part of this theater in the making. But the directors took their time during the long winter of talks to make the important decision about participants—for everything depended on the Chosen Ones. The actors had to have talent and histrionic skill; this was not to be an amateur or stock company. More important, they had to be capable of growth, had to be able to open themselves fully to the demands of the Group Idea. Those who finally gathered to take off for Brookfield turned out to be a remarkable, colorful, but very strange fellowship.

Carnovsky ruefully recalled that as they prepared to depart, "we must have regarded each other quizzically...wondering what potency, what magic, was going to summon us into some semblance of unity" (*Reunion*, 477).

A sampling suggests the unusual mix of personality, gender, ethnicity, religion, and class. The directorate itself seemed a "bizarre trio." Cheryl Crawford captured the characteristic Group composite when she quipped it consisted of "two Old Testament prophets and one WASP shiksa" (*Naked Individual*, 52). Several established performers willingly gave up individual commercial opportunities for the ensemble alternative, but there were striking differences among them. The statuesque, talented Stella Adler had been on the stage from the age of four with the "acting Adlers." Her father Jacob was the great star of the Yiddish theater, and her mother Sarah, a leading actress; all their children were thrust upon the stage at the earliest possible age. Although they were part of the immigrant culture of the Lower-East-Side, Stella was no product of the ghetto streets. She grew up on East 72nd Street in a luxurious, if chaotic, household. With her parents and her brothers and sisters, she appeared in the United States and abroad in a repertoire that included Shakespeare, Tolstoy, and Ibsen. She played in vaudeville, in Maurice Schwartz's Yiddish Art Theatre, and on Broadway, making a name for herself in the more than one hundred roles she played by the end of the 1920s. Well before the founding of the Group Theatre, she recalled, "I had searched for the craft of acting...There was something in the air that said there was one step further that the actor would go. He could go further in using his experience and in formulating an approach that would give him a greater sense of craft in a subjective, experiential, personal way" (*Reunion*, 507).

This search brought Stella to the American Laboratory Theatre. It was here that she met Strasberg and Clurman, who she would marry after a tempestuous romance that would last through the decade of the Group Theatre. Clurman described her as "poetically theatrical...with all the imperious flamboyance of an older theatrical tradition—European in its roots" (*Reunion*, 507). Her special quality carried with it the whole tradition of her father's theater. Jacob Adler's bold emotional acting was no casual entertainment; he appealed to the profoundest emotions of his audience. His roles expressed both the longings of the Eastside Jewish immigrants and the lofty mission that he saw for art. In the early years of the century, the Yiddish theater in America offered major plays from the world repertory performed by remarkable actors before a vibrant audience. For these newcomers to the "Golden Land," theater was a gathering place where the community looked back to the old world they had left and forged a place for themselves in the new world. The theater was a home for their problems and their aspirations. It was surely this family heritage that made the beautiful Stella responsive to Clurman's appeals, just as this same vital, communal art had inspired Clurman's own enthusiasm for theater.

Morris Carnovsky was also well on his way to success when he joined the Group Theatre. A son of immigrants, he, too, was inspired by Yiddish stars like Jacob Adler who toured to his native St. Louis. These versatile performers reaching out to their audience with powerful emotional acting stirred his interest in theater. But Carnovsky was utterly unlike Stella, the sexy, pampered but ambitious princess of

Yiddish theater royalty who never had time for regular schooling. Studious and scholarly, Carnovsky studied literature and did some acting at St. Louis University, where he made Phi Beta Kappa. Coming east to rid himself of his Midwestern accent, he went first to the Copley Theatre in Boston, where he learned what he termed "a genteel sort of behavior rather than acting," and then left this behind for New York City. Six of the next ten years were spent with the Theatre Guild where he became a successful young character actor playing good parts in plays by Shaw, O'Neill, and Maxwell Anderson with some of the best actors of the day, Edward G. Robinson, Alfred Lunt, Lynn Fontanne, and Clare Eames. Although Carnovsky appreciated both the plays and the players, he was not really satisfied with his work. "I was impatient in a nagging, vague way," he explained.

> I was possessed by idealism, even intolerance. The breeze that Filled my sails...came from France and Russia. The names of Jacques Copeau and Konstantin Stanislavsky vibrated in the air like the harp of Memnon, irresistible and mysterious. Even without fully realizing what they portended...we were drawn to them as to a promised land. It was that impulse, of course, that finally emerged as the inspiration for the Group Theatre. (*Reunion*, 481)

Equally idealistic but from a far different milieu, Franchot Tone also preferred what the Group promised. The wealthy, handsome son of the president of the Carborundum Company of America and a Phi Beta Kappa graduate of Cornell University, Tone was a witty, debonair man who might have played in light comedies but chose to associate himself with theaters where his intellectual, economic, and political concerns were engaged. His first New York appearances were in productions of the New Playwrights' Theatre, organized in 1927 by John Dos Passos, John Howard Lawson, and Mike Gold to stage radical, innovative plays about modern industrial life. In Lawson's *International*, the young Tone played the American hero, described as a kind of "adult Rover Boy," who sides with the downtrodden workers in a revolt against the world of his father. Seeing him in this part, Clurman invited him to participate in their early projects despite the fact that he thought Tone somewhat stiff in his acting. Tone continued playing roles in conventional productions while involved in the explorations prior to the founding of the Group. When invited to go off with the company to Brookfield, he, like Carnovsky, was under contract to the Theatre Guild, but both were released in a gesture of support by the Guild for the revolt that was brewing among its own young people. Tone's upper-class parents, reflecting an old prejudice, were happier to see him in the leftish Group Theatre than in crass show business.

Unlike these accomplished actors whose frustrating experiences in the commercial theater made them eager for a creative alternative, Margaret Barker, flushed with her first success on Broadway, was undecided. She had accompanied Franchot Tone to Clurman's talks; they had acted together in the *Age of Innocence* for Katharine Cornell's company, and Barker was now playing the ingénue in Cornell's highly successful production of *The Barretts of Wimpole Street*. It was, as she later observed, "probably the most exciting and wonderful part an ingénue could have had at that time" (*Reunion*, 520). But now she was torn between the attractions of becoming a star and the alternative of being part of a committed ensemble. She discussed the choices with Tone, who remarked: "If you *want* to be a good actress, then come with the Group. If you want to be a star, then don't." Crawford echoed: "If you want to play neurasthenic ingénues for the rest of your life, stay in *The Barretts of Wimpole Street*. If you want to be an actress, come with the Group."

Daughter of a dean of Johns Hopkins Medical School and a former undergraduate at Bryn Mawr, this fair-skinned debutante found Clurman's talks disturbing. He "was tearing down all my romantic notions about theatre—even attacking the Lunts." She sought Clurman out on weekends for answers to her many perplexities, but youthful idealism propelled her quest "to live for something bigger than the self." She said, "We had to find something. We weren't really sure what our values were, but we had enough of a common view of what we wanted theatre to be or what our theatre values were that we could come together. Harold in his strange, stuttering, overemphatic way really molded the whole group that winter" (*Reunion*, 521).

Before making her final decision, she had a long session with Katharine Cornell who, she said, "asked me all kinds of questions and I talked about... all kinds of esoteric things that Harold had talked about that I didn't really understand." Finally, Cornell advised her: "Beany, I think if I were ten years younger, it's what I'd want to do" (*Reunion*, 521). Barker sent a telegram at once to say that she would join the Group.

The contingent of educated, upper-class young women attracted to the experiment was a sign of the times. Dorothy Patten was a southern belle from Chattanooga, Tennessee. The only daughter of one of the leading families, she grew up in privilege and luxury. She acquired her interest in the arts from her mother, who remained content to be a gracious hostess. But Dorothy, like a number of other wealthy young women growing up in the 1920s, felt it appropriate to be more than a social dilettante. She dreamed of a professional career in the theater. After graduation from the same girls' school that Katharine Cornell, her idol, had attended, she enrolled at the American Academy of Dramatic Arts, played in stock in upstate New York, and, after the usual disappointments, in a few shows on Broadway. The turning point came when she was cast as Penelope in the Theatre Guild's production of Maxwell Anderson's *Elizabeth the Queen* starring the Lunts. Working with these master theater artists in New York and on tour was educational and pleasant; reviewers singled Patten out as "especially good" in this supporting role. Hearing about the meetings from fellow cast member Carnovsky, she became part of a small *Elizabeth the Queen* contingent to attend Clurman's talks. Before the founding of the Group she wasn't sure what to do next in her career. Here are some notes she wrote at the time: "Go to Hollywood? I had two 'movie offers' during *Elizabeth*. Give up the 'commercial theatre'? Wait around hoping the Lunts would have a part for me in every play they did? Or retire to Chattanooga and raise riding horses?" Joining with the others at Brookfield seemed a personally enriching alternative to a conventional career.

The circle of young women looking for a more meaningful experience included Eunice Stoddard. A pretty blonde ingénue, she gained her elevated ideas about theater from her parents, who were active in the society and cultural life of New York. She studied ballet and music in Paris, acting with Boleslavsky at the Actors

Laboratory Theatre, and even met with Stanislavksy when he was writing *An Actor Prepares* in Baden-Baden in 1930 through her parents' friendship with Elizabeth Hapgood, the Russian's American translator. When she played the role of Vera in the Theatre Guild's production of Turgenev's *A Month in the Country*, Katharine Hepburn was her understudy. They attended the famous talks together.

Far removed from the options and lifestyle of these all-American socialites were three lively, but decidedly unconventional bit players who did not fit the show-business image of the actor. They were Sanford Meisner, Robert Lewis, and Clifford Odets. For Sandy Meisner, as for his friend Bobby, Broadway was not a viable option. Both had considerable training in music, Lewis with the cello and Meisner with the piano, but in their teens found acting their true calling, much to the horror of their Jewish immigrant parents. Musicians at least could make a living teaching, but actors were a disgrace to the family! Meisner went to the Damrosch School of Music, but hard times forced him to work in a factory where men's trousers were made. During lunch hour he made the rounds of theater managers' offices, finally talking his way into a job as an extra in the Theatre Guild's production of Sidney Howard's *They Knew What They Wanted*. He was entranced by the acting of Pauline Lord, who was playing the lead; now he knew that "acting which really dug at me was what I was looking for." He attended the Theatre Guild's short-lived School of Acting, and before long met Clurman. His new friend told him he would learn much more about acting by working at Chrystie Street with Lee Strasberg, who became for him "a great uplifting influence." Meisner acted in early projects with Strasberg and Clurman so that when the Group was being organized, it was, for him, "just kind of a spontaneous move in one direction."

> I never had a choice, actually. I had no decision to make. Fortunately—because if it had been a decision between the commercial theatre and the Group Theatre, it would have been too bad. If I had decided in favor of the commercial theatre, I would have been in my father's fur business years ago. I wouldn't have made it in the commercial scene. Not because of my own temperament as much as because of the way the commercial theatre operates—the type casting, the working in terms of fixed clichés. (*Reunion*, 502–503)

Bobby Lewis studied the cello at what would become the Juilliard School of Music, although he really wanted to be an opera singer. He broke with his family in order to act with the Sue Hastings' Marionette Company, where the short, chubby actor could speak the lines of Romeo as well as Eeyore in *Winnie the Pooh*. He stole into the balcony at the Civic Repertory Theatre and quickly made his way as an apprentice in Eva Le Gallienne's company, where he had a chance to play small parts, watch the talented actress direct, pick the brains of the much-admired Jacob Ben-Ami, and test himself as a novice director. At the end of the season, Le Gallienne let him go, saying: "Bobby, I feel you definitely have a place in the theatre; but it is not as an actor" (Lewis, *S&A*, 33).

Although he did later make his mark as a director and teacher rather than as an actor, he was determined to prove Le Gallienne wrong. At the time of Clurman's talks, he and Sandy Meisner were playing together at the Provincetown Playhouse in Maxwell Anderson's *Gods of the Lightning*, a drama inspired by the

Sacco and Vanzetti case that had reshaped the social awareness of the decade. He was buoyed up by the good notices he had received as the "gentle anarchist" in the Anderson play.

Bobby Lewis's story of how he first met the men who were to change his life contrasts the intensity of their attitude to acting with the casualness of most performers. Clurman and Strasberg had come to see their friend Meisner in the Anderson play, and, Lewis recalled,

> they saw me, too. They came backstage after the show. I don't remember what Harold said, but I'll never forget what Lee said. Lee looked at me and said: "What were you trying to do?" I didn't know what the hell he meant. All I was trying to do was to give the best performance I knew how, and you know, I thought I was pretty good. I had gotten good notices and everything, but I could see they hated it. (*S&A*, 35ff)

Yet, they invited him to the meetings in Steinway Hall, and he went.

Like so many others, Bobby Lewis fell under Clurman's spell. One memorable evening he, Meisner, and others were sitting dejectedly over their coffee in a Steward's Cafeteria following a performance by the famed Indian dancer Uday Shankar. Clurman came along and shouted at them: "What's wrong with you? You just saw this beautiful dancer." They complained to him: "Well, we can never get to be like that. Because he's religious, and we're not. That extra purity he had in addition to his talent and technique was the spiritual thing that we can never achieve." Clurman nearly blew his top, screaming at them: "Don't you ever say that. Because you are believers. You believe in people, and what better religion is there than that?" They learned something very important from Clurman's humanistic fury. "We too could hit any heights. We didn't have to feel that we were 'just actors.'"

When Bobby Lewis was invited to come along to Brookfield, Crawford asked him to contribute 90 dollars to pay for the food for the summer. "I didn't have ninety dollars, and nobody in my family had ninety dollars, and none of my friends had ninety dollars. But I knew that this was going to be the most important thing in my life," he remembered. He asked the one rich man he knew to invest 90 dollars in his life. He did, but Bobby's salary with the Group remained so small that the man died before he could earn enough to pay him back. (*Reunion*, 485)

Clifford Odets was one of the oddest, but most revealing of the directors' choices. The high-strung Odets, who dropped out of high school because he was "crazy to act," had recited monologues on radio, toured with Mae Desmond's stock company, and played walk-ons on tour for the Theatre Guild, where he met the director Phillip Moeller and Cheryl Crawford. He wrote both of them long letters about his literary aspirations, which Crawford later regretted throwing out. She suggested that Clurman ask him to the talks. "I remember this peculiar man named Clifford Odets who didn't say very much," Clurman recalled.

> I felt he was a pretty bad actor. He never agreed with me because he thought he could do anything if he put his mind to it...One night he walked along with me and said: "You know, I've heard ten lectures of yours and now I'm just beginning to understand what you're talking about." When we had to decide, Lee asked me: "What about this Odets

fella?" I said: "Let's have him. Something is cooking with that man. I don't know what it is, whether its potato pancakes or what it is, but what's cooking has a rich odor, a fragrance, something is going to develop from that man." (*Reunion*, 474)

The diversity of the Chosen Ones is a striking feature of the group, responsible for many highly individual performances on stage and plenty of company tension offstage. Adding the remaining founding members also suggests the surprising extent to which these very different actors, nevertheless, had similar theater experiences before committing themselves to the Group. Most had been associated with schools and theaters that stood in opposition to what Eugene O'Neill called the Broadway "show shop." Hungarian-born J. ("Joe") Edward Bromberg, along with Morris Carnovsky, studied acting with Leo Bulgakov of the Moscow Art Theatre. He had an opportunity to play roles ranging from the dog Nana in *Peter Pan* to Mercutio in *Romeo and Juliet* for Eva Le Gallienne, who was known as the "Abbess of Fourteenth Street" for her dedication to a repertory of significant plays and artistic but inexpensive productions.

Paula Miller, who would marry Lee Strasberg, was a plump, strawberry blonde from a respectable but impoverished Jewish family. She, too, had her start in small parts with Le Gallienne.

Mary Morris acted first as an undergraduate at Radcliffe College under the direction of Professor George Pierce Baker, then with the Washington Square Players and Jesse Bonstelle. Her big chance came when Eugene O'Neill cast and worked with her on the complex role of Abbie Putnam in *Desire Under the Elms*. "No play has ever seemed difficult to me since then," she recalled. The mature actress left Le Gallienne's company to join the new Group.

Most of the other actors—from the west and from the east—also came to the Group through schools and theaters that aspired to serve art rather than show business. Art Smith, who spent his youth touring with his father's stock company, then roamed the country as a lumberjack, a longshoreman, and a bohemian, and Philip Robinson, who played in jazz bands, both worked at Chicago's Goodman Theatre, one of the oldest regional theaters with a professional company and a school. Ruth Nelson grew up backstage, touring in vaudeville with her mother, finally getting some education as a teenager in a convent in California. She came East to study with Boleslavsky at the American Laboratory Theatre, where she met and then acted with those who would found the Group. She was also in the large Group contingent in the Theatre Guild's *Elizabeth the Queen*, which in addition to Patten and Carnovsky included the well-trained, very pretty singer and actress Phoebe Brand, who would marry Carnovsky; the lively Gertrude Maynard, known as Mab Anthony, who was the girlfriend and then wife of Maxwell Anderson; and the dapper singer and actor Gerritt (Tony) Kraber, who had toured in Shakespeare and acted in Paris with Copeau. The handsome Walter Coy and the shy Herbert Ratner also found jobs on and off stage with the Guild. Mary Virginia Farmer, a busy radio and stage actress, had performed in Jasper Deeter's idealistic repertory at the Hedgerow Theatre along with her husband Lewis Leverett, who was playing in a production of *The Seagull* directed by the Russian emigré Leo Bulgakov. The spirited William Challee, who had played in stock and in Provincetown, was also in this production. Friendly Ford came to the Group from George Pierce Baker's playwriting course at Yale. Clement Wilenchick, a painter-actor, had worked on sets for Boleslavsky at the American Laboratory Theatre, where he became interested in the Stanislavsky system.

The coterie of young women included the attractive and politically committed Sylvia Feningston, who had participated in the production of Waldo Frank's *New Year's Eve*, and the rather troubled Alixe Walker, from a wealthy New York family, who had worked on Katharine Cornell's *The Age of Innocence*.

The companies in which these actors were formed belonged to the "New Movement" that had introduced major modern European theater artists to America and then had encouraged the new American drama of Eugene O'Neill and others. More than a decade before the Group came into being, George Cram Cook, founder of the seminal Provincetown Players, for example, had preached the doctrine that true theater must be based on the unity that sprang from "one shared fund of feelings, ideas, impulses" more than a decade before the Group came into being.

Those chosen by the Group or those who chose the Group—the selection process really worked both ways—did not fit the glamour image of Broadway. Clurman sometimes wondered why the Group attracted so many odd ducks: ambitious, talented people who felt homeless, who were seeking their identity, who wanted to locate themselves in relation to the world around them. He was describing himself as well as the others. He suggested that the Group's idealistic objectives tended to attract "people under pressure of some kind, troubled, not quite adjusted people, yearners, dreamers, secretly ambitious." Some of them hoped the unique acting process would release them from personal hang-ups. Most hoped to find some intensely personal yet meaningfully social and artistic expression. Their expectations would place a heavy burden on their theater. Even supporters like Theresa Helburn of the Theatre Guild thought them "fanatics."

From the point of view of show business, or dominant American culture, or some of Franchot Tone's upper-class friends, what they were doing may have seemed un-American. The members of the Group, however, thought of themselves as uniquely American. Their interest was in American life; all their plays were to be new, native dramas; their basic objective was to respond to what was happening to America and to themselves in the early years of the Great Depression. They were, in fact, acting on a profound but often obscured impulse in American life.

Although much is made of the Russian influence on the Group's experiment because of their dedication to the Stanislavsky system, their intellectual mentors included Ralph Waldo Emerson (Odets kept a picture of Emerson in his room and called him "the wisest American"); Walt Whitman, whom they often quoted, dramatized, worshiped; Alfred Stieglitz, the famed photographer and spiritual mentor about whom Clurman wrote a paper entitled "Alfred Stieglitz and the Group Idea," before founding the Group Theatre; and Waldo Frank, essayist-critic, who came to be associated with the Group.

Clurman believed that "one of the things that distinguishes us as actors and as a theatre is that we work in America and we believe in certain things, tend to have a certain type of character and ideals, whether we know it or not, because we are Americans." American wealth and resources have brought many aspects of our lives to a "high state of maturity," he argued, but "in a spiritual sense we are still new." He identified the Group with those uniquely American qualities found especially in Whitman—naïveté, iconoclasm, contradiction, the "show me" and "let's start everything from the beginning" quality. Like Emerson's Progressive men of "good hope," they wanted "to speak to the conscience." Although the members all had their theatrical roots in the social and intellectual life of the 1920s, they rejected the pessimism of the expatriate "lost generation" as decorative.

These attitudes led the Chosen Ones to question all aspects of life and to seek new answers with honesty and sincerity. Clurman liked to think of America as the land of opportunity not for conventional success, but for making a great civilization. During the years of struggle to build a Group Theatre, he confessed that along with his complaints, he had a great feeling of exhilaration. "I am American enough to say that the jungle which the American forefathers fought with tools, I will fight again in a new way, and just as they conquered the outer world, I can conquer the inner world." He confessed: "I believe in belief even tho I am not what would ordinarily be called a religious man." What he believed in was the creation of a "new American synthesis."

The Depression gave such a new synthesis a special urgency. The crash all but eliminated the possibility of the economic success that was the essence of the conventional American dream. While some gave up jobs to join the Group, the prognosis for theater, always a sensitive barometer not only of the audience's taste but also of its available cash, was grim. Each season from 1929 on, the number of productions on Broadway dropped. In 1929, there were 249 shows; in 1930–31, 190; in 1932, half the theaters were closed; and by 1939, only 80 shows. The boom that had made the expansive, varied theater of the 1920s possible—that had, indeed, made their beginnings in the little experimental theaters possible—was over. Meisner explained what, in part, drew him to the Group: "What else was there? There was no money. There was no making a good living. When the Depression eased up and people had somewhere to go that was more lucrative, they went" (*Reunion*, 502).

The failure of the economy to recover reduced most members of the Group and their families to hitherto unknown hardship. A few who came from well-to-do homes did not themselves experience the devastating poverty of the decade. In their very range, Clurman felt, they comprised "a perfect mirror of the Depression." None, however, could avoid the ugly Hoovervilles, the pathetic apple sellers, the long bread lines right on Broadway. "The world around you just wouldn't leave you alone" was the way Carnovsky put it.

Overwhelmed by a "sense of decomposition at every level of public and private life" never experienced before, many young people began to listen to that "different drummer" that had provided the rhythm for many American idealists. This alternative American dream emphasized collective responsibility rather than the unfettered individualism so often regarded as the American way. Looking back, Clurman celebrated the Group's finding "a solution to our dilemma in collective action for artistic experiment." The reawakened consciousness of this "Found Generation" led to a zeal for change so that, as Odets was to say in *Awake and Sing!*, "[l]ife shouldn't be printed on dollar bills." (*Reunion*, 475)

The Group could only offer a subsistence wage. For the summer rehearsals at Brookfield some, like Bobby Lewis, paid for their keep, but most were to receive room and board. In New York each actor in the permanent ensemble was to have the security of being paid as long as any Group Theatre production was running. The scale was to be based on the actor's need and his or her usefulness to the ensemble. In order to cover salaries and mount their first production, Crawford canvassed for contributions from, among others, Maxwell Anderson, Edna Ferber, and Eugene O'Neill. The major funding came from the Theatre Guild under whose auspices they were to do their first show.

At many times in the next ten years, Group members probably felt like Clurman's old Jew, but not in the spring of 1931. The 27 who were chosen were thrilled. They shared Lewis's feeling that this was the most important decision in their lives. They had awaited with great anticipation the letters inviting them to come to Brookfield for the summer. These letters were the only contracts the members received. They needed no legal ties; they were bound by that large vision they had shared during the preceding winter. It lifted their spirits that rainy day in June when they took off for Brookfield, and it sustained them not only during the decade of the Group but for the rest of their lives.

Economic issues were not paramount to the founders of the Group. As they were organizing themselves in the unsettled spring and summer of 1931, there was little discussion of the Depression or of politics. Ruth Nelson captured their mood. "We didn't really know the Depression was on. We always lived on nothing. I could put aside twenty dollars a week and take care of groceries and all the bills. . . . We didn't know there was a Depression; we were inspired with the theatre" (*Reunion*, 529).

It was through their belief in the theater, in their way of working, in the renewed idealism of the time that they became most fully aware of themselves and of their era. "It was that kind of inspired moment," Stella Adler believed, "where the actor responded to the social situation, to the group quality of not being alienated or alone, and to the depth to which he could experience his art." Their theater, Clurman told them in his talks, had to say something not only through individual productions but through a series of productions that would mark its whole career. "A theatre could not be one thing one day, another thing another day." It had to have variety, but had to convey "some sense of life which is typical of it as a collective." Theater with a meaning, he was to believe, was one of the Group's unique contributions. (See *Reunion*, 451–52)

That meaning, however, was not a simple slogan or even a philosophy. At a loss to come up with a better word, Clurman called it "our Idea," recognizing that the designation sounded "evasive and vague." Words seemed inadequate. He believed that the "Idea" was defined by the kind of people the leaders were and those they had chosen to work with them. "You know Cheryl Crawford, Lee Strasberg and me," Clurman explained. "You have heard what we think about the theatre; you have listened to our interpretation of plays, you know how we are attacking this project for a new theatre . . . If you are in sympathy with what we say and do . . . then you probably share our Idea. You have the first qualification for work in our theatre."

Dedicated to theater, the only art that would allow them to say what they wanted to say, they were not primarily concerned with innovations in stagecraft, or new styles, or doing "amusing" things. "Whatever novelty our work may show will inevitably derive from our message." Unlike the 1920s generation of artists, the Chosen Ones were not skeptics. They rejected the "cocky pessimism" of their predecessors as "abhorrent and ridiculous." They didn't see themselves as "the Pollyannas of a new day, nor its Messiahs."

> We believe that life is essentially tragic but the movement of our muscles is sufficient warrant for our belief that it is also "worth-while." We do not know—we believe. We have not found, we are seeking... not in the texts of ancient creeds or in those of the up-to-the-minute intellectual academies but in the maze of our own lives, in the lives of those closest to us, in the ordinary routine of our work and our pleasures.

They were prepared for a long "period of discovery" and for their work to be the record of their "continuous growth."

Morris Carnovsky would recall the power of their mission almost 50 years later:

> If we were finished actors when we came to it, the Group unfinished us. It forced us to examine all that we were and had attained in the light of a harsh insistence on basic truth... We of the Group can never forget that we were born as a group in the thirties, at the time of the Great Depression. We saw visible signs of it all around us, and since the experience of being a Group actor was intimately and organically bound up with the world we lived in, it followed with varying intensities of belief, that through our work we must effect, even change, that world. (*Reunion*, 481)

These artists, whose roots were in the wide range of the American middle class, believed they would no longer be condemned to the usual isolation of creators. They would have, for a while at least, a home. The intimacy of their lifestyle, their rehearsal process, and the resulting productions were to intensify both their collective identity and their conflicts with the theater world around them.

Looking back, Clurman pointed out that the Group was the "only theatre which recognized the possibility of pain and failure in the course of our work." Stella Adler when asked what she recalled most vividly about the Group experience, replied: "Trouble, conflict, lack of peace and quiet." The conflicts they were personally living through were to become major themes in their plays. They faced the "tragedy of choice" among crucial competing values. The ambivalence that many felt about this tension is captured in a joke Clurman used to tell. A troubled old Jew says to God, "Are we the Chosen People?" When God says, "Yes," the Jew responds, "Then choose somebody else!"

2. Summertime and the Living Is Collective ᥬ

Brookfield Center is still a delightful, green, and hilly retreat a little over an hour from New York, but in 1931, for the Chosen Ones, it was the place where dreams would come true. Their first summer together was a kind of mystic experience they could not wholly communicate. Ruth Nelson compared it to the first months of a marriage, and Clurman called his chapter in *The Fervent Years* on this period "Honeymoon" (*FY*, 39–54). The night before their departure from New York, some of them gathered at Strasberg's home. Their friend and publicist for the Group Theatre, Helen Deutsch, who had just published a history of the Provincetown Players, was eager for them to make a permanent record of their summer at Brookfield. She gave them a black, imitation leather Day Book, urging them each to take turns jotting down in it everything that took place. "Be as personal as you like, within the limits of conscience," she advised. This fascinating record captures what Brookfield meant to them. It includes many testimonials to becoming "whole," becoming "real," to "not knowing where work finishes and life begins," to "linking the individual and the group," to "giving birth to a new life." Odets, with typical literary flair, wrote ecstatically: "I have begun to eat the flesh and blood of the Group . . . I who cried from my inverted wilderness for strong roots with which to fasten to the swarming, sustaining earth have found them at last in 'The Group.'"

Cheryl Crawford had located what she called "a country enclave" on Hawleyville Road that had enough space to house them all. Overlooking a deep valley, it had five houses, one of which had a kitchen and a dining room, and a large barn perfect for rehearsals with a newly installed floor, electric lights, and benches. Here the company played classical records, drank illegal applejack, took long walks in the woods, and swam nude by moonlight. The men grew beards, some women fell in love with them, others tended children they had brought along. They were all "acting to live and living to act." With romantic ardor, they came to know one another, studied the new system of acting that was to give them a unified craft, and rehearsed Paul Green's *The House of Connelly*. Their actions, their style, and their animated talk, especially about strange Russians with names like Stanislavsky and Boleslavsky, made their Connecticut neighbors fear they were a free-love, anarchist commune.

On their arrival mid-afternoon that rainy Monday, June 8, they settled into the rooms assigned by Crawford. "What I did," she recalled, "was I gave myself a nice room and the rest depended on who lived with whom and needed extra beds." They were a sizable gathering, for in addition to the members of the company, there were, as Crawford calculated, "wives and children, twenty-one Victrolas, three radios and assorted cars and dogs" (*One Naked Individual*, 54). Shortly, there were also two horses brought along by Alixe Walker.

As they were settling in, Franchot Tone, ever a kind of left-wing Boy Scout, organized a baseball game between the "Hard Sluggers" and the "Cagey Bunters" on the soggy lawn. This was a good way, he believed, to help them "overcome the natural self-consciousness" of the first day of their high adventure. At eight-thirty that evening they all gathered in the barn to hear the three directors celebrate the beginnings of their life together. Everyone had a sense that something momentous was happening. In his diary, Odets tried to capture the mood: "A kind of hush falls on all of us and the habitual Strasberg suddenly goes leonine and paces around with his head in his hands. He opens the meeting…and admits that he's nervous." Clurman remembered that Strasberg was so overwhelmed by the occasion that at first he had difficulty speaking at all. Crawford wept.

But Clurman talked. He warned them against animosity or anything that would fracture the group. "We mustn't have it…This is a family. We can hate each other, but we've got to work together. We have to respect each other's faults as well as admire each other's virtues…I don't care if you kill yourselves, but not on the stage, not in rehearsals."

A few of the actors added brief emotional tributes at the short meeting. Lewis Leverett, seasoned by his exposure to alternative theater at Hedgerow Theatre, wrote on the first page in the Day Book that "the belief in the Group idea, half under-standing—half instinctive on the part of many in the company, was strengthened and deepened by this meeting. Not so much by what was said as by the humility and strength of purpose that evidently lie behind it." Odets caught the spirit of the moment with a telling metaphor. "The air is surcharged with a strong feeling to which I find it difficult to apply a name…It reminds me of nothing so much as saved souls giving testimonial at an evangelical meeting. It is true; there was an emotional upheaval there." When the first convocation was over, they went off and marked the occasion by filling the country night air with noble-sounding music played on some of the many Victrolas they had brought along.

The next morning, after breakfast supplied by Constantine Fabian, the one-eyed Russian owner of the camp, they gathered in the parlor. Crawford, who had put together Paul Green's script from various versions in the Theatre Guild office and was to serve as a sort of codirector, read them the play. The Group Theatre was off and running. Brookfield became their theatrical Eden. In subsequent summers of collective living and rehearsals and in winters of performances, the company tried to recapture—with varying degrees of success—the utopian spirit of their initial adventure.

Of course, they were not the first group of stage-struck young actors spending a summer together putting on shows, but others did not have such ambitious inten-tions as the Chosen Ones. Compare them, for example, with the University Players, begun in the summer of 1928 by Charles Leatherbee and Bretaigne Windust at Falmouth on Cape Cod. These two ivy-league undergraduates from cultivated, wealthy families met for the first time at the New York apartment of Elizabeth Hapgood, close friend of Stanislavsky and later the translator of *An Actor Prepares* and his other books on the system. She was giving a party for Vladimir Nemirovich-Danchenko, cofounder of the Moscow Art Theatre, and these young theater buffs from Harvard and Princeton were permitted to attend. Inspired by the Russians and by Max Reinhardt, whose company was then playing in New York, and by the native idealists Eva Le Gallienne and Robert Edmond Jones, they started the University Players the next summer and kept it going until 1932.

Among the members of this talented group were Joshua Logan, Henry Fonda, James Stewart, Margaret Sullavan, Mildred Natwick, Myron McCormick, and Norris Houghton, who told their history in *But Not Forgotten*. In 1931, Logan and Leatherbee spent several months observing Stanislavsky at work in Moscow. When they told him that their hope was to "duplicate the Moscow Art Theatre," he scolded them, saying, "You must not duplicate...you must create something of your own." Articulate and dedicated, they wanted to create excellent theater, but they had no special enthusiasm for particular kinds of plays, or high-minded notions about what acting could be, or big ideas about the relationship of society and self. They were just starting out; they were university trained, East-coast ivy-leaguers; their productions were lively but sometimes amateurish. As Houghton put it, they followed "the intuitive process of creation that is native to our American theatre." Individual members became stars, but the company did not make much of a mark and was soon forgotten.

When Norris Houghton told Stanislavsky about the University Players in 1935, the master could not comprehend the point of their organization. "To start a theatre you must be revolutionary," he explained. "Oh, I don't mean politically. I mean you must be motivated by dissatisfaction in some way with the status quo. Either you must want to produce plays different from those being done around you, or to present them in a different style, or in a different form of theatrical space, or for a different audience" (*Entrances and Exits*, 99).

The Group, inspired by the Moscow Art Theatre's first summer of rehearsal at Pushkino, could boast of the kind of large agenda Stanislavsky recommended. Their gathering involved a great deal more than youthful gregariousness, although there was plenty of that. They swam in the old swimming hole. Two of the women found a secluded spot to sunbathe in the nude, but fled when they discovered motorists could see them from the road. Some competed for free rides on Alixe Walker's horses kept conveniently below the barn. The "girls"—as they were called in those days—went off on picnics or car rides together. When one of the "boys" shaved off the full beard he had grown, his hair plugged up the less-than-high-tech plumbing. Some tried trout fishing with rods they found in one of the cottages. On their tennis court Guru Strasberg was a strong player, and playwright Paul Green, who joined them for a time, proved himself a real pro. The shy Herbie Ratner spent his free time rowing on the lake, playing classical records on his Victrola, and declaiming Shakespeare. Music seemed to be everywhere. Carnovsky played his classical records, Meisner the piano, and Odets banged out the few E-minor cords he knew.

At Brookfield, the company tried to become that close family they had been talking about. Clurman had told them again and again that the "unity of theatrical production...was a unity that does not spring...out of an abstract sense of taste or craftsmanship, but out of a unity that is antecedent to the formation of the theatrical group as such" (*FY*, 33). But he found that, in fact, this unity in life, which was to be the basis of their art, was the chief problem that first summer. The high ideals elaborated in his talks were being tested in the day-to-day activities of the high-spirited, independent, temperamental members.

"It was important for us to know each other and understand each other in order to get the effect we desired on the stage" was the way Cheryl Crawford put it. To help this process along, she became a kind of "big mama," despite her mannish trousers and cropped hair. She took care of things, saw that there were scripts, food, rooms, and so on. She scrounged for money although she did not feel well prepared for the job, and most important, kept her two volatile codirectors working together, a task that often left her in tears. Crawford also suffered creative frustration. Assigned as codirector with Strasberg on *The House of Connelly*, she found herself with little to do and complained of being an "appendage" not an "associate" in the creative process.

For all her "mothering," Crawford hardly fit the maternal stereotype. When she came marching along in her riding breeches, Clurman called her "Squire." Stella Adler's little daughter Ellen was amazed when she saw Crawford in a dress; she thought her a man. Crawford was involved and helpful, but removed. She had her private room and her books. "I had never lived communally with anybody," she reminisced, "and I often had to go off and be by myself because the excitement and the talking and the way people jarred on each other during that summer—it was hard to get used to. I never did get used to it." Thus, she kept to herself, retreating, she recalled, from the mostly Jewish gang that gathered nightly in the dining room below her room to drink tea or coffee or have milk and cookies and "argue and argue and argue and talk."

Clurman, of course, was part of that coffee klatsch. After spending the days "always out there talking, digging into the lawn with his stick, getting one more aspect of the Group into focus," he talked in the evenings to his pals. He worried about the "flock" that had followed him into the wilderness. They were, he believed, "fine, clean and essentially sound," but typically American in their eagerness for growth. His preoccupation with interpersonal relations in the company was so intense that it robbed him of all work initiative. In a reversal of the roles they played in the previous months, Clurman's lassitude was now compensated for by Strasberg's effective command of the rehearsals, which occupied the whole summer. Yet, Clurman gave important talks during the summer on the new method and on the Group spirit. Bobby Lewis confessed that "trying to record in a couple of pages the impressions gathered from a day of discussion with Harold is like inscribing the Lord's Prayer on the head of a pin."

About a month into their stay at Brookfield, Tony Kraber quipped that "Harold's talk today was mostly explaining to Stella what he meant yesterday." Stella Adler was very important to Clurman, but their relationship was difficult. "I supplied the storm and she the surprise" was the way Clurman put it. "She ran away and I ran after. I ran away and she called back. She was unkind and I was foolish... We ran round and round till it was difficult to know who was chasing or following whom. It all meant something." To him, the contradictory relationship with Stella was more than a personal pain. "She in her confusions, in her impulses toward good and evil, kindness and destruction, positive and negative, clarity and chaos represents to me all these things in the whole group," he wrote at the end of the summer to his friend, the photographer Paul Strand.

Stella Adler was an essential member of the company, its most experienced actress, heir to a great tradition. She wrote in the Day Book that "the thing that is most completely satisfying is that I don't know where the work finishes and life begins. It's all linked." For the first time in years she enjoyed rehearsals. "Is it possible that I'm a perfect specimen for the Group? Lee said 'no' a few years ago." But maybe Strasberg was right; she didn't really feel herself part of the Group. On the first night at Brookfield, Clurman described her as "sadly looking out of the window." In retrospect she would confess: "I didn't belong there. I was a complete stranger there because most of them were not very theatrical" (*Reunion*, 507). Yet, Stella had her circle who loved to hear stories about her family and the Yiddish theater, and she had Ellen, her little daughter from a youthful marriage, whom she would send off "to eat something healthy." Her dedication to better acting, to Clurman's philosophy, and to Clurman himself kept her involved in one way or another through most of the ten years of their existence.

Strasberg, still emotionally scarred from the death of his young wife Nora in 1929, was remote. The loss of his devoted bride locked the withdrawn Strasberg in his uncommunicative shroud. Carnovsky, always observant, remembered that "Lee had a curious priest-like quality...I recall him in that ugly yellow slicker that he wore as if that were his priest's uniform. He'd walk through the rain in that. He was so fanatically absorbed in his work. And this was good— very moving." In those early days, Odets thought both Strasberg and Clurman lacked "kindness" and appeared to their subjects as "Jehovahs with forked lightnings." Strasberg seemed to him "juiceless," but he soon realized that their director had a very good head for facts, which he could spew forth with clarity, and that he had a "certain awareness of people...but he was far away."

Strasberg certainly must have been aware that the young women all seemed to have tender feelings for him. One evening when he wasn't feeling up to par, "restoratives were applied by fluttering ladies," and, to cheer him up, Crawford told him that "three members of the F.S. [feminine sex] had voted him the most attractive man in the Group." Beany (Margaret) Barker, assigned the leading role in *The House of Connelly*, remembered that the complicated Strasberg was very gentle at this time. "I'll never forget the touch of his hands...people said he was a little in love with me, but I'm not sure. I used to take him for an ice cream cone at night after the show." Strasberg confessed being attracted to the beautiful, talented Barker. "If I'd had more gumption I probably would have made an approach, except I could never make an approach to anybody."

With Paula Miller, Strasberg probably didn't have to make the approach. Some thought her warm and friendly; others considered her aggressive. She set her cap for Strasberg. Mab Anthony, who was living with playwright Maxwell Anderson in a cottage nearby, claimed to have given Paula advice that summer. Anthony, who "prided herself on being able to capture any man she wanted," told people that she said to her friend: "Look, you listen to me, and I'll tell you every move to make...You want Lee Strasberg? I'll tell you everything to do." Whatever the advice, it worked.

Paula was married, but when her husband turned up at Brookfield, he found himself displaced by Strasberg.

Beany Barker was housed in the same cottage as Franchot Tone, who had been her friend and protector during the run of *The Age of Innocence*. In reminiscing about their communal life, she laughed; "I don't know how important it was that my room was here and Franchot's was there. He never paid any attention to me." That first week at Brookfield, Barker recalled, they were all austere in their dedication, no smoking or drinking. But before long, despite prohibition, they found a farmer nearby who sold them applejack. The drinkers gathered regularly to carouse in Tone and Barker's cottage.

For all his dedication to the collective idea, Franchot Tone remained their leading man and also their playboy prankster and hell-raiser. He complained in a Day Book entry that "this place is no bargain. It hasn't had its hair cut for a long time anyway." Tone often took off by himself; when he was bored, he was given to making mischief.

Barker along with Eunice Stoddard, Alixe Walker, and Dorothy Patten made up a little social circle. Although years later Stoddard, for one, looked back on their cliquishness as a mistake, they did have the special bonds of their class. Stoddard and Alixe Walker, who were sharing a room, had been together at Brearley School in New York, and Barker had attended Bryn Mawr, where many of the Brearley girls went. Stoddard described Dorothy Patten as "not eastern seaboard; she was definitely Chattanooga. But she was closer to us than to the others." The little band read the books Strasberg told them about and went off for rides in Stoddard's car. "We acted like college girls, like sophomores. I think other people resented it," Stoddard recalled. "But it didn't occur to us at the time because people were joining up in different groups anyhow." She and Ruth Nelson, from their very different east and west coast backgrounds, were great friends from their days at the American Laboratory Theatre, where they had alternated playing the lead in the production of Boleslavsky's *Martine*.

A number of couples comprised little units of their own. Ruth Nelson and Bill Challee, much in love, were often on their own. They married in the fall while others lived together throughout the 1930s—Morris Carnovsky and Phoebe Brand, Stella Adler and Harold Clurman. These liaisons were an accepted part of the artists' life. J. Edward Bromberg and his wife Goldie, who lived below Stoddard and Walker's room, were preoccupied with their baby. But Bromberg along with Carnovsky avidly joined in the discussions of the coffee klatsch, as did Lewis Leverett. His wife, Virginia Farmer, was staying at her mother's nearby country home. Their marriage was falling apart that summer. Mary Morris's greater maturity led her to caution the others that their kind of creative work required "patience and vision," but she was pleased to be spending the summer in the beautiful countryside with her son Richard and working with "such fine and lovely people." The unattached single men and women formed occasional alliances, some of them homosexual. Odets sent passionate daily letters to the beautiful Eunice Stoddard and took romantic walks with Beany Barker.

These clusters, with their differences of gender, class, religion, and temperament, occasioned some tension at Brookfield and much more later. One much-talked about blow-up was the confrontation between Tone and Carnovsky on the Fourth of July. Tone shot off fire-crackers, especially disturbing Carnovsky relaxing on his back porch, as always, playing his favorite Mozart records. Finally, Carnovsky cried out, "Franchot, for God's sake, I can't stand the noise." Tone shouted back: "And I can't stand your noise." Declaring "I am an American," Tone ran off to his New York girlfriends and pals, whom he kept apart from the collective life. (*FY*, 47)

As the weeks went on there were expressions of ambivalence, frustration, impatience, tension. The directors, acting in loco parentis for their colorful brood, seemed to take literally the lectures they gave about the actors' need to preserve a childlike creativity. Clurman noted the company's trust in the leaders and their playful innocence. But there was also a quality of overbearing, old world paternalism in Clurman and Strasberg that the actors found objectionable. The two men would beam like proud parents when visitors were around, but among themselves they "spoke to everybody as to pupils who had to be instructed, sinners who had to be saved, mental babies who had to be whipped into growing up," according to the somewhat older Mary Morris's view of life at Brookfield. (*FY*, 48) Virginia Farmer, more experienced like Mary Morris, complained in an open letter to Strasberg that "though we may and indeed must come as children to learn something, we must come also as adults to sift, digest, to make these new things our own, through the processes of our own beings."

Although the sense of the Group as a family satisfied their desire for a communal life to counter the loneliness and social chaos of an individualistic society, the Group was no idealized American family. What it most often resembled was an emotional immigrant clan with its shouting, its quarrels, its passionate devotion, and its many glasses of tea. Some who came from very different backgrounds found it difficult to adjust to what Beany Barker, from Baltimore and Bryn Mawr, described as the "closeness and warmth of the Jewish family" (*Reunion*, 524).

The point of their living together, of course, was to enable them to act together with unique rapport. The day was scheduled to maximize the time for work. With three directors involved simultaneously, no holidays observed, and all members present, the place was abuzz.

The Group was not constrained by Actors' Equity rules about how long they could rehearse. Their model was the Moscow Art Theatre, which sometimes worked for several years on a show. They also tried to be as disciplined as Stanislavsky's actors. No smoking in the rehearsal barn, not even on the porch. No drinking at all—at least during the first week. Later, they tried to keep one another from imbibing or smoking during rehearsals.

The rehearsal process reinforced the spirit of devotion. When *The House of Connelly* was read to the company, for example, the actors did not know who had been cast. This tactic kept everyone involved in the production as a whole rather than concentrating only on individual roles and interpretations. The collective exploration went on for about a week as they read the play together around the table, listened to Clurman explicate its dramatic and social intricacies in afternoon sessions, and began investigating with Strasberg the acting method they would all use. Only then were the parts finally given out and the casting set.

Having thus caught everyone's interest, the directors kept them creatively engaged by training them as an ensemble. Everyone, whatever his or her talent, was taught to act with the same personal reality, in emulation of the Moscow Art Theatre productions that had so inspired Strasberg. The leads, Tone, Barker, Carnovsky, Stoddard, Adler, and the others who played small roles and supernumeraries, were all instructed in the same craft and motivated with what Bobby Lewis, reminiscing years later, called the "ask not what the Group can do for you, ask what you can do for the Group" (*Reunion*, 485). The process held them together.

In the afternoons, Clurman gave inspirational talks, mainly about the need for "dynamic humility." He believed, as he put it, in concentrating "on what we could get from each other, and what we could give, too, through the love of what we were trying to do." He stressed the similarities among the members rather than the all-too-evident differences. He tried to prepare them for the problems they were going to face as actors working on Broadway. Clurman often decried "the tragic waste of talent in the American theatre," the deterioration of stars like John Barrymore, Laurette Taylor, and Jeanne Eagels. In their group, he explained, the directors were trying to understand the actor's life and not just technical or artistic difficulties. "The treatment of many artistic problems, we thought was often superficial because it limited itself to these problems alone for fear of infringing on more intimate matters." The Group wanted the actor to become aware of himself, as Stella Adler put it. "Did he have any problems? Did he understand them in relation to his whole life? To society? Did he have a point of view in relation to these questions?" (See *Reunion*, 506ff.) The directors said that they did not want the acting to be used in a "neurotic way for its therapeutic values, as self-escape, rather than for self-expression."

Despite some resistance, each actor's personal predicaments and hang-ups were discussed, especially with Clurman, but also with Crawford and Strasberg, who would explain that "we were making a group, not hiring a company, and that a certain closeness to the very pulse of the individuals composing the group was essential to real leadership in it." Central to these intrusions into the actors' personal life, which Clurman admitted some might consider "immodest prying into succulent privacies," was the belief that "the individual needed help and an objective aim beyond himself to avoid an isolation that would end in confusing and diminishing him." The actors cherished Clurman's insights, personal warmth, and concern. In turn, the summer made him realize that "human relationships are the most important thing to me and if they are not right, if 'art' doesn't affect them, if I do not feel that everything is sound and clear in that respect, then everything else becomes unimportant, even futile to me."

Clurman also explained the theoretical basis of their acting method by analyzing the vocabulary of the Stanislavsky system. On the afternoon of June 23, Lewis took notes as Clurman, sitting on the lawn, pointer in hand, explained the basic concept of "action" as "the reason for being on the stage" and illustrated how "one line can have 100 different actions." The session explored "beats," "adjustment," "affective memory," "long-distance mood," "relation," and "relaxation," suggesting appropriate exercises and connections with *The House of Connelly* rehearsals. In the next few days he introduced the central idea of the "spine," the action that "goes thru the whole play" and is "created by the interpretation of the directors." He pointed out how action, adjustments, and emotion were related to characterization, which as the "dress over the body" was the last thing to work for. He even reviewed the controversy about whether the actor should feel his or her part, placing the old question in the context of the psychology of the actor and the expressive function of the actor's art. Other talks ranged over Clurman's favorite social, philosophical, and psychological themes. He elucidated Gordon Craig's dictum that "[a]fter we've reformed the art of theatre, we must remake the life of the theatre" by linking the childlike creativity of the actor to the human desire to be part of "something outside us." The Group was important because it helped the actor to grow "out of himself" and "into the world" (see Lewis, *S&A,* 41–42).

It was Lee Strasberg's task to transform the 27 actors into an "artistic organism with its own special character and aims." He, too, gave a few inspirational talks that zeroed in directly on basic acting problems and the stages of rehearsal, which were to become his lifelong preoccupations. The actor must have a conscious technique, he explained, since creativity is bound by the rigid time limits of performance. "In studying any character the important thing is not how but why the person behaves a certain way—then find equivalent reason for such behavior in yourself." Substitution and use of feelings associated with the actor's own past were the means to link actor and role. Memorizing lines without establishment of a relationship with other actors, he considered a very poor use of the actor's much-needed energy. The actor must become "an IDEAL machine for transmission of emotion" by developing a sensitivity to objects that goes beyond their immediate quality to "see them as symbols of something more significant."

More important than Strasberg's talks were the rehearsals in which he taught them the craft of acting. Odets wrote in their Day Book. "Four days of actual work negate talks and talks and talks. A Miracle like to the bursting of a chrysalis."

Although teaching and directing were one activity for Strasberg this first summer, it is helpful to look, first, at the method he was teaching. Strasberg's objective for the company, in Eunice Stoddard's view, was "to eradicate bad habits, to loosen people up, to make them see that there were a great many facets to working in the new way that they hadn't worked in before." The actors felt that he was experimenting. His main effort, as Tony Kraber saw it, was "trying to get the actors to work together. Not to think so much of what you, yourself, were doing or trying to do. But to make a connection with the other people."

All aspects of the training—the mental, the physical, the emotional—were governed by the idea of "living through all soul states" in such a way that the results would occur as they do in real life. This was the basic objective Strasberg had taken from his teacher, Boleslavsky. To help the actor achieve this end, he gave each one exercises, beginning with an attack on his or her greatest enemy, physical or muscular tension. "Reeelaxxx," Strasberg would insist in his rigid, tight-lipped way. Despite his own tension, he showed the actors how to "shake themselves out" so that they could be relaxed but energized. He would have them sit in chairs alternately relaxing and tensing, learning to gain control over each part of the body. To combat the tension engendered by being on stage, he introduced a concentration exercise. "For three minutes each day we concentrate on an object," they reported.

The actor's principal problem, as Strasberg defined it, was "training himself to make imaginary objects or stimuli real to himself as they would be in life, so that they will awaken the proper sensory, emotional, or motor response." Thus, along with concentration, exercises in sense awareness or memory became a staple of his method. He would tell the actors to practice putting on shoes and stockings, combing hair, picking up a cup and saucer, or listening to a fog horn, a train whistle, a subway, jazz music, classical music, without the objects or sounds present. He would warn them not to be preoccupied with what they were showing the audience, but to concentrate wholly on bringing the moment alive to themselves.

Relaxation, concentration, and sense memory were also needed for what became known as "the exercise," the one that dug into the actor's personal emotional memory so that he or she could substitute true feeling for "clichés of stage deportment." Strasberg taught them that "every human being contains within himself the keys on which to play all types of emotional experiences." He would tell the actors to start by recalling "any unusual event that has happened to you...not too dramatic, but...sufficiently unusual to have made an impression on you." He instructed them to review their lives to identify those experiences from the past that still moved them. Since long-remembered childhood experiences had the strongest hold, in his opinion, these memories were the emotional keys to touch. By concentrating on the original objects and events and not on the emotion itself, the actor, Strasberg held, can become "so conditioned that he can command himself to experience any emotion."

After filling a "Golden Box" of varied, stored emotional memories, the actor could then "Take a Minute" to substitute some powerful personal feeling wherever his role called for sudden or strong emotional expression. As an example of the process, Ruth Nelson suggested she could have used her complex emotions when the much-delayed letter asking her to come to Brookfield for the first summer finally arrived. She recalled,

> If you were to be asked to reproduce that moment, or use emotions that you had at that moment, in a play, what you would do is to try and visualize everything connected with that moment. Not yourself, not what you were feeling, not your emotion, but what room you were in. Was it winter or summer, the environment, and who was around. As you begin to think and try to recall everything concerned with that moment around you, you find yourself receiving those emotions. You find the emotion of that moment coming to you without any effort on your part.

This exercise was carried out, Nelson explained, not only during rehearsals but also during performance so that moment by moment the actors would shift between the character and their personal past.

To further facilitate the actor "living through" an experience rather than "indicating it," Strasberg made extensive use of improvisation in training and rehearsal. Since the improvisations, like the emotional memory exercises, began with the actors' own lives, it is not surprising that "adjustments" to complicate and enrich scenes were often drawn from familiar situations in the 1930s—being fired from a job, competition for scarce work, tasks of relief workers, refugees on the run.

Improvisations, which were central to the idea of acting as a collective art, also helped the actors become conscious of individual problems. "It is continually amazing," Bobby Lewis wrote in the Day Book, "to see that each specific action of my work here...has such a concrete relation to my life." Odets confided to his diary that he dreamed "of the time when he will become untangled as an actor by the fanatic Strasberg, who in his relentless hunt for true emotion, it is said, 'can unlock doors within you didn't even know were there.'" Clurman, who promoted Strasberg as the master of the craft, was nevertheless amazed at the desperate eagerness of the Group.

> Our actors do want to become better – they do want to work (they follow me with pathetic eyes, the small part actors who want additional training)...And more astonishing still is the naturalness—one might almost say the casualness—with which the actors take Lee's direction.

Despite the willingness of the actors to follow their leaders, honing the special sensory and emotional sensibility required for their theater provoked considerable comment among the actors and also outsiders. Phoebe Brand recalled first seeing these kind of exercises on a visit to the American Laboratory Theatre long before the Group was founded. When Strasberg gave them similar exercises at Brookfield, she said, "we thought, well, here we go, we're gonna be those glasses of orange juice or a match box." (The match box exercise, in which the actor concentrates on every aspect of the little wooden box leading to a wealth of personal, social, and historical detail, goes back to the earliest days of the Stanislavsky system.) Herbie-the-Actor, as the withdrawn young Ratner was teasingly called, was given to practicing being a tree or an apple with endless dedication. And Carnovsky, so eager to learn, had puzzled: "What's this hocus-pocus?" (*FY*, 42).

It wasn't only the process that could be disturbing; some egos were wounded by the casting. Although Odets, for example, was made to understand by Strasberg that his abilities as an actor were not highly regarded, he was still chagrined to be cast in *The House of Connelly* as a tenant farmer with only one line. (Brenman-Gibson, 195) The emphasis on group process and group life also helped Ruth Nelson overcome her terrible disappointment when she, too, was cast in a bit part in *The House of Connelly*. She had played the lead in Boleslavsky's *Martine*, had acted in *Red Rust*, and had been one of the most enthusiastic attendants at Clurman's talks. Now she was asked to take on the role of a young mulatto girl who was scheduled to be played by a Black actress when they returned to New York. In the end Nelson loved the part very much, even rolling her hair tightly in leather curlers, and then brushing it out with Brilliantine to achieve an authentic image. (See *Reunion*, 528)

Two Black actresses had come to Brookfield to play women field-hands important to Paul Green's plot, but they were not considered members of the company. One was the greatly admired Rose McClendon, whom the critic Alexander Woollcott had described as having the "lost loveliness that was Duse." The other was Fannie de Knight, who expressed her gratitude in the Day Book for the opportunity to meet "this most interesting sociable group of aspirants in this Utopia." Crawford was assigned to direct their scenes since she knew the actresses from the Theatre Guild production of *Porgy*. She made no attempt to use the Group method with them, in part because she felt these very professional actresses would be offended, and in part because, as she put it, "what I knew about the method at the time was gleaned mainly from books." It was not until Strasberg allowed Crawford to observe him with the actors that she became more knowledgeable. (*Naked Individual*, 54)

Anecdotes abound showing how life and art were fully intertwined for the actors. A party at the nearby home of Eunice Stoddard's wealthy parents, meant to provide some much-needed relaxation, flared up into an emotional conflagration. Informal in their shorts and slacks, the Group trooped over to Washington, Connecticut, on a hot Sunday afternoon. They were met by Stoddard's parents in their beautiful white house set amid rolling lawns and looked after by a staff of formally attired servants. According to Stoddard, the company ate and drank applejack in abundance, toasted marshmallows, and played games on the lawn, wreaking havoc on the place and totally ignoring her parents. As they rushed back without so much as a thank you to their barn at Brookfield for a scheduled eight o'clock rehearsal, Strasberg was ready for them—cool and collected, his "face a relentless mask," according to Clurman. After a long silence, he asked: "Do you feel tired?" Fearful of his intense, autocratic rule over them, the actors assured him that they were not. He ignored their answers and in a controlled voice announced: "There will be no rehearsal tonight. You had such a good time today that you are in no condition to rehearse" (*FY*, 52). His lips were bloodless as he spoke, Beany Barker remembered. Suddenly, he screamed and shouted at them. His rigidity triggered a wild outburst among the somewhat drunken men who, in reaction to Strasberg's fierce rebuke, tore off their clothes. Naked and wild, some jumped into the pond; others threw up in the bathtubs. They tore pillows apart, slinging feathered sacks at one another in a noisy melee. Barker feared that "Lee was going to die. It was awful . . . He screamed, then something happened in the back of his throat and he was tongue-tied. I was terrified for Lee."

Clurman later explained the episode as "Lee's way of making a point the actors would not soon forget. The actor couldn't come to rehearsal casually; he had to be physically and mentally prepared . . . He wanted to teach them that alcoholic conviviality was not the proper preparation for rehearsal." But, in retrospect, Clurman felt there was more to Strasberg's harshness; perhaps "some scratch had been inflicted on his ego during the course of the afternoon" (*FY*, 52). Clurman's efforts to mollify the actors led to a tense exchange between him and Strasberg during which Strasberg spoke in anger, "You will please not speak to my actors," and later apologized for referring to "my actors." (*FY*, 52–53)

Much to their own surprise, the experiences of the summer were highlighting temperamental and even aesthetic differences between the two leaders. Clurman, whose inspirational force had brought the company together in the spring, was finding it hard to work at Brookfield. "What tied me up," he wrote to Paul Strand, "was being so close to and deeply concerned and pained with the personal-moral problems of the group . . . the endless, confused, tragic enigma of the personal human relations of the people." His troubled relations with Stella epitomized for him complications in the company and even in the "whole world." Strasberg, on the other hand, was now in his element, as Clurman saw it. "Lee doesn't really live outside the rehearsal hall; indeed, he hardly seems a person outside the theatre...Lee's 'silence,' his self-repression and his 'aloneness' give him a certain strength, a certain nobility and power," he felt. Although Clurman believed Strasberg had "great humility before his work," his "personal feeling of superiority" made any criticism of his efforts seem a personal affront. But, Clurman also realized, with considerable prescience at the end of their first summer together, that his collaborator was "unable to argue about his work unless he first gets sore and allows himself in his anger to feel 'superior.' "

Yet, there were very happy social occasions and relationships. Playwright Maxwell Anderson was a genial host at his close-by summer home. He really enjoyed his youthful, idealistic neighbors. The Group camp attracted a number of visitors, among them Paul Strand and Ralph Steiner, whose photographs over the years were to form an important record; Mordecai Gorelik, who was later to become one of their main designers; and Luther Adler, who came to visit his sister and "to flirt with available girls," and shortly joined up. (*FY*, 49)

Biblical language alone seemed appropriate to their aspirations, their accomplishments, and their difficulties. In mid-July, Paul Green spoke to the assembled company: "Ye are the brethren, ye are the sisters marching to Canaan land! May you live to bless the thorns and even like St. Francis be not angry with the fleas." Brookfield was their Paradise or Garden of Eden. The beauty of the country acquired mythic intensity. Rose McClendon thanked the company, saying, "I was a stranger and ye took me in."

Everything seemed rewarding, even the often painful one-on-one discussions with the directors during which each actor's faults were examined. To Odets, the care and concern gave the actors a sense of being special, of being part of something new and invaluable. Looking back many years later, Odets voiced a view most members shared that Brookfield was "the heartland of art and culture and creativity...and morality."

Despite their commitment to respond to the issues of the day, they were so caught up in their pastoral paradise that they forgot about politics and social problems. Clurman, too, was worried: "They act as if this were an eternal summer, as if they were going to be able to discuss their parts, do affective memory exercises, run the Victrola, swim, play tennis, and dress in pajamas for ever and ever." The members gave no evidence of understanding how hard it had been to set up their summer's "paradise" and how very difficult it would be to sustain it during the tough coming winter on Broadway.

Although the actors were blissfully enjoying the wonders of their summer, they were, of course, preparing in their rehearsals of *The House of Connelly* for their return to Broadway. After Crawford read the play to the assembled company in the parlor on their first full day at Brookfield, they immediately set to work. "The dark doings" of the Connellys, as Joe Bromberg put it in the Day Book for that date, were discussed, and "Lee clarified for all in a simple straightforward manner, the inner significance of the play."

The ideas for *The House of Connelly* involved their interpretation of the text, and also, perhaps more important at this time, the rehearsals and training in the new method that Strasberg was using to weld the disparate actors into an ensemble. That was the top priority of the summer. For, as Clurman realized, "at this time—and perhaps the only time in our history—concern over the play gave way to the actors' far greater absorption in it as a vehicle for the strengthening of their craft."

There doesn't seem to be any surviving statement by Strasberg of the significance of Green's play or his directorial concept for realizing it. He was not given to writing out his responses, and no one seems to have noted down details of what he said. His preoccupation in this initial Group production centered almost exclusively on acting problems rather than on ambitious notions about interpretive staging. Strasberg's comments tended to be psychological perceptions about roles or generalizations about style and theatrical anecdotes. It was not his way to dig into the words or immerse himself deeply in the text. When, in the 1970s, he lectured on "The Stages of Rehearsal," those sequential steps he first developed in the Group, he revealed that he normally read the plays he directed once and only once. What he considered important was the director's first impression because "that's what the audience is going to have," he explained. Reading and rereading, he believed, led the director to lose the perspective that paralleled the audience's immediate response. "Trust your first feeling," sums up his advice.

At Brookfield, the reading by the actors started after dinner on that first day as they began the preliminary study "around the table," as they called it. The schedule set that day held for most of the summer: Strasberg worked on scenes with the main characters during the days; the evenings were used for a general run-through that everyone attended. At the same time Clurman discussed the play with the company. His dramatic analysis ignited the collaborative production process in which all three founders were involved. Clurman and Crawford essentially divided the functions of dramaturg or script advisor between them, both having greater literary interest than Strasberg.

Clurman analyzed *The House of Connelly* as a drama of the decay of the old South. The cultivated but lifeless and racist plantation owners are being displaced by crude but vigorous tenant farmers. The two classes confront each other in the romance of the aristocratic-but-weak Will Connelly and the hardworking farmer's daughter, Patsy Tate, whose love ultimately rescues him from the inertia of his tradition. Played out in the run-down grandeur of Connelly Hall and on the neglected plantation grounds, the action juxtaposes social change and the timeless rituals of the earth and the poor farm hands, especially the elderly Blacks, who are rooted in the land. In Green's historical drama of southern change, however, Clurman identified a general theme the Group was to emphasize in many of its plays, namely, "the basic struggle between any new and old order." As the Group members became an ensemble, they hoped to make a positive, collective statement not only about the transformation of the South, but also an affirmation of the social and theatrical invigoration of contemporary life they themselves hoped to effect.

Clurman also applied the concepts of the Stanislavsky system to the script. He suggested that Patsy Tate, the farmer's young daughter who infuses Will Connelly with her eager spirit, has as her spine or basic action the drive "to build herself a new life." He told the actors to look to the end of the play for the meaning of the action and the proper spine for each character; thus, useless, inebriated Uncle Bob Connelly may voice some positive views in the early scenes but he must do so as a man who by the end will commit suicide. Clurman's emphasis on endings was to have important consequences for many of the scripts the Group produced.

As Strasberg's rehearsals progressed, those who had small parts would hang around the rehearsal barn, which Odets dubbed "the Vatican of the Group without Swiss guards." Here one could see Strasberg sitting at the table "with a stoic face," and Crawford sitting beside him at the table also "with a stoic face." Those, like Odets, who were not in on the individual rehearsals of the leads, had to content themselves with experiencing the new technique in the group scenes directed by Strasberg and in sessions run by Clurman or occasionally by Crawford. Odets complained that the rehearsals did not "refresh" him because he had so little to do. He was also sometimes bored at rehearsal "because Lee Strasberg, when he explains something, goes in for verbosity on a grand scale, forgetting in his zeal that we have intelligences too." Strasberg's run-on sentences and patronizing attitudes were already a source of irritation for some of his actors.

Bobby Lewis, who, like Odets, had only a bit part, talked Crawford into letting him be assistant to stage manager Alixe Walker in order to be in the rehearsal room when Strasberg worked with the individual lead players: Margaret Barker as the vibrant tenant-farmer's daughter Patsy Tate; Franchot Tone as the weak Will Connelly, scion of the Connelly family; Morris Carnovsky as his hard-drinking Uncle Bob; Stella Adler and Eunice Stoddard as the Connelly spinster sisters; Mary Morris as old Mrs. Connelly; and Art Smith as Patsy Tate's tenant-farmer father. Lewis would sweep out the barn vigorously with his broom and then sit inconspicuously in the corner watching Strasberg direct. "That's where I learned the 'big stuff,'" he recalled.

Beany Barker's preparation of Patsy Tate provides a glimpse of how Lee Strasberg worked with his leads. After a few rehearsals, she noted in the Day Book that "much had happened for the Connelly family." Yet, she was not sure what Strasberg wanted from the actors—a complaint that was to become frequent over the years. "Lee talked at great length after this last reading, claiming there had been a certain too-conscious seeking for mood and that mood alone had no drama—that it was the struggle to overcome a mood which creates drama." She confessed it wasn't easy to produce what Strasberg wanted. At the first reading, he came up behind her, relaxed her shoulders, and taught her a kind of energizing by totally shaking her out and "getting absolute relaxation" (*Reunion*, 522). Barker recalled that many of Strasberg's comments to the actors were impressive and was "delighted at the natural and wholly comprehensive acceptance of those who were criticized. I determined to profit thereby."

What this talented, upper-middle-class young woman was trying to learn from Strasberg was how to relax in order to open herself emotionally to the demands of playing the rather forward, sexy peasant girl, Patsy. Paul Green said he "couldn't believe" his eyes at this bit of casting. He told the directors, "[S]he won't do, she doesn't have it." But Lee said, "Now, never mind, she'll have it by opening night." According to her good friend Eunice Stoddard, when Barker found one section difficult, "General Lee helped her on her way to a deeper approach to the scene...in a private interview." Perhaps it was in this interview that Strasberg guided her, through the use of emotional memory and substitution, to create a personal truth for her character. "He didn't think my type of gentle lovemaking on stage was strong enough (which God knows in terms of my lack of experience must have been rather gentle)," Barker reminisced. "So he would have me do an exercise of anger recall. And the anger would get something that was as passionate as he wanted Patsy to be in the play. It was a total substitution of what the real emotion was, put in the mold of the scene" (*Reunion*, 522).

Even the often restless Franchot Tone became caught up in the rehearsal process, especially the improvisations, which Strasberg used extensively. "It's encouraging to feel again the stir in the bones of creative acting. It only lasts a minute but it's laboratory work that everybody takes courage from." Tone was less sanguine about the progress the cast was making. "Lee and Cheryl do all the work and sort of drag us after. I hope we can begin to act before Strasberg runs down." Yet, he believed, "this will be a great theatre—some day."

Art Smith was pleased that they were rejecting the conventions he had known in routine, touring productions. "Now we throw out the well-oiled but useless machinery and start painfully with building blocks. Simplicity is elusive and the truth hard to tell." Even Carnovsky with his wide-ranging experience in some of the finest Broadway productions recalled: "We were ruthless in tearing ourselves apart in order to build ourselves up again" (*Reunion*, 481). Playing the superfluous, dissolute Uncle Bob Connelly, he worked hard to bring "a different personal life" to the role by examining in himself some "interior facet of emotion that I had never consciously tangled with before."

Although she often felt out of step with the Group, Stella Adler, nevertheless, found strong personal reinforcement in the rehearsal of this initial production. Noting parallels to her own life in the behavior of Geraldine, the disappointed older Connelly sister, she realized that "the problems that I have are the problems the play has." Taking courage from the theme of positive personal and social change, she wrote in the Day Book that "the things that are truest for the play can be so for me, perhaps for everyone." Strasberg had explained that every object and every moment on stage, like the famous little matchbox in their exercises, should transcend mere casual utility to express a larger life. For the actor who "becomes a symbol thru which all life comes," as Strasberg put it, there need no longer be a separation of life and art. Stella felt the force of this artistic ideal.

It was not only the leads who were having a personal creative experience. The group scenes of poor Blacks and tenant farmers played by Bobby Lewis, Tony Kraber, Ruth Nelson, Phoebe Brand, Clifford Odets, and others were rehearsed in Strasberg's special way, which combined individual emotional memory exercises with improvisation. To intensify Group action, relationships, and characterization, Strasberg had the supers improvise scenes unrelated to the text. In one they improvised being trapped in a burning mine shaft. The desperation of crawling in the dark "created a group sense," Barker recalled. "When you all play in a mine together, you have to have some sort of relationship. Is it dark? Who is to help me see? Does somebody have a light? Do you have a match? Dare we burn up that much air?"

The Christmas Eve dinner in the second scene of Act One of *The House of Connelly* was put together through improvisations. The scene juxtaposed the debt-ridden, desiccated Connellys vainly trying to recreate the lost elegance of 150 years in the house with the vitality and joyous abandon of the tenant revelers who intrude on the masters. The first rehearsal for the serenaders began with a "lot of hop, skip and jumps interspersed with spirituals," wrote Ruth Nelson in the Day Book. In high spirits they "took a moment" to think of jolly parties they had attended and took an "adjustment" to neighbors complaining about the noise; they drank imaginary gin and played spin-the-bottle to kiss embarrassed girls. Everything contributed to a wild scene. Nelson believed that Strasberg was working to get real play as the foundation upon which to build the scene.

With a word from Strasberg, the revelers returned to being serious Group actors. Their director was pleased. He explained that the spontaneity of the improvisation was necessary to play the actual scene. "What makes a group scene effective is not what all the people are told to do at once but what each individual does and his relation to the scene and the other actors," he cautioned them, enunciating one of his basic principles.

"What an interesting way to go about the making of such a scene," exclaimed the experienced Virginia Farmer. "What a multitude of possibilities it opens up—how much there is to try and to learn about it and through it." Strasberg himself was pleased by the end of the first month with the authentic "life" they were creating. That meant more to him than their lapses in dialect or their becoming incomprehensible when carried away by the moment—inconsistencies that were later to be noted by reviewers. As the director of this new company, he was experiencing a rare moment of satisfaction.

> To watch life being born in any object is always a fascinating thing—but to watch it transform one person into another under your very eyes—and to know that you have helped to do it—that the thing is so near for you and yet so far—I wish the actor would sometimes realize how much the director's joy and happiness depend on him.

Even though Strasberg missed the "do or die quality" that the actors had shown in some of the projects undertaken even before they decided to start a company, he felt that their work was progressing "along definite lines —nothing is important today that will not be so tomorrow—nothing is important that will not create an entire person—not just an actor but an artist... the actor is the craftsman in the artist— the artist must be developed—the actor must be trained." There is no magical formula, only struggle, he told them. "We'll work on it" became his lifelong refrain.

The actors themselves were amazed at the whole process. The identity of life and art that they so devotedly struggled to realize during the rehearsals not only transformed them but also the meaning and text of the play itself. Paul Green's original script emphasized a brooding sense of doom by juxtaposing the romance of Will and Patsy with the weird rituals of the two ancient Black crones who serve as Fate figures. In the final moments of the drama these representatives of the old South choke the life out of Patsy. After working on the script, the three directors invited Green to join them in Brookfield in order to convince him to rewrite the ending. Instead of the rather poetic, folk drama denouement, they wanted Patsy's lower-class, earthy vitality and love to rejuvenate the weak Connelly heir and the land. Although Green saw his drama as tragic, he believed a positive ending could be justified historically. Giving in to their pressure, even thinking that their point of view might be interesting to explore, he wrote the alternate close the directors requested.

The company had made Green's play their own. Through their rehearsal process they had infused the play with their hopeful, collective spirit. Patsy's "spine," the need to make a new life," was also the spine of the Group Theatre. "In a sense, we felt," Barker said, "that Patsy represented what we as a theatre wanted to do to the old theatre, which was to take its

> values and restore them with blood and life...That play was to me what I felt I was in theatre for...If people from such a varied background, some miserably poor, some very close to stardom, were somehow willing to put a theatre before themselves, then it had to be mystical. There was some spiritual power [there]. (*Reunion*, 522)

That power manifested itself at a run-through at the end of their stay at Brookfield. In their barn, without a stage, sets, or costumes, they "poured forth a concentrated stream of fervor that was like the pent-up rivers of all their young life's experience and the aspirations awakened and released through the summer's efforts. The company was exalted by its own transformation," Clurman declared. (*FY*, 53–54)

After 12 weeks of rehearsals, they were ready to return to New York. On the last night Clurman spoke, giving a "salute to the future." He reminded them of Beany Barker's exchange with a producer who asked her how long she would be busy with her present engagement. Her response: "If our play is a success—twenty years. If not—twenty years" (*FY*, 54). They were elated, Clurman recalled, but he warned them that they were headed for Broadway. "It's a tough job. The theatre is very trying. Your life is going to *be hard!*" In his closing remarks, Clurman spoke of the "resistance that we might encounter...not so much through mischief as through indifference. This resistance would not embitter us, but would serve as a challenge. Our heat would melt the city's ice" (*FY*, 54). The company now felt prepared to take on whatever might come. In this high spirit with its slightly anxious subtext, their extraordinary first summer at Brookfield came to an end.

Part II   Performance ❧

3. Early Rehearsals ❧

Brookfield stands apart. It was the Group moment. During the rest of the decade as the company was forced to jump-start itself again and again, the first summer survived as their ideal alternative community, an American utopia. Their collective experience had given new meaning to what it was to be an actor, laying down basic principles and cementing personal bonds that would guide them through many upheavals. The 12 weeks of rehearsal could also boast another very important achievement: the debut of Lee Strasberg as a director on Broadway and the Group's redefinition of the idea of the director.

When the three founders were organizing the company in the spring of 1931, their Broadway friends promised them, "We'll get you a good director." Philip Moeller of the Theatre Guild or talented foreign directors were among those suggested as appropriately experienced for the adventure on which they were embarking. Nevertheless, Harold Clurman told all the givers of good advice, "I don't want anybody—no great names—I want our people. It's our company—ours." That such proposals were being pressed made the founders realize that most people did not appreciate what they were up to. Clurman wanted their position understood:

> If Cheryl Crawford, Lee Strasberg and I feel that we are at the present the only possible directors for our group, it is not from any mere egotistic assertion of our personal ambitions but because we know that only through our technique of direction will the group be able to say what it has to say. Other directors might be able to turn out "good shows" with it—but only through us who have formed it, can it become a Theatre.

The director as the artist of the theater rather than as a glorified stage manager or efficient processor of commercial products had only recently begun to penetrate the American theater. In the experimental little art theaters of the teens and early 1920s there had been much talk about the director as someone who would liberate the American theater from provincialism and commercialism and initiate a theatrical, social, and spiritual transformation. As early as 1912, the possibilities of this New Movement or New Stagecraft, as it was called, were glimpsed in America in the pages of Edward Gordon Craig and in productions such as Max Reinhardt's pantomimic spectacle *Sumurun*. The notable visit of Jacques Copeau to New York in 1917–19 and then of Konstantin Stanislavsky and the Moscow Art Theatre in 1923–24 richly demonstrated the accomplishments of the new artists of the theater. Although Broadway was not congenial then—or now—to the idea of either the art or the artist of the theater, in the 1920s some important, diverse American directors began to make their mark, among them, designer Robert Edmond Jones, producer Arthur Hopkins, Theatre Guild director Philip Moeller, actress-director Eva Le

Gallienne, and the two Georges, Abbott and Kaufman, who then worked for the idiosyncratic producer-director Jed Harris.

Despite these developments, the founders of the Group had something else in mind. They wanted to go beyond what Strasberg rejected as "the tasteful organization of the stage performance" to "a conscious, unified vision of a play" by a permanent company with something special to say. Perhaps they recalled the kind of distinction that George Cram "Jig" Cook, founder of the Provincetown Players, had drawn for his company. Cook had contrasted the unity imposed by the director who uses his collaborators as obedient instruments with the spiritual unity that springs from "one shared fund of feelings, ideas, impulses" among a group of people. The Group founders were impatient with what seemed to them the vague, romantic search of the preceding generation. They intended to establish a new technical, social, and political basis for theater.

Although each of the three founders contributed to the Group's special vision, in 1931 only Strasberg had any significant experience as a director. This meager background hardly made him seem the person to direct shows for Broadway under the aegis of the prestigious Theatre Guild. Yet, Strasberg alone had the know-how and the self-confidence to turn the Group's large Idea into viable stage productions. As early as 1925, his conversations about theater had greatly impressed the bookish Clurman as they waited together for their cues in the Theatre Guild's *Garrick Gaieties*. This pale-faced, thoughtful bit player explained that theater was not just the hand-maiden of the dramatic text but an independent, distinctive art. The largely self-educated Strasberg had read all the books about the new art of the theater that were being published at the beginning of the 1920s. He was especially intrigued by *Continental Stagecraft* by Kenneth Macgowan and Robert Edmond Jones, which, he would later recall, introduced him to a whole new world. Above all, he fell under the spell of the visionary Edward Gordon Craig. "It would be no exaggeration," Strasberg reminisced in *A Dream of Passion*, that Craig's writing "became the strongest intellectual stimulus for me to devote my life to the theatre" (27). In Craig's seminal *On the Art of the Theatre*, Strasberg discovered not only the art of theater but also the artist of the theater—the director. It was acting, of course, on which Strasberg "seemed as concentrated as a jeweler over the inner mechanism of a watch," as Clurman put it, confessing that he himself never "dreamed that there was that much to it" (*FY*, 11).

Strasberg's confidence in his ability to work with actors, to understand their problems and produce startlingly true results for them, intrigued the more diffident and less experienced Clurman. Sitting together on one occasion, watching the actress Helen Westley struggle through a frustratingly unsuccessful rehearsal at the Theatre Guild, Strasberg whispered to Clurman, "I could get it out of her" (*FY*, 15). He had found the way to do it at the American Laboratory Theatre, where Boleslavsky and Ouspenskaya offered the Stanislavsky system as a pragmatic structure for his fascination with actors and acting.

Although he only attended the Lab for some months in 1924, Strasberg acquired the basis of his lifelong method there. In addition to acting technique, however, he gained what he called "theoretic insight" into the nature of theater from lectures by Boleslavksy preserved in the notes that Strasberg himself took. Theater was analyzed as a collective art in which "everything should be done by the group." The director does not exercise control by "artistic tyranny," according to Boleslavsky, but by his skill and his willingness to share in the collaborative construction of the theater event.

By his precepts and his practice, Boleslavsky contributed to the slowly evolving conception of the modern director. In 1926, he offered a course in directing; both Strasberg and Clurman took advantage of the rare opportunity, although Strasberg attended only a few classes before he dropped out. Clurman, who was certainly influenced by this class, believed that by 1926 Strasberg was already "set in his own methods."

"I came to directing through knowledge of acting and working with actors," Strasberg explained in later years, confessing that "my understanding of directing arose a good deal after I was a director, not before I became a director." He believed that for directing "we cannot lay down quite as distinctively as we do in the acting field basic procedures which we consider to be...correct." Directing involves "vaguer" results dependent on the "vision and taste of the people involved." Moreover, he faulted Clurman for poor coverage of the training and of rehearsal procedures in *The Fervent Years*, but he offered only a few brief illustrations of his directing in the posthumously published *A Dream of Passion*. The notes for a book on directing, about which he talked frequently in the last years of his life, provide generalizations and favorite anecdotes about the great modern directors, but few details of his own work. Yet, the founding of the Group gave him an opportunity to bring new American plays to life in a way that would be followed not only by others in the Group but by generations of American directors.

Directing *The House of Connelly* allowed Strasberg to realize some of the Group's large performance objectives. Although the production was destined for Broadway, Strasberg was no hired hand of commercial producers and was even free of Actors' Equity restrictions on the length of the rehearsal period. At Brookfield, he tested his new training and rehearsal processes with the lively company that was willing to share the work of creation with him and make sacrifices to collaborate in realizing their idea of theater. The actors had made a good beginning in their 12 weeks in the country. As their director, Strasberg was pleased, although he did not often tell them so. He had thought that it would take two or three years before the ensemble would be fully ready and perhaps longer before people would begin to understand what it was they were striving for.

The sponsoring Theatre Guild Board, for whom the company did a run-through of *The House of Connelly* on their return to New York, were among those who did not understand their accomplishment. Theresa Helburn, who was most sympathetic to their endeavor, realized that the touching performance had unusual "mood" and "emotional substance." Other Board members insisted on accommodations to their more conventional taste. They wanted Morris Carnovsky and Mary Morris replaced and the original ending Paul Green had written restored. If not, the Guild would not provide the $10,000 required to open the show. Clurman remembered that "Lee Strasberg went white as he asserted that he wasn't going to tamper with the ensemble" (*FY*, 55). The show was produced under the Guild's auspices, but with only half the money coming from the Guild. Crawford raised the rest of the financing from other sources to allow the show to open.

Given this painful setback, Crawford remembered that they "were all terribly nervous" on opening night (September 23) at the Martin Beck Theatre. Standing at the back of the theater with Crawford and Strasberg, Clurman felt that the company was not "up to their usual pitch," and the audience seemed a bit "subdued" (*FY,* 58). When the curtain fell, the overwhelming response was a wonderful surprise. There were more than 20 curtain calls; Paul Green came on stage for a bow. There was no elaborate opening-night party because they just didn't have the money. In the early hours of the morning after Clurman and Odets brought back the newspapers in which the New York critics confirmed their success, a few members gathered. Paul Green "read from the Bible about the alpha and omega and in the beginning was the word." Beany Barker said she "went out and lay under a bush in Central Park. I don't know how I got home. It was all a dream. Just a great dream."

The unexpected enthusiasm of the audience and the critics gave the Group public confirmation that theirs was the right way to achieve true theater. John Mason Brown hailed Green's poetic folk drama as "the first grown-up play of the season." Yet, the fact was that the dramatic structure of the play was widely recognized—with praise or condemnation—as not "well made" and "contemptuous of the common formulas." It was the ensemble acting and the spirit of the young company that won the reviewers: "They play . . . like a band of musicians . . . so smooth, so finely dovetailed a performance . . . they must have convinced the fascinated audience that their way is the only way to prepare a play for all its worth." "A pellucid performance, the expression of an ideal." "I cannot remember a more completely consecrated piece of ensemble work since the Moscow Art masters went home." "Jaded Broadway seems finally to have found the young blood and new ideas for which many of us have been praying" (see *FY,* 59–60).

In keeping with most reviews of the period, there was little rich detail about the acting and the direction, which the critics did not realize was the unique accomplishment of Lee Strasberg. The program credited Cheryl Crawford and Lee Strasberg, although some thought all three directors had collaborated. There were the usual brief accolades or occasional strictures. As part of the ensemble, everyone drew some praise, and Fannie de Knight and Rose McClendon, playing the elderly Black crones, made such a striking impact that one critic considered them "the stars of the cast." The faults found in Strasberg's first staging for Broadway were to become standard criticisms. The Southern accents were a jumble of inauthentic noise, and the production as a whole failed to suggest the flavor of the South. The actors could not be heard even by those seated fairly close to the stage and the pace of performance was erratic—"either sleepy, hysterical or both" (*FY,* 61).

Only a few reviewers went beyond routine comments to link the production's "strenuously alive" scenes and characters with a new creative process of acting and directing. Brooks Atkinson of the *New York Times* praised the company for being "arrogant enough to regard acting as an art" and contrasted the Group's approach with "the glib, superficial competence of Broadway acting [that] would hurry across the surface of 'The House of Connelly' without once touching the quickness of its poetry." He suggested that they "play at a tempo that is almost dull" because they are determined "to keep their performance honestly subdued" even if their truthful acting makes them hard to hear in a large theater. Headlining his review in the *Herald Tribune* "A Good Show, Though Presented by a Group of Eager Idealists," Percy Hammond also saw that there was more to this performance, concluding that "some bits were so graphically played that they will almost convince you that stage direction is an art." John Mason Brown credited the unique process of "long summer rehearsals" for the rare "group feeling" communicated by the "smooth," "adult," "touching" performance. (All reviews dated September 30, 1931)

Strasberg justified the flaws noted by critics as artistic choices. He took the blame for complaints that Margaret Barker could not be understood in one explosive moment. "Yes, I can slow her down but then I won't get the emotional power." Believing the actress did not have the training to control both the words and the emotion, he was willing to give up intelligibility for a real experience on stage. Some of the very slow moments "mesmerized" the audience without their knowing how, he explained. The scene at the Connelly dining table, which many critics admired, had very few lines, but Strasberg explained that the long pauses were "filled with inner emotional experiences...People said that they didn't know how it was done, some magic" (*Reunion*, 548).

To keep the performance fresh during the run of the show, he instructed the actors to continue using individual and group improvisations sparked by emotional memory. Will Connelly, for example, was left alone on stage after his uncle exited to kill himself. Every night Franchot Tone improvised to find in himself the exact moment when he would be emotionally prepared to take in what had happened and respond by running toward the door where the farmers were coming in with the body of his uncle.

During the performances Bobby Lewis as assistant stage manager had the responsibility of leading the tenant-farmer's serenade. Well before their cue, each actor would "take a minute" to become "emotionally prepared." At a signal from him, the off-stage improvisation would begin, assuring that the entrance would be the result of a real experience. The actors also improvised "digging potatoes" both in rehearsal and later during performance to find an authentic rhythm for the regional work-songs that the farm hands sing. Phoebe Brand remembered that people used to say,

> Oh, well, they just spend their time digging potatoes in the cellar—those crazy people...
> We were the laughing stock of the theater during the first year. I guess people couldn't
> understand why we preferred this work to becoming stars. And also in some ways...we
> were the envy of many people...our acting...was startling to the audience. Because they
> had not seen real emotion used to that extent on the stage before, they were flabbergasted.
> (*Reunion*, 514)

All of this energetic off-stage acting certainly flabbergasted stage hands at the show's first rehearsals in the Martin Beck Theatre. There was much "weeping and wailing" when the community discovered that Uncle Bob Connelly had shot himself. Strasberg had arrayed his actors up and down the backstage stairs where they could build a crescendo from distant sounds cumulatively rising till they all rush onto the stage carrying the dead body. During one rehearsal Dorothy Patten remembered that the theater's doorman ran in "wild-eyed with a towel and bucket of water" to help out at what he was convinced was a real accident. (*Dorothy Patten Story*, 38) "My God, why doesn't somebody do something," he shouted, "a man is dying." (Adams, 127)

The actors themselves were amazed at the whole process. It was only Strasberg's close collaborator Clurman who truly appreciated the daring and originality of Strasberg's teaching and direction.

> He is like a doctor who refuses to treat his patient except with the most natural, the most inevitable remedies and turns with disgust and even anger from the suggestion of some patent medicine, let us say, an obvious piece of business, a technical suggestion, a bit of external characterization or any preconceived means of expression. The patent medicine, says our doctor, may produce immediate relief but it may injure the patient's heart.

Clurman was "convinced that no director—not even Stanislavsky—directs this way."

Certainly, no other American director was directing this way. With his first production, Lee Strasberg took a giant step forward. Innovative directors from the 1920s like Robert Edmond Jones, who were inspired by the New Stagecraft, were more comfortable using sights and sounds than their human medium. For all their spiritual aspirations for theater, they left their actors floundering on their own. Jones, by the way, considered *The House of Connelly* the "most creative show he had seen in New York in years." John Williams, producer of *Beyond the Horizon*, Eugene O'Neill's first play to reach Broadway, boasted that "I believe in leaving the acting to the actors... They are all allowed to work out their interpretations of the part they play."

The Broadway directors most characteristic of the 1920s, including George S. Kaufman and George Abbott along with their producer Jed Harris, caught what they thought to be the spirit of the Jazz Age by directing shows with lots of business, forceful action, and insouciant satire. They made speed the hallmark of successful staging. At the opening of the traumatic 1930s, however, as the world seemed to be collapsing, Strasberg slowed the tempo down. He replaced the popular whiz-bang external action with expanded moments of inwardly felt real life and explosive emotional memories that vividly projected larger historical forces of the drama.

No one else was using the rehearsal period to train actors systematically to seek personal authenticity, to react to one another with improvisational spontaneity rather than with clichés and conventions, and to interpret a play as the collective response by a cohesive ensemble to their own time. Years later, Carnovsky described what it felt like to work in this way. As the "unit" of this collective art, the actor on stage "turns his eyes outward to behold his brother actor... When their eyes meet, the scene begins. When their ideas collide, they move forward in the service of the play, and possibly to a common shared point of view about life and art" (see *The Actor's Eye*). Through *The House of Connelly* the actors spoke out in a very personal way about the need for action to force social change. With their penetrating method and their all-consuming life together, they felt they were transforming themselves, the art of theater, and society.

The Group's ambitious approach, however rewarding, was hard on the actors and on their director as well. Strasberg confessed to his brother Arthur Strasberg at the end of the first summer the "great strain" he felt bearing the responsibility for this difficult process. (Adams, 127–28) Strasberg evaluated their work in a production post-mortem, the first of many often painful critiques.

In the four years that followed their debut, Strasberg as their main director and the Group as a company rode a roller coaster of highs and lows. Carrying out their objectives on Broadway during the depth of the Depression proved incredibly difficult, and Strasberg's direction of nine new, distinctive American plays between 1931 and 1936 was part of this herculean Group endeavor. All the problems they faced impinged on using their method properly, finding the right plays or any plays, locating "angels" and audiences, negotiating an equitable organizational base and the correct political stance, confronting failure and success, and dealing with the individual temperaments of the three directors and the increasing number of company artists. In addition, Strasberg's own complex personality, which seemed by turns withdrawn or outgoing, silent or hysterical, authoritarian or concerned, ambitious or selfless, dabbling in overarching generalizations or digging obsessively into minutiae, colored everything he did with his Group collaborators.

The process Strasberg initiated that first summer at Brookfield set the pattern for his later productions. Combining actor training and rehearsal, each staging— the successes and the failures—involved an exploration of some aspect of the art of theater in the context of the social and political dynamics of their time. It was an approach that would later influence many major American directors exposed to the Group heritage. The acting nurtured by this process introduced the method of work and mode of performance that would become known as the American style.

The Group's second production was in many ways a triumph for the Group Idea and especially for Strasberg's directorial craft, but it was a complete failure at the box office. Rehearsed for eight weeks, *1931–*, by Claire and Paul Sifton, opened in December 1931, and lasted only ten days. The critics said it was "a most ungrateful play as far as entertainment for the average theatregoer was concerned." For the Group and the small audience that filled the balcony seats, while the orchestra remained largely empty, the production was "extraordinary, memorable."

With *1931–*, the Group came closer to doing what they had been created for: they transformed the drama on the streets of America into a professional theatrical event. The trauma of a modern Everyman named Adam was documented against the background of the collective calamity suffered during the Depression. The descent of a robust freight handler from youthful confidence in his ability to find work to the desperation of unemployment alternated with expressionistic scenes of larger and larger mobs of jobless men locked out in front of shut factory gates. Clurman had originally found the script "dry and thin," "too full of reportage and journalistic touches," but he was reminded of something Strasberg had been telling him since the mid-1920s, namely, that "the manner in which a play is done is itself a content" (*FY*, 11). That was the meaning of theater; any other view was merely literary. To draw a sharp distinction between a "bad play" and "a fine production" was "mechanical and aesthetically false." Especially for the Group Theatre as well as for the new workers' theaters then emerging, the true significance had to be found in the "complete production not in the nature of the written play alone" (*FY,* 73).

Whatever their reservations about the writing, neither Clurman nor carping critics could ignore the electrifying effect of Strasberg's direction of his ensemble. Using emotional memory and group improvisations, the twin principles of the method he had worked out in *The House of Connelly,* Strasberg orchestrated the performances with powerful mass movement by the whole company plus several hired extras. Mordecai Gorelik's striking unit set allowed the action to move through the many scenes of grim urban devastation, and the complex construction of corrugated iron warehouse doors that framed the stage rose and fell with terrifying force like the terrible blows of the Depression itself. The lines and texture of his scenic art made the audience feel the rough misery of the times. Yet, on stage the play "glowed with a stern beauty, sensitive, vibrant, full of heartache and mute love," wrote Clurman, who, looking back, considered *1931–,* together with *The House of Connelly,* Strasberg's finest creation. (*FY,* 73)

During rehearsals Strasberg had worked very hard to make the rather schematic script pulsatingly alive. It wasn't always easy for him or his actors. Phoebe Brand, for example, was acting her first major role. Strasberg explained:

> I took the responsibility. I said, "I'll get the performance from you." After four weeks or so, I couldn't get the things that I wanted. I wasn't getting it. I remember the Theatre Guild people came in and Terry Helburn said, "When are we going to see that performance?" I can finish it now, but then I'm not going to get from her what there is still a chance of getting. And as long as there is a chance I'm not going to set that, because I'm still working for some things…With Phoebe, we finally got it in the last week. But if we hadn't gotten it, I would have been in a pickle. (*Reunion,* 547)

Brand recalled rehearsing The Girl whose life is destroyed by the hard times and trying to interact with or "work off" Franchot Tone, cast as the devastated young Adam, rather than "digging into" herself. Tone, on the other hand, was following Strasberg's injunctions. At each "beat" in the play, he would remove himself from Brand to take an "exercise" to link the horrors of the play with his own life. Despite his involvement in radical theater since the late 1920s, he could not easily escape his upper-class background and habits. Seesawing between private emotion and dramatic character created that curious rhythm of alternating slow moments with intense, hysterical ones that critics observed in most of the early Group shows. When Tone and Brand connected, the scene worked very well, but she became distressed when her partner removed himself into his "private moments." Strasberg, in turn, was irritated that Brand was not "enriching and enlarging the part." "He was very angry with me, but at the same time, he was stroking me as if to say, 'I'm not really mad at you.' All this was very confusing" (*Reunion,* 516).

To deepen the vital life of the scenes, Stella Adler, Morris Carnovsky, and J. Edward Bromberg, who had played major roles on Broadway, doubled in some of the small parts, becoming workers and the unemployed in the hungry mob whose struggle was crosscut with that of Adam and The Girl. The actors knew they would not be handled like conventional supers. For Strasberg "a crowd reaction, even off stage, had to be as true as anything in the play." He used his skill, for example, to make the dynamic protest of the masses at the finale deeply felt by each participant. Dorothy Patten, the debutante from Chattanooga, who acted as a gum-chewing stenographer and other bits in the crowd that provided off-stage sound effects as well as on-stage characters, also played the factory leader of the hunger march that climaxed the play. Her recollections vividly document how effective Strasberg's crowd could be. During these last scenes, she said, the "workers...started down in the cellar of the theatre with speeches and heckling and marching and singing and policemen and sirens, and running back and forth up and down the dressing-room stairs." It seemed so real that the stagehands feared their lives were in danger, and the doorman regularly locked himself in the bathroom. (*Dorothy Patten Story*, 41) The actors themselves worried that a misstep might find them beheaded by the guillotine-like metal factory doors. No wonder the actress Helen Westley of the Theatre Guild quipped that seeing a Group production was like witnessing a real, live accident. Once on stage, each emotionally aroused actor became part of the protesting mass that Adam joined as it surged across the stage to confront and some to fall before the machine guns of the police. As he marched toward the footlights on opening night, Tony Kraber noticed the millionaire Otto Kahn sitting in the second row. "I saw his face, it was like a sheet. The revolution was happening right before his eyes!" (see Adams, 134).

For Strasberg this passionate stage activity took precedence over the concerns of the playwrights. The Siftons complained when Strasberg spent time in rehearsals explaining minor points to a very minor actor. He was urging Friendly Ford, who shortly left the company, to make the desperate experience of being unemployed real to himself. Paul Sifton called out from the back of the house, "If you want to give lessons in acting do it somewhere else. We've got to open the show in ten days and the production isn't ready." Strasberg was furious. "I am responsible for the opening of the play, which will take place at the scheduled time. As for what is going on here now, please don't interfere with what you don't understand" (*FY*, 73–74). He announced, "in his iciest manner," that "there are some things even more important than your play. We are a Group Theatre and this is a moment of teaching and I shall pursue it until I am finished" (Adams, 133). Dealing with the playwrights was the least of Strasberg's concerns and he usually relied on Crawford and Clurman for that. But it was he, alone, who made the playwright's words come to life on stage as the Group's message.

The Broadway critics described the impact of the production with such phrases as "stunned," "grimly moving and a little terrifying," "harrowing," the "mass groupings and moving are thrilling," "quivers with a sense of living tragedy," and "alive with the real thing." Critics found the message unacceptable or confusing and the play crude propaganda. The production challenged the very purpose of show business as well as conventional values and aesthetic standards. *1931–* stirred considerable discussion in the press about propaganda and art, about what is "too real to be a play" (reviews dated December 11, 1931).

For the Group the fact that the regular Broadway audience did not want to listen to their message despite the power of the production was the first of a number of blows to their Idea of theater.

The failure of Maxwell Anderson's *Night Over Taos*, in March 1932, was another blow. Their good friend Anderson had written this new play especially for the company. Inspired by Racine's *Phaedra*, he transplanted the classic story to New Mexico in the early days when the old-world Spanish aristocrats resisted purchase by the egalitarian Americans. It seemed an unlikely vehicle for the Group, but Clurman managed to articulate a "spine" that linked the heroic life of the past to the aspirations of the Group. They had little confidence the show would succeed, but they needed to continue active production; it lasted ten performances.

Strasberg's production lacked "the spark of life" despite his intense efforts. The austere sets, costumes, and lighting by Robert Edmond Jones inhibited Strasberg from carrying out some "special effects ideas" he thought would enliven the script. Strasberg confessed, "I could not yet afford to have such strong ideas about scenery, so I didn't push it" (Adams, 136). Strasberg pushed some of the actors almost beyond endurance in his misguided effort "to bring something" out of them for the lifeless play. Ruth Nelson was crushed by what she felt was the wholly inappropriate preparation Strasberg was demanding for the simple ingénue she had to play. He had been against casting her, despite strong endorsements from the author and from Robert Edmond Jones, who knew her from her success with a similar role in *Martine*, directed by Boleslavsky at the American Laboratory Theatre. She recalled the terrible pain of hearing Strasberg say, "It's unfortunate that you're doing the part, but...we'll work and see if we can't get something from you which will help on this role" (*Reunion*, 528–29).

There was some praise from critics who were coming to expect a high standard from the Group, but the general feeling was that both the author and the actors were "standing outside of the material"—a harsh judgment for a company that struggled so valiantly to penetrate their characters. Only Bobby Lewis triumphed. He was distressed to be assigned yet another bit part, a wordless one of an "old Indian" whose sole action was to finish cleaning the fireplace as the curtain opened. He determined to turn the whole play into a drama about an old Indian. Taking advantage of the extensive improvisational rehearsals, he introduced his old Indian into every scene. "Lee was delighted with my inventiveness," he remembered; "his only objection being that I was too comic. Every day on his page of rehearsal notes I'd see the same entry: 'Bobby—not funny Indian.'" Bobby, decked out in a brilliant costume Jones helped him put together, stole scenes shamelessly with his mime. During the curtain call of the first preview, Tone, who was furious at his pranks, paid him back. As Bobby liked to tell it, Tone "left his place in the center of the full company call, walked all the way to the end of the line where I, the least of the characters, was standing, and pulled me back to the center with him and, locking my arm under his, forced me to bow alongside the principal actors. They never gave me a walk-on again" (*S&A*, 53–55).

After these two flops and a brief, unrewarding tour, the Group Theatre, as it was now officially known, had to face the future on its own. The company had severed formal connections with the Theatre Guild and the directors had to scrounge for new sources of income. Those at the top of their salary scale had to take cuts to keep those at the bottom of their collective payroll from destitution in the increasingly difficult Depression days. Yet, what they all felt was what the ever-scribbling Clifford Odets poured out to Clurman in his heightened prose:

> Here comes the Group and all the time I kiss the ground where it walks. Here stand The Group, with convictions; here is a communal life from which already richness has resulted...when I think of the thirty of us I want to weep with joy and remind myself constantly that we are we and there is no earth or world without us.

On June 19, 1932, the Group once more abandoned New York for the summer, making their way in their cavalcade of cars to Dover Furnace, near Pawling, New York. With the money Crawford and Clurman had managed to collect, they set themselves up in an old hotel complex with a main house, some cottages, and two rehearsal spaces. There was a place to swim, a baseball diamond, a croquet lawn, and a billiard room. A more elaborate undertaking than that of their first summer, Dover Furnace involved about fifty people, including eight paying apprentices and a number of visitors who also paid for the privilege of being part of their community. Ben Slutzky, a friend of Strasberg's with family experience in the hotel business, was in charge of running the extensive operation. It wasn't quite like Brookfield. Odets noted that he didn't feel the same "old turbulence, the old swift inner running" as he drove up from New York with Clurman and Stella in Crawford's car.

With considerable difficulty, the three directors had come up with two plays to work on during the summer: Dawn Powell's *Big Night*, to be directed by Crawford; and John Howard Lawson's *Success Story*, to be directed by Strasberg. Clurman, as usual, gave the company the inspirational welcome when they assembled their first night. He recalled "what the Group meant, what it was destined to do, what position it must fill in American society." Years later, Clurman's fervor was remembered:

> Harold was able to make us believe that a Group Theatre was the only course that could give our lives worth...He taught ethics for the theatre artist, spoke words the masters of religion have used, railed in the grand manner of a visionary, calling into being what does not exist. I believed that a great theatre had been born and that it would be unlike any other that existed in this country. When he was through, I was an altered man. (*A Life*, 62)

That is how one apprentice remembered Clurman's opening talk. He had come down from the Yale Drama School and paid $20 a week for room and board to be with the Group. His name was Elia Kazan, destined to become a powerful figure in the Group and later one of America's most famous stage and screen directors.

4. Early Classes ✑

W hile John Howard Lawson's play was being revised when they arrived at Dover Furnace in upstate New York in 1932, Strasberg devoted his full attention to classes for the actors. At Brookfield, where the training had been done mainly during rehearsals rather than in separate classes, his emphasis had been primarily on sense and emotional memory. These exercises remained the cornerstone of his instruction. Roman ("Bud") Bohnen, who had enthusiastically listened to Clurman's talks but had not been able to join them the first year, wrote to his father from Dover Furnace about the exciting experiences he was having with the Group, which seemed close to the mainspring of contemporary culture in America (see Theatre Collection, NYPL, Lincoln Center). In addition to the rehearsals, he pointed out that the actors spent a great deal of time "training, like athletes—as instruments." He described the sensory exercises:

> We feel various materials, cotton, silk, etc., and sensitize ourselves to it; then in panto-
> mime, without the material, we learn to suggest to the onlookers by the way our fingers
> move what kind of material it is. I am very fortunate in my native ability in this sort
> of thing. We also learn to pound a nail in the wall so that in pantomime we really feel
> the weight of the hammer and every detail. Then we do it without the nail and ham-
> mer. Then we take an "adjustment," which means we assume there is someone asleep in
> the next room; another adjustment is to pretend we have hit our finger the time previ-
> ous...there are a million ways to pound a nail in a wall, and one must sharpen one's
> senses to be able to first perceive the essential differences, and second to make them
> articulate to the watcher through technical facility.

Elia Kazan, the energetic and methodical apprentice, said that he "worked like a beaver" doing his sense memory exercises every day at dawn: "shaving without a razor or soap, feeling cold sitting in the summer sun, smelling a lemon, then smelling the space where the lemon had been held to my nostrils, still smelling the lemon...And so on." He took "a minute" to concentrate and "awaken his emotional resources." He collected the memories that worked for him in a notebook, which became the "Golden Box" where he filed pertinent memories away so that he could easily find just what he needed for particular scenes. Kazan confessed in his autobi-ography: "I still have the notebook, with my store of emotions in it" (*A Life*, 64).

For the old-timers, however, who had their initiation the summer before, Dover Furnace stands out for the new approaches that Strasberg developed to stir the imag-ination, emphasizing theatricality and modes of interpretation. He began to explore the new type of work from the very first class. He gave the actors exercises in "inton-ing, or making the words project themselves" and "taking attitudes and realizing the full force of the human body in action, the power of expression contained in hands and the carriage of the body." One evening, an apprentice made a brave effort to be a monkey in an animal improvisation. Since the result was very conventional, the actors offered criticism for about two hours—a standard Group tactic. When Morris Carnovsky did his monkey, however, he created "a beautiful sad portrait that has for me all the essence of a caged animal that wants to be back in the forest. Very good and arousing in all of us a deep emotional experience," wrote Odets in his diary of that summer, from which much of the detail here is drawn.

In a class the next morning the actors tried "taking attitudes from pictures, working for ease of voice-production and feeling." Bud Bohnen described imitating the postures in a Giotto, a Rembrandt, or an El Greco. "After we have succeeded in suggesting such a character, we characterize him, make him live, make him walk out of the picture, as it were. Then we improvise dialogue."

The following day Odets began exploring Robert Frost's poem "Home Burial" for a class project. Since the preparation Strasberg expected was intended to be done outside of class, Odets, easily distracted by his playwriting, by his Beethoven music, by his sexual fantasies, berated himself in his diary for "not working enough on my exercises for voice...attitudes." Inhibited also by "what people will think of him" and a "fear of being silly," he counseled himself to toss aside all thoughts of appearances. "Cut off all my hair, for instance, forget how or why to dress, forget about the girls here and the desire for them...get to real honest work."

In class after class with Strasberg the actors experimented with all sorts of improvisations. In the guise of student and teacher, Phoebe Brand recalled improvising the gravedigger scene from *Hamlet* with Sandy Meisner. Poems were recited in three different ways—as originally intended, then going against the obvious meaning, or finally giving a personal interpretation. Another innovation was the use of gibberish. "It was supposed to liberate you and free you so that you didn't have to be stuck with the lines," Brand recalled. (*Reunion*, 517)

Ruth Nelson especially remembered those expert actors Carnovsky and Bromberg concocting gibberish improvisations that became "classics." But the playful, liberating exercises also helped novices. Tony Kraber tried some highly theatrical sketches to build esteem for apprentice Kazan, who had been known as the handy "Gadget" since his undergraduate days at Williams College. Kraber remembered that the directors considered Kazan a "no-talent guy":

> They were gonna drop him at the end of the summer. I went to them. I said, you guys are out of your mind. This guy is loaded with talent. And to prove it, I did two things. I did a sketch with Gadget in which we took all the Sir Toby Belch and Sir Andrew Aguecheek bits of *Twelfth Night*. I'd always been in love with Sir Toby Belch, but of course I'm the wrong shape for it [being long and lean]. But there it didn't matter. So we did it as a couple of itinerant Irish acrobats. We would do leap frogs, I carried him on my shoulders, I swung him around. We did all kinds of things. And recited the Aguecheek-Sir Toby Belch lines with the wildest Irish brogue you've ever heard.

The two also acted a *commedia dell'arte* scenario that Kraber found in the New York Public Library. In it Harlequin goes to Paris, becomes pregnant, and comes back to Italy to give birth. Mab Anthony played the baby and Kazan played the Doctor. The exercise was such a hit that they repeated it for the Theatre Guild board when the Group returned to New York.

Very rapidly they would make little playlets out of three unrelated words, an exercise Stanislavsky himself had used. "Spaghetti, flower, and beast" was a triad Odets and Willi Barton tried. (Wilhelmina Barton was an apprentice that summer who later married Tony Kraber.) Strasberg had criticized Odets for not establishing a relationship to objects outside of himself. "He said I had a certain level of emotion but not connected with my partner, not recognizing her presence and purpose and potentiality," Odets noted. Strasberg set them to inventing little dramas of proverbs. "Honesty is the best policy" became a man gripping jail bars and staring out. They also improvised a single word like "religion." Odets recalled a very "comical" improv by Joe Bromberg and Luther Adler, Stella's very talented brother who had joined them in the spring. In it, Bromberg tried to dissuade Adler from suicide and finally overcome by the unfortunate man's despair, killed himself.

As the classes continued, Odets, after several tries, finally came up with a very successful "visualization" based on a single word. In his epitome of "America," a man rushed madly from his bed to his office only to arrive there and throw his feet up on the desk with nothing to do. The class rocked with laughter and it became another of the frequently performed sketches that grew out of the summer's endeavors.

"The experimental nature of some of the work in these sessions was for me," Bobby Lewis asserted, "the most exciting activity of the whole Group project." He emerged as something of a maverick who, in the manner of the politicized 1930s, was labeled a "theatrical Trotskyite" by the orthodox "Stanislavskyites" because of his interest in style and the means by which truthful feeling can be projected in theatrical form. Trained in music, he relished the exercises in sound and movement that Strasberg gave them and often turned them into comic gems that were performed at the many left-wing benefits and fund-raisers they were called upon to do. His "Red Hamlet" became a hit. Interpreting the "To be or not to be" soliloquy as a political speech to rouse a mob, he gestured and moved like an animated cartoon by William Gropper of the radical *New Masses* magazine.

> Starting with the attitude of a worker in chains (what else?), on the first line I broke my bands, flung my arms in the air and proclaimed a victorious "To be! or not to be." I sank into a sitting position thumbs under my armpits and assumed the manner of a fat, capitalist bastard (those two words were always spoken as one). "That is the question" propelled me up and into my character of a mediator, making the contrasting points of capital versus labor—and so on to the end. At the finale, "And lose the name of action," the word *action* accompanied by a raised fist, was a thunderous cry to revolt.

Lewis pointed out that "you can't imagine how popular this number was during the depression" (*S&A*, 66). The journalist Heywood Broun, who was master of ceremonies at a benefit where Bobby Lewis later performed this sketch, quipped, "I didn't know Shakespeare was a Communist."

Equally popular were Bobby Lewis's rendition of Walt Whitman's "I Sing the Body Electric" in the guise of a sleepy "old Milquetoast of a man" being hit by the freezing water of his morning shower, and his interpretation of Browning's "Pippa

Passes" as a confused political speech by a grotesque Herbert Hoover that he created with "little balls in my cheeks to stretch out my face and the highest stiff collar I could find."

Out of this varied experimentation, little productions began to take shape. Art Smith developed a stylized scene based on drawings by George Grosz, the German expressionist painter, that various actors had been using in class exercises. Teams of actors portrayed 12 grotesque tableaux of the decadent rich and powerful. At the same time Smith trained 12 male actors in what Bud Bohnen remembered as "a choreography of military movements, such as saluting, marching, charging, dying." The "exhaustive improvisation," worked on most of the summer, began with actions and realistic characterization and became intensive sessions in dance classes to test out and then control different movements, including a rhythmic pattern of death throes for soldiers.

For Odets, the point of this work was "to show that the words say one thing which the overt action criticizes and adds devastating comment to those words...in a purely theatrical manner." He noted that Strasberg was pleased and Odets decided to juxtapose readings from the Book of Psalms and a song by Marlene Dietrich as further ironic counterpoint to Smith's images, which then communicated a potent antiwar message. This strange experimental satire, originally performed on the tennis court, was subsequently shown to more than 50 unions and workers' clubs. In 1934, Ralph Steiner made a film of it, entitled *Café Universal*, with Smith and Kazan as the soldiers and Group members filling out the cast. Unfortunately, the film has been lost, but the stills that survive suggest vividly the class exercise upon which it was built. (see Steiner, 118–19)

In contrast with this "stylistic result with Meyerholdian dimensions to it," as Bud Bohnen called it, the actors' efforts to capture the essence of the powerful, humane drawings of the German artist Kathe Kollwitz required affective memory and justification exercises. "The actor had to generate an emotional condition in himself, such as he might need for the performance of a great role in a play, in order to convey the vexed purity of heart of the Kollwitz people." The experiments with the two artists provided important insights about method and style.

In an explosion of creative activity, Odets planned to direct a stylized version of Robert Frost's poem "The Fear" with Bill Challee, Ruth Nelson, and Philip Barber, a Yale designer and playwright who had joined them as technical director. Odets put the Frost poem aside for a time in order to devise other imaginative class exercises. "I'm going to do a visualization of a Beethoven symphony later, but now I am beginning work on a young man in a prison cell waiting to be electrocuted within the quarter of an hour. In the electric chair he recites a poem," Odets noted in his diary. "Everyone is teeming with ideas around the place. Lots of us have to digest what we're thinking about, but the overflow is a very healthy sign."

They also needed to digest Strasberg's critical comments about Bobby Lewis's amusing interpretation of Whitman's "I Sing the Body Electric" and other class projects. "We must try—despite our disbelief in current coinage—to make anything that we do have a positive value," Odets reported Strasberg saying. "There was little use in tearing down destructively. It is our work, our prerogative to build, to state positively." Odets confessed that he, too, had been troubled about the tone of some of the projects. "In my own things I want always to say that life is good."

In August, as Strasberg turned his full attention to rehearsals for Lawson's *Success Story*, Clurman, who had been working with the apprentices, took over the classes. In the spirit of the summer's work, he developed additional innovative exercises and even cautioned the actors about excessive dependence on emotional exercises. "The time is over," he said, "when we get up and do an improvisation just for the sake of emotional truth. Some of us who are just using the method properly for the first time are a little drunk with our abilities to play a scene with true emotion."

According to Odets's jottings, Clurman undertook to spot "these little self-indulgences, insisting that we go ahead and work on what is not so easy of accomplishment." Clurman challenged the actors to relate the emotional memory practice to characterization and stylization, his special concerns. The arrangement of the classes was changed from group attendance to two-hour sessions for pairs of actors with whom Clurman could work more closely on individual problems. Odets thought the new schedule would be better than their current classes, where, as he put it, "one lolls and yawns and smokes and only sometimes gets a valuable thing."

In his sessions, Clurman emphasized especially the expressive value of musical rhythms, costumes, and objects. After listening to a Chopin mazurka, for example, Phoebe Brand and Joe Bromberg became a young man playing music as he dreams of a dead girl dancing behind him. Carnovsky transformed himself into an elderly mother who was seeing her daughter off to her first dance. Virginia Farmer and Odets planned a vignette about a woman visiting her husband in jail and telling him about their daughter's first dancing lessons, but class time was up before they could show it.

In another session several people improvised to a Bach piece recorded by Myra Hess; Carnovsky became an old Jew at prayer mourning for the world. Later in the summer, Odets, Bromberg, and Grover Burgess, who had acted with the New Playwrights and had become a Group member at the end of the first season, improvised to the slow movement of the Brahms Double Concerto. They became three doctors operating on a patient who dies. Odets realized that music inspired both movement and emotion. Everyone was impressed. Even the ever-critical Max Gorelik proclaimed that this project "was the most moving thing he had seen on the stage in the last five years."

Objects were manipulated to make them expressive; each actor, for example, had to use a pillow in some special way. No one loved using objects for class projects more than Bobby Lewis. In addition to having music in his presentations, he always had "millions" of props.

> I was prop crazy. Phil Loeb once did an impersonation of me, and the scene was that my hat fell off to the ground. That was the whole scene—took him one solid half-hour. The hat fell off and he'd get down on the ground, and all the pens would fall out of his pocket. Half-hour, just to pick up my hat. So that's how in love with props I was.

Quickly put together costumes provided another kind of challenge. Clurman assigned people roles: Othello, Shylock, Don Juan, Mephisto, Cleopatra, a Toulouse-Lautrec street girl, and so on. In 15 minutes each actor had to concoct an expressive costume made from any materials available, a bathrobe, a table cloth, and perform a one-word improvisation that caught the spirit of the clothing. These impromptu creations live in the photographs Ralph Steiner snapped of the exercise. At tea one day, Strasberg emphasized the value of these improvisations. "The trick," he observed, according to Odets's notes, "was to make the costume part of the acting, to make it express emotions. So everything on the stage becomes to the actor not a static object, but something alive to help the actor in his expression." Odets concluded that "to get something from one's shoes, a pencil, a glass of water, a chair, to drive all these things to express the actor's task, that is almost an ideal, but one that we get closer to each day." Everything was avidly and heatedly discussed during meals, walks, and drinks in this unique university of the theater. "All things are moving onward here, nothing and no one stays behind."

Helen Tamiris's dance classes were a challenge. Odets described her as "a goodly woman, a Jewess who has obviously struggled up from a Jewish meanness to be what she is now, amazonic and clipped of speech, looking for all the world as if we might be brother and sister." Indeed, Tamiris, whose original name was Helen Becker, was very much the sister in dance to her "brothers" in the Group Theatre. She had eclectic training in Italian and Russian ballet and Isadora Duncan's natural dance as well as experience in opera, night clubs, and theater before finding her own idiom as a modern dancer. She made her concert debut a year after Martha Graham in 1927, but only came into her own in the 1930s with dances like "Mass Study" and "Cycle of Unrest," choreographed for her dance group. Her association with the Group Theatre involved a reciprocal arrangement. Tamiris taught movement classes to the actors and in turn her dancers were given acting classes. She later choreographed dances for Melvin Levy's *Gold Eagle Guy*, and group members turned up in the casts of her dance concerts. She credited Strasberg's version of the Stanislavsky method with showing her how to evolve movement from individual motivation. Like the Group, too, Tamiris would be caught between criticism from the right for the obvious propaganda in her programs and attacks from the left for being too bourgeois and aesthetic.

Odets welcomed Tamiris's afternoon classes, noting in his diary that "the sluggish body takes on color and warmth." Very quickly he confessed being "woefully stupid" in her class where he found that "the body is not so easy to control as once I thought." Other things put him off: the "male odor of sweat," which emanated from Tamiris, made her lose some of "her allure," seeing her body in her thin silk dance suit destroyed "the Delphic mysteries" for him, and perhaps her comment to him that he "had no sense of rhythm"—this to the man who felt that he was Beethoven. Odets kept at it for a time saying, "I may never learn anything from these classes, but they will always be good workouts." Soon he complained of waking up "twisted and pained" because Tamiris made them use "unusual muscles and these hurt." Then for weeks he simply skipped the dance classes; busy writing his play was his excuse. When he returned to class, he chided himself: "It was really not right to miss the classes. I can get much from them, and they should be looked upon as a necessity to actors such as we are growing to be." When he and Tamiris discussed the importance of the classes, he found her gentler and said, "We have partly tamed the Diana."

When Franchot Tone, ever the bad boy, figured out how much hard physical exertion Tamiris wanted from them, he never went back to her sessions. (He also did not attend the experimental classes Clurman offered.) Nevertheless, Bud Bohnen and his wife Hildur struggled on, painting their scratches and bruises with mercurochrome. Kazan, dedicated to self-improvement, attended all the classes. Of Tamiris, he wrote, "Her specialty was something called the pelvic thrust...On the down part of the movement, standing above me, she'd put her foot on my spine and press. Her footprint is still on my back. And I can still recall her voice screaming: 'The floor is your friend!' as she pushed me down" (*A Life*, 65). Yet, he and Lewis especially liked the summer dance classes and became adept at the tasks she set them. Lewis, like many others, admired Tamiris, whom he called a "lusty companion" who "developed the actors' creaking bodies relentlessly, until some of us could actually move with genuine authority."

When a sampling of this varied craft exploration was later shown on a double bill with *Waiting for Lefty* as a benefit for the Group early in 1935, many of the leading critics responded with enthusiasm to this laboratory of acting, which, among other things, revealed that the long-haired intellectuals of the Group had a sense of humor. The presentation quickened John Mason Brown's "devotion to the Group ideal" and gave him "some sense of what it is as actors its players are driving at." John Anderson found these "artist's sketches" more interesting than most of the Group's formal Broadway productions. Brooks Atkinson called it an "invigorating revelation of their skill and force as a company...which is most stimulating when it is not competing with the entertainment business on Broadway, which is not interested in the studio craft of acting nor in the drama of social revolution" (reviews dated February 20, 1935).

The Group's whole intention was to make their method and their message one and to change Broadway. The remarkable theaters of the Soviet Union provided instructive aesthetic and social models. The experimentation at Dover Furnace in their second summer grew in part from the greater knowledge the directors were gaining about the adaptations of Stanislavsky's training made by the radical younger generation of Russian theater artists. Strasberg kept Mark Schmidt, a Russian anarchist friend who was working in their Dover Furnace kitchen, busy night after night translating recent Russian theater books and articles, including a volume by Eugene Vakhtangov, who died in 1922 but whose influence remained only second to that of his mentor Stanislavsky. In class and at their late-evening tea times, Strasberg read from these books as most listened to these essentially technical essays with "romantic awe." Vakhtangov's socialist values inspired their organizational development and his theories of acting influenced Strasberg's evolving method. When the Vakhtangov material had all been typed up, Clurman used readings from it to demonstrate, as he wrote, "how a certain ideal was translated into actual technique and that all the noble sounding words were possible of actional counterparts." Vakhtangov's "fantastic realism," which brought together the emotional truthfulness of his mentor

Stanislavsky and the theatricality and intensification of his peer, the iconoclastic innovator Vsevolod Meyerhold, appealed greatly to the Group. From Vakhtangov they also picked up those impressive sounding phrases that became part of their vocabulary: "agitation from the essence" and "ideologically cemented collective," a scientific Marxist label for their group identity.

The productions of Meyerhold, who was still active in 1932, fascinated Strasberg. Little was then known about the great Russian's avant-garde stagings and his original technique of "bio-mechanics," a scientific physicalization of movement for the stage. From his voracious reading Strasberg regaled the actors with descriptions of the theatrical brilliance of Meyerhold's *Camille* and *The Magnificent Cuckold*. The actors then related Meyerhold's experiments to their own. Kraber noted the Russian's theatrical use of objects or roughly put together symbolic costumes. Kazan long remembered the challenging principles Strasberg transmitted from Meyerhold, especially that *words* were only the "decorations on the hem of the skirt of action" and that the director alone is responsible for creating stage life.

Linking theatrical revolution and political revolution was an obvious step for many in the Group to take this summer of 1932. Part of their schooling dealt with the larger world around them. Isolated in the country and involved with their training as they were at Dover Furnace, the violent events that made headlines, nevertheless, struck them with force. The brutality and horror of the attack on the Veteran's Bonus Marchers in Washington, DC, appeared several times in Odets's diary. All shades of leftist views were aired, and radicals, espousing various "isms" came through their camp, including a friend of photographer Paul Strand's who had been an officer in the Irish Republican Army (IRA) and regaled them with his revolutionary exploits. They argued among themselves and some proselytized. Kazan remembered that the first day he arrived at Dover Furnace he saw one of the actors making his way to the swimming hole with an open book in his hands entitled *Left-Wing Communism: An Infantile Disorder*.

Even the informative lectures on theater history that Strasberg gave on various occasions during that summer were not just background talks. He found in the past the large idea of theater they were trying to realize in their Group. Drawing on recently popularized sociological and anthropological interpretations of the origins of theater, on Marxist theories, and on the historical essays of his idol Gordon Craig, Strasberg talked about primitive ritual, collective vision in the Greeks, rhythmic action of the *commedia dell'arte*, and, above all, the primacy of the actor in the evolving performance-centered history of early periods of theater. Bohnen wrote his father that their study of primitive theater "amounts to an examination of the very fountainhead of the religious impulse in man...[which] grew out of REALITIES [and]...was a very immediate and practical thing." The view of "art as a necessity without which we cannot exist" was reinforced in lectures by Boleslavsky, which they read and discussed.

The invaluable classes at Dover Furnace set a pattern followed over the years. For audiences and critics it was the productions that earned the company acclaim. For the members, many of whom were disappointed to have only small parts in productions that had short runs, the exercises, experiments, discussions, readings, and lectures—the whole process—kept them entranced. "It was 'extraordinary,'" recalled Eunice Stoddard. "You felt that this was so much more important than anything being done on Broadway in the thirties, that you stayed." For the directors, too, the training in classes was in some ways more important than the productions. Strasberg told one class: "A production is always limited—a certain number of weeks, considerations of audience, and other artists..." What actors needed, he believed, were opportunities to practice their craft and reach for new goals. Properly structured, classes could free the imagination more effectively than productions and develop the actor's capacity for independent creative effort. "We can set aside 5–10 minutes a day for technical exercises, and that is good," Strasberg told the actors, "but for these other artistic problems we need...a different kind of class—a laboratory with no limitation—where we can do what we want."

In the middle of their fascination with the classes, rehearsals for *Success Story* finally got under way. The company responded enthusiastically to the script, which Lawson still had to complete. The drama of Sol Ginsburg and Sarah Glassman, young lovers who are Jewish radicals from the Lower East Side caught up in the advertising world of the WASP Raymond Merritt Company, seemed the play for them. Ambitious and angry, Ginsburg ruthlessly seizes control of Merritt's business and of his sexy girlfriend Agnes Carter, but he loses his soul and the love of the faithful Sarah. In a final moment of hysteria, she kills him because he has already killed himself.

Clurman gave an "illuminating" talk about the play, according to Odets's 1932 diary. He interpreted it as a drama about

> what happens to an idealistic force when it finds no effective social form to contain it. The protagonist of *Success Story* becomes a desperately destructive man because he sees no way his unusual energy, imagination, and sense of truth can operate in harmony with the society that confronts him. It is only by becoming society's enemy and the betrayer of his own deepest values that he can succeed in it.

There was considerable speculation about who would play Sol Ginsburg, "a Jew who goes from communism to riches and then realizes that his life has been lost on the way," as Odets put it. He thought Bromberg would be cast, but would have loved to play Ginsburg himself. "I doubt it much," Odets confessed to his diary, "for the directors have told me my worth and it doesn't seem to measure in any way to the requirement of such a role. Every day would be a catharsis if I played that part, for it is much my own problem."

The choice of Luther Adler for the important role of Sol Ginsburg disappointed some members, who considered Adler a relative newcomer. Combining the tough looks of a kid of the streets with the self-confidence and talent of someone who had been on the stage all of his life, however, Luther Adler seemed perfect for the role of the aggressive but sensitive ghetto boy who destroys himself in the fight to become an all-American success. Stella played opposite her brother as the radical young secretary who loves Sol but despairs as she loses him not only to another woman but to the corrupt values of the business world. Strasberg recalled that Lawson had wanted Stella to play the glamorous Agnes, but the directors saw her as Sarah. They "perceived in Stella...the presence of the emotional colors needed to create a controlled but dynamic character." Franchot Tone was the obvious choice to play

Raymond Hewitt, the handsome WASP executive who is defeated by Luther Adler's ambitious young Jew. The only trouble was that Tone kept taking off from Dover Furnace and rehearsals. Finally, at a meeting of the company on July 30, Clurman and Strasberg announced to the shocked members that Tone was leaving the Group for Hollywood, but he would remain long enough to play Hewitt for the first five weeks of the *Success Story* run. Roman Bohnen would replace him. The other leads were played by Morris Carnovsky, who appeared as Sonnenberg, the cynical, sophisticated, older Jewish tycoon; and Dorothy Patten, who was Agnes, the grasping glamor girl. Strasberg began private rehearsals with the actors cast in the central roles. Minor characters, who did not appear until the second act, were not cast until August, when Lawson sent them the completed script.

Success Story, with its small cast, did not call on Strasberg's unique approach to staging group scenes, but allowed him to refine ways of creating true emotion, the cornerstone of his directing. Odets, who listened to an early reading of Act I, was amazed at the progress that was being made. "Stella is using some sort of adjustment to people in the play that gives her a quality I've never seen her have before on the stage. I wonder what she's using. It's good, giving her a kind of human warmth."

The "adjustment" Odets observed was one that Strasberg himself described frequently in later years. For the part of the dedicated Sarah, Strasberg recalled, "I wanted a deep emotion—which Stella had—but contained in a pure, lovely ethereal quality. It was very difficult to get this from her because of her natural tendency to 'burn up the stage.'" He wanted her to show "concealed longing" for Sol, but, as he saw it, "the notion of a repressed, hidden, calm romance was alien to her own behavior. All of her attempts were overdone, or without any personal truth." Strasberg believed that Stella succeeded in the role because he gave her what he called the "shipboard adjustment." He suggested that she act her part as if she were sharing her feelings in a casual shipboard romance, which is "very real," "very pure," but "it doesn't seek anything else." It "worked for her," creating, in his view, "probably her most distinguished performance" (Adams, 147–48).

Strasberg also gave Luther Adler an adjustment to help him reach the intense anger Sol felt at the abuses of the upper class. When Adler admitted that he did not react strongly to "personal wrongs," Strasberg tried to discover what would raise his ire. The actor confessed, "When someone does something awful to someone else, I get furious." According to Strasberg, using this substitute enabled Adler to "produce the character's destructive energy."

Having his actors use a "substitute reality different from that set forth by the play" was, according to Strasberg, one of his "chief discoveries" in directing the Group productions. Influenced by Vakhtangov's reformulations of Stanislavsky, he urged his actors to find "equivalent reasons" in themselves for the behavior required by the character. But at Dover Furnace, Odets, a keen observer, made the perceptive suggestion that these indirect adjustments reflected Strasberg's personality more than any acting theory. "In directing, Lee gives clue after clue as to himself and the kind of inward life he leads," Odets wrote in his diary.

For instance, talking about a character, Odets said: "Suppose you're bursting to tell some piece of good news that has happened to you. When a good thing happens you want to share it, but you are afraid of how the other person will receive the news. So you approach him cautiously and if he makes the smallest start toward scoffing or laughing at your enthusiasm you'll shut up like a clam." And another observation: "People don't approach one another directly and say what is on their minds. Say you want to ask a girl to go somewhere with you, but you can't approach her directly with such a question. So you ask her some casual thing and then finally manage to ask her in an off-hand manner if she'll go walking with you." He continued: "Those things are indicative of Lee, of what he does in life. I am curious now to see what else will turn up as he goes on. I'll write them down. He is like me in that he wants to join in with people, but some inner thing often forbids it."

The innovations of Vakhtangov and Meyerhold, which Strasberg was analyzing in the classes at Dover Furnace, also inspired his staging. He told the actors that he was tackling new directing problems in *Success Story*. Odets tried to make sense of Strasberg's comments; it had something to do with finding typical, social characteristics for each character. "Frozen behavior," Strasberg called it, and it involved "visualization." Odets was impressed:

> What a job, what a job! I don't really understand it all yet, but give me time. I mentioned that it was difficult to understand, and Lee answered, "Well, I don't expect you to understand yet." I suppose that he himself is not yet clear about it in actual performance, that he knows only broadly what he wants, but not yet particularly.

A few days later, Odets observed one of the innovations when Bill Challee, playing Jeffrey Halliburton, read his lines to a jazz rhythm with interesting effect.

This exploration in rehearsals was going on while the company was still waiting for the rest of the play. Lawson's cuts and revisions were intended to conclude the drama with an effective and meaningful dramatic moment, but just how to interpret the final action was a question the Group members debated. Some insisted that a more frankly political interpretation of Sol Ginsberg's conflict was needed. Clurman recalled that his psychological insights into character were termed sentimental by some of the budding Marxists in the company because they did not expose the division of the world into capitalist and working class. The controversy about *Success Story* reflected new political passions that would flare up again and again as they chose the plays that would speak for them and then made dramaturgical and directorial decisions, complicating even further their already difficult creative process.

Nevertheless, the rehearsals at Dover Furnace seemed to be coming along on schedule. "We're not supposed to see the rehearsals yet," Odets wrote, "but some of the people look in thru the windows and report an amazingly exciting production. Lee does something to a script so that it becomes, finally, his property as much as the playwright's." When Odets saw the third act, he found it

> horrible in its intensity, never letting up for a second, and Stella, letting her own hysteria come thru, does nothing to add joy to watching and listening. But, I hasten to add, that the acting is distinguished in each part, the least of them being Dorothy Patten. I don't think that ever before has there been such acting on the American stage.

They had all known from the beginning that Dorothy Patten was "disastrously miscast." Over the years there was the recurrent complaint among the women in the permanent company that the Group did not have anyone to play the "femme fatale." Patten was chosen, it was implied, to please Cheryl Crawford, with whom she had a long-standing relationship. Clurman confessed, however, that they believed in those days that proper direction could make any competent actor give a satisfactory interpretation of a role. When Lee Shubert, who came to view the show prior to investing in it, complained of Patten's inadequacy, Strasberg went to work. He coached her privately, trying to inspire her with an elegant style taken from advertisements and fashion models. Finally, in desperation, Strasberg "played the part of the sexy *shiksa* himself, then asked to be imitated," according to apprentice Kazan. (Heresy from the master of the new method of acting!) "So great was Lee's hypnotic power that summer" that Patten, Kazan understood, "emerged from the privileged rehearsals glowing with confidence." Her acting of the 1930s material girl was, nevertheless, a failure, although she seemed to improve during their short season in Boston. Bud Bohnen, who was playing opposite her there, felt she was "not so far out on a limb," having "forgotten some of the complexes that Lee endowed her with." She showed a simpler quality when she no longer had to run the "gauntlet through a system of taboos set up by Lee." Bohnen concluded, "She is still not so hot...and neither is the part—its really a shell...an indicated role of great possibilities which the author didn't fulfill."

Shubert also suggested modifying the image of the Jew, which he found too "harsh and bitter." Odets noted in his diary after a rehearsal on September 4 that the play seemed different; "a false note" had "crept" into both the writing and the acting. He believed that Lawson had made "what seemed unfeeling and unthinking dialogue changes," and that Strasberg had altered the intent of Luther Adler's performance. "Where before he was playing Sol with arrogance and bitterness, now that is all softened and a romantic soft note has crept in, so that in the third act Luther sounded like the Music Master patting a little girl on the head." It was an off night. Franchot Tone was "half cocked," but Odets still felt the production was "neither here nor there." He wondered if this was caused by the many script changes or by "indecision in Lee's mind"? He hoped the show would be "jacked up and tightened speedily."

It was an intense and hectic summer. They swam and played tennis. A few men cut their hair off to semibaldness and grew beards. Innumerable cigarettes were smoked. Some of the fellows competed with Tone for his good bike, his pretty women, his roles, and his ability to get away with things. Tone had difficult moods. Sometimes before dawn he would drive his Ford over the lawn, into the outdoor furniture, through the fences, and the tennis court; cavort in nothing but a loin cloth, fire shots from a gun he carried with him, and drink heavily with a circle of "pretty good bottlemen." One of the turning points of the summer was his showdown with the directors that led to the shocking revelation that he was leaving the Group for Hollywood. It was the first defection, although he stayed on to open in *Success Story*.

It was the summer Beany Barker broke her toe playing tennis and Bobby Lewis took her to the insane asylum (the nearest hospital) to have it set as she recited "Oh, What a rogue and peasant slave am I." (Adams, 143) Odets thought he might be in love with her. At the end of August, he went to Virginia Farmer's room for some farewell drinks and drank as he had never done before. At two in the morning, he banged wildly on the piano and then threw two billiard balls at Barker's door, badly frightening her and her roommate, Dorothy Patten, and making permanent dents in the door.

Steamy hot weather raised tempers to the boiling point. Times were bad and political argument was rife. The actors seemed at an impasse, especially those not in the small-cast show. Yet, when they readied themselves to leave Dover Furnace in early September, spirits revived, ready to face the next challenge. Odets, for example, observed a new closeness and maturity. He himself had grown confident about his writing ability and he'd been told he would understudy Luther Adler in *Success Story*, the part he coveted. Although he realized he was not the actor Adler was, he thought that he might come closer to the vision of the playwright. He never had an opportunity to act the part, but his close study of the script was to pay off handsomely in his development as a playwright.

Bud Bohnen characterized this hectic summer encampment with its actors, directors, playwrights, wives, and children crowded together in "close quarters" as bringing "the notion of ensemble training smack into your private life." The company was finding it difficult to "face the fact that a collective behavior off-stage was prerequisite to being able to stay together long enough to train for an ensemble on-stage." At first, everyone complained about the assigned rooms, about the food, about the noise from the many competing Victrola records, and about one another's failings. "The place was breathless with discipline during acting hours and bristling with irreconcilable egos between times." Bohnen thought the directors were following a laissez faire policy, hoping that the problems would sort themselves out. And, indeed, this is what happened. Respect emerged from the challenging work they had done together.

Aware of the foibles of their leaders, most of the company still responded to their magic. They were fascinated by Strasberg's method in class and in rehearsal, even though he irritated them when he seemed dogmatic or mean-spirited. Clurman's brilliant analysis of their plays and his inspirational rhetoric continued to draw them, even when he seemed lethargic or erratic. Although the directors reluctantly agreed that they could support only 18 people in the coming season rather than the whole company, Clurman wove a web of new plans. He and others considered opening a Group restaurant, starting a magazine, a school, or film projects. All this in the depths of the Depression! But, as Clurman would say more than 50 years later, "we weren't depressed, we were full of beans."

Clurman described the end of the summer of 1932 as one of "Rabelaisian playfulness." Broadway gossip columns hinted that the Group was a free-love farm. The actors did a take-off on their directors: Beany Barker played Crawford as a "kind of female cowboy"; Art Smith was Strasberg weighed down with books stuffed in every imaginable place in his clothing; and Carnovsky was a bearded Clurman angel with lightning on his brow and a stuffed silk lady's stocking under his arm.

In this heady atmosphere, the mixed critical reception of *Success Story* when it opened in New York on September 26, 1932, was a devastating disappointment; in

Clurman's words, a "blow to the solar plexus, a kind of moral defeat in which we sorrowed for the world as much as we did for ourselves" (*FY,* 102). The provocative play had aroused the emotions of the company deeply. The initial response of the first-night audience made them think they had a triumph, but the confusing final act did not work as they had hoped. Once again a Group production stirred considerable critical discussion, but the reviewers seemed so inept in dealing with the play that Clurman for the first time found himself "indignant" with the press. Critics took Strasberg to task for a certain lack of "expertness" in casting and direction; yet, the acting of the Adlers in the two leads was highly regarded. The final moments, after Stella has shot her brother Luther in a struggle, were the sensation of the season. Actors in other shows would slip into the back of the theater for the ending just to see her cradle her lover in her arms. Bobby Lewis remembered:

> Stella set up a kind of keening that was shattering to her and to the audience. She had taken as her emotional reference the legend that, during World War I, young British soldiers, under the unbearable pressure of relentless shelling, had been heard to speak Chaucerian English...Anyone who witnessed that acting feat of Stella's might well wonder when he would see the like again. (*S&A,* 78)

Although Lawson found the production the best that could be had on Broadway, the work on the script with Clurman and the interpretation by Strasberg and the actors shook him profoundly. His high hopes for collaboration with artists who shared his views were deeply disappointed. Yet, he greatly admired the performances of Stella and Luther Adler. He observed that they "were more affected by their early training with their father, Jacob Adler, than by the Stanislavsky method" and that Strasberg's direction was probably influenced by "the special intensity that Stella and Luther brought to their performances." He also wondered how much Strasberg's immigrant background contributed to his orchestrating the performance around the Jewish theme, one that would become prominent in the plays of Clifford Odets.

There was some sense even among its ardent supporters that the production was both "uneven and remarkable," as Clurman put it a decade later. He had high praise for the three leads: for Stella's combination of poignant sensitivity with "something of the grand line of the heroic tradition"; for Tone's humor and dignity in the face of "bewildered defeat"; for Luther Adler's combination of "theatrical flair" with close observation in transforming Sol from an "impetuous, uncoordinated boy" to a "mordant and precociously leonine captain of industry." Nevertheless, there was the unevenness that resulted not only from the problem of casting Dorothy Patten in the fourth lead, but also from Strasberg's experimentation with "social interpretation and theatricality" à la Vakhtangov and Meyerhold. The result was "colorless" performances in the supporting roles. Although rhythmic and highly physical forms fascinated Strasberg, they seemed ill-suited to his handling of Lawson's play and also to his strengths as a director and as a man. Kazan, still only an apprentice that summer at Dover Furnace, concluded in retrospect that Strasberg's personality imposed "a kind of psychological restriction, which made a wild fling into experiment, humor, or fantasy impossible" (*A Life,* 64).

Yet, Strasberg gained a great deal from the classes and productions during this second year. The experiments he initiated at Dover Furnace greatly extended and intensified the company's range of expression, providing an extraordinary technique for the many different productions that followed, all of which aspired to a kind of theater poetry. Without abandoning emotional truth, the actors were encouraged to explore vivid, imaginative ways of showing with their bodies, their voices, with poetry, art, music, dance, and improvisation the human and the aesthetic meanings of theater art. In the next season, Strasberg would be able to integrate highly theatrical, almost choreographed staging, with psychological probing to great effect, turning Sidney Kingsley's hospital melodrama *Men in White* into a theatrical work of art.

5. Lee Strasberg: Artist of the Theater ✧

The real "success story" for Strasberg came a year after the tepid reception of *Success Story*. On September 26, 1933, Sidney Kingsley's *Men in White* opened to rave reviews and excellent business at the box office. In the interim the Group had passed through what Clurman called the "Winter of our Discontent." The years 1932–33 were the nadir of the Depression. Although the members had returned from Dover Furnace with uplifted spirits, many could only survive in New York by living together collectively in a run-down flat they had rented on 57th Street near the river. They thought of it as the Group poorhouse, although they dubbed it "Groupstroy" in the fashionable Russian manner, linking themselves ironically with the heroic labors on the great new Soviet dam, Dnieperstroy. The need to cling to one another and to their theatrical and political idealism was great as they suffered one blow after another. John Howard Lawson's *Success Story*, for which they had such high hopes, had its disappointingly short run, and Dawn Powell's *The Big Night*, directed by Crawford which followed, was the flop they had all anticipated. Production came to a standstill and members had to take jobs and handouts wherever they could find them. The Group seemed to be falling apart. To stem the tide of dispersion, they pleaded with Strasberg to teach some classes for them, but "Lee was wan and they were listless," Clurman remembered. In his view the Group "did not need classes so much as relief."

Despite this very grim winter, by summer of 1933 the company was off again to Warrensburg, New York, near Lake George. They had been rescued by a most unlikely combination—a script that Cheryl Crawford retrieved from the office of Lee Shubert; a benefit organized by Bobby Lewis; the enterprise of the owner of Green Mansions, an upstate New York summer camp for adults; and the generosity of Franchot Tone, who had written to Clurman that winter from Hollywood that the Group had been "the most important influence in his life" (*FY*, 125).

At Green Mansions, they quickly threw themselves into rehearsals for *Crisis*, a hospital drama that Crawford said she found in a huge pile of scripts on the floor in Lee Shubert's office. She found the theater owner "still somewhat enamoured of what seemed to him our crazy fanaticism" (*One Naked Individual*, 62), and he helped them produce *Success Story*. Despite little enthusiasm among her codirectors and many Group members for the script, they decided to work on it since nothing else suitable was available. With Sidney Kingsley, the young playwright on hand, and Strasberg directing, they transformed his script into *Men in White*. It was their first hit, a triumph for Strasberg's directing, and one of the most successful productions in the Group Theatre's ten-year history.

Green Mansions was something new in the Group's summer experience. For the first time, the actors were performing publicly at their retreat, making them seem more like a summer stock company than dedicated experimenters. Even the "gossip columns in the New York newspapers kidded us and made disparaging remarks about our services as 'entertainers,'" Clurman recalled. These services evidently included the actors dancing with the female guests, taking guests out in canoes, and even getting into bed with them, according to the memories of handsome Alexander "Billy" Kirkland, who had come from Broadway and Hollywood successes to link his fortunes with the company. The daily schedule was so hectic that Clifford Odets complained in his diary that he couldn't find time to write regularly. He did note that he was having voice and articulation lessons with Evelyn d'Angelo and that he "would have to do much work in that department," although he felt that Strasberg caused the "tightness" he suffered from on stage. Since, according to Clurman, the speech teacher was having a nervous breakdown, it's not surprising that Odets didn't make much progress. The dance teacher didn't work out either, and there wasn't a great deal of time for acting classes. (*FY*, 128)

What kept them busy was the combination of regular rehearsals for the Kingsley play and organizing entertainment each weekend in return for room and board for a very large contingent of actors, designers, teachers, wives, and children. Lena Barish's popular summer camp for adults had a small theater that became the focus of their lives for more than eight weeks.

The experimental classes and productions of the previous summer made it possible for them to succeed at Green Mansions. They drew heavily on the exercises and class sketches developed at Dover Furnace for what amounted to a show every weekend. As early as Memorial Day, part of the troupe went up to Green Mansions with Clurman, who was to be responsible for arranging the complicated work schedule for the season, something he did not do terribly well. On that occasion they offered a one-act play by John Galsworthy and an improvised revue based on the Dover Furnace work. As soon as the others arrived, on June 20, 1933, the Group featured Joe Bromberg and Morris Carnovsky, the "gibberish" experts, in improvisations, along with Tony Kraber singing cowboy songs and playing his guitar, a specialty that became part of their summer programs. Kraber added Yiddish songs to his repertoire to the enthusiastic approval of the guests. For the upcoming weekend of July 4, Odets and Lewis Leverett prepared a cutting of *Ten Nights in a Barroom*, which they immediately put into rehearsal as their Saturday night show. It did not go over very well, but the Fourth of July revue on Sunday night became a big hit. Beany Barker and Stella Adler were part of a "deconstructionist" chorus line that opened the show. Wearing khaki shorts and a kind of brassier-sash fashioned out of an American flag, they did a military routine to the tune of "Dixie." They sang,

Let's pledge allegiance to the Flag
That freed us from oppression
And also freed us from our savings
During the Depression.

For that's the best solution
Save the dollar for it is
Our sacred institution.

The veterans are all heroes though
They're getting thin and bony
Some folks think heroes ought to eat
But that is all baloney
So buy American and save
Our sacred institution
[as they skip off "very cutely"]
But don't blame us if dollars turn

Another revolution!

With Bromberg, Carnovsky, and Strasberg limping along as a very decrepit Spirit of '76, the chorus reprised its song and added "Volga Boatman," "Columbia the Gem of the Ocean," and "The Caissons Go Rolling Along" for a wild finale. The owner Lena Barish was pleased and came backstage to shake hands with everyone.

Bobby Lewis was heavily involved in putting the revues together because, as he put it, "I was musical and dance and all that." He recalled that by working all through the night they managed the feat of a full-length play on Saturday night and a revue on Sunday night while rehearsing *Men in White* the rest of the week. For their musical numbers, they "had a chorus consisting of...three girls who were pretty, or pretty enough...who could dance. It was Phoebe Brand, I think Eunice Stoddard, and I'm not sure of the other." For the sketches, they relied on their acquired skill in improvisation. For example, Philip Loeb, a Theatre Guild friend and later an occasional Group actor, taught them sketches from shows like the *Greenwich Village Follies* and *Garrick Gaieties* in which he had appeared. They rehearsed what he showed them the same way they rehearsed with Strasberg, that is, by improvising scenes. Bobby Lewis remembered, "We didn't need to learn every word and every cue so that if we forgot it the thing would be a bust. Not at all. We knew what the situation was, you see. All night long, we rehearsed...and all the next day." What they produced, according to Eunice Stoddard, one of the chorines, was not quite the *Chauve Souris*—the famous Russian theater cabaret Nikita Balieff had brought to New York in the 1920s. Yet, the lively foolery of the talented Group actors greatly pleased the guests at Green Mansions.

Just as they rifled recent shows that some had appeared in, so they rifled much of recent theater history for the plays they put together each week. They staged Eugene O'Neill's *The Emperor Jones* out-of-doors in a natural amphitheater. Meisner and Odets sat in trees and beat the drums, providing "the sound and fury," as Meisner put it, for Bromberg's impressive Emperor Jones. One day, when the two of them learned that they had been cast in very small parts in *Men in White*, they drove around in Meisner's car, got drunk, and at that night's performance wouldn't stop drumming and wouldn't come down out of the trees. Nobody spoke to them for days. They did several other O'Neill pieces, Maxwell Anderson's *Gods of the Lightning*, Chekhov's *The Bear*, one-acts by Sean O'Casey, and some segments from their own repertoire, including one act of *Big Night*, and two acts of *Success Story*.

The most significant production at Green Mansions was one that can be credited in large part to the nurturing of playwrights that had occurred the previous summer. In a cottage reserved for playwrights at Dover Furnace, Odets had started a play about the Greenbaum family. Like the acting problems he had struggled with in classes, his writing, he realized, would have to grow out of his personal truth. At Green Mansions he gave Clurman the first act and a half of the Greenbaum play, having labored on it at Groupstroy the previous winter. Odets indicated in his diary that Clurman liked it, made good critical observations, and suggested that the first act be put on one weekend. He was also pleased that Crawford too praised his play. On August 26, they staged what they called "the second act." The author believed it would play "like a house on fire," and it did. (Brenman-Gibson, 272) The audience and the actors loved it, but, much to the distress of Odets, no move was made to place it in rehearsal for a regular production. A year and a half would pass before the Greenbaum play, called *I Got the Blues*, would become *Awake and Sing!*, the signature play of the Group Theatre.

One of the bit parts in Odets's show was taken by Elia Kazan, who confessed that he "snared every small part" he could. He had been brought along to Green Mansions to be the all-purpose technical person for the heavy production schedule they had undertaken. His former Yale teacher, Philip Barber, a playwright who also served as a technical director for the Group, had promised that his former student, rightly nicknamed Gadget, "could build, paint, and light scenery, prepare the props and costumes as required, stage-manage the productions, and have everything ready in good working order and on time." Kazan said frankly that all he wanted to do that summer was "to make the Group feel they couldn't get along without me" (*A Life*, 102). He succeeded. He was asked to be the assistant stage manager for the fall production of *Men in White*, and by the end of the summer, he was made a Group member.

A special project Kazan worked on at Green Mansions grew out of the Dover Furnace classes. The photographer Ralph Steiner, who had been part of their circle ever since the talks given by Clurman in 1930–31 when he had offered his studio for some of the meetings, came with them to Green Mansions to make a movie of the sketches based on George Grosz drawings that had created a stir the previous summer. Antiwar in content, *Café Universal*, as it was called, was experimental in both its acting and in its filming. Steiner observed that "the direction and acting were not realistic, but more like posters come to life." The wordless film had a poetic, dreamlike quality. Stills of the no-longer extant film reveal its highly stylized quality; all the men in the film are without shirts, but the capitalists wear ties and the soldiers helmets. The lead actors were Art Smith, who had originated the improvisation, and Kazan, with whom Steiner had recently made another experimental film, *Pie in the Sky*.

These Group Theatre films offer a glimpse of the unique approach of the early class projects. Improvisation based on the actors' ideas and the immediate physical background rather than written scripts supplied the scenarios. *Pie in the Sky*, indebted to the famous hobo song, juxtaposed a pious preacher at the Grace and Hope mission with images of decay and debris found at the New York City dump, where most of the project was filmed. "The thrown-away things of the dump furnished rich props and costumes and presented us with ideas for sequences," Steiner remembered. The film had a Brechtian opening that showed the Group crew shooting the film with Steiner at the camera, Kazan lounging on the ground getting ready for his role, and Molly Day Thacher, Group play-reader and Kazan's wife, studying notes on her clipboard. With its political implications, this film, which has survived, combines cinematic experimentation with agitation-propaganda techniques and content. Interviewed about it years later, Kazan seemed to link it to the communist cell that he said had already been established in the Group to promote Marxist views.

Political commitment among the members increased during the summer; some had begun working with the new proletarian theaters, whose young actors became hangers-on at Green Mansions. The spirited actions of the newly elected Franklin Delano Roosevelt, who promised a "new deal for the American people," intensified their activism. Their increased well-being at Green Mansions spurred them on. The company was thriving; they were eating well, sleeping deeply, and keeping themselves busy with many different projects. Odets, always the emotional barometer, noted with considerable ambivalence the changes among his friends: "Our Group people are all getting a sort of fat-belly quality. I can hardly explain. They're freer, more relaxed, more satisfied with mere life divided from idealistic yearning." He explained the change this way. "First, it seems, Lee colored the Group with a kind of stern, disciplined bit. Now it seems that they're taking (since Lee these days has little contact with us, living off on the other side with Paula) their quality from Cheryl and Harold. There are no ideals or visions wasted around here these days. These things slumber here these days." Yet, Odets concluded, "It is just as well." He felt more certain of himself, his talent, his girlfriend in the city, and his sexual adventure with a guest at the camp. He observed "a certain sexual laxity" at Green Mansions with liaisons both hetero- and homosexual and sometimes both simultaneously. Yet, he also noted an important change: "[P]eople are not so ashamed of life as they were." Some lived quietly off by themselves like Strasberg and Paula Miller, Carnovsky and Phoebe Brand, Joe and Goldie Bromberg, Art and Degan Smith, Eunice Stoddard and her husband, Julian Whittlesey, who came up weekends. Others were going through personal crises. Virginia Farmer, her marriage to Lewis Leverett having broken up, was bitter, and the speech teacher was in the process of leaving her husband. Clurman and Stella seemed to have separated. Although Clurman kept his pain to himself, his deep unhappiness was apparent to his friend Odets, especially when in a somewhat drunken state Clurman allowed himself to be hypnotized by a young psychiatrist who had been entertaining the lodge guests with his psychic tricks. (Brenman-Gibson, 267) Clurman's behavior under hypnosis was frighteningly bizarre. It was a time of personal, political, and creative ferment and change.

The hectic entertainment activities were fitted in around the major task of the summer—rehearsals for *Men in White*. The decision to undertake its production had been made reluctantly. Despite brief references to class differences in access to abortion and the need for socialized medicine, Kingsley's melodrama did not seem an appropriate play for the artistic, socially committed Group Theatre to produce in the bleak days of 1933. Strasberg argued that they had to do it just to keep going as a theater and challenged their play-choice procedures, saying that they couldn't wait for "the great plays that are expressive of the ideas everybody stands for." In addition, he believed the weaknesses in the script were not that important. Reiterating his aesthetic, he argued: "A play is not in the text. It's on the stage. This is a sound work about idealism. It can do well. With this we can make our statement" (Adams, 158). Others were not so sure. Clurman, unenthusiastic himself, had to deal with actors who begged him to stop the production because "it would surely ruin the Group" (*FY*, 127). But, since Kingsley's script was the only practical option they had, he supported the decision.

Rehearsals started upon their arrival at Green Mansions. Within the authentically recreated environment of a busy city hospital, Kingsley had dramatized the conflict between success and selfless dedication to the medical ideals embodied in the Hippocratic oath. Young Doctor Ferguson, played by Alexander Kirkland, is torn between his beautiful, wealthy girlfriend, Laura Hudson, played by Margaret Barker, who wants to share with him a life of comfort and power, and the dedicated surgeon Hochberg, played by J. Edward Bromberg, who urges him to undertake medical research that would benefit mankind. The idealistic but overworked Ferguson yields very briefly to the emotional and sexual attractions of the sweet, young student nurse Barbara, played by Phoebe Brand. In a climactic operating room scene, Laura witnesses her fiancé assist Dr. Hochberg in trying to save Barbara's life after a botched abortion, the bitter fruit of her one night of love with Ferguson. Her death renews Ferguson's dedication to medicine, and the curtain falls on a positive note as the young doctor reassures a weeping mother that he will save her son.

Although Strasberg was disturbed by the attitudes to the script, he set to work, according to Clurman, resolutely and well. (*FY*, 127) The four shows he had directed and the many classes he had conducted no doubt gave him increased confidence, but there was something deeper involved as he undertook to stage this play on which a third season and their very existence seemed to depend. Perhaps it was the need to prove to the doubters, who had to be forced to rehearse, that he could do it or the need to concentrate in the face of the distractions of the other performances being prepared for the weekends. In addition the dedication of young interns bucking the medical bureaucracy, an obvious parallel with the Group's story, must have appealed to the tense, authoritarian, but idealistic, even sentimental personality of "Dr. Strasberg." Even his notoriously erratic temper improved during the rehearsals. "Lee is working differently with the people now," Odets noted in his diary. "No whip, but explanation and relaxed goodness. I enjoy working with him on my small part in the play. One can get near to him, like him, be helped."

To young Kingsley, however, the Group at Dover Furnace seemed "the wildest bunch of radical fanatics you ever saw." He remembered that one day Strasberg had the actors cutting each other's hair. He wasn't sure whether this was being done because barbers were the original surgeons or because Strasberg thought the actors benefited from intimate physical contact. The rehearsals troubled and amazed him. "One could hardly call it rehearsal," he observed, "because they very seldom rehearsed the scenes, but they did some marvelous things." After a few readings, Strasberg's ensemble tossed his script aside and spent most of the summer improvising. Although Kingsley resented the "disrespect for the script," he eventually realized these peculiar means were the director's way of readying his play and the actors for staging. Strasberg seemed to him "a mysterious man," whose work was "great."

Although some actors patronized Kingsley, he got on so well with Strasberg that he dared to make suggestions about how the actors were saying lines or developing their characters. He was troubled, for example, that Bromberg was acting Dr. Hochberg in an angry, self-important way. "I whispered to Lee, 'I wouldn't let this man operate on my little toe. He seems so menacing.'" He asked Strasberg to tell Bromberg to smile, even though he knew that the director never told his actors what to do. According to Kingsley, around the big lunch table later that day, Bromberg said, "You know, the most wonderful thing happened to me today. I don't know where it came from but suddenly I found myself smiling sweetly; and Lee, if you don't mind...I'm gonna play it that way." Lee nodded yes. At that moment, said Kingsley, "Lee did something I never saw him do before or since. Lee winked at me. He had somehow conveyed to Joe Bromberg what the actor should do without Joe realizing that he had been told." Another ploy that Strasberg used to modify the character was to give Bromberg what he called the "FBI adjustment," suggesting that the authority of the head doctor be indirect like the questioning of an FBI agent. (*A Dream of Passion*, 89; also Adams, 162) Bromberg won praise for his performance, which one critic rated the best of 1933 in competition with Henry Hull in *Tobacco Road* and George M. Cohan in *Ah, Wilderness!* Strasberg credited Bromberg's subsequent success in Hollywood to this performance.

The magic Kingsley came to admire was the direct result of Strasberg's rehearsal process. Describing his usual practice years later, Strasberg said he gave the actors "an idea of the play as a whole—the kind of experience it embodies and conveys—how it should move—what problems it sets for us, actor and director—how it differs from other plays in feeling—in mood—in rhythm." He did not indulge in extensive thematic or conceptual discussion, preferring to analyze the structure of the play so that he and the actors could proceed directly to the acting problems. "What we would do in the first session and in the reading rehearsals," he recalled, "was block out the actions, without acting them. Then we would start to work so that as the reading rehearsals went on, we almost began to have a performance in the chair. The actors would have a sense of what it was that they were working toward." Actors did not start memorizing lines, but would put the script aside as Strasberg worked individually with each one "to find the main elements of the character he is to portray, and to search for the best way of translating the impression of the whole into the medium of each actor's individual talent."

For *Men in White* the novel problem was the unusual hospital locale, one that has since become a clichéd backdrop for television melodramas. Just as the young author had extensively researched the hospital environment, so Strasberg, the actors, and their designer Mordecai Gorelik also went to hospitals and interrogated nurses and doctors in order to capture the general atmosphere and the details accurately. In turn, doctors visiting Green Mansions gave them advice: one was the brother of Margaret Barker, whose father was Dean of Johns Hopkins Medical School. Nevertheless, it was Strasberg's theatrical choices rather than any attempt at literal realism that made a hit of the hospital environment, especially the preparatory "scrubbing up" in the operating theater where Kingsley had placed the dramatic climax of his play. Doctors told Strasberg that this unusual scene was absolutely accurate, but Strasberg confided years later: "I felt that I could stage something that would be better than what I found. I thought I had done rather well in producing something that was more than a reproduction" (*Reunion*, 551).

What Strasberg had produced was a stylization that seemed more real than the real thing. Kingsley had imagined the sequence as "having the beat and rhythm of some mechanical dance composition," and in rehearsal it became a kind of ballet. "When an actor washed up in the operating room it was a kind of poetry," Carnovsky reminisced. Playing Nurse Jamison, Eunice Stoddard, who had dance training, staged or choreographed her sequence of laying out the instruments for the operation. Strasberg, however, insisted: "We never intended it to be a ballet." Fascinated by the origins of theater as well as the experiments of symbolists, Strasberg had something else in mind. "We did intend it to be a heightened kind of ritualistic procedure in which some people represented life and others, death. The doctor was almost a preacher or a priest, who fought for life." Kirkland vaguely remembered the ensemble improvising as Incas worshiping at a pyramid temple. Strasberg told the actors: "Wash as if this were some great achievement. Don't wash your hands one, two, three. Wash slowly, methodically, carefully ... the whole thing moves as in a sense of ritual" (Adams, 160–61).

Actors recalled improvising this operation sequence over one hundred times at Green Mansions, practicing the scrubbing-up ritual each morning on awakening. To find a rhythm for the operation, Strasberg had the actors improvise to the second movement of Beethoven's Seventh Symphony, an exercise they had done in classes at Dover Furnace. They would also pantomime an operation in which the patient died. This tragic version would be followed by *commedia dell'arte lazzi* to music by Offenbach in which the actors opened up the patient, then stitched him up again, leaving the instruments in his innards. Strasberg pointed out that "neither exercise had any direct connection with what was actually done in the play, but they helped to stir the actors' imaginations and thus enable them to get behind the words of the play and into the event that was taking place." During one improvisation Luther Adler, as the anesthetist assisting Bromberg as Dr. Hochberg, examined Phoebe Brand lying on the table about to be operated on and then said: "She's dead." Bromberg countered, "She's not dead." "Yes, she is." "That ended the improvisation right then and there," laughed Brand. "I knew I wasn't dead, but he was insistent. I think he was being funny." Obviously the operation scene was neither replica nor ballet. "What it was really," concluded their director, "was the way it should be."

Along with the highly theatrical ritual structure, rhythmic movement, and authentic details, the actors motivated each moment with the kind of inner reality and conviction for which they were becoming famous. Their skill using intense, often traumatic personal experience filled out and overwhelmed the types that served Kingsley's drama. Even the minor parts were played by members of their trained ensemble. Luther Adler, who had the emotionally powerful lead in *Success Story*, played one of the interns; Meisner doubled in two small parts, Odets played a board member, and Bobby Lewis played his first real character, the comic intern. Strasberg direction to Lewis went something like this: "Bobby, in this scene I want you to do ten funny things." Humorous as he was, Bobby had trouble coming up with something that would work until Clurman helped him out. "Stop worrying. He's just the kind of kid who sees a pretty nurse coming toward him in the corridor

and calls out. 'Hi, sweetie. Gettin' plenty? Oops, I'm sorry. I forgot you're Catholic'"
(*S&A*, 78). Elaborating on that clue, Bobby made a hit of his small part.

Margaret Barker remembered that improvisations helped her to explore her character, one whose comfortable background was familiar but whose personality was utterly unlike her own. She wasn't always sure what Strasberg wanted, especially when he told her to play Laura like "seaweed"—a description he had read about Eleonora Duse's acting in *Lady from the Sea*. Barker confessed that she had a "terrible time" because the character was "so unlike Duse." She was "a kind of a modern girl Sidney Kingsley had written, who expected her boyfriends to take her dancing and so on." It was all "far away from seaweed" or from some of the intense improvisations Strasberg's devised. In one, her Laura became so furious with her young doctor that she slapped him. When Kirkland slapped her back really hard, Barker started to cry as Strasberg shouted out to his overwrought actors, "Hold it, hold it."

Kirkland recalled that he improvised a desperate sequence of meeting Barker in Amalfi, where he had to confess to her that he had contracted syphilis. This aspect of Strasberg's acting process fascinated him because, as Kirkland put it, "it caught out all kinds of feelings in you...Lee was very good at giving you things that would come in as association later when you played other scenes." Playing the lead, although a newcomer, Kirkland had to absorb Strasberg's training during these rehearsals. He had walked out on his Hollywood contract when Crawford urgently invited him to join the Group as a replacement for Franchot Tone. An old Theatre Guild friend, Crawford had taken him to see *Success Story*; the acting overwhelmed him. At Green Mansions he thought it wonderful to be using the process that had produced their "magnificent" acting—improvising on practically every beat and doing the emotional memory exercises with Strasberg, which he found an effective, revealing way to "particularize" sudden emotional moments in a script.

Max Gorelik's sets reinforced the combination of realistic and emotional detail with evocative stylization that made the show a down-to-earth, yet almost mythic rendering of the gleaming, impersonal, but mysterious world of modern medicine. He imagined the hospital as a "piece of surgery," constructed like "a scientific toy...of rooms coming off of long corridors." A permanent set with sliding vertical panels upstage and a long sliding platform parallel to the proscenium made quick cinematic shifts possible for the little vignettes—in the hospital's library, board room, nurse's night desk, intern's room, and the operating theater. (Gorelik, 296–97) But, as Gorelik pointed out, the "sense of precise movement along interminable corridors of a hospital" was always maintained. This functional, dynamic, highly theatrical space was created with "an almost antiseptic cleanliness of design, emphasizing the modernistic, polished areas, contrasting deep blue to white, bringing out the glitter of surgical instruments."

Patiently, slowly, through Strasberg's method and his instinctive skills and that of his collaborators, the play began to take on a special life. Clurman pointed out that if they had to open the show after the time usually allotted to rehearsals, the production seen later would have not been in evidence. The famous three-minute surgical preparation was originally only a "purely atmospheric" improvisation intended to intensify the actors' awareness of hospital reality. Clurman asserted that he urged

Strasberg to include it in the action of the play. Most of the final version of the third act grew out of improvisation, according to Kirkland, who reported that the actors "didn't have any written down lines for a long, long time," but they worked with a "skeleton of beats." Walter Coy, who played one of the comic interns, felt that Kingsley's script provided a "framework" for Strasberg's "brilliant" work. "Sidney's play was created not just by Sidney, but by the whole Group, by everybody working in it." According to Kingsley, however, it was only after the success of the show that the actors took the credit rather than recognizing the playwright's contribution.

Yet, tinkering continued. The first run-through before one of their backers on a rainy night at Green Mansion's tin-roofed theater seemed disastrous to everyone. Crawford, who had been the chief booster of the script, had to comfort Strasberg, who was "very disturbed." He told her: "I don't think I can go on with this." She remembered suggesting that their technique of emotional identification had undercut the "professional objectivity" required of doctors and nurses and also preempted the audience's opportunity to be moved. (Crawford, 64–65)

Strasberg realized what was wrong:

> Because everything was correct—how you put on the gown, what you do with the glove—everyone said it was exactly as it is in a hospital, but it wasn't. No real doctors behaved like that. It's how they like to *think* they behaved. Real surgeons yawn and scrub up while cracking to the next guy, "So how was that dame you were with last night?" Very casual, very ordinary...everything we were doing was actually right but the delivery was too heavy...it appeared the play wasn't coming over." (Adams, 161)

Recalling his original impression of the script as one that "moved more easily, quicker, seemed exciting," Strasberg decided that in pouring life into the action, he had gone "overboard, that everything was...too deep, too intense, unprofessional." With his sharp critical instincts, he sensed the disparity between his method of work and Kingsley's script, which could not bear the emotional weight the actors were putting into it. "If you have a very deep reaction and you take a pause and then, after it, you say, 'Gee, that's too bad,' people will say the writing is very thin." Having learned how to be "deeply moved," the actor wanted to share his inspired "moment" on stage, but Strasberg realized that "different words" would be needed, not Kingsley's journalistic dialogue. The actors thought he was "going back on the method" when he urged them to take a "professional adjustment" appropriate to medical mores and the casual language of the script. (Adams, 161)

The company kept adjusting the show through the previews at the Broadhurst Theatre. For example, Eddie Kook of Century Lighting focused powerful lights without colored gelatins on the white surgical table-sheets and doctors' costumes to stunning effect. But, Strasberg shouted for more and more light for the final moment of the scene. When no lighting they had available seemed to satisfy him, Crawford and Kingsley bought a gooseneck lamp they had seen at an Eighth Avenue drugstore. They put a very strong bulb into it, and set it on stage where the assisting physician could turn it on unobtrusively when he handed over the instrument as the surgeon called, "Scalpel." In Crawford's opinion, "the sudden excess of light did the trick, creating an effect as painful as the scalpel making the incision" (65).

Barker became upset by all the changes after the long months of rehearsal and, in a moment of emotional frustration, threw her handbag at Strasberg, fortunately missing him. Other versions of this story have Strasberg slapping her when he could "not communicate what he wanted." Yet, even after the first preview, they kept at it. They decided that the ending of the play, in which the curtain came down on the dejected intern abandoned by his wealthy fiancée, didn't work. After a conference with the author, they added a concluding upbeat telephone call from the Italian mother, played by Mary Virginia Farmer, of one of his patients. Young Dr. Ferguson, overcoming his personal despair, was heard comforting her, telling her not to cry, promising that despite all, her son would live. (65–66)

With the script and the acting adjusted, their meticulously crafted production was ripe for critical acclaim on Broadway. Audiences enjoyed the stylization of melodramatic thrill, scientific voyeurism, authentic, emotionally fresh characterization, high-minded sentiment, and hopefulness. Joseph Wood Krutch, *The Nation*'s usually severe critic, pointed out that "the effectiveness of the production can be credited ... to its remarkable wholeness, to the way in which everything in the acting and direction, as well as the script itself, works with everything else to produce an unbroken continuity of interest and to leave behind a complete, unified impression." This wholeness led him to call the production "a genuine work of art" (October 11, 1933). It was essentially the director's triumph, and Strasberg was credited by the knowledgeable *Theatre Arts* for "the unity and fluency, the quiet and tension of the large company's playing" (December 1933). Shortly after the opening Clurman, in one of the moral curiosities of the period, reviewed the Group's accomplishments in the *Daily Worker*, writing under his pseudonym of Harold Edgar. He held that *Men in White* is "chiefly noteworthy for the fact that it is the first [production] which has brought the Group's collective technique prominently and successfully to public notice ... [and] reveals this technique which is not a trick that can be applied indiscriminately and at will whenever desired, but an accumulative theatrical discipline for the organization and the individual within it" (October 3, 1933). Clurman concluded in later years that *Men in White* was Lee's "masterpiece" and the Group's "most finished production" (*FY*, 128–29).

In retrospect, Strasberg acknowledged that Max Gorelik "had as much to do with creating the vision of the play on stage as any of us." He credited the designer with important contributions to the evolving Group style, "an approach to the treatment of reality on stage not only in acting but also in production." Gorelik, who had studied in the 1920s with Robert Edmond Jones and Norman Bel Geddes and had designed the striking vaudevillesque sets for Lawson's expressionistic labor play *Processional*, was more theatrical as well as more theoretical and radical in his approach than the Group directors. He applied to the theater the Marxist thesis that "as societies" change, their "art forms change." In his view the modern theater was passing from being a commodity for the individualistic, introspective middle class to an immediate ceremony for a working class concerned with communal effort to change society. The older drama with its limited, unified analysis of action fitted easily into the realistic illusions created within the box set. The new dynamic drama required a frankly theatrical stage design for its simultaneous action, representing a multiplicity of views and places such as he had created for *Men in White*. In his designs Gorelik hoped to show that the purpose of theater is to "influence life by theatrical means." A Guggenheim Fellowship awarded in 1935 and renewed in 1937 allowed him to explore his evolving views with designers and critics in major European theaters. His innovative analysis of theater history from the perspective of production was published in 1940 as *New Theatres for Old*, an important landmark in theater studies.

Although Gorelik's theories often made him critical of the Group, especially of what he considered the directors' middle-class vacillations and political naivete, he believed that the company was the only one creating organic theater in America. "My designs for the Group were never just added to the play, but grew organically... It was fascinating to watch the rehearsals and develop with the ensemble something that had single impact." He could make the scenic details of a seemingly realistic play like *Success Story* the vehicle of a larger meaning: metallic texture, diagonal placement, and golden color transformed the office into an emblem of inhuman but alluring values. His *Men in White* set facilitated the almost cinematic movement without sacrificing either the sense of realistic locale or the overall impression of the antiseptic medical machine. (Gorelik, 296–97)

Although the staging and sets were influenced by radical political theory and the principles of abstract modern art, Strasberg believed that audiences and critics did not seem to recognize that the Group had a unique theatrical style in part because of their highly organic creative process. Since no aspect of production stood out as obviously "theatrical," people thought everything on stage simply belonged to what Strasberg called "the particular reality that we created." What was true for the limited perception of the Group's visual style was also true, to a certain extent, for the acting. It seemed "real," especially in contrast to the artificiality of most stage behavior. The actors looked to personal emotion and individual psychology instead of theatrical convention for the truth they could bring to the characters in their plays—an important source of their strength. But, for all the emphasis on truthful emotion and being real, it was a special notion of theatrical truth and reality they were aiming for. Strasberg believed that "the greatest poetry has invariably come from life." The ensemble experimented with songs, dances, sound effects, choreographed movements, socially defined characterization, and somewhat abstract sets. Improvisations in rehearsals, on stage, and in classes may have been intended to make scenes seem more real, but they also gave their work immediacy, surprise, and turbulence that is essentially theatrical. That all the actors in the ensemble, from leads to supers, performed with the same integrity and intensity resulted in unique theatrical concentration and consistency. The fervor of their shared convictions about art and life charged the productions with a larger-than-life dimension.

In addition there was plenty of old-fashioned theatricality. For all the emphasis on versatility and alternating roles, the casting often followed the kind of acting lines associated with the old stock companies, leading to decisions that sometimes engendered jealousy and hurt. There was Tone, later replaced by Bohnen and Kirkland, for the WASP male leads; Margaret Barker for the attractive, often wealthy female; Phoebe Brand for the struggling or abused sweet young woman; Morris Carnovsky and Joe Bromberg for juicy character parts; and Stella and Luther Adler for strong emotional, often ethnic leads. In *Men in White* the conjunction of the real and the theatrical along with both conventional and novel touches suited Kingsley's mix of the melodramatic, the scientific, and the innovative very well. Strasberg's accomplishment filled the coffers of the needy company.

Yet, the very success of *Men in White* brought about a number of ironic consequences. As the actors played in their hit, they gained recognition and reaped substantial benefits (regular salaries and even vacations-with-pay) during its run of 311 performances, but their disdain grew for the show, the author, and the middle-class Broadway audiences who loved it. The disparity between their challenging aesthetic and political ambitions and the creative and ideological accommodations of this hit show rankled. Indeed, Clurman's pseudonymous *Daily Worker* review took the Group to task for the play's lack of "social comment or intellectual value" and hoped the company would apply its fine methods to the ultimate goal of creating the "drama of a classless society, which, in terms of the present, must be a revolutionary drama" (October 3, 1933). Kazan, who stage-managed the show, later wrote that success precipitated "an exodus of Group actors downtown to the newborn 'workers' theatres,'" where they could do their "'real work' south of Fourteenth Street" (*A Life*, 105). He and Art Smith used actors in the cast of *Men in White* when the agit-prop *Dimitroff: A Play of Mass Pressure*, which they had written, was performed at one of the radical "New Theatre Nights" at Eva Le Gallienne's Civic Repertory Theatre.

Success on Broadway also brought Strasberg to Moscow, the workers' fatherland. There he saw productions by the Russian masters that made him realize what directing was really about. His enlarged understanding inspired his subsequent, ambitious productions for the Group. The trip was a gift from the grateful Kingsley, who accompanied Strasberg and learned that he had won the Pulitzer Prize for *Men in White* amid the tumult of the Moscow May Day parade. The long run of the show also made possible a holiday in Moscow and Europe for Clurman and Stella. It was this trip that ended in those famous Paris sessions with Stanislavsky that were to challenge Strasberg's method.

Before that fateful jaunt, however, Stella, for whom there had been no part in *Men in White*, was cast in the central role in John Howard Lawson's *Gentlewoman*, which, flushed with success, the Group quickly put into production. Carnovsky and a few others were replaced in *Men in White* so they could act with her, along with a number of non-Group actors including Lloyd Nolan, who was recruited for the male lead. Strasberg again directed and Gorelik designed the sets for this radical drawing-room comedy in which, in the words of one critic, the "political soap-box is cretonne-covered."

Gwen Ballantine is the refined gentlewoman of the title, whose comfortable but empty life collapses with the suicide of her husband, a businessman who has kept from her the deceit and decay of his financial ventures. She tries to continue her now somewhat impoverished life with a hard-drinking, rough-hewn working-class poet, Rudy Flannigan. Each is attracted by the qualities of the other, but they cannot resolve their personal and class conflicts and frustrations. Together they cannot find "where reality lies." He goes off to help farmers organize in Iowa; she remains alone to bear their child whom she hopes "will take sides" and "make a new world."

Clurman recalled that the company really felt the play seemed to echo their own middle-class confusions and yearning. When *Gentlewoman* opened at the

Cort Theatre in March 1934, however, it lasted only nine days. The burden of the critical response was that Lawson, despite occasional impassioned brilliance, suffered from confused intentions. This parable of the stock-market crash came out as a rather boring, inflated, and unconvincing drama. (*The Nation*, April 11, 1934; *FY*, 133–34) It opened just after the Guild production of Lawson's *The Pure in Heart*, which also closed in a few days. These traumatic rejections and the critical exchanges with Broadway pundits and the *New Masses* left-wing columnist Michael Gold radicalized Lawson's personal life as well as his objectives as a dramatist. (*New Masses*, April 10, 1934)

There was also substantial criticism of the production itself. What little comment there was on the direction suggested that while Strasberg's contribution was "intelligent" and "generally competent," it was marked at times by "an almost morose uneasiness." The unease was real; lacking social grace himself and resentful of those who had it, Strasberg did not connect with Lawson's ideological drawing-room drama. It was not his forte, or Clurman's, or the company's. "We felt that the production needed a lighter touch and quality. We weren't sure that our own people could give us that in a short space of time" was how Strasberg remembered his explanation for why outside actors were hired. (*Reunion*, 550) The result was that the company did not do its usual acting preparation.

In *Gentlewoman*, there was not the slightest Method work, Strasberg insisted. (*Reunion*, 550) Lloyd Nolan, who was a rising young performer in whom they were interested, did not seem to respond to the play at all. "The play's issues were a closed book to him," Clurman wrote; as a result, his acting seemed "predictable," emphasizing only what was "crude" in the character. Perhaps they should have cast Odets; he was dying to play the role of the "poet, vagrant, rebel, misfit" with whom he felt a strong kinship. Or, Walter Coy, who was kept on the hook about playing the part for which he did not feel himself "quite right," but not "too wrong." He believed the Group was turning to stars; he complained that he had also been displaced by the better-known Kirkland for the lead in *Men in White*. Even the usually admired Carnovsky seemed to be "colorless" in *Gentlewoman*. For Stella the show was a disaster. She didn't know what Strasberg wanted from her and could not herself make contact with the character. Although a few critics considered her playing "properly tremulous" and "lyrical," others found her "presiding over the role" and "obscuring the character with a maze of mannerisms." Perhaps they should have cast Eunice Stoddard who had the background and talent for the role.

Few members have commented on this show; it seemed eminently forgettable. Yet, this flop, like the hit before it, had wide-ranging consequences. At the end of this third season, serious tensions surfaced within the company; they had become disgruntled with Strasberg's direction and with the use of non-Group actors. (See W. Smith, 164–65) They began to clamor for a greater voice in creative and organizational decision-making. Stella's unhappiness at playing in *Gentlewoman* as well as the growing unease of the actors with Strasberg's approach stirred her plea for Stanislavsky's help a few months later in Paris. Their sessions would transform the Group and have a profound impact on subsequent generations of American actors.

6. Strasberg versus Adler ❧

O n the day Lee Strasberg died, February 17, 1982, Stella Adler asked actors
in her class at the Stella Adler Studio to stand for a moment of silence.
After the stunned quiet, so the gossip goes, she said, "It will take the theatre decades to recover from the damage that Lee Strasberg inflicted on American
actors" (a variant of this quote in *Kazan, A Life*, 143).

Whether this widely circulated rumor is true or not is unimportant; the fact is
the feud between these two charismatic teachers had gone on for almost 50 years.
It began in the summer of 1934 when the actors' quietly simmering malaise about
Strasberg's interpretation of the Stanislavsky system first boiled over in a steamy
confrontation between him and Stella on her return from sessions in Paris with
Stanislavsky. Things would never be the same for the Group and for American
acting. At issue were the growing tensions in the Group, the complex transmission
history of Stanislavsky's theories, and the roots of what would become the world-
famous "American Method."

Ironically, Stella Adler and Lee Strasberg both learned about Stanislavsky's systematic training from the same source and about the same time. As early as 1925,
Stella saw the first public presentation by Stanislavsky's disciple Richard Boleslavsky
at the American Laboratory Theatre. It seemed to her the most beautiful production she had ever seen, "a miracle performance." Although she was an experienced,
professional actress, she immediately went to the Laboratory school and asked to
study with Boleslavsky and his Moscow Art Theatre associate, Maria Ouspenskaya.
Despite the teasing of other members of the Adler clan, she accepted a scholarship
in the fall of 1925 and threw herself into the work. The following spring she was
chosen to be a member of the Lab's acting company, where she played several leading parts but reluctantly resigned in order to seek more secure work. Stella remained
enthusiastic about Boleslavsky as the one who introduced American performers to
the concept of acting as a craft that could be developed through the Stanislavsky
system.

About a year before Stella discovered the Lab's classes and productions, Strasberg
had also found his way to this first American center for training in the Stanislavsky
system. He did not complete the course, but, like Stella, acknowledged that
Boleslavsky was "decisive" to his career. He confessed that "Boleslavsky actually
represents for me a major post in the history of the American theater" (see *A Dream
of Passion*, 63 ff.).

Yet, Stella and Strasberg ended up with conflicting views of crucial aspects of
Stanislavsky's system. There was more involved than the evident personality conflict
and the fact that the system was susceptible to various interpretations even among
Stanislavsky's close Russian disciples. The differences between Stella and Strasberg

grew out of the training and practice in the Group, which was the laboratory for Strasberg's controversial interpretation of the Russian master's system.

As director and teacher, Strasberg's most intense interaction with the members of the Group was inspired by his lifelong fascination with true emotion—the Holy Grail of acting history. His quest seemed to have been driven by his deeply personal malaise as an introverted, shy loner as well as by his aesthetic ideals. He began his search in earnest in 1924 when he realized that the admired actors of the Moscow Art Theatre were doing something that every actor could do—even Americans—despite the fact that some critics insisted that the ensemble intensity of the Art Theatre was purely Slavic. He gave up his share of the family's wig business in return for 25 dollars a week to be paid over the next year and enrolled in the rather conventional Clare Tree Major School of the Theatre. But, he quickly concluded that the school offered only "routine work—not necessarily bad, but not very invigorating or stimulating." His interest in acting might have come to nothing if a fellow student had not suggested that he try the recently founded American Laboratory Theatre. After passing the challenging three-part audition, which consisted of a sense-memory exercise, an improvisation with an older student, and a speech by Shylock from *The Merchant of Venice*, he was admitted to the Lab. "Thus began my life in the theatre" was how he remembered the decisive moment. (*A Dream of Passion*, 64)

When Strasberg first heard Boleslavsky talk to the students, he was thrilled. Years later he regretted that the notes he made during his first classes at the Lab did not fully capture his "strange exhilaration" and "excitement." Yet, the "precise but cryptic" jottings he kept all of his life recorded those ideas and practices that made the greatest impact on him. Boleslavsky's proclamation that "art is universal" must have thrilled Strasberg, who, then, as later in his life, was searching for basic principles. Boleslavsky taught that theater was a collective creation intended to express human longing for a better life.

In precise detail, Strasberg captured the fierce but perceptive tutelage of Madame, as Ouspenskaya was called. The wizened actress from the Moscow Art Theatre, who smoked her black cigars and surreptitiously drank vodka, often reduced her students to tears in her effort to unleash fresh emotional responses—an intimidating but efficacious technique Strasberg may have copied. Students tried the famous Yoga exercise of examining a matchbox with such intensity that the little packet yielded up the whole history of man. They enacted various imaginary situations: walking past the half-open cage of a lion without arousing him; awaiting with others for arrival of a much-delayed boat bringing a favorite aunt; stepping on stones to cross a rivulet at a picnic; impersonating animals or characters unlike themselves; and other sense-memory exercises. The attention Strasberg paid to Madame's comments on his class participation is striking: "Now you are explaining to us what you feel," she told him; "don't do that. You just get the affective memory, really feel it, and we'll understand without your telling us, either by words or gestures... Don't imitate the tiger, but try to feel what the tiger feels. See the bars of your cage, feel the unrest." He listed her guides to handling what he called "basic, recurrent" problems: "Always have a reason, a cause for appearing on the stage; don't show the result of the moment instead of living through the moment; take time to realize what it means to you" (*A Dream of Passion*, 67–74).

Strasberg noted the underlying values as well as the various elements of the system, but it was bringing the memory of unconscious emotions under the actor's creative command that truly engaged him (entries from Strasberg's notebook are included in *A Dream of Passion*, 63–82; Strasberg papers are in the Library of Congress).

Strasberg no doubt believed that the precepts and practices he carefully jotted down were essential truths about acting discovered by Stanislavsky, although there was little reference to Stanislavsky in his hand-written notes. Boleslavsky and Ouspenskaya had both been part of the famous First Studio of the Moscow Art Theatre along with Eugene Vakhtangov and Michael Chekhov, who were also to influence the Group. From 1912 on, these Russian actors participated, under the supervision of Leopold Sulerjitsky, in experimental productions to develop Stanislavsky's system. The senior artists of the Art Theatre had begun to accept the system as something more than Stanislavsky's "crackpot" preoccupation. But, it was the talented and dedicated young artists, working in their tiny Studio theater until the early hours of the morning after performing in the regular Art Theatre repertory, who demonstrated Stanislavsky's innovative technique. More than a decade later, during the New York tour of the Art Theatre, Boleslavsky, who had already emigrated, spread the word about the Russian approach, first in lectures, articles, and then in the classes of his newly organized American Laboratory Theatre. In 1933, he published his version of the system in *Six Lessons in Acting*, which became a widely used text.

During these years, Stanislavsky, the least dogmatic of theorists, put off publishing "definitive statements" from his voluminous notes on his evolving science of acting. He had begun his inquiry during a holiday in Finland in 1906 out of frustration with his own acting and continued till his death in 1938. Adding, changing, rethinking, and revising, he was gradually extending his early "psycho-technique" with its use of affective or emotional memory, validated by his readings of the French psychologist Theodule Ribot, into a "psycho-physical" technique. Linked to Pavlov's studies of conditioned reflexes, Stanislavsky's later experiments identified physical action as the springboard for "living the part."

Little about these developments was in print when Strasberg was studying with Boleslavsky. There was Stanislavsky's hurriedly written *My Life in Art*, initially published in the United States in 1924 to take advantage of the popular interest generated by the Moscow Art Theatre's international tours. The narrative contained a sketch of the beginnings of his system, but Stanislavsky considered this autobiography a "botched job" and rewrote it for the subsequent Russian edition. Carrying on his teaching and directing during the difficult times of war, revolution, and the complicated twists and turns of the evolving Soviet society, he remained reluctant to codify his ongoing investigations. In 1926, the *Encyclopaedia Britannica* carried a poorly translated article on acting and directing by Stanislavsky that did little to clear up the confusions about his system. In Russia there were diverse interpretations by Stanislavsky's innovative followers—Vakhtangov, Meyerhold, Michael Chekhov. In New York there were a growing number of emigré teachers and directors—Leo and Barbara Bugakov, Tamara Daykarhanova as well as Ouspenskaya and Boleslavsky.

Each one had a particular perspective on Stanislavsky's ideas depending on when he or she had studied with the master. Boleslavsky had been trained in the earliest period when Stanislavsky had been particularly fascinated by emotional memory as the means of making acting real and true. He offered his American classes a somewhat simplified, popular answer to all their problems in place of the complex, ever-shifting investigations of Stanislavsky.

During his studies at the Lab, Strasberg, like other innovators before him, quickly put his personal spin on the system he was learning from Boleslavsky. The new depth psychology of Sigmund Freud was very much in the air and in the theater, too. Everyone was reading about suppressed desires, sublimation, the unconscious, and the healing power of psychoanalysis. Subjectivity was in. From the pages of *Good Housekeeping* magazine to the plays of Eugene O'Neill, the newly important professional middle class learned to value the depth of inner experience above all else. Strasberg, an alert, intellectually curious young man of his time, was obviously keeping up with the widely publicized theories and therapies. As he listened to Boleslavsky say that even the actor's knowledge of psychology "must be more than theoretical," he made this note: "Thus if he reads in Freud that recollection (remembrance) of childhood fantasies will bring back a certain emotion, he must use it practically," that is, must "live it thru." Strasberg elaborated his strong response to this observation in a parenthetical comment clearly marked with his initials. He wrote: "This is very interesting. The way of working on a part is very near to the psychoanalytic method" (Adams, 80–81).

"Suddenly, I knew, 'That's it! That's it!' That was the answer I had been searching for," he recalled years later of the "theatre of real experience" to which Boleslavsky introduced him. Strasberg knew all about "action," "spine," "beats," control of voice, body, and nerves, the more analytical elements of the Lab's curriculum important to the production process. But, he had never been directed by Boleslavsky and had not been responsive to Boleslavsky's lectures on directing where the Russian applied theory to production. He was already piecing together his own method, combining Boleslavsky's acting lectures, Ouspenskaya's rigorous exercises, and his reading about Freud and the psychoanalytic process. Strasberg was soon off and running.

Convinced that nothing much would come of the Lab's various plans, Strasberg decided to try his luck on Broadway. Through Philip Loeb, whom he knew from his amateur acting stints, he was taken on by the Theatre Guild. There, in the next few years, he played all kinds of walk-ons and bit parts and even danced and sang, and then stage-managed the *Garrick Gaieties*, the wildly popular revue fashioned by the young Guild performers. On tour with the Guild, he urged fellow actors to enliven their roles by using improvisation, which he believed to be essential for imaginative spontaneity. In his projects with the SADs (students of arts and drama) at the Chrystie Street Settlement, he staged plays in different styles influenced by innovators he greatly admired: Meyerhold, Vakhtangov, Reinhardt. Here, he tested affective memory exercises, improvisation, and especially adjustment as solutions to acting problems. Bit by bit, Strasberg assembled a scheme for actor-training that bore the imprint of his ideas and his own personality. He was also putting his life into shape. In 1927, he married Nora Krecaun, an admiring young SADs actress; her tragic death from cancer two years later was a devastating blow. When the Group was founded in 1931, Strasberg was still mourning the loss that turned his withdrawn personality more deeply inward, but, creatively, he was ready for the challenge.

"To get poetry out of the common things of life...and see more in the lives of human beings" was the "whole idea" of the Group, as Elia Kazan put it. Combining Marx and Freud, "it became our mission to reveal greater depths" (*Reunion*, 536). Stirred by the bleak chaos of the Depression, the Group would use Strasberg's evolving version of the Stanislavsky system to relate the inner life of ordinary people—both the actors and the characters they created—to the painful, complex reality of their daily life. It allowed them to combine the popularized psychoanalytic notions that was their legacy from the 1920s with the radical materialism of the 1930s. For the actors, the improvisations and affective memory exercises used to conjure up their own deepest feelings for the imagined life of their socially committed productions seemed a "miracle." Clurman explained:

> The system...represented for most of them the open-sesame of the actor's art. Here at last was a key to that elusive ingredient of the stage, true emotion. And Strasberg was a fanatic on the subject of true emotion. Everything was secondary to it. He sought it with the patience of an inquisitor, he was outraged by trick substitutes, and when he had succeeded in stimulating it, he husbanded it, fed it, and protected it. Here was something new to most of the actors, something basic, something almost holy. It was revelation in the theatre; and Strasberg was its prophet. (*FY*, 44–45)

Despite his years of professional experience, Morris Carnovsky was overwhelmed by the initial impact of the new method of work. "The value of it was...that it acquainted you with yourself. You began to be attentive to the movement, so to speak, within yourself." He confessed, "If we were finished actors when we came to it, the Group unfinished us. It forced us to examine all that we were and had attained in the light of a harsh insistence on basic truth. 'Be afraid to lie,' says Michael Chekhov, and we took these words literally" (*Reunion*, 481).

This subjective, self-revealing process was central in the development of the Group actors and the Group style, but, from the beginning, there were "difficulties and confusion," as Strasberg himself put it. At issue was the use of the emotional memory exercise. In his final assessment of his years with the Group in *A Dream of Passion*, Strasberg identified one of his "chief discoveries" to be the "reformulation" of Stanislavsky's "creative if." Instead of asking the actor, as Stanislavsky had done, how he personally would feel or act if he were the character in the play, Strasberg used what he liked to call the "formulation" of his idol Vakhtangov, whom Stanislavsky considered his most gifted disciple. To create a heightened theatricality justified by the actor's personal emotional responses, Vakhtangov was said to put a slightly different question to the actor: "What would you the actor have to do in order to do what the character does in this situation?" In this way, he substituted for the direct appeal to the actor's personal experience an indirect approach that would motivate the actor to behave in the particular way required of the characters in the given circumstances of the play (*A Dream of Passion*, 85–86).

Although Strasberg did admit to using both the Stanislavsky and Vakhtangov formulations, he thought later that the problem in the Group stemmed from his "unwillingness as a director to accept the actor's own natural behavior in that set of circumstances dictated by the play. Rather, I was intent upon searching for adjustments and conditions not necessarily related to the play, but still coming from the actor's own experience." No doubt Strasberg had complex theoretical justifications in mind as he tried first one approach and then another in classes and rehearsals. Moreover, he had trouble communicating his ideas effectively to the actors.

The ordeal of two young women apprentices in one of the 1932 summer classes demonstrates Strasberg's probing. After a difficult improvisation, the two turned to Strasberg for his reaction. Kazan, an apprentice that summer, vividly recreated this moment.

> He said nothing. They waited. He stared at them. His face gave no hint of what he thought, but it was forbidding. The two actresses began to come apart; everyone could see they were on the verge of tears... Finally one of them, in a voice that quavered, asked, "Lee, What did you think?" He turned his face away, looked at the other actors present. No one dared comment for fear of saying the wrong thing and having Lee turn on them. Finally, speaking quietly, he asked the stricken actress, "Are you nervous and uncertain now?" "Yes, yes," one actress said. "More than you were in the scene you played?" Lee asked. "Yes." "Much more?" "Yes, much more." "Even though the scene you did was precisely about such nervousness and you'd worked hard to imitate it?" "Oh, I see, I see," the actress said, getting Lee's point that now they were experiencing the real emotion whereas before they'd been pretending. He wanted the real emotion, insisted on the "agitation of the essence," as he called it. (*A Life*, 63)

"Agitation from the essence" is a phrase derived from sections of Vakhtangov's writings that Strasberg had translated for the Group at Dover Furnace. Vakhtangov pointed out that "an actor who is a mere journeyman becomes agitated (emotionally aroused) from the very fact of coming out on the stage, and he accepts this 'professional agitation' as the 'feeling' of the character." Such "muscular experience," which is what Stanislavsky called it, does not deeply move the audience.

Strasberg introduced the Group to the techniques that led to those first gains in self-knowledge and in performance power. Yet, creative practice with Strasberg, although stimulating, was not easy. He revealed himself early on as a stern, unforgiving, and often hysterical taskmaster. Virginia Farmer pointed out that while some of the exercises used during the first summer at Brookfield worked out well, some were frightening. Strasberg would become "very excited and very annoyed," she recalled. "It got very, very difficult for a number of us to work... He was quite harsh... Some of the exercises led to explosions between people." As one of the older and more experienced members of the company, Farmer wrote Strasberg a letter of complaint, which, not surprisingly, enraged him. Yet, she felt it had some effect on their work. "We wound up in the end very much better off than we were in the beginning. I think I was not the only one to write" (Farmer, Daybook, July 4, 1931).

Strasberg no doubt encouraged extreme responses in the exercises and manipulated his tantrums in order to drive his actors to explore fuller and truer spontaneous emotion. Clurman agreed that "liberties of manners in rehearsals...as a technical means to create freedom for emotion" could be permitted occasionally. In his view, emotion, had to be "connected with something or somebody" in the script, which was always his preoccupation. Vehemence and lack of manners were probably more than pedagogic ploys for Lee Strasberg. They were aspects of his contradictory temperament, which was tender, generous, and sentimental at one moment; irascible, dogmatic, hysterical at another. Strasberg's admirable qualities were readily acknowledged by his followers; his brilliance as a student of theater theory, history, and practice and the breadth and range of his interests awed them.

Yet, Strasberg's outbursts were more than the amusing foibles of their theory-driven teacher who wanted to discard the words of a text in order to penetrate to life itself. His often uncontrollable reactions intimidated the actors, making the group dynamics during rehearsals tense. Although the company had its share of "opinionated and temperamental" people—to use Strasberg's own description—the complex and contradictory personality of their teacher-director also contributed to complaints that the atmosphere in which some of the Group work was done was loveless. Strasberg recognized that he was "harsh, cold, and dogmatic," but seemed unable to accept criticism or challenge to his authority. Nor could he give criticism in a spirit of professional exchange. Strasberg sometimes raged at people with such violence that his victims, instead of feeling anger toward him, feared for his health or sanity.

Odets suggested in his 1932 diary that Strasberg's acting techniques were as much reflections of his psychic make-up as of his high-minded notions about theater art. It is almost as if Strasberg projected his own emotional needs onto the acting process, perhaps finding some release in the explosions he encouraged in his actors and yet hounding them to gain a control that he himself did not have. (Odets's 1932 diary, in Papers and Diaries, 1926–1963, NYPL, Lincoln Center)

"The emotional thing is not Freud, as people commonly think," Strasberg would later challenge critics of his approach. "Theoretically and actually, it is Pavlov." Yet, his youthful observation that the new "way of working on a part is very near to the psychoanalytic method" remained central to his work. In the posthumously published *A Dream of Passion*, Strasberg would still write, "Part of the therapeutic value of art generally, especially of the acting profession, resides in the ability to share experiences and emotions that are otherwise locked and blocked, incapable of being expressed, except under artistic and controlled conditions" (140).

The notion that acting transforms the actor—with bad or good results—is as old as Plato's prohibition against imitation and Aristotle's rejoinder that catharsis purges the ill-effects aroused by drama. These ideas recurred—modified, of course—in Freud's doctrine of psychoanalysis and also in Stanislavsky's psycho-technique. Their theories, evolved independently at the turn of the century, share the modern fascination with inner life and the efficacy of emotional memories to release what is beyond our conscious control. Nevertheless, the doctor and the director had different objectives. Freud's abreactive process was intended to discharge psychic tension by exposing or talking out repressed traumatic experiences. Stanislavsky did not know Freud's theories and indeed he believed that the forcing of emotion was unnatural and dangerous to mental health. Stanislavsky's subtle and shifting explorations were meant to lead actors to "the threshold of the subconscious," a term he used in what has been called a "pre-Freudian physiological sense." In the early days of the Group, the Freudian and Stanislavskian approaches to emotional memory became confused.

What at first was hailed as a liberating exercise turned for many in the ensemble into a destructive burden as Strasberg, convinced he was on the right track to "total emotion," worked with fanatic deliberation to achieve powerful results from emotional memory. Looking back, almost everyone had a painful tale to tell. Ruth Nelson found the "analytical" Strasberg "very trying to work with, very difficult, very theoretical" and contrasted him with the warm-hearted Boleslavsky who dealt directly with her not with the theories in his head (*Reunion*, 528). "The Group took introverted people and intensified their introversion" was Sandy Meisner's view. The older, more experienced actors, such as Stella and Carnovsky, "flourished," he asserted, because "they knew what to pick and choose... The younger people, who were full of dedication and commitment and rather thoughtless, gave themselves over to the authority... and were hurt by it" (*Reunion*, 504).

Beany Barker recalled that "Lee asked me, the first time I met him, whether I had a strong emotional memory." For Patsy in *The House of Connelly*, Strasberg "had her going over and over a painful experience—my roommate had been killed the year before—until I thought I was going to crack... he reduced us to a pulp" (*Reunion*, 523). The inexperienced, vulnerable Herbert Ratner tried to "follow this procedure and this terminology," as he put it, but friends believed that he was "just murdered" by Strasberg's intense probing.

The actors used to "take a minute," Bobby Lewis reminisced. "We prepared ourselves emotionally by finding some emotional reference for every goddamn entrance we made onto the stage. We'd come up before our entrance and sit in a chair on the side and get in the mood." Listening for cues while regressing to early traumas was a challenge. Lewis and his friend Sandy Meisner complained that Strasberg and later Clurman as well thought of themselves as "amateur psychiatrists." There were a number of physical and emotional breakdowns among the members; some claim never to have fully recovered. "You and Gadget were the only two who came out of the ten years of the Group Theatre completely untouched," Katharine Hepburn declared to Bobby Lewis later when they worked in Hollywood together. His reply: "Well, you're right, Katharine—outside of three or four complete nervous breakdowns, it didn't touch me at all" (*Reunion*, 484).

Even Carnovsky, dubbed the "Dean" by Meisner, wandered around like a white ghost after some emotional memory sessions. He came to believe that the constant repetition of the affective memory exercise dissipated its effectiveness. "The attempt to reproduce the same emotion night after night, performance after performance, led to something stultifying," he contended. "Like rubbing the same spot... it led to a lack of self-confidence because your own sense of truth told you that the emotion you were striving for in the 16th performance was a strained and imitated thing based on the first successful accomplishment." Barker reached a similar conclusion: "It was awful with Strasberg because you felt that once you cried and had a full emotional thing, you weren't acting if that didn't happen every time" (*Reunion*, 523).

"You were digging into your subconscious life and not with a trained psychiatrist" was how the introspective Phoebe Brand viewed the process (*Reunion*, 516). The affective memory exercise "assumes an actor is an emotional mechanism that can just be turned on," she contended, sensing Strasberg's efforts at building up conditioned emotional reflexes. "We were always going backward in our lives. It was painful...too subjective...it makes for a moody, personal, self-indulgent acting style." To her "the golden box" of memories was really just everyone's "store of experience." The Group work "put the cart before the horse." Brand concluded:

> We spent all our time in the early days working for emotion first, and then came the action...we were going backwards, and succeeding in spite of ourselves. Nobody had been using emotion at all in the theatre, hardly—indicating—suggesting—and when we began to laugh, and cry, and have a ball as we did in *Connelly*, people were amazed. But we couldn't continue that way without killing ourselves—and I think a lot of people were killed by it. (Chinoy interview with Phoebe Brand)

The personal and creative costs catalogued in these retrospective accounts were deeply felt, but the actors were too intimidated to openly challenge their overbearing teacher. Initially, they felt empowered by Strasberg's fierce focus on their creative dilemmas, benefiting from his keen insight into their acting problems and their repressions. They believed that following Stanislavsky, Strasberg understood the psychology of acting in addition to knowing all there was to know about actors and the history of theater. The actors were willing to pay whatever price was necessary to gain self-knowledge and creative growth under his tutelage. But, even as their acting won critical acclaim in the six shows Strasberg had directed, by the summer of 1934, the inner turmoil created by his confusing and painful obsession with emotional memory was undermining the confidence of the company in themselves and in their director.

No one felt more strongly that Strasberg's ways were harming the actors than Stella Adler. She complained that Strasberg was "a kind of fanatical, unsocial personality—untheatrical—and that made a big difference to people who had a certain theatrical flare. I had a flare." Tall, extraordinarily beautiful, she had a queenly bearing, aristocratic tastes, and an elevated idea of theater. She had been nurtured in the larger-than-life romantic world of her parents' Yiddish theater to which adoring Jewish audiences came. She was attracted to Clurman and to the "fanaticism" of the Group. Its large social ideals and dedication to the actor's craft were important to her. (*Reunion*, 507)

Stella recognized that Strasberg had talent, that, indeed, "he was a very good director." As an actor she could deal with his demands because she felt herself to be smart, self-reliant, with considerable professional experience. "He didn't have to struggle with me. I could guess what he wanted." Having studied with Boleslavsky and been directed by him in productions, she was "deeply disturbed" by the way Stanislavsky's system was being interpreted by Strasberg. She considered the overemphasis on the actor's personal emotion "schizophrenic." Even though she believed herself "an instrument that was emotionally fluent," she, too, became troubled by the "sick" approach. (*Reunion*, 508)

These pent-up feelings exploded when Stella met Konstantin Stanislavsky in Paris in the summer of 1934. Stella and Clurman had stopped in Paris after a brief trip to Moscow made possible by the success of *Men in White*. It was Clurman's old mentor Jacques Copeau who told them Stanislavsky was in Paris recuperating from a heart ailment, and suggested they should try to meet him. Clurman, who had sent Stanislavsky congratulations from the Group on his seventieth birthday the year before, arranged for them to call on him. Clurman recalled that when they entered the Paris flat, Stanislavsky was thumbing through his dictionary for French words to use in explaining the special vocabulary of his system. "When he looked up and saw Stella with me, he rose to his great height—he must have been six foot four—and addressed himself first to her, saying, he had heard that her father had been a wonderful actor." Stanislavsky invited Stella and Clurman to accompany him to the Bois de Boulogne, where he sat with his doctor a few hours each day to aid his recovery. It was there that Stella told him that she had lost her joy in acting and that perhaps this was due to his "cursed" method. To which he immediately replied, "If the system does not help you, forget it. But perhaps you do not use it properly" (*FY*, 138).

To help her comprehend his methods, he volunteered to rehearse her in a scene from her repertory that had not gone as she wished. She chose Gwen's ten-minute farewell to her lover from Lawson's *Gentlewoman* and had it translated into French by Mlle. Gould, who assisted and took notes as the director and actress set to work. It was an obvious choice, not only because of her recent failure in the role, but also because Lawson's play is, in part, about the inability of Americans—those of the upper and middle class—to confront their feelings. (The Stanislavsky-Adler meeting is cited in Stella Adler's interview with Mel Gordon in W. Smith, 178–80. A shorter version is in Adler's *The Art of Acting*, 235–37.)

Stella and Stanislavsky arranged to meet in the Bois de Bologne over the next few weeks as Clurman, restless to return to the Group, departed for New York. During these weeks, Stanislavsky elucidated the basics of his system as they rehearsed the *Gentlewoman* scene. Stella had arrived at a propitious time. Stanislavsky was working on the manuscript of the first volume of his projected series on acting and was struggling to find a format that would integrate the various aspects of the system, including his latest exploration of physical action as the impetus for creative release. Although they explored Stanislavsky's general theory, they worked together "in a practical way because he was a very practical man," Stella recalled. (*Reunion*, 508)

First, Stanislavsky had Stella and Mlle. Gould, who filled in roles opposite her, play the scene without the words, to allow the physical actions to take command. He helped them divide the "big idea" of the segment into "beats," to be carried out in a quiet, relaxed way, and pointed out that improvisation could release lively action only if the beats were carefully planned. In improvisation, he explained, "the conscious and the sub-conscious work together." He cautioned Stella when she was forcing her feelings. "Don't squeeze it so from inside," he advised. When she tried pacing up and down, he warned against clichéd action. (See Clurman notebook on Adler's talks with Stanislavsky, Rare Book and Manuscript Division, Butler Library, Columbia University, quoted here and later.)

Stella asked the basic questions: "Can the conscious enter into the memory of the subconscious?" Stanislavsky answered:

> One must put that differently. Here are the given circumstances. Have you never gone through an experience of this kind—saying goodbye to someone you do not love? If you can remember these things...the feelings will follow...If your director wants you to or says, please feel and then you will be able to play, tell him—"When I know how to swim then I will go into the water." Can one swim without going into the water? One cannot feel and then do the problem—first act the problem for the physical action and then you will be able to feel...The actor can force the cliché, he can feel emotion, of course, only the corpse feels nothing. But *what* have you felt?

Stanislavsky encouraged her to imagine the life of the character she was playing and that of her lover as well. "If he stays, what will your life be like? How does she get up in the morning, what was she like yesterday, what is the plan of her house? Live in that house a 100 times. Have you really seen it? Where? Paris? New York? In your affective memory...it will remain forever." His generalizations grew out of rehearsal problems.

> For emotion, I search in the *given circumstances*, never in the feelings. If I try and do the psychological, I force the action. We must attack the psychological from the point of view of the physical life so as not to disturb the feeling...*In each psychological action there is some physical element*. Search for the line, *in terms of action*, not in feeling. (See W. Smith, 179, for a variant of this account)

Stanislavsky talked with Stella about the books he was writing. The first was to be a grammar, covering what a beginning actor should know. In 1929 at Baden-Baden, he had tested the clarity of his presentation on a very young Eunice Stoddard, who had been privileged to join him and his translator Elizabeth Hapgood, a friend of her parents. Stanislavsky believed that "such a book is needed if only to put an end to all the twisted interpretations of my so-called 'system' which, in the way it is presently being taught, can put young actors on quite the wrong path." Over 70 and ailing, he was eager to pass on to the younger generation "the fruit of a lifetime's research in art."

Eager to set the record straight for Stella—and, through her, for others in America—Stanislavsky elucidated the system from an elaborate chart intended as a concise, clear, diagrammatic summary of his whole system. As they discussed the chart at length, Stella asked him, "Does one ever take the emotional memory as an exercise?" He responded:

> *Never*. But, as we did yesterday, take a simple physical act, surround it with given conditions...One can tell someone to walk, to open the door, but not to feel...Each man has in him all the faults and all the qualities of all men. You will find them in you. It is like the notes of an instrument. You only take those which you need. The right notes exist in the action of the role. Above all, the system is made for the action, the transaction, and the super-problem. (Quoted in Clurman's notebook; see citation earlier)

Stella now knew with certainty that Strasberg's work was a distortion of Stanislavsky's approach. Yet, she wondered whether there might be some special need for explicit emotional work in the United States. This vibrant daughter of the titanic Jacob Adler told the Russian that "in the American soul there is a certain frigidity. The director needs to make his actors feel." Perhaps Stanislavsky's awareness and acceptance of cultural differences in the use of his system conditioned his response. He drew a flower. "The director says make this flower. Can you make a flower with paper? One must start with the roots. It is of the roots of feeling and not the feeling itself that he must speak."

Stella understood that, for Stanislavsky, the roots of feeling were in the rich humanity of the actor. For him, acting was a conscious process in which the actor used his mind, his body, and his emotions in an organic way to facilitate the subconscious fusing of his inner life with that of the dramatist's creation. In the last years of his life, Stanislavsky was still changing and rearranging the segments and sequence of this complex creative process to provide the actor with a better method of work. Whether "emotional memory" was used to initiate the process, as it was in his early formulations of the system, or was subsumed in the method of physical action that he was exploring at the time of Stella's visit, it was always, for Stanislavsky, only part of the overall unified approach to creation that had to be used with the greatest care. In *An Actor Prepares*, he described illusive emotional memories as "wild animals" that had to be delicately coaxed or lured from their hiding place in the actor's soul. In the last years of his life, according to Jean Benedetti, his British biographer, he came to feel that "the evocation of past experiences produced negative results—tension, exhaustion, sometimes hysteria"—and should not be used (see Benedetti, 315 ff.). This was the message—one that confirmed Stella's own unhappy experience in the Group—that she brought back from her extraordinary sessions in Paris.

In early August, Stella returned from Paris to rejoin the Group, carrying with her Stanislavsky's words as well as a few Paris hats and other "frills and furbelows." Cheryl Crawford, who had remained behind in New York while her codirectors were abroad, had rented what Alexander Kirkland called a "desiccated kind of Charles Addams place" halfway up a mountainside in the Catskills near Ellenville, New York. Its main virtue was that it was cheap enough to relieve the actors of singing for their supper, as they had at Green Mansions, and yet big enough to accommodate the collection of people with their dogs, cars, and Victrolas that gathered to work on Melvin Levy's *Gold Eagle Guy* under Strasberg's direction. "It was damp, full of mists, and I'm sure, ghosts," recalled Crawford. (*Naked Individual*, 68) Beany Barker remembered that the floors were slimy and the actors almost broke their legs as they tried to run to the sound of dance instructor Helen Tamiris's drum. The dogs developed ringworm, and the people did too. Despite the grim location, the actors were enjoying Carnovsky's verse class, in which he continued to "revive a sense of rhythm and word color" to compensate for the "diminished sense of fine language" in naturalistic drama. Clurman led a playwriting course covering the whole history of dramatic technique. And Strasberg reported on all he had seen in the Russian theaters as his avid listeners made notes that some kept the rest of their lives.

In the memories of most of the Group, however, what stood out most about this summer encampment was the very special class given by Stella Adler. On August 7, 1934, on misty Mount Menagha, she shared with the company what Stanislavsky had taught her in Paris about the "whole problem of acting." She did not mince words. In her dramatic way, on a hazy afternoon, she let them know that Strasberg's insistent use of the emotional memory exercise was wrong. Stanislavsky was now emphasizing action in the given circumstances of the play, rather than emotional memory. On the wall of the recreation room she tacked up the very large, complex chart and accompanying outline Stanislavsky had given to her. This unique summary, drawn up by Stanislavsky himself, gave Group members unique access to the synthesis of all aspects of his system that Stanislavsky devised in the last years of his life.

Notes taken by several of the actors at Ellenville show a sketch and a numerical listing of all the salient points on the chart. Ever the energetic student, Bobby Lewis revised his diagram, bringing the numerical listing and the sketch together as one impressive chart, which he subsequently published in 1958 in his collection of talks, *Method-or-Madness?* (Labeled "The Stanislavski System, 1934," the chart is inserted as a fold between pages 34 and 35.)

Taking the form of a pipe organ, the structure Stanislavsky devised not only included over 40 elements but also the dynamic interrelationship among the parts. Thus, the whole organ had as a basic pedestal "work on one's self"; the next level included "action," followed by "truth of feeling...under the given circumstances," "creation of life...with conscious technique (beats) which arouses the subconscious," "creation on stage of life of our soul...not of body." Next came "Mind, Will, and Emotion," conceived as the "three motors of our psychic life." Pipes numbered 11–27 were devoted to the "process of feeling internally"; 28–40 to expression of emotion. At the top of the chart the complete internal and external preparation join together to become "The Part."

Although many of the items on the chart were familiar to the Group actors from their work with Strasberg, what was of greatest interest, of course, was item 17—Emotional Memory. Making emotion dependent on the sequence was an illuminating clarification. So was the injunction that after feeling is found, it must be expressed; "it must be given out...to draw the spectator in." Two jottings on Stella's chart were telling: "Feeling for feeling's sake in life? Abnormal." And, "If you go to your memories, you create your own play, not the author's."

Stella's report came as a great relief. All the "digging, probing, kvetching" that had been troubling them had turned out to be a misinterpretation of the Russian master. "It was like a great load had been taken off us," said Bobby Lewis. Eunice Stoddard, recalling what Stanislavsky had read to her in 1929, seconded Stella's report. Carnovsky was relieved to hear that Stanislavsky was no longer interested in "capturing dead, or distant emotions." Meisner's contention that the Group's work had become unhealthy, "not organic," was confirmed. Phoebe Brand's sense of the moment remained vivid years later. "Stella challenged Lee openly. It was not done, you know. Lee was really an authority, and we all thought he was God. When she challenged him, we all said, 'Good, good, go ahead.' That was the beginning of our loss of faith in his approach" (*Reunion*, 516).

Some radicalized actors leapt to their feet and sang the "Internationale." For them, Stanislavsky was not only the source of theatrical wisdom but also stood for the admired accomplishments of Soviet society. The new emphasis on physical action and the "given circumstances" seemed consonant with the doctrine of Socialist Realism recently promulgated in the Soviet Union. Thus, to follow Stanislavsky was "politically correct" in addition to being creatively satisfying.

What was Strasberg's reaction? "I couldn't speak," he recalled for his biographer, Cindy Adams. "I just had a great feeling of being insulted" (Adams, 179). He told others in later years that he thought that either Stella had not understood Stanislavsky or that the master "had gone back on himself." Strasberg was not totally wrong in the latter statement. When Stanislavsky was on to something new, he tended to make light of or even disavow his earlier approach. Nor was Strasberg wrong when he claimed that the Group had learned all the right things. It was a question of priority and emphasis.

Some of the Group actors remember a more violent response from Strasberg. According to Bobby Lewis, Strasberg did not attend Adler's presentation. Instead, he called a meeting of the Group the next day, August 8, 1934. "It was ugly," said Lewis. "Instead of saying 'thank you,' which is what we all said to Stella, he lit into her and into Stanislavsky," saying, "I teach the Strasberg Method, not the Stanislavsky System" (*S&A*, 71).

In his emotional declaration of independence, Strasberg insisted on the distinctions and improvements made by the Group, according to Lewis's written notes of the traumatic day. Although Strasberg found agreement on basics, he denigrated the accomplishments of Stanislavsky and the Moscow Art Theatre, asserting that only their performances of Chekhov and Gorky were successful.

Stanislavsky's comments on his meetings with Stella Adler, like everything else in this unusual international exchange about a dramatic method, have been variously reported. One source has Stanislavsky describing Stella as "a completely panic stricken-woman," begging him to save her from the effects of the system (W. Smith, 178). It would seem to support Strasberg's view of Stella as highly emotional in life and on stage, with the implication that Stanislavsky muted the emphasis on emotion because of her excesses. Another source provides a less hysterical image of Stella in these words attributed to Stanislavsky:

> They say my method is being introduced in America, yet suddenly this talented actress who has studied my system "withers away" before everyone's eyes. I had to take her on only to restore the reputation of my system ... It turned out that everything she had learnt was right, but certain aspects of the system had been overemphasized ... [Stanislavsky] turned his attention to the through-line of action ... and the various tasks she had to perform in order to create that line. Truth on stage was still the goal ... They made a chart of the main stages in the role. When she had learnt this, he recalled, she acted so brilliantly that we absolutely "howled with delight." (Filippov, 59; also, W. Smith, 179–80)

This statement jibes with Stella's report of her Paris sessions, with some notes Clurman made, and also with Stanislavsky's teaching. Stella mistakenly assumed there had not been changes in Stanislavsky's system over the years. Strasberg, on the other hand, did not know what Stanislavsky was up to in the thirties. Although he had visited Moscow with Stella shortly before her sessions in Paris, he did not seek an opportunity to speak with Stanislavsky at that time because of his disappointment with the productions he had seen at the Moscow Art Theatre. In a characteristic reaction of withdrawal, Strasberg felt that he could not face the master whom he could not praise but did not want to criticize. The year 1934 was, in fact, a low point in the Art Theatre's history, perhaps accounting in part for Strasberg's attack. When in 1936 *An Actor Prepares* was, like *My Life in Art*, published first in the United States, Strasberg was not impressed. He said, "We knew all that." What Strasberg probably didn't know at the time is that the book was a greatly reduced and edited translation of Stanislavsky's manuscripts, and did not fully reflect his thinking. Stanislavsky had intended to include in this one volume both the inner preparation and the external expression of the actor. Poor health, the excessive length of the manuscript, and pressure to complete the work resulted in two volumes. *An Actor Prepares* was followed eleven years after his death by *Building a Character* in 1949. *Creating a Role*, a compilation of pieces from different periods of Stanislavsky's career, appeared in 1961. At the end of the twentieth century [when Chinoy was writing this study], scholars were still struggling to clarify, first, Stanislavsky's true intentions as revealed in a twelve-volume *Complete Works* in Russian, and, second, to sort out the oral and written transmission of his legacy, in which the Group's quarrels played a part.

What seems clear at this time is that both *action* and *emotion* were central to Stanislavsky's teaching. In his late theory, based on the analysis of physical action, emotion was divided into a sequence of actions, and in his early emphasis on emotion, action was also part of the process. He had never intended the emphasis on emotional recall Strasberg encouraged. The consensus among the early Russian teachers of the Stanislavsky system in New York is that Strasberg's approach was a perversion of both Stanislavsky's teaching and Boleslavsky's. A set of Boleslavsky's typed lecture notes, belonging to Stella Adler, supports their contention.

The immediate consequence of the clash over Stella's report that summer at Ellenville was that she began to give classes based on Stanislavsky's tutorial with her. She set the actors very simple tasks: "To look for glasses; to look for one lens lost from glasses... To pour and drink coffee." Insisting that they feel the truth as they executed each simple physical activity, she explained: "In a *problem* there is always *action*, an *object*... the *feeling of truth, connection* (this is done unconsciously), and *adjustment*, everything that belongs to the imagination" (see the "Afterword" in Adler, *Art of Acting*). Stella's stress on action and imagination changed the process significantly, reducing the "hysteria" that she believed resulted from the excessive use of affective memory exercises. The actors were excited by her pragmatic approach, even proposing she be placed in charge of handling acting problems for the company.

Did Strasberg modify his training and direction of the actors after the harsh confrontations of the summer of 1934? Clurman claimed that he did (*FY*, 139). "It was Stella who changed, not our method," Strasberg insisted years later. "It went on just the same. But I feel that she does not know and understand what the work was, because she thinks that it was to create emotion. But the problem was not to create emotion, but to define emotion." He added, "Stella had a way of being very emotional, personally. She had a very full, vivid emotion, but one which frankly rubbed me the wrong way. I remember one moment saying to her in *Success Story*, 'If you cry, I'll kill you!' And I meant it. Obviously I wanted her to have the emotion, but not to cry the way she personally would cry" (*Reunion*, 550).

Stella may have reported accurately what Stanislavsky said, but Strasberg maintained that her complaints to the master about the problems in playing her role in *Gentlewoman* were "erroneous." "We didn't do any kind of emotional work with her," he recalled. "Stella gave a reading…that was perfect. That's all that I wanted. I wanted her to do what she did at the reading. I don't know what the hell I told her; I just wanted to get her not to do the things that she wanted to do to fill in her characterization." He concluded that under his direction, she did her best work. "The greatest performance she ever gave was in *Success Story*. So if it was done by going counter to Stanislavsky, I'll do it again" (*Reunion*, 550).

For all of his later protestations, Strasberg's approach did undergo important changes after the confrontations at Ellenville and his own exposure to Russian theater on the 1934 trip. Indeed, much in the Group changed after that fateful summer, which emboldened the actors to challenge his authority. At the end of the year they refused to accept the directors' decision to close the theater after the debacle of *Gold Eagle Guy*. In defiance of Strasberg's strong disapproval, the actors forced the company to stage Clifford Odets's *Awake and Sing!* with Clurman as director and Stella Adler playing her greatest role. They also triumphed with their own production of *Waiting for Lefty* for the New Theatre League. In 1936, Strasberg directed his two final productions with the Group and that summer at Pine Brook Club in Connecticut, he taught his last class for the company.

At Pine Brook on July 10, 1936, Strasberg opened his class with a defensive comment that reflected Stella's challenge. To the "new people," he explained: "What you will learn here is not a method that goes by the name of Stanislavsky, or Lee Strasberg, or anything, but simply what we do in the Group Theatre in the process of production." Strasberg described the class as constituting a "return to pure origins, much in the way an accomplished pianist will intermittently revert to elementary finger exercises." The process that would become famous at the Actors Studio seemed to be taking shape. "The only way to train an actor to watch himself is to teach him to watch others," Strasberg explained by way of justifying both his pedagogy and the presence of observers. The actor's inability to judge his creation with objectivity because he is both the artist and the material with which he works was one of the central problems Strasberg planned to address. The basic exercises in the training must be done again and again over the years, Strasberg reiterated, not in order to be able to do them well but because they "will lead to other, more valuable things." He also told the actors in no uncertain terms that "there is no such thing as genius and talent that shows itself without training."

In trying to clear up the misconceptions about the Group's work, Strasberg's general comments and his individual critiques concentrated strongly on "doing very real, concrete, simple things." He told the actors, "It is easy to get the audience's applause when we give them what they want, but we want to get the applause when we give them what *we* want. That is not so easy."

Each actor's problem was broken down into simple segments that could be worked on in order to achieve "something which only the actor can give." To Phoebe Brand, who was having problems determining the action of Nina in the final scene of

Chekhov's *The Seagull*, Strasberg indicated that technique would provide a "definite series of steps that we can take, even if we don't know the answers. If they don't succeed, we are no worse off than before." If the actor does the simplest things, he urged her, "that will start the process." Strasberg warned, "You cannot be a great actor by doing great acting—only by doing very real concrete simple things... Fix your pin, look at the lamp, fix it, turn it out... That will lead you to bigger things... It at least gives the person who is doing it the feeling of being alive... The choice of the things you do is your talent" (Chinoy interview with Phoebe Brand).

While Strasberg was refining basic technique in his classes, Stella was offering instruction in "problems of acting." "One doesn't know how to work on a part," as she put it, "another doesn't know the difference between emotion and emotionalism; another understands it all but is tense, etc." Each member was required to prepare 15 minutes from a familiar play by breaking down the script according to the following instructions: "Beats/G.B. [general background]/mood/problems." The actor must have "a routine for mapping out a part quickly, whether he has three hours or three months to work on it."

Exercises in sense memory and in the use of "given circumstances" were central to her classes. Working with objects, she handed her large vanity case to some of the men, asking them in turn to describe it "with as many seen details as they possibly could. Art Smith confided that "substitution" worked better for him than the "given circumstances," "Is it that I have made the problem too simple. Should I work in the conscious imaginative way?" Her answer embodied an important dimension of her teaching. "There is no distinction between memory and imagination; if a thing is in your memory, it is in your imagination. In all of life there are common denominators of experience. When the actor goes to a particular experience of his own, he doubles the work."

Temperamentally, the contrast between the "emotionally fluent," expansive star of the Yiddish stage versus the obsessive student from the East Side has been remarked upon. On the basic orientation of the actor, they were profoundly divided. Stella made actors look primarily *outward* to their partners, the objects, the action, the text, the social context. Strasberg made them look primarily *inward* for painful emotions to be used and also stored in each one's "golden box" to be released as needed. He used emotional memory to penetrate the individual psyche for "the real thing." She stressed the relationship of memory, imagination, experience, and looked to the given circumstances of the play.

Clearly, Stella and Strasberg shared a great deal in common as teachers of acting, including attention to detail and the moment-to-moment life out of which the words come, concentration, use of objects, and the need for a dependable way of working. Later, when they became famous opponents, they were both known for terrorizing their actors. In her eighties Stella would still say, echoing Strasberg, "I'm tough. I ask a lot. There is no kindness in my demands. You better do it my way" (see *Art of Acting*, 262).

Their schism over the use of emotional memory must itself be put into context. Despite the charge that he had wrongly interpreted Stanislavsky, there is little question that what Strasberg had achieved in the initial training of the ensemble and in the early plays he directed was an unprecedented accomplishment. He knew that the early preparation of the Group was achieved in a unique personal, artistic, and social collaboration. His individual, subjective approach was mediated through an ensemble of players with whom he staged the collective, objective action of new, socially significant American plays. As he envisioned the systematic study of acting in the Group it included voice and movement, experiments in style, lectures on theater, literature, and society as well as participation in professional productions—a varied education that was unique in American theater and held the company together in the 1930s—and even brought them together for projects in later years.

With his close study of histrionic history, Strasberg must have realized that the controversial "emotional memory exercise" was only part of Stanislavsky's legacy, which was not a rigid regimen but a many-faceted heritage. Strasberg's approach was not as expansive. It was not that Strasberg never concerned himself with the remaining dynamics of the system— action, spine, and so on—indeed, it was he who initially introduced most of the company to these concepts. He suggested late in life, however, that his main preoccupation had always been with the "talent of the actor." But his own fascination was with the training of raw talent—whether working with the young people of the Group or later with experienced members of the Actors Studio.

Strasberg became artistic director of the Actors Studio in 1951, after it was founded by Cheryl Crawford, Elia Kazan, and Bobby Lewis in 1947. It was here that Strasberg's approach became famous as "The Method." The objective of the Studio was to provide professional actors with a place where their talent could be nurtured and trained away from the demands of the commercial theater. Neither a theater nor a school, the Studio became Strasberg's personal laboratory for working with an extraordinary generation of American actors using his method. His work, which became the most famous and, for some, infamous, version of the Stanislavsky system, struck a responsive cord as actors in post Second War American theater retreated from the collective, social commitment of the 1930s to the troubled psyches dramatized in the 1950s.

Many others in the Group contributed over the years to the unique technique and style of acting—Stella Adler, Harold Clurman, Robert Lewis, Sanford Meisner, and the many talented, willing actors who lent themselves to the experiment and later also became important teachers and directors. Strasberg, nevertheless, could rightly take credit for getting them all started. Sandy Meisner, who at 17 began studying with Strasberg at Chrystie Street, quipped in 1977, a few years before Lee Strasberg's death, that he was now his *oldest* student. Meisner vigorously opposed Strasberg's "introverted emphasis"; yet, this respected teacher of acting paid an important tribute to his mentor: "I think that the biggest single influence in my life was Strasberg and I say so gratefully. The fact that we went in different directions—well, that's life, isn't it?" (See *Sanford Meisner On Acting*.)

7. Testing the Theatrical ✦

Lee Strasberg's disappointment in the Moscow Art Theatre and his reluctance to seek out Stanislavsky during his summer visit in 1934 by no means extended to Stanislavsky's most famous students, Vsevolod Meyerhold and Eugene Vakhtangov, and their theaters. Strasberg had admired the theories and productions of both artists from afar. In Moscow, he had the opportunity to assess their work for himself. It was a transforming experience.

Strasberg saw *Turandot*, Vakhtangov's extraordinary production created in 1922, at the end of his all-too-brief life. Although Strasberg felt himself to be "personally more of a realist" than Vakhtangov, he attributed his experiments at Dover Furnace and his efforts to heighten the theatricality of his recent productions to Vakhtangov's synthesis of Stanislavsky's "inner justification" with poetic/theatrical staging. He made Vakhtangov's reformulation of Stanislavsky's question about the relationship of the actor and the role central to his own evolving theory.

Yet, Strasberg reported that his greatest experience in Moscow was the discovery of Meyerhold. He saw Meyerhold's challenging masterworks (*Camille, The Magnificent Cuckold, The Forest*), visited with the director, watched him rehearse, was unafraid to ask him questions, and observed his associate teach biomechanics— Meyerhold's scientific system for training the actor's means of expression. From these contacts he concluded that Meyerhold's directing was unparalleled as an illustration of the possibilities of the theater and as the basis for understanding the director's possibilities in the theater.

Strasberg admitted that prior to his Russian visit he could not really explain what the principles of directing were or just what the director's task really was— and this despite the fact that he was, as he said, "theoretically inclined." During his exposure in Moscow, he realized that the showy or eccentric staging, usually hailed as evidence of the director's hand in the United States, was completely beside the point. The director's creative contribution involved fresh interpretation and comment using the total expressive power of theater. [For Strasberg on his Russian visit, see *TDR* 17:1 (March 1973): 106–21.]

Strasberg was overwhelmed by the daring theatrical imagination evident in Meyerhold's productions. Although his reading had prepared him to admire the Russian's work, when confronted with Meyerhold's production of Ostrovsky's *The Forest*, Strasberg at first did not like what he saw. His initial disappointment with the set and the acting, however, quickly gave way to amazement. "You are caught by the scenic action, by its imaginativeness, by its flair. The entire life of the people begins to unfold...It actually makes possible more reality than would be possible in a realistic set." He made detailed notes in his diary (see *TDR*, above) on how Meyerhold developed a scene in his production of *Camille* so that it "brought alive the entire epic"; he marveled that the Russian could conceive events in a way the author himself had never imagined. Comparing these productions with those at the Moscow Art Theatre and the Vakhtangov Theatre helped Strasberg understand the genius of Meyerhold and enabled him to confront the limitations of routine realism for modern theater. The Moscow Art Theatre seemed to him technically excellent but no longer animated by the search for truth that had so inspired Strasberg in the 1920s. Even Vakhtangov's famed stagings could not compare with Meyerhold's inventive business. "Vakhtangov's are finished perfect jewels," Strasberg said, "Meyerhold's are magnificent boulders."

On his return to New York, Strasberg determined to apply what he had learned. "There is no reason why such acting and direction as I saw at the Meyerhold, the Vakhtangov, and the Moscow Art Theatres should not be brought into the American theatre," he declared. He was ready to make a change.

While Strasberg, Stella Adler, and Harold Clurman were abroad absorbing inspiration from the Russian innovators, at home the Group ensemble was exploring a more theatrical approach on their own. The actors were playing in the long-running *Men in White*, which brought them rewards, although the radicalized membership continued to look down on their hit show, their two-week paid vacations, and clamor for a greater voice in the organization's decisions. Since the Group would not be able to leave Broadway for a full summer session, as they had in the previous three years, the actors arranged to have a "pastoral retreat" in the basement of the Broadhurst Theatre where *Men in White* was playing. Modeling themselves on Stanislavsky's First Studio, the company offered classes that explored facets of theater that they had not yet been able to master.

Despite his evident enthusiasm for Russian innovation, Strasberg had been unfairly berated over the years for ignoring theatrical experiment in his own productions. Beginning in the fall of 1934, and through to his resignation from the Group in 1937, Strasberg tried to fashion a style that he hoped would be a synthesis of Vakhtangov, Meyerhold, and Stanislavsky. In carrying out his intentions in *Gold Eagle Guy*, *The Case of Clyde Griffiths*, and *Johnny Johnson*, he confronted serious obstacles. During the second half of the 1930s, there was the growing threat of war and fascism in the larger world, mirrored in the smaller world of the Group by increasing personal and political friction exacerbated by critical success and defections to Hollywood. Strasberg's authority and mystique, already undermined by the feud with Stella, was on the line.

In this troubled period, Strasberg seemed to be suffering from the very affliction he had tried to cure in his actors, what he called a "lapse between what you try and what you are actually able to do." His very ambitious, final Group productions lacked some of the emotional complexity, realism of detail, and improvisational vibrancy that had distinguished much of his work thus far. Moreover, there was no significant gain in conceptual insight, theatrical brilliance, or sheer staging flair. Although critics came down hard on what didn't work in these productions, there was considerable appreciation for his and the Group's artistic aspirations. Broadway offered no comparable experiments. Indeed, a curious disparity developed between the respectful reviews, which often only served to keep Broadway audiences away, and the painful, internal anguish of the company grappling with a new approach.

Despite Strasberg's insight into acting and his knowledge of modern innovators, he seemed to be losing what he himself considered essential: the ability of the director to inspire his collaborators rather than tyrannize them. Kazan, who stage-managed many of these productions, came to believe that Strasberg lost his grip on his own method as he tried to ape the Russians he so admired. Clurman, in remarks deleted from *The Fervent Years*, suggested that Strasberg, fearing that his personal "limitations" would keep him from becoming the kind of director he wanted to be, attempted to alter his artistic personality with unconvincing results. These aspirations, confusions, and conflicts were apparent in Strasberg's three final productions with the Group.

Strasberg threw himself into the challenge of Melvin Levy's *Gold Eagle Guy* while still in Moscow. In preparations for the upcoming production, he sent a note to Cheryl Crawford asking her to have people find songs, dances, costumes, customs, manners, and interesting events of San Francisco at the turn of the century to enlarge the historical context of the upcoming show. When Strasberg joined the rest of the Group at Ellenville in August, he began rehearsals at once. He considered Levy's panoramic costume drama about the rise and fall of Guy Button, a steamship magnate, in the years from 1860 to the San Francisco earthquake in 1906, a perfect vehicle for innovation. Dealing once again with the human failures resulting from the American success myth, Levy's script offered an episodic chronicle of the colorful era in which a large cast in an exotic setting could use more of the theater itself to project their drama. In planning his staging, Strasberg evinced a far "greater concern with movement and the expressive value of physical materials than he had ever had before," Clurman recalled. (*FY*, 139)

Strasberg's new interest revealed itself in his attention to sets and costumes. Donald Oenslager, who was chosen to design the show, had apprenticed under Robert Edmond Jones at the Provincetown Playhouse and was on his way to becoming one of the most sought-after designers of the 1930s. Strasberg, inspired by the constructivist designs of Meyerhold, told Oenslager that the Group wanted "levels for acting" and "scenery that contained ideas." Oenslager tried to give them what they wanted. The space was crowded with levels! Combining realistic detail that recalled David Belasco settings to some critics within an overall constructivist structure, he also tried to project significant meaning through textures, colors, and dynamics in the five scenes that chart the growing wealth and power of Button followed by his sudden demise. Oenslager used rough materials like bits of wrecked ships for the opening dockside locales and covered the subsequent scenes in luxurious gold tones to reflect Button's material success. When the huge triumphal arch from which an emblematic gold dollar was suspended came tumbling down on Button in the elaborately orchestrated replay of the 1906 earthquake at the finale, audiences were impressed by the vivid symbolic action, although, for some, the heavy physical production seemed more dramatic than what the actors did within its spaces.

The production was ill-fated from the start. Melvin Levy had never written a play, only novels and short stories. It was Bobby Lewis, whom Levy had met through Rose McClendon when they were protesting the infamous Scottsboro case in Harlan, Kentucky, who suggested the writer ought to turn the historical novel he was planning about San Francisco into a play for the Group. Then, Cheryl Crawford worked with Levy on the script in New York while Strasberg, Clurman, and Stella traveled abroad. When the first draft was read to the company, they were not at all enthusiastic, mainly because, as Clurman reported, they found it "not hotly contemporaneous in subject matter or feeling." In trying to sell them on the play and quiet other discontents among the members, Clurman wrote a long paper in which he tried to justify his view that "our aim was not and never had been to become a political theatre, but to be a creative and truly representative American theatre" (*FY,* 135–36). Nevertheless, the company was not convinced of the play's merits. Ruth Nelson, playing several bit parts in Levy's play, found it pretentious. Stella, despite her colorful role as the "divine Jewess," the historical actress Adah Isaacs Menken, introduced as the amorous object of Guy Button's lifelong pursuit, complained, "No one wants to see a play about bills of lading" (*S&A,* 82). And, during the increasingly difficult final rehearsals, her brother Luther delivered the coup de grace: "Boys, I think we're working on a stiff" (*FY,* 142).

During rehearsals Strasberg lectured the cast on Meyerhold's bio-mechanics and had Helen Tamiris teach the young women dances for the barroom scenes and make them practice walking in period bustles. The huge cast required for this lavish saga made it necessary for many members of the company to double, even triple, in bit parts. Nelson, Brand, and Stoddard played Can-Can girls in the rough dockside bar of the opening scene where Guy Button begins his ruthless climb, and then later society women in his wife's elegant drawing room. Luther Adler acted a mad, elderly drunk who calls himself the Emperor of Mexico, and Tang Sin, a rich Chinese businessman who made a deal with Button to import thousands of Chinese to work on the railroads. The effort to bring these many roughly sketched types to life using the Group's familiar psychological technique combined with the new physical expressiveness made the acting seem self-consciously painstaking and puerile. Even a usually sympathetic critic wrote: "The players have practiced conscientiously until they are mechanically perfect. But their pat doings on the stage mean very little. They are automatons" (unidentified review).

Negative critical reactions reenforced what the actors themselves perceived, namely, that neither they nor their director was doing what they were best at. Bud Bohnen's detailed account to his wife of the try-out rehearsals on the set in Boston captured the disjuncture between Oenslager's elaborate, beautifully built structure and the pedestrian play into which the actors were desperately trying to breathe some life.

> We rehearsed on the set...a great island of scenery that turns like a gun turret on a battle ship, revealing every so many degrees a new bunch of steps and levels to play on. Act one is O.K. Scenery and acting meet. The audience won't know what the hell its all about, but the general effect will be excitement...Act two will startle them. The office scene is played about 15 feet up in the air. The language and the movements are so puny that they don't justify the extravagance...The 4th and 5th scenes are again up on high places— actors stuck in the air with 10 square feet of playing space while the scenery fills up 1000 feet of playing space—dead, unused...Lee is beginning to realize that some directing will have to be done pronto to give realistic emotions a pictorial co-efficient in scale with the sweep of the set. (NYPL, Lincoln Center)

Some of the reviews reflected upon this sense of inappropriateness in the unusual attention paid to Strasberg's directing. "The staging of Lee Strasberg is splendid enough. He is a gifted director. But the whole business remains stiff and self-conscious and hollow…an amalgam of thousands of tiny fussy details." The accolade of another generally admiring reviewer seemed inappropriate for the Group's guru: "Strasberg deserved 'a marshal's baton' at the very least." Joe Bromberg, in the title role, was commended for his "flesh and blood" performance (*NYT*, November 29, 1934). Stella Adler as the famed actress and Margaret Barker as Button's long-suffering wife were also admired by the critics. (*New York Post*, November 30, 1934)

For actors, trained as they had been, working on the play was difficult. They were all terrified by having to act on the narrow platform eight feet above the stage. The actors' confidence in Strasberg, already shaken by the challenges from Stella's report on the Stanislavsky system, disintegrated. The show demanded highly organized blocking and choreography, which was not Strasberg's strength. He was exhausted by the effort to put the huge show on its feet and by the increasing antagonism of the actors to what they felt was his "impossible tyranny." (Adams, 175) Yet, they remained cowed by his autocratic control, all, that is, except young John Garfield, who is remembered as the first to dare to talk back to Strasberg. He did it innocently since, as Lewis put it, "he didn't know that Lee was the Pope." Even Kazan didn't talk back when Strasberg scolded him publicly one night. As stage manager he had missed the complicated set of cues that set the impressive "earthquake" in motion— something Kazan claimed Strasberg had never clearly determined. Strasberg tore into him before the company. Devastated, Kazan "rushed down into the cellar, to the wardrobe mistress's room and burst into tears. I hadn't cried since I was a little boy, and I resented Lee for causing this evidence of weakness" (*A Life*, 111).

By the end of the preparatory period, there was an explosion on stage more traumatic than the earthquake that brought down the last-act curtain. During a rehearsal of the big social gathering in scene three, Margaret Barker, wife of the now wealthy Button, was pouring tea when one of her guests fainted in the crowded room. Uncertain if this was part of the scene or a bit of reality, the well-bred Barker rose to see what happened, but then changed her mind and continued to pour the tea. "Why did you do that?" shouted Strasberg from the back of the theater, stopping the rehearsal. "I'm sorry, Lee, I'm sorry, I won't do it again," she apologized and restarted the scene. (Barker realized Strasberg wanted her to be the kind of woman who just went on doing whatever she was doing, although her own good manners had made her stand up.) But, he said again, "Why did you do it?" "I'm sorry, Lee. It was a mistake. May we go on?" she urged. Strasberg yelled at her again and again from the back of the theater, reducing her to tears with "a rage so absolute that he became unintelligible" (*S&A*, 82).

Ruth Nelson, playing one of the guests, could not take it any longer. "With that, I got up from my table, walked out there, and said in a calm, steady voice, 'Now, I'm going to kill him. I'm going to kill him.'" Lewis recalled that "with outstretched hands aimed toward Lee's throat, she started across the footlights, oblivious of the great void of the orchestra pit between herself and her target. Had the other actors not grabbed her and held her hard, she would have taken a bone-smashing plunge." Strasberg, whose ill-mannered harassment contrasted with Barker's instinctive courteous behavior, seemed genuinely fearful. He ran out of the theater and did not return. Clurman took over rehearsals of a Group production for the first time (*S&A*, 82–83). It would be two years before Strasberg directed again.

Strasberg's dominance as the Group's director ended with Nelson's attack, a devastating blow following his loss of authority in the conflict with Stella. Clurman recalled that Strasberg "retired into a state of impassivity" (*FY*, 164). On Broadway that winter, *Gold Eagle Guy* lasted for 68 performances. The company again faced the grim prospect of closing down, but the actors, led by Stella, refused to accept defeat. They forced their directors to produce *Awake and Sing!* by their own Clifford Odets, with Clurman undertaking his first directorial assignment. About ten days into rehearsal, activist members of the cast performed Odets's agit-prop drama *Waiting for Lefty* for the New Theatre League to thunderous audience approval. The wild success of *Waiting for Lefty*, followed quickly by the strong audience and critical response to *Awake and Sing!*, revived the spirits and fortunes of the Group, despite Strasberg's disapproval of both plays. The triumph of Clurman as director and champion of Odets, coming on the heels of Stella's emergence as a teacher, no doubt pushed Strasberg further into psychic withdrawal.

Yet, Strasberg remained involved in the general operations of the Group. He was still their teacher, although no longer the only one. Under the assumed name of Lee Martin, he acted in Odets's *Till the Day I Die*, written to alternate on Broadway with *Waiting for Lefty*. This was his only acting stint with the company. When, in the winter of 1936, the Shubert organization suggested that the Group stage *The Case of Clyde Griffiths*, Strasberg's positive evaluation persuaded the company to undertake the unusual script. In dramatizing Theodore Dreiser's *An American Tragedy*, retitled *The Case of Clyde Griffiths*, Erwin Piscator had transformed the novel into a Marxist drama in the epic style that he and Bertolt Brecht had experimented with in Berlin in the 1920s. Instead of the conventional sequence of dramatic confrontations and resolutions, Piscator structured a cinematic collage of brief episodes whose meaning was reenforced by the Speaker, a didactic interpreter. These innovations intrigued Strasberg who thought the script had great potential for the director's creative input and would provide his highly skilled actors with an opportunity to use exercises that utilized rhythm, music, and art to reach for a more intense, poetic form of expression.

Piscator's Marxist reworking of the plot—the drowning of a pregnant girl by her working-class boyfriend, lured out of his class by hopes of marrying into wealth—challenged conventional values and dramatic structure as well as the handling of stage space. Following Piscator's text, Strasberg explained that the four levels of the space—rising 12 feet above the stage—represented different strata of society. In addition, the horizontal space was also class-coded, with the left for the lower classes and the right for the upper class. In the middle was a cave-like opening representing "No Man's land" where crucial scenes in Clyde Griffiths's struggle to find a place for himself in the highly stratified society were enacted. On the symbolic, sculptural set, Strasberg had to orchestrate the action of his large cast in some 40 scenes. Once again, the actors were terrified of falling off the complex maze, and the stage hands complained about having to make scene shifts in the dark in the split seconds between changing the many spots used to give the show a cinematic feel.

Looking back almost 50 years later, Strasberg remembered his disappointment with the set. The Shuberts, who were financing the project, insisted that the Group employ Watson Barratt, one of their house designers, best known for Shubert musicals. Strasberg recalled that Barratt was intelligent, a good designer, and a nice person, eager to realize Strasberg's intentions. (*Reunion*, 551) What he created, however, was a sentimentalized background for the didactic play. Strasberg had hoped to take advantage of the skills and interests of Max Gorelik to design the show. The previous fall Gorelik had created the sets for the Theatre Union production of *The Mother*, a Gorky novel adapted by Bertolt Brecht, who made his first visit to New York in October 1935 to oversee the ill-fated production. Gorelik became Brecht's friend and disciple, championing the playwright against the Theatre Union's team, which was as ignorant of and antagonistic to epic staging as were Broadway's reviewers.

Recognizing that for each production Gorelik designed for the Group he "had as much to do with creating the vision of the play on stage as any of us," Strasberg believed that the designer would have been invaluable to *The Case of Clyde Griffiths*. "We really had no idea of our own," Strasberg confessed; "it was something new for us." Gorelik recalled that he had suggested epic staging for *The Case of Clyde Griffiths* that would have turned the whole play (and stage) into a trial of Clyde Griffiths with the audience-as-jury seriously considering evidence that the class-based society was as guilty of the tragedy as the hapless Clyde. "The action would be the immediate and actual one of the trial itself rather than of a nostalgic, make-believe story viewed beyond the proscenium." A Brechtian demonstration with the characters-as-witnesses would have provided dramatic justification for the miming of props and for the Speaker who explicates the social significance of the drama. (*New Theatres for Old*, 433–34) But Gorelik was not available. Drawing on his experiences with the Group and Brecht, the designer won a Guggenheim Fellowship for the study of European innovations. His travels led him to rethink the history of staging as man's effort "to influence life by theatrical means," which became the theme of his landmark study, which he published in 1940. (*New Theatres for Old*, 5)

Strasberg confessed that he began the production "without a complete idea" not only for the design but, more importantly, for the overall concept of the show. He seemed to be hoping to combine what he was best at, which was adding "life from the characters' point of view" to a simple but dynamic schematization that would "show the individual in a wider relationship." In page upon page of verbatim notes taken during rehearsals from January 30 to March 13, 1936, Tony Kraber documented every aspect of the process and the problems of staging, from the schedule and organization of the work to the acting and the design of the space. (See *The Flying Grouse* (February 1936): 5). In the six weeks to which he was limited by the Shuberts' budget, Strasberg planned the first two weeks for readings and discussion; the second two weeks for work on scenes, improvisations, problems, and the last two weeks for final staging. In prior shows Strasberg had been aided by Clurman and Crawford. For this one, a new Production Committee was put into action; its members, Stella, Lewis, Kazan, and Mike Gordon, were all budding directors who hoped for an opportunity to develop their talents. Carnovsky was cast in the challenging part of the Speaker. The love triangle repeated the successful trio of *Men in White*: Phoebe Brand as Roberta Alden was the sweet, loving, poor youngster; Alexander Kirkland as Clyde Griffiths was the handsome, ambitious young man Phoebe Brand loses to Margaret Barker, once again cast as the rich girl Sondra Finchley. Other founding members, Art Smith, Roman Bohnen, Ruth Nelson, Sandy Meisner, Bobby Lewis, Walter Coy, Dorothy Patten, Eunice Stoddard, Paula Miller, Tony Kraber, Lewis Leverett, William Challee—plus old timers, Luther Adler, Elia Kazan, Grover Burgess, and ten other actors hired for the occasion, played the mothers, fathers, sisters, cousins, workers, rich partygoers, and legal staff. One news story carried the rumor, quickly squashed, that Stella Adler might play the Speaker one or two performances each week, to satisfy women's rights organizations who questioned why the speaker should necessarily be male. (W. Smith, 256, offers a slightly different version)

Aware of the need for a different approach, Strasberg told the actors that they would not have to do their usual digging into each character because the motivations were explained by the didactic Speaker. The play, Strasberg told the actors, did not "call for psychological progression of acting but the strictest kind of relationship to stage space." The staging problems would be simple ones, to be solved by "full, precise actor's energy" (*Flying Grouse* (February 1936), 5). Nevertheless, the problems turned out not to be so simple. Much of the relatively short rehearsal period was given over to alternative ways of dealing with the Speaker, a problematic character used "to make clear to, rather than affect, an audience." As the assembled cast energetically contributed alternative interpretations and actions—including Stella's quip that she could find a hundred ways to play the role—Strasberg reminded them that "our plays have to begin with a collective idea shared by everyone, not just the director."

Improvisations for individual characterizations and for the important group scenes followed the readings. Many moments were pantomimed from sense memory exercises because few props were to be used in the spare, abstract staging. Hot, tired, and singing their bits of popular songs, Roberta and other girls mimed sewing at machines in the Griffiths collar factory. They also vocalized the sound effects of their machines. In another mimed sequence, dirty, sweaty, disgruntled workers introduced Clyde to the routines of vats and drums used to shrink fabric. Later, they sang Wobbly union songs in preparation for a strike. Margaret Barker's Sondra Finchley mimed driving the car in which she picked up Clyde. For the final court room scene, the actors arrayed themselves as the varied classes to witness the death sentence of Clyde Griffiths sacrificed to an unjust society. Many of these improvised segments worked so well they were written into the script.

As he analyzed the acting demands of the epic dramaturgy, Strasberg distinguished between "narrative emotion," which presented the play's events as remembered events from the past to be used, on the one hand, by the characters involved in the action, and, on the other, the Speaker was to feel real emotion in the present as the "soul of the people." When Carnovsky said of one moment, "Then it is like the Brecht thing," Strasberg responded, "Yes, except that I want more color" (*Flying Grouse*, February 1936).

The costumes reinforced thematic values. Clothing changes encoded Clyde Griffiths's movement up the social ladder in highly effective sequences that often required a style of acting that extended beyond realism. In one instance, Strasberg gave Bobby Lewis carte blanche to improvise and stage a scene on his own. Lewis first appeared as a well-dressed storefront mannequin. As Griffiths came into the shop to buy clothes for an upper-class party, Lewis came to life as a tailor, who with robotic movements dressed Griffiths in emblematic evening clothes, thus, with a vaudeville quick-change, transforming Clyde Griffiths into a "mannequin" of the upper class. Strasberg thought of the moment as "the ritual of passing from one world to another," and Lewis's interpretation was hailed as a "masterpiece of stylized acting and staging worth all the rest of the show put together" (*S&A*, 88).

Despite Strasberg's detailed analysis, replete with his many references to different theatrical and artistic styles, and despite the challenging improvs, the actors often did not know just what Strasberg wanted or how to achieve the results he had in mind. They tried to pin him down with specifics, asking, "What is my spine?" "What is the actor's problem?" "What are we working for in these readings?" But, Strasberg did not seem able to clarify his new approach. Perhaps mindful of unrest in the company, he kept telling the actors to carry out activities on their own. "I want the actors to feel that the things are theirs not mine. We will agree on the basis, the point of view, the particulars will be your own." Yet, when one of the hired actors didn't see things his way, Strasberg asserted his right to be "the sole judge of what is important."

The concentration on the role of the Speaker in rehearsals paid off when the show opened. The critics admired Carnovsky's eloquent, mellifluous, earnest acting but hated the character, who, they felt, turned the murder-drama into a lesson taught with a "pointer." In general, most found the play to be didactic, simplistic, obvious. "If the Group Theatre, under Lee Strasberg's direction," one critic wrote, "were less versatile as a stage organization, this abstract of a vast novel might be a floundering bore. The style of the production puts an enormous responsibility on the actors. They are equal to it." Strasberg was credited with creating "wonders... The complicated trick of it runs off like a Houdini special" (*NYT*, March 14, 1936; *Daily Worker*, March 17, 1936).

Despite the theatrical experimentation that gained the reviewers' attention during a conventional Broadway season, *The Case of Clyde Griffiths* closed after 19 performances. Within the Group, feelings about the show were grim and even dismissive of Strasberg's efforts. Not so Kazan, who remembered Strasberg grappling with "Piscator's concoction." He felt it was "as far from Lee's own character and talent as he could go... which was intimate and cloistered—not suited to too many plays" (*A Life*, 151). Then, too, Clurman rightly concluded that half of Strasberg's "talent was enough to give the production a certain fluidity and sensitivity, an aura of quasi-nobility, that were distinctive on the Broadway scene" (*FY*, 174).

Inspired by the Russians, Strasberg realized that much was expected of the modern director who must use the actor, the ensemble, and the production as a whole "to convey truthfully the image of a world passing before our eyes." In an important essay on the work of the director that he wrote in the 1940s, he explained that the director must "suggest that environment out of which the life of the play arises, and that angle of viewing the play from which the actions of the characters will appear most plausible, most meaningful, and... most truthful and exciting." Yet, he himself had difficulty articulating and working out effective "angles for viewing" the somewhat schematic, abstract or epic plays he directed. In his early, more psycho-logically based productions, his fierce preoccupation with emotional truth in acting, complemented by the Group's collective perspective, and articulated by Clurman, had been enough. Now the foundation of his very personal work had been shaken by the confrontation with Stella, by his desire to emulate Meyerhold's accomplish-ments, by the contact with Brecht and his "alienation effect," along with the dissen-sion among the directors and an increasingly radical company. All of this in turn exacerbated Strasberg's always painful personal relations with the company. Things were coming apart for him and for the Group as well.

In the summer of 1936, the company bravely started out again; their ability to reincarnate themselves and their organization was extraordinary. They went off to another adult vacation spot, Pine Brook Club in Nichols, Connecticut, where the company performed once again in return for room, board, and rehearsal space. Clurman brought along for discussion a major reorganization plan. Much energy was spent deliberating his suggestion that he become their managing director, assisted by a newly elected Actors' Committee (Stella Adler, Roman Bohnen, Morris Carnovsky, and Elia Kazan). During cantankerous deliberations, they restructured the company. With Strasberg and Crawford in agreement, Clurman became man-aging director with the power and organizational backing that they hoped would solve their many problems—with money, people, plays, and productions.

Hope was kindled by an unusual project in which Cheryl Crawford served as the "sparkplug" igniting a creative collaboration between playwright Paul Green and composer Kurt Weill, the distinguished refugee composer whose *The Threepenny Opera* they all admired. (Crawford, 94) The company hoped to develop a script that would become an American version of *The Good Soldier Schweik*, the antiwar satire staged by Piscator in the new epic style in 1928 Berlin.

Gathered for this anxious but expectant summer session were 26 members and 12 apprentices. Again, they drew on their own experiments in acting and on scenes from their earlier shows—*Awake and Sing!*, *Men in White*, and *Success Story*. A Variety Evening produced under the supervision of Art Smith and Crawford with settings by Herbert Andrew boasted a full orchestra, musical numbers by Weill's wife Lotte Lenya accompanied by Sandy Meisner at the piano, Tony Kraber and his guitar, a dance number by Felicia Sorel, and sketches featuring the whole company with titles like "Culture at Macy's," "The Lower Depths," and "Ginsberg on the Pines."

In addition to acting classes by Stella and Strasberg, a special class on musical theater was offered twice a week by Kurt Weill. The composer shared his radical aesthetic with the actors, insisting that all great art is the expression of economic and human conditions. He viewed musical theater as a popular form that, unlike ossified operatic classics, encouraged people to experience works of art. Rejecting realism as more suited to popular movies, he celebrated musical theater as "the purest form of poetic theatre." A musical is not a play with songs or musical scenes interspersed, he explained, but a fusion that makes possible an easy shift from "the spoken to the sung word" as well as successful blending of serious drama and comedy. (Quoted in Hirsch, *Kurt Weill on Stage*, 139, 144–46)

As the actors waited for Green's script to be finished along with two other scripts (Odets's *The Silent Partner* and Lawson's *Marching Song*) to be delivered, the question arose: Who would direct their first musical play? Clurman had introduced Kurt Weill to the Group and his standing was high after the success of the Odets play, but he was ambivalent about staging the show. He did not think either he or Strasberg was really right for the task, although he sensed a preference for the more experienced Strasberg. Clurman proposed the unlikely combination of Stella and Kazan as codirectors. Strasberg rightly considered it a poor idea and Kazan did not want to make his debut as a Group director as Stella's "caddy." (*A Life*, 154) Clurman initiated the rehearsals with Stella, Kazan, and Meisner as a Production Committee, but, after a week, he claimed that he was overwhelmed by his new management position and asked Strasberg to "take over." (*FY*, 187) This transfer from one to the other was no simple cooperative gesture; the two men were barely speaking.

Although difficult to document, the maneuvering was surely not a good way to start their fifth season and one of their most ambitious productions. Indeed, in the retrospective evaluation of the Actors' Committee, the resulting disorganized approach to staging *Johnny Johnson* led to "embarrassing failures in every aspect of the production process, from finalizing the script to running the lights" (Actors' Committee report at NYPL for the Performing Arts; major sections are quoted in W. Smith).

To design the Group's one and only musical play, Donald Oenslager, who had made his initial reputation designing such musicals as George Gershwin's *Girl Crazy*, seemed a very good choice. Clurman, beginning as the director, invited Oenslager to come up to Pine Brook Club in order to start the complex design for the show's kaleidoscopic scenes. At a meeting in the house that Cheryl Crawford shared with Weill and Lotte Lenya, Clurman explained to Oenslager in a general way what he had in mind. He was always somewhat vague in talking about sets, and since he probably had already decided not to direct the show, Clurman's comments were faltering about settings with a "miniature quality" for this antiwar play about a little man who tried to turn the guns of war off. (W. Smith, 277) The tension between the two "boys," as Crawford called Clurman and Strasberg, left it to Crawford to give some direction to the discussion with Oenslager. With the technical need to make quick scene shifts, Oenslager came away with the need for a turntable as the main priority in his design.

Oenslager's scenic solutions for the three acts and thirteen scenes of this parable of the common man's struggle against war ranged from poetic realism for the sentimental opening scenes in Johnny Johnson's hometown, to fantasy for the battle front sequences in which three cannons sing to soldiers in the dugout below, to extreme distortion for the "mad unreality" of the psychiatric hospital in which Johnny Johnson is incarcerated for trying to bring peace to the world, and a final symbolic street "leading nowhere" for the little man's closing moments. In a mishap that may be taken as prophetic of the disasters that were to overtake the production, Oenslager lost his initial ground plans and sketches at Woolworth's Five and Ten Cents Store. When the company learned that he had been shopping for props for George S. Kaufman's *Stage Door*, which he was also designing, they felt that Oenslager was too busy with his own career to devise creative designs for them. Strasberg evidently wanted to make some design changes when he took over the direction from Clurman, but it was late in the process and he was, as usual, intimidated by outsiders. In the end, the many sets, involving some nineteen scene changes using a raked stage and a turntable, had to be built quickly for the vast 1,400 seat Forty-fourth Street Theatre. The set, so important to total theatrical expressiveness, became "monstrous" to the cast negotiating it. The musical director Lehman Engel recalled that "the chief problem suddenly became one of self-preservation in climbing out of First World War trenches and making costume changes with no allowable time" (L. Engel, 94). Ironically, once again, the critics thought the set, which dwarfed and defeated the actors, to be one of the best features of the production along with Weill's stirring incidental music. (e.g., *NYT*, November 20, 1936)

Strasberg believed that *Johnny Johnson* required a special theatrical interpretation. The Green-Weill "musical autobiography of a common soldier whose natural common sense runs counter to a sophisticated civilization" was, in his view, an "American folk legend, full of the humors of old vaudeville and the provincial family album, sharpened with poetic comment on the madness of contemporary life" (quoted in W. Smith, 280). All this, plus the first music in the American idiom by the very continental Weill, was a unique creative challenge. Strasberg hoped to eliminate what he called the "strange distinction...between the play of ideas and the play of pure entertainment." *Johnny Johnson* was intended to be artistic *and* popular—a tragicomic musical play with a philosophical view of war. (*Daily Worker*, January 5, 1937)

This timely piece about the man of peace in a world at war was thus no ordinary musical, but combined song, poetry, caricature, and surrealistic scenic touches. Johnny Johnson, the quintessential, good-natured, "Aw shucks" American, is a stone-cutter who very reluctantly joins up to fight in order to please his patriotic sweetheart. From the recruiting office to the trenches of France, where he makes a peace pact with a German sniper he was sent out to capture, he marches out of step with the insanity of war. Wounded unheroically in the rump, he steals a laughing-gas tank from the hospital, uses it on the Allied High Command to turn a major offensive into a peace initiative, and ends up spending most of the rest of his years in a mental hospital. In the last scene he is a broken man selling wooden toys, but not toy soldiers, to children. Despite sounds of a growing militarism around him, he goes off stage singing, "We'll never lose our faith and hope and trust in all mankind."

The members of the large cast had their work cut out for them: to give life to the unusual characters and actions, which, like the settings, comprised a hodge-podge of styles. The naive, small-town iconoclast Johnny Johnson was played by Russell Collins with deep, direct feeling, and his girlfriend, Minny Belle, who is always in his mind during his military mishaps, was interpreted by the warm and appealing Phoebe Brand. Around them, however, were grotesques from every walk of life: the hometown folks with Bobby Lewis as their zany Mayor; the Army brass with Art Smith as a comic recruiting sergeant, and Tony Kraber as a soldier who sings a cowboy song Weill wrote for the actor's folk-singing talents; the terrified German sniper movingly characterized by Jules Garfield; the mad psychiatrist played to the hilt by

Morris Carnovsky; and the asylum inmates, the Allied High Command, and many other bit-parts played by members of the company with additional men drawn from the studio classes.

In the rehearsal notes, one senses Strasberg's struggle with what often seemed like contradictory aims. He wanted the actors to interpret the play and live through rather than indicate the experience of each character; even those in the crowd scenes were told to retain the "color" of their responses. At the same time he wanted them to speak the lines clearly, sing in unison, be precise in physicalizing moments of fantasy, and deliver the music with vitality and punch.

Strasberg believed that they were "trying to establish a new form," using actors rather than singers for songs, which were in themselves dramatic and integral to the action. Some of the director's detailed guidance was familiar Group work. For example, Strasberg scolded Russell Collins, struggling with his role as Johnny Johnson, for not coming up with fresh activities. Many were chastised for "indicating." He used improvisation over and over again to help the actors penetrate the lines. In early Group productions, Strasberg had often been willing to sacrifice words to the truth of the activity. For this musical, he told them, "You must be very careful about the words." He even quipped, "I am going to ask you to do a peculiar thing, that is, for us. I want you to learn your lines."

It was Bobby Lewis, once again, who pulled off the trick of being able to "justify" and "give meaning" to a highly stylized comic character. As the Mayor in the opening scene, he modeled himself on Boss Tweed, manipulating his padded stomach as an emblem of power. In the Allied High Command scene, he satirized the French Premier Georges Clemenceau, the "Tiger" of France, with eyebrows and lips covered with "enough crepe hair to suggest that animal and gestured with great over-the-head clawing movements." Later, one reviewer observed: "Bob Lewis' contortions as the French Premier and the Mayor add the quality of dance to the poetry and music of the drama. His rhythmical voice and movements serve as an example, in a perfect though small unit, of the aim of the play form as a whole" (quoted in *S&A*, 91).

Years later, after Bobby Lewis had staged very successful musicals, he attributed the "miserable" direction of *Johnny Johnson* to the fact that Strasberg was "helpless to find musical staging" and would not permit those more knowledgeable to help. Lewis had ventured a suggestion intended to eliminate a very awkward exit for Paula Miller, playing the Red Cross nurse. She had to sing "Mon Ami, My Friend" as a solo, center stage, in front of the "tab curtain" while the sets were being changed. Her rendition of the song, which Lotte Lenya later sang, was not, as he put it, "a show stopper … and not two hands were put together in the form of applause. At the end, she side-stepped off stage left in deathly silence, smiling foolishly." With his extensive experience as an entertainer, Lewis couldn't stand it. He went to Strasberg. "Lee, I hope you don't mind a simple suggestion to help Paula." Couldn't she "travel" with the last four bars so that the music takes her off the stage? Strasberg, who was usually "very nice" to Lewis, was furious: "This was theatre, not vaudeville!" (*S&A*, 91).

As they reached the end of the rehearsal period, everyone felt a great sense of pressure. Because of the confusing rehearsal process, the actors, despite their enthusiasm for the material, found *Johnny Johnson* a very dull show to rehearse. They sharply criticized each other's way of working and felt they had let the director down, but also that many of their difficulties were his fault. Thus, it was not surprising that the dress rehearsals and previews at the Forty-fourth Street Theatre were disastrous— "the most distressing experiences I have ever gone through in the theatre," Clurman recalled. In the intimate, 500-seat Belmont Theatre where they had rehearsed, "the production seemed charming: informal, unpretentious and sweet." Those who saw it there loved its delicate treatment of an important idea. In the large Forty-fourth Street Theatre, the untrained voices of the actors, Clurman recalled, "sounded so small they were occasionally inaudible...the performances now looked amateurish." The staging and the orchestra were under-rehearsed, and "the actors were lost" (*FY*, 188–89).

During the two-day postponement of the opening, they desperately tried to whip the show into shape, reducing the number of sets and scenes from 19 to 13, cutting musical numbers in a state of desperate hysteria. Clurman remarked that the always sensitive Strasberg became "a veritable sacrifice." At one late night conference the beleaguered director shouted, "I know more about acting than any of you," as he tore into the weakness of the script and the music. (*FY*, 189) Some of the Group's friends sent letters begging them not to open the show. Even though nightly previews showed improvement, Clurman confessed, "I felt as if everything was giving way underneath me—not only the production, but six years of work" (*FY*, 189).

Once again, contrary to their own sense of failure, when the show officially opened, the audience seemed enthusiastic, calling the playwright to the stage. Although there were few "money reviews," most of the critics greeted the high ambition the production exemplified with respect and praise. Strasberg was again acknowledged as staging an unusual show. The thoughtful critic Arthur Pollock found this "hopeful and discouraging, bitter and sweet, derisory and tenderly compassionate" production "the most satisfactory play on Broadway at the moment." The stylized battle scenes were dubbed impressive, and the moment when the cannons sing as a sleeping soldier below reenacts the descent from the cross was praised as a moment of direction that "must have come from some half heaven." Almost universal praise for Weill's "delectable score" was, however, tempered by frequent remarks about the absence of singing voices among the cast. With the exception of Russell Collins, Morris Carnovsky, and Bobby Lewis, the actors came in for considerable criticism. Their efforts at comedy seemed self-conscious, "as if they were members of an ancient Greek chorus who had wandered onto the stage at Minksy's" (see reviews of November 20, 1936).

The anguish of the actors was understandable at reading such epithets as "amateurishness" and "exterior professionalism." In an interview with Strasberg after his resignation from the Group, it was pointed out that Strasberg's technique was as "far removed from the Abbotts, the Kaufmans, the McClintics and the Connellys as Broadway is from Moscow" (*World Telegram*). They identified his approach to directing as "naturalistic" because his basic premise was, as he told them, that "you cannot be a great actor by doing great acting—only by doing very real, concrete, simple things. And acting that is acting is something done...that means something to the person doing it." He had turned his actors away from acting clichés to projecting their own inner experiences into the minute details of the inner and outer reality in which their characters find themselves.

This essential credo had made Strasberg's staging unique. Although he told the interviewer that, of course, a director must have the power of "visualization" and must work through rehearsals toward his vision of a script, it was the director's ability to reach his actors through acting that he emphasized, even claiming that "a good director must be either consciously or unconsciously an actor." Until the end of his life Strasberg continued to talk about directing primarily in terms of exploring acting problems, telling an American Theatre Wing class in the 1950s that the director creates "the atmosphere in which the actors can do their creative work."

Yet, Strasberg did aspire to a more comprehensive theatricality. In talks, articles, and letters he expressed eloquently that the great directors he admired used their brilliant inventiveness "to mirror and explore life more fully by means of the theatre." He never put himself or Clurman in the same league with Vakhtangov, Meyerhold, or Stanislavsky as directors, although he believed the Group could hold its own as a theater company. His own efforts to follow the lead of the Russian directors, however flawed, were in many ways original attempts to explore the possibilities of theater art, something he felt every production of worth ought to do. Even the critics, whose respectful reviews often condemned the shows to box office failure, recognized the interest of the work. Nevertheless, the gap between what Strasberg hoped to accomplish in his last three shows and the mixed results was no doubt bitter to him and destructive of the Group spirit.

The Actors' Committee Report struck at crucial contradictions. They credited Strasberg with giving "the first artistic shape to the Group" through his method of work, which made him in the first years the "greatest artistic force in the American Theatre." To forge his revolution, however, "necessitated (as it tended to further harden and bring out) Lee's great courage, his doggedness, his arbitrariness, his necessity for being right, his cold scorn of artistic compromise, his clannishness, his removal from life, his hysterical force...and above all, *the brute domineering of his will.*" The report expressed admiration for Strasberg's brilliance as "student and teacher of theatre" and for his "many lovable and admirable qualities," but regretted that he had become "so protected" in recent years that he no longer realized the deleterious impact of his behavior. They recommended that he be "relieved for some time to come of all but purely artistic tasks" and that his productions be organized not only to assist him but also to "take care of" his "faults and deficiencies." (*FY*, 194) It is not surprising that this evaluation led to his resignation in April of 1937.

In looking back on Strasberg's contributions as a director more than 50 years later, his former Group people were able to applaud his accomplishments while recognizing his limitations. (see *Reunion*) Elia Kazan, who attacked his faults and whose opinions can be sensed in the criticism of the Actors' Committee, came to feel that "Lee was blamed for the failures—uncharitably; he'd given the Group so much of himself for so long" (*A Life*, 156).

After leaving the Group, Strasberg directed a number of productions in the next few years with many Group actors and writers, but he did not have the career his brilliant beginnings in the early 1930s promised. He would make his mark—and a very prominent one—doing what suited his talent best, teaching "The Method" at the Actors Studio and at the Lee Strasberg Institutes.

What Strasberg accomplished with the Group was crucially important. In addition to his productions, he placed acting at the center of theater and made the process of rehearsal more important than the product. Teaching a conscious craft, he nurtured a new kind of actor for whom the work became part of a continuing, shared exploration in which the failures were as significant as, or maybe more significant, than the hits. In classes and productions he encouraged the beginnings of a new, contemporary American style—improvisational, concentrated, connected, subjective, emotionally truthful, and poetically real. Harold Clurman's assessment in *The Fervent Years* remains one of the fairest and most insightful:

> Lee Strasberg is one of the few artists among American theatre directors. He is the director of introverted feeling, of strong emotion curbed by ascetic control, sentiment of great intensity muted by delicacy, pride, fear, shame. The effect he produces is classic hush, tense and tragic, a constant conflict so held in check that a kind of beautiful spareness results. Though plastically restricted, his work through the balance of its various tensions often become aesthetically impressive, despite its crushed low key and occasional wild transitions to shrill hysteria. Above everything, the feeling in Strasberg's production is never stagy. Its roots are clearly in the intimate experience of a complex psychology, an acute awareness of human contradiction and suffering, as distinguished through perhaps a too specialized sensibility. (*FY,* 60–61)

When Clurman found himself the sole director of the company, he was able to stage those shows for which the Group is probably most famous because he had been left with Lee Strasberg's greatest accomplishment—*an ensemble of players.*

8. Harold Clurman: Author of the Stage Production ⌁

"I was a late developer," Harold Clurman remembered his friend Aaron Copland saying of him. The retiring young man who went off to Paris with the studious composer in 1921 was a precocious but timid doctor's son from the Lower East Side. He was so shy with strangers that he trembled when he talked, hardly able to get his words out. In the years between his adventures in the continental art capital in the early 1920s and his charismatic lectures at Steinway Hall in 1930–31, Clurman remained withdrawn although persistent, not, as he himself quipped in later years, "this loudmouth blowhard you see before you." But conviction carried him away. Once he started talking to his eager listeners about the idea of theater that he, Strasberg, and Crawford had in mind, he became a new man. Although he transformed himself into a spell-binder, something of the emotional bumbler was always there. He was both the sophisticated, elegant, fedora-hatted Maecenas of young artists and the awkward, intuitive, suffering Prince Myshkin out of Dostoyevsky's *The Idiot*. In short, he became the fascinating Harold Clurman many remember and revere.

As a director, Clurman was also a late developer and a complex master. It was not until January 1935 that he directed his first full-scale production, *Awake and Sing!* by his protégé and close companion, Clifford Odets. It was the making of both of them and of a unique director-playwright relationship preceded by a long, painful apprenticeship. In Paris, Clurman wrote a thesis on drama for a degree at the Sorbonne and studied the inspirational lectures and innovative productions of Jacques Copeau; yet, he had no career aspirations in mind. His parents, whose lack of tenderness toward him, he felt, created his timidity, put no pressure on him to choose a life's work or even to earn a living. He was like a secular Yeshiva boy, reading Joyce and Ibsen instead of the Talmud. If he showed any bent, it was for literature. His one try at playwriting in his teens, however, turned out to be an unconscious plagiarism of Ibsen's *An Enemy of the People*. Essays seemed a better outlet for his literary and critical flair as well as for his fascination with theater, which he had loved since childhood when at his father's side he saw the titanic Jacob Adler at the Yiddish Theatre.

When Clurman got around to working, on his return to New York, he tried the stage. "My flesh had a natural hankering for the atmosphere of the theatre, even when the plays were contemptible" (*FY*, 6). His dogged persistence landed him several modest jobs, bit parts, stage-managing stints, and play reading. From these obscure vantage points, he, like his friend Lee Strasberg, had a chance to observe some of the most interesting American directors and producers of the twenties, among them Robert Edmond Jones, George Abbott, Jed Harris, and Philip Moeller. What he discovered stood him in good stead in his own creative development and also in reconfiguring the role of the director to suit the Group Idea.

Clurman told friends that it was his ambition to be a director, and went off with Strasberg to the American Laboratory Theatre to take Boleslavsky's directing course the 1926–27 season. Strasberg, more experienced and already somewhat set in his ways, left after a few sessions, but Clurman stuck with it, despite the fact that Boleslavsky went to England leaving the actual teaching in the hands of others. "I learned many things about handling actors through Boleslavsky," Clurman said later. "Observing him was a first step in my education as a director" (quoted in Carrington, 118).

It was Clurman who initiated the projects that preceded the founding of the Group, but feeling himself "insufficiently secure, technically speaking, to convince the actors of the validity of our methods," he turned over the task of training the company and directing the productions to Strasberg. In the summer of 1931, Clurman, still believing that Strasberg was the only person among them who could forge the ensemble and realize the script on stage, asked him to direct *The House of Connelly.*

Yet, beginning that very first summer, Clurman made a number of abortive forays into directing. He planned to stage *The Man with the Portfolio*, a Soviet play that he suggested be adapted by Gerald Sykes, a good friend who was at Brookfield with the company. In preparation Clurman read Soviet novels, took in Soviet newsreels, cast the play, and evidently started to rehearse. But the challenges unnerved him. He received little help from the more experienced Strasberg, of whom he wrote in a passage deleted from *The Fervent Years*, "his peculiar silences, his perhaps unconscious patronizing, his momentary asperities, did not reassure me." Looking back he dismissed the whole effort, realizing that in those days he didn't really understand what the Soviet Union signified and that "the play was inappropriate, the adaptation weak; and I was still unready to direct any play" (*FY*, 50).

The second summer at Dover Furnace, his codirectors urged him to direct Lawson's *Success Story*, "the content and manner of which they thought suited my temperament," Clurman recalled (*FY*, 87). Nevertheless, he insisted that Strasberg take charge in order to extend the training of the company. In the fall Clurman took over from a dispirited Crawford the final rehearsals for Dawn Powell's *Big Night* but he could not rescue the production, which closed quickly.

By the spring of 1933, Clurman made the painful discovery that his codirectors no longer thought him capable of directing. He suggested that he might stage Lawson's *The Pure in Heart*, but Strasberg stopped him cold, saying that Clurman "had given no evidence of directional capacity or enterprise" (*FY*, 124). When Crawford agreed with Strasberg, Clurman felt utterly betrayed. That summer at Green Mansions, while the Group was at work on *Men in White*, his stock with the company seemed to plummet. The word was "the Group has only one director," and, as Clurman put it, "they didn't mean me" (*FY*, 128). Strasberg declared to Clurman in front of others, "You can't direct." This, despite his work with Odets on the promising second act of *I Got the Blues,* the hit of the summer entertainment the company offered the guests at Green Mansions, and his rehearsing of *Gallery*

Gods, a German script brought to them by its adaptor, John Houseman. For this play about the theater, Clurman had cast leading players Stella and Luther Adler, among others, but Houseman could see that the play was "Harold's personal project and that it was unlikely to be produced unless something went wrong with *Men in White,*" and that seemed unlikely. (Houseman, 93) Clurman's ever-critical girlfriend Stella told him that these false starts had seriously diminished him in the eyes of the company.

As Clurman struggled to find his way, he realized that he did not really have much to learn from the successful directors whom he had observed. His views about directing and about theater had little in common with theirs. At the same time he concluded that although he admired Strasberg, it was "disastrous" to copy him. The brief trip he made to join Stella in Russia in the summer of 1934 provided the release he needed. "For four years I had lived, theatrically speaking, in Strasberg's shadow. My failure to achieve my own style of direction derived from my falling into an imitation of Strasberg's method" (*FY,* 139). Just as it had stimulated Strasberg, the rich variety of directors' interpretations in the Soviet repertory theaters opened the way for Clurman to discover his own creative identity.

Unlike Strasberg, however, who, even as a director, was ever honing acting talent through his method, Clurman's inspiration was the Group Idea and the playwright's creation. It was the effort to "link the actor as an individual with the creative purpose of the playwright" that Clurman believed was the truly innovative objective of the Group. (*FY,* 23) Important as the acting technique was, a number of the actors had already been introduced to the basic approach either at the American Laboratory Theatre or at the Neighborhood Playhouse, where Boleslavksy had also given some courses. But as Clurman saw it, neither the American Laboratory Theatre nor the Neighborhood Playhouse had "much understanding of plays or any special attitude toward them" (*FY,* 23). In his talks before each production, in contrast, Clurman would set the action of the play in its social and cultural context, and he would excavate its inner structure with the analytical tools of the Stanislavsky approach. His interest in dramatic structure went back to his teens when he pored over William Archer's critical works, and continued through the 1930s in the various classes for playwrights he offered. Influenced in part by Strasberg, he had gradually integrated his literary predilections with Stanislavsky's method and with Gordon Craig's theatrical theories that placed the text in the context of a totally new creation: the stage production. Play after play, his discussions fascinated the company. As Strasberg began the rehearsals for their early productions, he would be translating Clurman's insights as well as his own into stage life.

Thus, it is not surprising that what finally propelled Clurman into his first independent production was his enthusiasm for a playwright. "A feeling for Mr. Odets's work," he recalled, finally got him going and kept him going as a director. With Odets, he realized the vision embodied in his early talks, that the Group would nurture its own playwright. Of the seven plays he directed for the company, five were by Clifford Odets and two by Irwin Shaw, who inherited the mantle of Odets after the success of his powerful antiwar one-act, *Bury the Dead.* On stage these plays—some successful and others not—all revealed Clurman's distinctive concerns: insightful psychological characterization, vibrant language, relevant life-affirming American themes, and heightened or poetic realism in both acting and design. Dedicated to making the stage a place "where artists have a right to express something more than the 'naked facts,'" he saw these plays as organic to the articulation in theatrical form of the ensemble's comment on the time in which they lived. He worked closely with the playwright as he undertook to unify all the elements of production by his interpretation of the script. In the Group's cohesive community he became what he thought the director should be, "the author of the stage production."

Awake and Sing!, which opened on February 19, 1935, at the Belasco Theatre, became the Group's signature production, the one in which the organic Group Idea became a reality. Like everything else in the Group's history, however, the play's passage to Broadway had been stormy. During the second summer at Dover Furnace Clurman, who had become Odets's mentor, tried to turn the budding playwright away from writing a play inspired by Beethoven, urging him "not to deal so much with imaginative things." In the spirit of realistic observation and self-exploration that characterized Strasberg's acting exercises, Clurman told Odets to pin himself "down to reporting actual and real things, such as people around here, what they look like, how they dress, etc." (see Brenman-Gibson, 236–37). That advice started Odets thinking about "the Greenbaum family play," one he had begun earlier. Realizing that this subject was "much nearer to the truth of my own feeling and reality," he began jotting down "desultory notes" for the new play. (Brenman-Gibson, 242)

In his cubby hole at Groupstroy the following bitter Depression winter, Odets worked hard on the aptly titled *I've Got the Blues*, interweaving the crises of the Greenbaum family he was creating with the plight of the Group family with which he was living. In the original typescript the character of the mother Bessie, for example, is occasionally called Stella. Clurman found these early drafts talented but troubling: a first act full of coarse Jewish expressions and humor and what he called "messy kitchen realism" and a "masochistically pessimistic" last act, but a brilliant second act. (*FY*, 127–28) By the following summer at Green Mansions, Odets convinced Clurman to test that second act of the play in one of their weekend productions for the summer vacationers. He promised the audience would love it—and they did. But Strasberg maintained the play was in bad taste, and it would take another "*Wanderjahr* in the land of might-have-been," as the critic Gerald Weales put it, "before it came home to a Group ready to receive it" (Weales, 57). The producer Frank Merlin optioned the play for a series he was planning with funds the wealthy benefactress Bess Eitingon had initially offered the Group. But, Merlin lost the money on another production and could not find further backing, in part because the Odets play, people said, needed an ensemble to make it work. Edith Isaacs noted in *Theatre Arts Magazine* (April 1939) after it opened that "no company of players picked up casually in the Broadway manner could make those unhappy individuals look and act like a family."

Still the Group family for which the play was intended was not ready. Yet, when the actors protested the decision of the directors to end the run of the lackluster *Gold Eagle Guy* and close operations for the season, their battle cry became, "Why don't we put on Clifford's play?" Stella, cast as the heroine, championed the twin causes of the actors and Odets's play. Strasberg, the antagonist, tried to stem the growing tide of revolt. Through clenched lips he reiterated those infamous words: "You don't seem to understand, Cliff. We don't like your play. We don't like it" (*FY*, 144). Clurman kept his enthusiasm for the play to himself, according to the various versions of what happened during these famous January meetings in the basement of the Belasco Theatre that often served as the Group's home. He evidently thought it politic to present a united front with his codirectors. Finally, the actors swept all objections before them. Odets read his now revised script to the company. Clurman, relieved that the actors had won the day, was no longer non-committal. He overrode the objections of his co-directors and announced that Odets's play would be the next Group production. In mid-December he had written to photographer Paul Strand that he felt ready to direct and he told the company that he would direct *Awake and Sing!*, as the play was retitled. To this decision Strasberg responded with a characteristic laconic one-liner: "It would be very beneficial" (*FY*, 145). And it was—for everyone except Strasberg.

Ironically, it was Strasberg's four-year reign as the director of the Group that was "beneficial" for the success of *Awake and Sing!* Clurman would now be able to drive the "Cadillac that Strasberg built." That was the way Michael Gordon described Clurman's first venture directing the Group actors. Gordon, a Yale Drama School alumnus who had directed shows for the Theatre Union, had come into the Group in 1935 as stage manager and technician, just to be part of Strasberg's ensemble. Strasberg had given them a "common lingo and a common frame of reference," Odets observed later. "It was very easy for Harold Clurman to direct *Awake and Sing!* or *Golden Boy* with this company that Lee Strasberg had put together" (*Reunion*, 497).

With these assessments Clurman would readily have agreed, often acknowledging his indebtedness to Strasberg. Yet, he was totally different in temperament and technique; he did not direct like his mentor and did not consider himself the kind of director Strasberg was, one who not only gave actors their basic training, but also drove them to dig deeper into themselves. Clurman tended to allow actors to work through problems on their own; he never really "saw things as an actor," Odets believed. But Clurman respected, honored, and loved actors. "He didn't hector his actors from an authoritarian position; he was a partner, not an overlord, in the struggle of production," recalled Kazan (*A Life*, 121). From the beginning Clurman had enriched Strasberg's intensive, obsessive search for emotional nuggets by nurturing the company with his special diet of wide-ranging intellectual, philosophical, psychological talk. For him, the system of acting was not an end in itself, but a means employed for the true interpretation of plays. Now Clurman was finally ready to see what his ebullient spirit could accomplish with these disciplined actors on behalf of the original script his ever-scribbling friend Odets had been begging them to do.

By the time the news that *Awake and Sing!* would be the next Group Theatre production was made public on January 13, 1935, Odets was no longer just a bit actor and unproduced playwright. He had been hailed as "a dramatist to be reckoned with" by Henry Senber, the second-string reviewer of the *Morning Telegraph*, who happened to be the only Broadway critic present at the New Theatre Night on January 6 when *Waiting for Lefty* exploded onto the stage of the Civic Repertory Theatre before 1,400 wildly cheering theatergoers (*Morning Telegraph*, January 7,

1935). He wrote Odets's first Broadway review as word spread quickly, especially among the workers' theater groups across the country, that this was the play they had been waiting for. It is difficult to say with certainty that the success of *Waiting for Lefty* spurred the decision to produce *Awake and Sing!* but the two shows had a symbiotic relationship. All the actors in *Awake and Sing!*, with the exception of Stella, had been in the original production of *Waiting for Lefty*, and, they were not only among the most committed to the Group Idea and to political activism, but also paradoxically, as one critic put it later, they were the "stars" of the ensemble. The actors ran from rehearsing *Awake and Sing!* to playing in *Waiting for Lefty*. After *Awake and Sing!* opened, a second company took over their roles in *Waiting for Lefty*, then playing on Broadway with the quickly written *Till the Day I Die*. The January triumph of *Waiting for Lefty*, produced with a vibrant radical spirit by the actors without the aid or approval of the Group directors, animated the preparation of *Awake and Sing!*

The rehearsal period for *Awake and Sing!* was short, a little over three weeks, in contrast to the extended months given most of the prior Strasberg shows. Yet, it was enough time for Clurman to transform his chosen cast into Odets's emblematic, lower middle-class Jewish family. He didn't have to do a great deal with the actors since the parts were written for them. The cast, most of whom had been in the sample act performed at Dover Furnace, was small but very strong. They were all eager to act out the "fundamental activity" that Odets had assigned the Berger clan, the "struggle for life amidst petty conditions" (Odets, *Six Plays*, 37). Clurman persuaded Stella to take on the role of Bessie Berger, the overbearing, sharp-talking but spirited Jewish mother, for which she was in part the inspiration. She never really forgave Clurman for aging her prematurely with this maternal role. She felt too young, too beautiful to be playing the matriarch whose love of life and her family has been deformed by the harsh circumstances of the Depression. "I was a looker," she liked to quip. Stories abound about how during the run, Stella would eliminate bits of the substantial padding to reveal her svelte figure, or push back her grey wig at the curtain call to let her blonde tresses show through—to the wild applause of the audience and the horror of her very professional fellow actors. Her brother Luther played Moe Axelrod, the wise-cracking, bitter, libidinous, one-legged veteran, a boarder in the Berger household. Condemning life as a racket but still burning with passion for the daughter Hennie, the character allowed Luther Adler to project the smoldering inner fire beneath a rough exterior that had made his Sol Ginsberg in *Success Story* so powerful. Those who had been at Groupstroy when Odets was writing with them in mind filled out the good parts he had promised them; every member of the ensemble contributed something very personal to the pulsating stage life. Phoebe Brand, who had become expert at embodying the pained but sexy thirties ingénue, played with strong emotion the daughter Hennie, who frees herself from despair by leaving her husband and child to run off with Moe, the real love of her life. Despite his youth, Morris Carnovsky made a convincing grandfather Jacob. He became the ineffectual but idealistic, radical ideologue who teaches that "Life shouldn't be printed on dollar bills." It was the role that gave him the greatest understanding of the "actor's job and technique," Carnovsky said later, "because it was the closest to myself of any realistic part I've played" (*Reunion*, 518). That was true for the whole cast; each actor brought some unique personal aspect to the role. J. Edward Bromberg, who despite his radical views was given to good living and good dressing—he loved to wear spats—turned Uncle Morty, the vulgar, successful cloak and suit entrepreneur into a vivid capitalist grotesque. Art Smith's middle-American background gave just the right touches to his portrait of Myron, the hapless father of the Berger household, vainly trying to grasp the American dream. Even the smaller roles were richly detailed as Sanford Meisner disclosed Odets's complex poetry in the immigrant Sam Feinschreiber, whom Bessie had tricked into marrying the pregnant Hennie, and the skilled Bud Bohnen breathed life into Schlosser the janitor. At Green Mansions, Herbert Ratner had played Ralphie, the young son who, after the suicide of his grandfather, turns the disappointments of his life into collective activism. He thought he owned the part, but Odets and others in the Group had discovered Julie Garfield at the Theatre Union and in their classes. Odets insisted that he be given the part in the Broadway production, despite promises to Ratner, who was devastated. There was also strong personal and political rapport between the "Dean," as the knowledgeable, helpful Carnovsky was called, and the eager-to-learn young Garfield, who seemed truly to be graduating from his grandfather's university at the close of the play.

It was at the beginning of the rehearsal period, in the "work at the table," that Clurman was at his best. "He was marvelous...at analysis of the play, understanding of each character in terms of action," recalled Brand (*Reunion*, 518). Odets admired Clurman's ability to "talk from every point of view about the play. Cover the ground backward and forward. And if the actor's imagination was touched somewhere, which was his intention, then the actor would catch something and begin to work in a certain way, with a certain image or vision of how the part should go, with Clurman here and there giving him a nudge" (*Reunion*, 500). Clurman considered this sitting around and talking the "real discovery period" in which he stimulated the actors to think of their parts and of the whole script in terms of his interpretation.

Clurman's inspiring talks on all the Group plays, but especially on those he directed, grew out of his own intense engagement with the scripts. His involvement with *Awake and Sing!* had continued on and off over the two-year gestation period. He recalled in an interview [with the author] that his inexperience as a director had kept him from realizing at first how easily the script could be improved. The first twenty pages were cut and the ending changed from defeat to affirmation. The success of the revisions emboldened Clurman to play an ever-increasing role in the development of Odets's subsequent plays. But he considered his contributions to this first play relatively modest. Once the basic structural changes were made, Clurman and the cast, as well as the rest of the company, found themselves at one with the play their fellow actor had written for and, in a way, about them. The intimate fusion of text and performers brought out the best in Clurman.

The actors responded fully to Clurman's intuitive vision of the production. "My first reaction to Clifford Odets's *Awake and Sing!* was a sense of chaos," Clurman later explained. He saw the world of the play in "terms of conflicting colors laid on 'cubistically' in uneven patches one over the other, or of incongruous combinations of objects, of voices in cacophonous counterpoint." From his gut response he spun out a larger social-psychological analysis that also implied a theatrical means of expression. The "disorder" was the consequence of years of economic struggle in big cities; it had "a comic side" but was "essentially melancholy." In *Awake and Sing!*, as in the plays of Sean O'Casey, whose "tenement tenderness" Clurman found more apposite than the many comparisons made to Chekhov, the tragic-comic reality derived from an "improvisatory spontaneousness" that the Group actors could well understand. (Odets, *Six Plays*, 421)

The chaotic, sad, but funny life-force Clurman found in the play was very close to the spirit of the Group members themselves, especially during that winter of 1932 at Groupstroy, when the play took on much of its form. The actors were woven into the identity of the characters that sprang to life under Clurman's guidance with extraordinary vitality. Rich in sensory details and improvisational immediacy, the life on stage resembled the life of the Group off stage. The actors, like the characters—talkative, histrionic, suffering, despairing, and idealistic—improvised the crosscurrents of the play's subtext out of their own life experience together. Even the anger, disappointment, violence, and harshness of the characters in this Depression-era drama reflected the Group's life off-stage. The through-line of the script was the through-line of the Group: "Life should not be printed on dollar bills." Their objective was young Ralph's famous concluding words: "My days won't be for nothing. Let Mom have the dough. I'm twenty-two and kickin'! I'll get along. Did Jake die for us to fight about nickels? No! Awake and Sing, he said" (Odets, *Six Plays*, 100).

Faithful to the approach of his first teacher, Boleslavsky, and to the method his friend Strasberg had evolved from Boleslavsky's training, Clurman analyzed the spine of the play and then that of each character, suggesting the dynamic relationship of part to the whole. He marked into beats the moment-to-moment activities that moved the action forward. The dynamic force of his interpretation is demonstrated in the following analysis he offered of the opening scene in *Awake and Sing!*

> During this conversation everyone is finishing dinner, but eating is only an incidental activity of the scene, not its main action. Ralph is calling attention to his problem; his action here is "to demand his due." This is directly related to the spine of his part, which is "to get away" from his environment. Myron's action is "to quiet him," also closely related to the spine of his part, which is "to make things good." Hennie's action here is "to provoke everybody," for she is in trouble herself and frustrated in her desire "to wrest joy from life," which is the spine of her part. Jacob's action is "to make Ralph understand something," for the spine of his part is "to find the right path for himself and others."

> Finally, Bessie's action is "to stop the argument," for she has to deal practically with the whole complex of the household's problems. The actions come to a climax with Ralph's leaving the table. The "beat" for him is over. His next beat is probably "to brood about his problem"—it is a silent beat: he has no lines. For the others the beat changes too with Myron's line, "This morning the sink was full of ants." (*Collected Works of Harold Clurman*, 48)

With their strong training, the actors knew just what Clurman was looking for as they worked out "moment-to moment adjustments," which he described as variations of the spine that the actor has to play in each sequence. Two or three days were spent on improvisations, which Clurman did not use as extensively as Strasberg had. Indeed, Clurman later came to consider improvisation as "self-serving," tending to distance the actor from his character rather than pull him closer. He was guided by Stanislavsky's caution to Stella: "[I]mprovisations are only good when they are close to the line of physical actions." Clurman believed that the Group had been in error in not indicating clearly to the actors the "correspondence between the line of action in the improvisation and the line in the play." He asked his actors to create small scenes related to but not found in the script that would force them to "watch, to listen, to react in character." By making the actors think, Clurman expected them to find their inner action for themselves. His job was to "prod...with questions and suggestions." The give and take between actors and director was "the dynamic factor in rehearsal" for Clurman.

Clurman and Odets worked closely together during the rehearsal period. Odets wrote several memorable new speeches around scenic elements that Clurman visualized. There was the alarm clock for which Odets penned the touching words for Bessie, "The clock goes and Bessie goes. Only my machinery can't be fixed" (Odets, *Six Plays*, 96). Instead of creating a separate living room and dining room, Boris Aronson designed one large, partially divided space in which all the daily activities of the family happen simultaneously. Jacob gives his rich son Morty a haircut in the living room, which also contains the daybed on which Ralphie sleeps, while Bessie prepares the dining table for their holiday duck. Upstage, through the open door to the grandfather's bedroom, we glimpse a framed picture of the anarchist martyrs, Sacco and Vanzetti, and listen, at times, to the old man's gramophone playing his favorite Caruso rendition of "O Paradiso." Years later, Strasberg liked to quip at Clurman's expense, that the then novice director was "a little unsure about Boris's set." "I felt very annoyed with him," Strasberg continued, "because I thought, 'My God! Boris is handing him something I would have given anything for and if I'd known he was going to do this, I would have directed the play.' Here was Harold, who always spoke of going beyond realism and he didn't at first see the possibilities of what was being handed to him. Fortunately, we went with that set, and it added greatly to the show" (*Reunion*, 552).

Clurman, who had met Aronson through Boleslavsky and critic John Mason Brown at the American Laboratory Theatre, said he had promised himself to have one of the designer's "turbulently dramatic" sets if ever he directed his own production. In turn, Clurman was to be the stage director Aronson worked with the most in his long, distinguished career. In Russia, the young designer had assisted Alexandra Exter, the brilliant abstract artist who pioneered Constructivist sets in collaboration with the iconoclastic director Alexander Tairov. On emigrating to the United States in 1923, Aronson quickly earned recognition for his avant-garde designs for Yiddish theaters, but it would be 40 years before he fully realized his brilliant concepts for such American musicals as *Cabaret*, *Company*, and *Follies*. He was just finding his way on Broadway when he designed *Awake and Sing!* He had admired *Waiting for Lefty* for its agit-prop form, and, on their first meeting, Odets asked him to design *Awake and Sing!* It was a challenge since Aronson knew little about American Jewish life but he did not believe that Odets's essentially realistic script could support an abstract set that would universalize middle-class life. The simultaneous set he designed elevated the action beyond the literal, making possible a moment that Strasberg would later praise as one of the "really great scenes in the theatre." In the middle of the first act Carnovsky's Jacob and Adler's Moe have only a few lines together, but finding themselves alone in the open space, listening to the Caruso recording of "O Paradiso" coming from the old man's bedroom, they seemed to epitomize the human spirit, caught between aspiration and despair. "It was partially accomplished by the setting and the space relationships in which the figures were isolated, lonely, and in shadow," Strasberg said. "It was extraordinary" (*Reunion*, 552).

For Phoebe Brand, it was Clurman's understanding of the play "from A to Z" that gave the production its richness and the actors a sense of professional accomplishment. (*Reunion*, 318) Rehearsals progressed, Clurman recalled, with remarkable efficiency and harmony. Of course, there were problems. They had a desperate time raising funding for the show. Franchot Tone saved the day, answering their appeal with $5,000 wired from Hollywood. Joe Bromberg wanted to leave the cast for a larger role in another show and was told that he couldn't destroy the ensemble. Stella fought what she deemed were Clurman's dictatorial directions, and her brother Luther made Clurman so mad one day that the director threw a chair at him. But, Clurman "loved to fight with the Adlers, brother and sister; he valued contention," Kazan recalled, remembering these exchanges from his vantage point as Clurman's stage manager. "Those tiffs were great fun to watch. After they were over, one never felt that the actor had been cowed into obedience or forced to agree" (*A Life*, 122). When the show had been running for some time, Clurman critiqued his actors: Stella and Sandy were "too subjective," Luther has "no Group technique...does not know how to improvise," Phoebe has "difficulty playing actions," Julie suffers from "unchanneled energy," and Morris displayed "conduct exemplary." Clurman praised good work, but chastised them for lack of discipline and excessive involvement with outside activity, a code phrase for political activism. Yet, in rehearsals Clurman was easygoing almost to the point of disorder and even disrespect, in contrast to the authoritarian, paternalistic Strasberg. Kazan characterized Clurman's rehearsals "like parties, at which he was the guest of honor" (*A Life*, 121).

How would audiences and critics respond to the production that was created within this special inner circle? On opening night the folks in the balcony "went wild," Odets remembered. Although the orchestra was less vociferous, the actors received 15 curtain calls. The critics on the whole welcomed the "genuine talent for drama" that Odets revealed in both *Awake and Sing!* and in *Waiting for Lefty*. What they most admired was the playwright's ability to project characters that had usually been comic or villainous stereotypes into an authentic American Jewish family caught in the upheaval of the Depression and his poetic power to give them fresh colloquial speech that was both true and theatrical. Most critics on March 10, however, faulted Odets for not containing the volcanic life he thrust on the stage within a neat, logical, forward-moving plot. Also troubling was the disjuncture many felt between the first two acts of frenzied family life and the final act with Ralphie's hortatory call to action. There were brickbats thrown from ideologues of the right and the left, but New York audiences, eager for a reflection of themselves and a timely, socially significant message, responded enthusiastically. With *Waiting for Lefty* and *Awake and Sing!*, Clifford Odets became the playwright of the 1930s.

Surprisingly Clurman's direction received mostly perfunctory notice. The fact that the Group's well-known spokesperson was finally staging his first show did not draw much comment. Stark Young, always alert to direction, commended it as "intelligent, full of a stage sense," but needing "greater variety in pitch" (*New Republic*, March 13, 1935). On the other hand, Edith Isaacs in *Theatre Arts Monthly* (April 1935), which also paid more attention to direction than the daily press, thought the staging too busy. "By the time the play is over, "she wrote, "you are worn out, not by the story and its despair, but by the nervousness of the performance."

Clurman's efforts to orchestrate the chaos he found at the heart of the play were more sympathetically reviewed in the left-wing *New Theatre* by former Group member Virginia Farmer. Nevertheless, she, too, found that the "the handling of this harmonic aspect of the play is not always expert" (March 1935). Given Clurman's view that "staging is the surface, direction the core," it is not surprising that for *Awake and Sing!* he left many details to his stage-manager, the ever-handy Gadget Kazan.

As for the Group actors, critics found them "at home inside Odets"; they had "never been so good." Carnovsky's grandfather seemed so perfectly "balanced" and "authentic" that one reviewer thought it "almost an impertinence to praise such a performance" (*NYT*, March 10, 1935; *New Theatre*, March 1935). Luther Adler was universally admired for his complex, tough but moving gambler, considered the best performance of his notable career, and Phoebe Brand's Hennie was voted one of the best performances of the season in competition with those by Elizabeth Bergner, Lynn Fontanne, and Katharine Cornell. Brooks Atkinson in the *New York Times* suggested that the actors "pitch into the play with none of the misgivings they have felt about other scripts, because they and Odets as members of the same company have a shared point of view" (March 10, 1935).

The actors had abandoned all pretense of being conventional "ladies and gentlemen of the stage." In this "folk play" about urban Jewish life in the Bronx, the ensemble headed by five remarkably talented Jewish actors revealed with poetic insight and intensity the lives of ordinary men and women, especially lower middle-class urban ethnics. "Sitting in the Belasco Theatre," wrote the literary critic Alfred Kazin about attending the original production, he felt as if he were "watching my mother and father and uncles and aunts occupying the stage in *Awake and Sing!* by as much right as if they were Hamlet and Lear, I understood at last...Art and truth and hope could yet come together...I had never seen actors on stage and an audience in the theatre come together with such a happy shock" (*Starting Out in the Thirties*, 81–82).

To other Broadway critics, the Bronx Jewish family life so vividly and faithfully animated on the Belasco stage seemed unfamiliar, even exotic. The critics' attempt to confine the actors and the playwright in an ethnic straitjacket was a troubling, recurrent problem. *Awake and Sing!* was a success but not a hit. Odets was struggling to discover whether the Jewish world he wrote about would appeal to Broadway, and, more important, whether that world could be generalized into a poetic metaphor for American *life*. *Paradise Lost*, on which he was then working, was intended to solve this dilemma.

Just as the quickly written, agit-prop *Waiting for Lefty* beat the long-worked-on *Awake and Sing!* into production, *Till the Day I Die*, the anti-Nazi melodrama hastily put together to make a full evening on Broadway with the popular *Waiting for Lefty*, reached the stage before the slow-simmering *Paradise Lost*. Cheryl Crawford was credited in the program with staging *Till the Day I Die*, but few remember her presence or her contributions. She herself claimed she was "elected to direct it…by sort of an eenie-meenie-minie-mo game" (*One Naked Individual*, 71). On opening night Odets played Dr. Benjamin in the accompanying *Waiting for Lefty*, the best and last role in his career as an actor. When *Paradise Lost* opened in December of 1935, it was the fourth show by Odets on Broadway in a year—an extraordinary record for a new playwright.

Clurman came to *Paradise Lost*, his second production, with new confidence as a director and renewed enthusiasm for the Group's endeavor. That he and the Group were creating that theater he had dreamed of was confirmed by the warm reception of the trio of Odets's plays. In addition, his creative understanding was enriched during a five-week trip with Crawford in April–May 1935, to study the theaters of the Soviet Union. Moscow offered them opportunities to experience the productions of Stanislavsky and Meyerhold, with whom they met, and the legacy of the Vakhtangov Theatre. Although they enjoyed these rich theatrical offerings, their main objective was to determine how the Group could profit from this exposure. Clurman noted in his diary of the trip that the Group needed to add to its organic process the innovative formal achievements and creative discipline perfected in the Russian experiments. The main lesson Clurman determined to take from the important Soviet sojourn was "daring to work in our way." (Excerpts of the diary are in *The Collected Works of Harold Clurman*, 6–15.)

Staging *Paradise Lost* would take all the daring Clurman and the Group could muster. This unfinished early work hardly seemed the right one to follow Odets's plays that had stirred audiences and critics. Disappointed at the Group's failure to option what was then called *I Got the Blues*, Odets had started making notes for *Paradise Lost* at Green Mansions in 1933. At a deep psychic level, in the view of Margaret Brenman-Gibson, the play was his response to his feeling of having lost the Group as his artistic home, his "paradise." On a more conscious level, Odets had set out to write a "a richer *Awake and Sing!* that the Group *must* produce." It was to be what he would call a "de-Jewished" play, one that Clurman and Strasberg could not criticize as crude, sentimental "Jewish kitchen drama." He later explained to Strasberg that he had intended *Paradise Lost* as a "better" version of *Awake and Sing!* that he thought the Group would never produce. Although he undertook to revise the play along lines suggested by Clurman, he did not want *Paradise Lost* to follow *Awake and Sing!* His recent acclaim as both Broadway's darling and the playwright of the revolution had not made it easier to solve the problems of the script or to work on *The Silent Partner*, the new labor play. He was going through a period of depression after all the hoopla of his sudden fame. Pressure from the Group for the new play weighed on him as he hid out at the Half Moon Hotel at Coney Island.

Nevertheless, amid political and organizational turmoil, the Group had rejected Maxwell Anderson's *Winterset* and was not sanguine about Nellise Child's *Weep for the Virgins*, which they had undertaken without serious consideration. Their determination to produce *Paradise Lost* became firm when Metro-Goldwyn-Mayer provided $17,000 in backing, probably in an effort to woo a reluctant Odets to Hollywood.

With his second production, Clurman came into his own. His direction, like the playwriting of Odets, was seen as central to the "theatre of the Left," which was now acknowledged by Brooks Atkinson as the main "trend in today's theatre." Clurman described his method and his message shortly after the show opened in articles that revealed his directorial process and offered his interpretation of the many characters and themes in Odets's new parable of the collapse of middle-class illusions and dreams. (See *New Theatre*; *Theatre Arts*, April 1935)

The Gordon family is at the heart of *Paradise Lost*: Leo (Morris Carnovsky), Clara (Stella Adler), and their children—the athletic hero Ben (Walter Coy), the ailing stock broker Julie (Sanford Meisner), and the pianist Pearl (Joan Madison). Around them is an extended family of relatives and neighbors along with assorted workers, politicians, and street people played by: Gus (Roman Bohnen), whose daughter Libby (Blanche Gladstone) marries Ben (Walter Coy); Kewpie (Elia Kazan), Ben's tough friend who steals Libby and destroys Ben; Sam Katz (Luther Adler), the artistic Leo's neurotic business partner, and his browbeaten wife Bertha (Frieda Altman), who share the Gordon's two-family house. It is out of the interplay of these many characters, rather than conventional plotting, that Leo Gordon finally salvages hope for humanity from the harsh pain of bankruptcy, eviction, and death caused by the Depression.

Following the Strasberg approach that Clurman had adapted to his personal needs in rehearsing *Awake and Sing!*, he began with his intuitive response to the script. Letting the play work on him before he worked on the play—advice he later gave to all directors—he hit upon a metaphor for *Paradise Lost*: "[A] crystal ball revolving in space, with various refracted lights and shadows revolving about it." This image, he realized, captured the "fundamental activity" of the play, which was restless, shifting, and vague. "Every character...was seeking for reality, for something to depend upon, without being sure what that reality, that substance, was: that each person portrayed was, in fact, slightly crazy." But the crazy world of Odets's characters seemed to Clurman to be "the world we live in—or to be more exact the middle-class world of our daily experience." In contrast with the "impressive sanity" of the people of the Soviet Union, where he had visited earlier in June, the people in New York struck him as "a bit mad," inconsistent, suffering from "an inner chaos" (*FY*, 166).

Like Lewis Corey, who diagnosed the "split personality" that resulted from *The Crisis of the Middle Class*, Clurman realized that only the middle class lived in a world "where nothing is altogether real." The upper class operated in the real world to protect its interests while the struggles of the working class were unavoidably in contact with a harsh reality. For the middle class, living between the two with the "illusion of complete freedom," he believed, real life "enters upon the scene like a fierce, unexplained intruder." From this personal interpretation, which Clurman recognized as a strongly social, class-conscious reading capable of being attacked for having a "propagandistic slant," he planned what he called the "production quality"—the setting, the style or spirit of each character, and the business of the play. Analyzing his "intuition" and "reflection," Clurman set in motion the process that would help him "translate the script's words into the language of the stage."

In the first rehearsals, Clurman urged the actors to open themselves to the play. He explained that the style of the production was to be that of Vakhtangov's "fantastic realism." The casual entrance into the seemingly realistic scene of the weird pyromaniac Mr. May, who comes to make a deal to burn down the business of Katz and Gordon as a way of saving them from bankruptcy, illustrated what he had in mind. Bobby Lewis caught the style perfectly, playing Mr. May with wild red hair, a stiff collar, a menacing black finger-guard, a strange Scandinavian accent, and a "Mephistophelian gleam."

Like the Russian masters he admired, Clurman moved from his interpretation to motivation, business, dress, and make-up that created a subtext of directorial comment that he said was "distinct from, though compatible with, the play's lines." For each of the characters he found behavior and imagery that would emphasize his sense of the "contradiction—the craziness" of this middle-class world. For example, he saw Leo Gordon, the artistic father, in a more humorous light than he seems in the text. Indeed, the picture Clurman painted of the liberal, sympathetic, but inept and passive Leo, seems a self-portrait. He pictured Leo as very aware and eager to do good, "but being typically middle class he does not know how." He is "embarrassed and clumsy" and even tipsy with wine when he has to deal with the details of real life. His movements are aimless, incomplete, but become stronger and more direct as he is forced to confront the loss of his children and his business, his whole bourgeois world. A physical change at the end suggests, as Clurman put it, that Leo Gordon "may become an integrated person," when he speaks the final words: "There is more to life than this!...the past was a dream. But this is real!...Everywhere now men are rising from their sleep...and *no man fights alone!*" (Odets, *Six Plays*, 229–30).

Readings and discussion of each of the characters, for whom Clurman offered similar analysis, along with dissection of the beats or actions in the complex pattern of this almost plotless play, were followed by improvisations. Clurman had Kazan, who played Kewpie, the street-kid turned gangster, improvise playing ball during his boyhood in such a way as to show that he was not intrinsically bad but a victim of his impoverished background. It was central to Clurman's interpretation that "the chief motivation or spine for each character must be conceived and stated from the character's own viewpoint"; at the same time, the character's "spine must be conceived as emerging from the play's main action." Thus, in addition to character improvisations, the whole cast would run through the action of the play several times using their own rather the author's dialogue. Without being aware of it, playing the action would lead the actors to say the author's words.

In the six-week rehearsal period, the longest ever for Clurman, the more they worked, the more touched and engaged they were. Even more than *Awake and Sing!*, *Paradise Lost* seemed to be about the members and the spirit of the Group. When Odets began the script in December 1933, he listed a Group actor opposite each of the characters he was envisioning and wrote out a spine for each one in the approved Group manner. The casting followed some of the author's early creative notions, although there were problems. Odets had visualized Carnovsky as the artistic, impractical, but liberal Gordon and Stella as his pragmatic but devoted wife Clara even before he had settled on the final names for these characters. Both actors fought the casting. Odets himself worried that using them in these roles would make the production seem like *Awake and Sing!* revisited. Carnovsky wanted to play the nostalgic Gus Michaels, but the role was given to Bud Bohnen, and Stella refused to be cast yet again as a Jewish housewife. Clurman appreciated her fears of being typecast in what was to her an uncongenial image, but insisted such notions should not prevail in the Group, where the actor's versatility was valued. (*FY*, 165–66)

Despite her anxieties, Stella liked to stress how different Clara Gordon was from the padded, aging Bessie Berger. Her Clara was very up-to-date. "She went shopping, went to Saks, smoked cigarettes...was completely assimilated into the American scene. She went to high school; the children are artists or in stock companies; they don't work in the factory. They own a big house" (*Reunion*, 511). In addition to being of a higher social class, Clara and her family represented for Stella both the middle-class aspiration and artistic temperament of the Group. She felt that from the first moments of the play when the daughter Pearl, frustrated in art and love, strikes out in anger, Odets had captured "the position of every young artist in the Group Theatre." Stella believed all the contradictions of their middle-class world were dramatized in the Gordons' living room—lots of people and heated arguments

> between intellectuals, socialism, communism, liberalism, all the political aspects of a society which was stranded economically...in another corner, people were playing chess, quietly thinking...in another they were playing quartets or four-handed Beethoven...in the center of this somebody was constantly serving tea, have a piece of fruit, which meant, have something...what one can give you to keep you in this paradise, which was breaking in front of his eyes.

To this abundant life, she believed that Odets brought "his growing political understanding," which provided the "great hope" that the Group artists could not live without. For her, one of the most powerful moments was the quiet opening of Act III, when Clara comforts her dying son Julie, played by Sandy Meisner, by retelling in her housewifely way the story of Moses, the Ten Commandments, and the Golden Calf—a parable of their own lives. Adler felt in herself this mother's anguish for her dying child and the moral force of the family and traditional values that were unfortunately being discarded with the rest of the furnishings of the bourgeois world. The truthful enactment of this warmth, love, compassion, and hope in the face of adversity strengthened Stella as it did most of the company.

For Kazan, playing his first major part as Kewpie, there was personal release. The audience loved him and the critics praised him, but the performance was more than acting a role. Like Kewpie, Kazan felt himself an outsider, from a Turkish Greek family, with an angry, intimidating face that did not fit into the New England world of Williams College where he had waited on tables during his student years. Like Kewpie, Kazan could have said, "I'm sore on my whole damn life." Clurman recalled that when he described Kewpie's background to Kazan, he "struck something very vital" and tears came to the actor's eyes. In playing the role with the "complete emotional openness" learned in Strasberg's classes, Kazan later recalled, he acted out all the complex feelings of "hurt" and "humiliation" he had concealed in life. He was even able to cry as required by his role as he never had in his own life. "I was offering the world everything I'd always masked, feelings I'd stored up for years and not let anyone know existed…Now I decided to enjoy being what I truly was, even if that proved to be a son of a bitch" (*A Life*, 148–49).

In this introverted, emotionally charged atmosphere, it was not until the final days of rehearsal that Clurman began to worry over the possible audience reaction to the play. They went through the usual desperate, Broadway attempts to inject the play with greater audience appeal—speed it up, brighten it, make it clearer. Clurman knew that some of his directing inspirations had not worked out. He had tried to give a somewhat tragic interpretation to the "comic explosiveness" of the character of Mr. Katz, who, as the business partner of the artistic Leo Gordon, was driven mad. As a small capitalist he is unloved, looked down upon, rendered impotent just doing what must be done to keep the business going. Clurman pushed Luther Adler to take his cue for the character from a strikingly, grim self-portrait of the painter Paul Gauguin. The result was rather crude exaggeration, unusual for this very good actor. Clurman blamed himself for this mistake.

Clurman also blamed himself for the failure of the stage set to provide an environment that would support and communicate the larger symbolism of his interpretation. He confessed that because of his own inexperience he had not given Boris Aronson instructions that would result in a set that "would create immediately the sense that this is a play about real people, but a poetic and symbolic rather than a literal play." Clurman explained that the characters were "fumbling about in an environment they didn't control or understand"; the Depression overcast their lives with a "dreamlike unclarity" (*FY*, 166). He told Boris that the play wasn't about Jews necessarily, but about the middle class. But Boris considered *Paradise Lost* another version of *Awake and Sing!*—which, indeed, it was—only he found that now the people "were in some sort of disguise." Aronson found the play difficult to design because he did not see in the text the abstract or symbolic qualities Clurman wanted. He also believed that Odets had sacrificed his own authentic voice in an effort to be "modern." (*New Theatre*, January 1936; see also Rich and Aronson, 56)

The problem with the set for *Paradise Lost* was only one manifestation of the show's larger problem of style and meaning. A defensive preopening letter comparing himself and Chekhov that Odets sent to the critics raised a critical storm about dramatic form and about the critics' responsibility in reviewing a challenging but imperfect work. Nothing very insightful was said about the staging, which Strasberg, by the way, thought Clurman's best. Brooks Atkinson noted the challenge of the uneven script for the director, concluding that Clurman had "not succeeded in orchestrating the script in every scene." John Gassner, identifying the method of the play as that of "realistic symbolism," on the other hand, felt that the Group's collective acting under Clurman's "sensitive and forceful direction" did realize the abounding life of the play. The general sense of most of the critics on December 10, however, was that the actors, many of whom had been so good in

Awake and Sing!, were right for their parts, but could not rise above the awkwardness of the script.

The disparity between the actors' experience working on the play and its critical and audience reception led Odets and the company to conduct an extraordinary public relations campaign. Appeals for support were sent to over a hundred celebrities from Eleanor Roosevelt and Albert Einstein to Mayor La Guardia and Harpo Marx. The show survived for nine weeks. It was during this difficult time that Odets succumbed to the Hollywood temptation; he needed to earn money for himself and the company and rescue his tarnished reputation.

Almost two years passed before the next Clurman production. Clifford Odets's *Golden Boy* in 1937 would be the Group's greatest success and Clurman's most famous Odets production. Between *Paradise Lost* and *Golden Boy* traumatic changes occurred. Clurman became managing director in an effort to hold the company together as internal tensions, financial pressures, and scarcity of plays kept it on the verge of collapse. Despite the disarray in his professional and personal life that followed the failure of his direction of *Paradise Lost*, Clurman made a start as director of *Johnny Johnson* before turning the show over to Strasberg. (*FY*, 187) After much pressure on Odets to finish *The Silent Partner*, Clurman, despite his misgivings, cast and started rehearsing the still incomplete labor drama. Surviving rehearsal notes reveal Clurman's struggle to help the confused actors ignite the creative spark—a character detail out of Nadezhda Krupskaya's book on Lenin, a scene that should be played like a Group meeting with "great excitement, action, and bickering." Despite many suggestions from the cast, the company concluded the play should not be done at that time. They had other things in mind. The Actors' Committee was drawing up its devastating critique of their leaders. Crawford and Strasberg resigned early in 1937. Odets, Clurman, and a number of others ended up in Hollywood, where Odets married Luise Rainer, the talented but delicate star. When they returned from Los Angeles to produce *Golden Boy* the next fall, it was to a totally reconstituted Group. It had become Harold Clurman's theater.

9. Odets in Clurman's Theater ◦○◦

Harold Clurman initiated an even closer collaboration with Clifford Odets when the Group came to life again in the fall of 1937. His accomplishments as a director were totally tied to the playwright he had nurtured, who, in turn, confessed that he remained with the Group because of his friend's special grasp of his plays, his needs, and his problems. While they were both in Hollywood, Clurman encouraged Odets to develop his idea for a play about a boy who wants to get rich quick as a prizefighter in opposition to his immigrant father's hopes for him as a musician. The fighter's triumph in the brutal boxing ring destroys his humanity, and in the end he destroys himself and the girl he loves. *Golden Boy* would not only dramatize the great American struggle between economic success and spiritual life, but also the immediate, very personal conflict between the lure of Hollywood and the idealism of the Group that Odets and Clurman, along with Elia Kazan and Luther Adler were confronting. Working in concert, they stole time from their studio assignments to confer on the script, determined to make it the first play of a reconstituted Group Theatre.

At the urging of Kazan and Adler, Odets left for New York to complete the first two acts. Upon his own return to New York, Clurman was enthusiastic about the script, believing it Odets's finest dramatic conception. Odets was not so sure; writing it to be the hit the new Group needed, he thought he had sacrificed "subtlety and depth" for plot. No matter, Clurman replied, "I had little time for these aesthetic fine points at the moment. I wanted the play finished and redrafted according to the many suggestions I had in mind. Odets and I held long conferences at which I pointed out the means by which the play's theme could be sharpened and the dramatic structure strengthened." He convinced Odets to change the father from a professional musician to a humble immigrant, and the boxer's brother from a physically defective fellow who sells score cards at the Polo grounds to a fighter for social justice. Odets came up with a nurturing fruit vendor and a union organizer. (*Collected Works*, 982) Director and dramatist had long discussions about interpretation and cuts. So extensive were Clurman's contributions to Odets's plays that his friend Boris Aronson thought he should list himself as coauthor. Odets himself would later say that Clurman understood *Golden Boy* better than he did.

With his sure sense of what the play was about, Clurman insisted on casting Luther Adler as Joe Bonaparte, the young fighter-violinist, rather than Jules Garfield or Elia Kazan, both talented actors who were more obvious choices. Although these two actors fit the type and would both later try the role—without great success—Clurman stuck to his choice. Despite innuendoes that he cast Luther to please Stella, he insisted that Luther was the only one who could carry out his interpretation. As he saw it, the role was not that of a "fighter" but that of an artist or "sensitive" human being caught in a struggle in which we are all involved, whatever our profession or craft. (*FY*, 209) Luther had the right emotional temperament and the necessary histrionic skill to illuminate what really became the Odets-Clurman allegory. Although there were some disagreements about other roles as well, Clurman cast the parts as he envisioned them and most likely as Odets imagined them: Morris Carnovsky playing Joe's gentle, idealistic father; Phoebe Brand as his simple, sexy sister Anna; Jules Garfield as her vulgar taxi-driver husband Siggie; Lee J. Cobb as the philosophical Jewish family friend Carp; Roman Bohnen as the besieged fight promoter Tom Moody; Elia Kazan as the homosexual gangster Eddie Fuseli; Art Smith as Joe's caring trainer Tokio; Bobby Lewis as the crude side-kick Roxy Gottlieb; and Frances Farmer as Lorna Moon, the tough "broad" loved by Moody and Joe. Small parts were played by talented newcomers brought in mainly by Kazan. For these young actors—Michael Gordon, Martin Ritt, Howard Da Silva, and Karl Malden—the production was an inspirational beginning.

At the first rehearsal of *Golden Boy*, Ritt, who took Luther to various gyms to learn to box, remembered his amazement when Clurman told the large cast that the Group was the greatest acting company in the world. "I looked around to see if anybody was smiling. Nobody was, so I guess he meant it." Looking back from years as a successful Hollywood and television director, Ritt still thought that *Golden Boy* was the "best acted play I've ever seen in my life" (a similar quote appears in W. Smith, 320). Under Clurman's benign tutelage, the carefully selected core of Group actors, most veterans of the 1935–36 Odets triumphs as well as the original Strasberg-trained ensemble, was ready to realize whatever acting challenges Odets had prepared for them. Resisting outside pressure from potential backers, the anger of disappointed actors who suddenly found themselves out of the company, and even suggestions from Odets, Clurman insisted on drawing the ensemble from their trained and experienced inner circle, with the exception of Frances Farmer, the young Hollywood star brought in to play the female lead. Kazan, then very close to both Clurman and Odets, believed that Odets not only had these Group actors in mind as he wrote the play, but that "Clifford was casting the play as he wrote it; into each part he put what he thought of the person he wanted to play it" (Kazan, 161). An interesting comment in light of the fact that Odets himself chose Kazan for Eddie Fuseli, providing him with a sketch of the gangster that emphasized the character's desire to dominate, his furtiveness, and his loneliness. Odets even had his graphologist analyze the handwriting of the actors to give him tips about their personality. (*A Life*, 161) The fit of actors to roles seemed near perfect.

Clurman remembered the rehearsals of *Golden Boy* as "long, intense, hard-driven. I had great energy due to my sense of do or die." He worried about how people would react to Odets's return from Hollywood; no backers had been found; the life of his theater was at stake. (*FY*, 210) Clurman spent the first two weeks of the five-week rehearsal period in talks and readings. "The actors were alarmed by the hours I spent talking about the play, but they were relieved to find when they began to act that my talks had been productive of a certain freedom and sureness in their work," he confessed. They had done much more than just review the text again and again. Clurman had served them his "banquet of ideas" about the importance of the task they were undertaking, about the play, how he saw their roles in it, and even what he called the "color" or the "flesh" covering the spine of each part. (Gassner, *Producing the Play*, quoted in *Collected Works*, 43)

"To win the fight of life" was the spine Clurman determined for *Golden Boy*. (*On Directing*, 76) In opting for the fist rather than the fiddle, Joe Bonaparte makes a choice destructive to others and especially to himself as he "becomes a commodity," but he does it in a "somewhat adolescent manner." Clurman saw his occasional "poetic" speeches as an effort to express "gropingly like a kid...what he feels but does not altogether comprehend" as the allegorical fight-racket turns him into a killer of others and of himself. Papa Bonaparte, "a lusty, smiling, immovably moral person in love with the world in its humblest aspects," chooses as his spine "to preserve the integrity of those around him." Despite her tough manner and her street smarts, Lorna Moon, too, is moved by the need "to help others." Siggie's spine is "to enjoy the attributes of comfort and position due his estate"; for him this means trying to get a new taxi cab. Joe's devoted trainer, Tokio, who speaks little and quietly, wants "to work honestly." To Kazan, Clurman suggested that his gangster Fuseli's spine is "to possess," to be a predator whose activity is "to hunt for possessions." "That is what I played," remembered Kazan, "circling the young fighter I wanted 'a piece of' like a hawk, then 'stooping' to pick him up. I couldn't take my eyes off Luther; he was what I craved" (*A Life*, 163–64). But the manner of this gangster is "poised and polished," Clurman cautioned, a "sort of 'Renaissance prince,'" well dressed, with "the faint hint of the homosexual in his masculinity" (*On Directing*, 36–37).

Max Gorelik's set made the boxing ring the unifying metaphor of the play. "It was," he explained, "as if each scene were set up in a prize ring, as if a gong rang for the start and finish of each scene, as if the actors came toward each other from opposite corners each time" (Gorelik in Gassner, 318). Using a diamond-shaped floor plan rather than a square one, he increased this sense of tension in each scene. Gorelik made his very spare, small sets suggest specific environments for the many scenes of the play—warm wood for the Bonaparte family home; a bench and section of stone wall for Joe and Lorna's tryst in Central Park; and stark, harsh brightness for the fight locales. Each scene, however, was rolled out on a platform that recalled the fight ring. Friends warned Odets that the absence of realistic detail would ruin the show, but Gorelik's design accentuated the abstract, larger idea while allowing the actors to live fully in a specific locale. (Gorelik in Gassner; also see W. Smith, 320–21) Gorelik, recently returned from his year in Europe on a Guggenheim Fellowship, was once again the Group's designer. Given to arguing with directors over contracts, money, and politics, he nevertheless loved working in the Group's organic way, where his sharp observations were considered creative stimulation and his innovative ideas were valued.

In the same integrated way, during the long sessions around the table, "the actors were wooed, prodded or inspired by the director," Clurman explained. "They became ever more imbued with the sense of themselves as characters in the play and of the play itself." Transformed, even while still clinging to scripts, the actors "sprang to their feet...accosted one another, pleading or threatening, warning or soothing, teasing or provoking—in other words, *acting*." The actual blocking, according to Clurman, took only five days. As they continued to rehearse, Clurman recalled that "a concentrated glow began to spread over the company which forged ahead, mindless of all the darker aspects of the theatre's situation." He rehearsed at the Belasco all day and then at night he explored script problems with Odets. They were tinkering with it until the end of rehearsals.

Encountering his usual third-act problems, Odets suddenly decided in the final week of rehearsals that the last act had to be rewritten; it didn't follow logically from the first two acts, he insisted. One notion he wanted to try when they were almost in dress rehearsals was that instead of lashing out at Lorna for turning down Joe, the gangster Fuseli would take out his gun, ready to shoot her. Clurman went wild, according to the Brenman-Gibson Odets biography. "That's all wrong! You can't change it now! That's not what you meant at all!" he screamed.

> Finally, as in an epileptic convulsion, he fell upon the floor, rocking, rolling, screaming, and in his misery, pounding the floor with fists and feet. The cast, thinking their director was truly in a fit of epilepsy, or psychotic, looked on aghast. No one moved until Odets said quietly, "All right we'll do it the way it is." Clurman arose with dignity and continued the rehearsal.

Sandy Meisner, witnessing this explosion, concluded, "I wouldn't be in any other business" (Brenman-Gibson, 482).

Everyone experienced the exhilaration of working on the show. Even the newcomers playing very small parts received Clurman's full creative attention. Karl Malden, making his New York professional debut as the manager of the fighter Joe Bonaparte kills in the ring, remembered that Clurman's talks would make you "ready to tear the walls down." Before he said his first line, Clurman conferred with him privately about the emotional moment he had to play as he came on stage to accuse Joe, "You murdered my boy!" He began by reminding Malden of the long bus trip he had taken to come to New York from Chicago, and then invented a vivid drama about an accident on the bus in the dark of night. He described how Malden lost his belongings, how he helped passengers out of the rubble as the fire engines and ambulances rushed by, how amid the hysteria, he heard that someone had been killed. Taken off by another bus, Malden, settling into the same seat he had had earlier, suddenly realized that the man who sat next to him was the man who had died. "That's the moment I want. That realization is what I want—not a completely hysterical kind of thing that would normally be done. No, I want that moment when you just look over ... and you say, 'He's dead. You killed him.'" Malden never forgot Clurman's power. "It was the greatest piece of direction I think I've ever had" (quote from *Golden Boy* in *Six Plays*, 314. Karl Malden tells this story in a documentary by Alan Kaplan and Thomas Klein, "Harold Clurman: A Life of Theatre," broadcast on PBS, July 3, 1989).

Others felt freed, for the moment at least, from Hollywood mediocrity, which they, like Clurman, recognized as the "inner theme" of the play, "its true subject matter." Lee J. Cobb, playing Mr. Carp, realized that "it became, for all of us, back from Hollywood, a time to take a unifying second breath." Kazan spoke of it as "the high point" in his experience as a performer. It was a new Group, "a company of equals," he called it, freed of "Strasberg's paternalism" and the immigrant family model he represented. Kazan spoke of himself as the "vigilante of the production team," the one who kept after Odets, propelled the sometimes lethargic Clurman into action, and introduced the younger actors he knew from the Theatre of Action, a workers' theater founded by Gorelik, as more suitable for the cast than some of the Group's old-timers. (*A Life*, 164) Could it have been Kazan who put up the sign on Clurman's door reading, "Nobody's in the Group Theatre except the cast of *Golden Boy*" (*Reunion*, 525). This unfeeling rejection of some of the founding members was an especially painful blow to Margaret Barker, who never worked with the Group again.

Clurman and Odets were terrified that, despite the Group's intense feelings about *Golden Boy*, this production, like *Paradise Lost*, would fail at the box office and with the critics. But the show fascinated the audiences as it had the actors. Clurman, who never attended his opening nights—he had gone to see a Federal Theatre Project production of Lawson's *Processional*—was told that the opening night "proved a swank affair. The Group was almost fashionable now; a long line of big cars drew up to the Belasco Theatre and handsomely outfitted ladies and gentlemen emerged to make a noisy, coughing, generally rude, first-night audience" (*FY*, 210). Among them were Crawford and Strasberg; it was the first play he saw after resigning from the Group. "I didn't know whether to like what I was going to see or dislike it, or to be sad or anything like that," he said in later years.

> Was it worth it? I was now out of it. Was it worth whatever I spent or whatever it was that I did?...I came away with the feeling that if I had the same thing to do over again, knowing that I would leave, I would do the same thing because what I saw on the stage was worth it...It was beautiful, and for me a very strange and moving experience...the characterization that Luther Adler did in *Golden Boy* was based on the characterization we did in *Success Story*. So a lot of things were already worked out, and the people had learned to use themselves. (*Reunion*, 546)

The critics were far more welcoming than the Clurman-Odets team had expected. The feeling about Odets was that "it's good to have him back where he belongs." Their praise brought patrons to the box office, filling the Group's coffers enough to keep the company going for two seasons. When mentioned at all by the critics, the direction was dubbed "consummate," "perfection." What received the most comment and praise, however, was the "heart-breakingly real and moving" characters and the "superlative performance given by the group of actors," for which, of course, Clurman deserved much of the credit, although the critics did not always say so. Fully realizing Clurman's expectations, Luther Adler showed the cockiness of youth, plus the moodiness, tension, and temperament of the pugilist who is on the climb; he seemed "to be Joe Bonaparte, not to play him." Luther felt in himself the ambivalence his close friend Odets had articulated especially in the intimate scenes in the park with Lorna. "I know what the author means there more richly than I do in any other part of the play," he told an interviewer, "and when you thoroughly understand an author's intention, it's far easier and more of a joy playing those scenes" (transcript of interview in Group scrapbook; quoted also in W. Smith, 321). There was good chemistry between Adler and Frances Farmer who, despite her Hollywood background, was "straight-forward and sincere" as the "tramp from Newark" (*Six Plays*, 138). And Carnovsky was simply "perfect." (Reviews, dated November 5,

1937, include *New York Journal American, New York World Telegram, New York Daily News,* and *New York Times.*)

Several critics noted with pleasure the skillful creation of the smaller roles that gave the Odets play "fullness of body and related his story to the life of his times." Joseph Wood Krutch, theater critic for The *Nation,* not given to superlatives, captured what was so moving about the production:

> No one that I know can more powerfully suggest the essential loneliness of men and women...and the powerlessness of any one of them to help the other...His dialogue is brilliantly suggestive, especially when he puts it into the mouths of ignorant or uncultivated people...and he involves the spectator in the agonies of his characters until the palms sweat and one goes out of the theatre tense with an emotion which the author has been unwilling or unable to resolve. (*The American Drama Since 1918,* 272)

The powerful impact of the intimately intertwined text and acting ensemble was created by the Group's unique American style—topical, tense, rough, romantic, sexy, violent, vulnerable, improvisational, tortured, and aspiring; that is, the familiar reality and the subtext of 1930s America transformed into stage poetry.

Krutch was one of the few critics to recognize the underlying political implications of Clurman's production, but was pleased these were "in the background where they belong." Others—and not only those from the left-wing press—faulted what they took to be a Hollywood melodrama for its lack of social significance. Odets seemed to confound the critics, as a writer in the *Sunday Worker* noted with glee. "When he tackles a social theme they lament the limitation of a roaring talent to political prejudices; and when he attempts to penetrate the so-called popular realm, they sigh for the halcyon days of the overt Class Struggle themes." In their final productions, Clurman and Odets felt themselves increasingly caught in these paradoxes.

Golden Boy was a high point and a turning point in the life of the Group and in the relationship of Clurman and Odets. Success allowed them to fulfill some of their many dreams for making the Group a vital center for their lives and that of many other creative people. One of the promising projects was a Group Theatre School set up by Bobby Lewis. They recruited students who paid tuition of a hundred dollars for ten weeks; they gave ten full scholarships and several half scholarships. In addition to acting classes taught by Lewis, Kazan, and others, there was instruction in fencing, movement, and speech. The school only lasted one season, however, because of the company's need to tour. But individual members continued to teach in theaters, schools, and colleges in and around New York City: Bobby Lewis at Sarah Lawrence College, Sandy Meisner at the Neighborhood Playhouse, and Stella Adler at Erwin Piscator's Dramatic Workshop at the New School for Social Research.

The intimate interdependence of Odets and Clurman, however, began to change after their popular success. Although the Group's need for plays had stimulated Odets to turn some of his many ideas into completed works, he now began to resent what he felt was the pressure on him to write plays on the Group's schedule rather than follow his own creative time-table. Moreover, he was now sought after by many others—film studios, newspapers, magazines, and other theaters. He and Luise Rainer were good copy wherever they went, first for their romance and marriage and then for their stormy separation and divorce. It was a heady and troubled time in his personal life, and, in the world around him there was the despair of Republican Spain, the horror of the Nazis's "final solution," and fear of an impending war in Europe. Although Odets gathered material for an anti-Nazi play, it would become increasingly difficult for him as a writer and for the Group as a theater to find those links between the deeply personal and the larger social-political world that had been their special creative accomplishment. Clurman appealed to Odets "as the Best Voice we have in America today... to rouse our sad bewildered, bloody, horror-stricken world." He also needed Odets to help him realize his own "great desire to shape the world in my own way to the realization of what is the truth about the life of our times and all times." As writing plays that answered these large needs became harder and harder for Odets, carrying on the life of the Group became ever more arduous for Clurman.

For all the closeness of these two, there were differences and frustrations as they worked together. Clurman nagged Odets about his defection to Hollywood, where the distractions would inhibit his much-needed playwriting. Odets, though always generous with money and other gifts to the man he called "his favorite character outside of fiction," complained that Clurman was a "schnorrer" who didn't repay debts, was unable to raise money needed by the Group, lacked discipline, was often spacey and frequently lethargic. Even as the company was playing *Golden Boy* to great acclaim in London in the summer of 1938—the production was discussed in Parliament, hailed by the left Unity Theatre, and prepared the way for John Osborne's angry young men—the two men had their first fierce, open fight. Odets had been devastated on his arrival to learn that Luise Rainer was planning to sue for divorce and turned some of his unhappiness and anger against Clurman. He complained to his cronies, Kazan and Luther Adler, "Why does Harold talk, talk talk? Why does Harold raise no money?" He then attacked Clurman directly: "You're lazy. You don't respect your talent... The Group actors don't do anything to make artists of themselves" (*FY*, 227). The shouting match ended with blows and breaking of china in an elegant Mayfair hotel suite. Things would never again be the same.

Rocket to the Moon opened a year after *Golden Boy*, again at the Belasco. On their way back from London Clurman had urged Odets to write "the dentist play" on which he'd been making notes since the early days of his marriage at the beginning of 1937. Clurman was not sure that the story of a nonaggressive dentist who falls for a rather silly secretary would be exciting, but needing a play for the new season, he had encouraged Odets by saying that it could be "infinitely tender and humbly truthful." Odets was so dispirited about his separation from his wife and the general world situation that he was not able to complete the script, as promised, for a reading in Chicago where the Group was on tour with *Golden Boy*. When he did catch up with the cast in Detroit, he had only completed two acts. The company was deeply impressed by the three central characters: Ben Stark, the dentist; Mr. Prince, his father-in-law; and Cleo Singer, the young girl for whom the two men compete. Clurman was concerned, however, that the drama had shifted from the original focus on the loneliness of the disappointed dentist to the aspirations of the romantic young girl who now embodied the play's theme—"the difficult quest for love in the modern world" (*FY*, 234). He hoped that the third act would make clear where the play was going and what it really was about.

When Odets showed up in Boston for the start of rehearsals, while the company continued its tour of *Golden Boy*, he still had not completed a third act, and the first act ran over an hour. Clurman and Kazan went to work cutting the script in preparation for their first rehearsal. Although Odets agreed to the cuts, he felt assaulted by the speed with which they were made. Clurman, in turn, believed Odets would have to adjust his creative process to the exigencies of the production.

Clurman energized the company with his usual talk about the text, heralding the script as "the first love play the Group has ever done, but more extraordinary is the fact that it is the first love play by a modern playwright." In a spiral notebook Clurman had been jotting down his responses to the script since September. Years later in his book *On Directing* (1972), he published part of these detailed notes on *Rocket to the Moon*, the only Group production included in the book. He found it important to write out in detail how the meaning of the play would be theatrically "embodied," a process followed by most of the Group directors. For *Rocket to the Moon*, he imagined a mood of "loneliness" that is both individual and social and proposed as the "spine" for the play "to seek love (search for love)." Unlike most plays where love is "an entertainment—a relief" or "a vicarious sex experience—a peep show," he saw *Rocket to the Moon* in a philosophical, human, and social dimension. (Notebook kept by Harold Clurman during *Rocket to the Moon*, Lincoln Center. See also, "Director's Notes for *Rocket to the Moon*," *On Directing*, 179–88.)

Although much was made by critics and commentators of the play's psychological rather than social or political significance, Clurman identified what he called the Group's "line," namely, that the loneliness propelling the drive for love is "also a social phenomenon" (*On Directing*, 179). The play, as Clurman interpreted it, is about the limitations of love in middle-class life: "Stark's office, his practice, his daily pursuits and habits, his income and his marital life create his need for Cleo or someone like her. These are all part of the play's poignancy." For each character he elaborated a personal history to explain the desperate search for love: Ben Stark, the dentist played by Morris Carnovsky, was imagined as orphaned, emotionally immature; Belle, his wife played by Ruth Nelson, having come from an unhappy family and having lost a child, wants love to provide security and middle-class propriety; Cleo Singer, Stark's sexy young secretary, played by Eleanor Lynn, recruited from Hollywood, disturbs the long sleep of Stark's marriage with her desire for a fulfilling love that will help her become a woman; Mr. Prince, Belle's cynical, but sharp-witted father played by Luther Adler, wants love as a final fling in a frustrated life. The remaining characters in the small cast, played by Art Smith, Leif Erickson, and Sanford Meisner, are also lonely seekers of love. (*On Directing*, 180–88)

In an unpublished segment of his notebook, Clurman analyzed the problems in the script and the revisions necessary to communicate the themes clearly to the audience, who, he insisted, must not be left "puzzled" as they had been about *Paradise Lost*. Clurman's very specific comments range from snap judgments like "these three pages stink" to repeated injunctions to Odets not to be vague, to detail and clarify his meaning. The background as well as the inner life of the characters needed especially to be filled in, he felt, so that the audience would realize that the play is about more than an illicit affair. Only by enriching the parts would the characters acquire universality and general poignancy. The scene between Ben and his father-in-law Prince, Clurman found "too general." The exchange should open Ben up, show his doubts, his questionings; it should be like Iago and Othello. Clurman's comments on the need to clarify the relationship between Ben and Belle Stark are particularly insightful. He was bothered by the scene of Belle's nagging Ben. "As the scene is written we assume she is just a mean bitch, which hasn't much value since the theme is not a triangle but the middle class and love." Perhaps Belle should have another scene in which to reveal more of her character, he suggested. "I believe the author's point of view is not clear here on his material since there is the unconscious assumption that because a woman nags and a man simply wants to get along with his work that she is a pest and wrong. Whereas what has to be studied actually is the concrete situation." He was also troubled by Prince's hackneyed jabs at his dead wife. It may be in character for him to say these things, but Clurman believed that the audience should understand something different from the author and the play. "A general misogynism becomes the basis of all remarks which will provoke superficial laughter but hurts the theme of the play." He concluded that "the whole play is written too emotionally and not materially enough."

Clurman also jotted down notes on the set, what he called "the physical environment" that were meant to convey a "sexiness" that "must express the basic loneliness." He wanted the set to "suggest a kind of mystery." "Always the feeling of night, of secrecy, a hidden place, an enclosure, 'mysterious' sounds: the gurgle of water from the cooler, the hum of the electric fan, rain" (*On Directing*, 179). His instructions to Max Gorelik, again designing a Group show, must have been very close to this description. Gorelik recalled that "Harold had no visual sense...he was so vague...He said: 'I want it warm, and enveloping like a womb. You know what I mean?'" Gorelik responded with one of his famous quips. "Yes. I've been in one once but I never took any notes" (quoted in Group Theatre (American Masters) documentary, PBS, 1987; also cited in Fletcher, 156). What did guide him in designing *Rocket to the Moon* was his sense that "Odets...likes to start with a piece of reality and then leap at the cosmos. My problem as a stage designer...consists in expressing this movement in the play." Gorelik did this by letting the background of his sparsely furnished set seem to disappear into the darkness created by black velvet drapes while thrusting the actors forward into the space of the curved apron of the stage. He believed that combining such unrealistic use of the space with realistic doors and a few set pieces would suggest a drama larger than the constricted life of the dentist seen on the stage.

Through most of the rehearsal period, Odets struggled to resolve his third-act problems. He did not provide the cast with the last act until ten days before the opening and kept rewriting even after the show opened. He couldn't make up his mind how he wanted to conclude a play that not only reflected the terrifying ups and downs of his own marriage but had come to symbolize his deeply personal struggle for artistic and personal liberation. Agitated and depressed about his creative vacillation and also about financing the show—he, Luther Adler, and Luther's wife Sylvia Sidney put up most of the money—Odets believed that the production would fail. He was not satisfied with the form of the play or the shape of the production, and he dreaded the critical attack he was sure would follow. On opening night he was down in the basement toilet of the Belasco throwing up. His cry against the ensuing mixed reviews of both his work and that of the Group was an hysterical but not inaccurate assessment: "I'm *not* a genius. I can't write like a genius. With these reviews, they're driving me out of the theatre. Whatever I do is not good enough for them. They want me to write a masterpiece!" (quoted in Brenman-Gibson, 539).

Many critics believed that they were watching something close to a masterpiece—at least for the first act. "Ferociously alive; a play torn out of the quivering fabric of life" (Brooks Atkinson, NYT, December 4, 1938). The eminent Joseph Wood Krutch, writing that the show "makes the best of the other new plays now current on Broadway seem pallid indeed," analyzed its unique qualities:

> Not one of the personages is a story-book cliché; not one of the situations seems other than freshly imagined; and Mr. Odets exhibits, among other things, two gifts not often combined—the gift for a kind of literal realism which makes his characters recognizable fragments of reality. (*The Nation*, December 3, 1938)

The importance of the director and the actors in achieving these rich, contradictory, and piercing human qualities was, as usual, only briefly acknowledged. In tribute to their accomplishments, Brooks Atkinson recognized that "in its eighth season the Group Theatre has become our leading art theatre by sheer persistence and hard-won ability. If Mr. Odets is its greatest asset, the Group Theatre is just as valuable to him. It knows what he is writing about and believes in it" (*NYT*, December 6, 1938).

In this production the emotional identification of actor and role took on new meaning. If, in the earlier plays, art had imitated the Group life, now personal life was imitating art. The reserved, genteel Carnovsky had fallen in love with his diminutive leading lady, Eleanor Lynn, causing great anguish to Phoebe Brand, with whom he had been living for many years. But, as in their stage roles, according to Odets's version of the scandal, Lynn realized that Carnovsky "was not strong enough to see it through." The pains of love were there for others as well. Ruth Nelson was performing with her ex-husband William Challee; Leif Ericson was acting in a play by the man with whom his wife Frances Farmer had fallen in love. And, the very special love between the director and the playwright was being put to the severest test.

The high praise found in almost every review was accompanied by ubiquitous negative criticism to which Odets and Clurman reacted strongly. Some critics chastised Odets as a social writer who had settled for frivolous subject matter; most judged the dramatic structure seriously flawed and the meaning confused. Odets went on the attack, offering a social defense of his decision to write about love: "The roots of love and the meaning of it in the present world need surely to be comprehended as much as the effect of a strike on its activists." Clurman, in turn, lashed out at the "new time-table school of criticism" that faulted the play for being too long and unresolved. (*FY*, 235) After the opening Odets cut the original last scene. He had tried to resolve the drama by introducing a new character, a contented salesman whose eagerness to race home to his wife was meant to "demonstrate that love is possible." Odets wrote to the critics, begging them to see the revised show.

Nevertheless, inserting cuts and even redirecting scenes did not diminish a deeper frustration that troubled Odets and others in the company as well. They believed that Clurman's staging had not done the play justice. Odets restaged a scene in Act II that he felt Clurman had not "directed with sufficient point." He was unhappy with the casting of Eleanor Lynn, whose small, delicate physique Odets thought undercut the final strong scenes, and he even questioned Clurman's early advice to add a second scene for the wife. (*FY*, 235–36) Early in the planning of *Rocket to the Moon* he had complained that "Clurman was full of ideas as to what my play was about," and expressed a desire to direct the play himself. In an interview two years before his death, Odets recalled the painful ambivalence in the relationship of the two men.

> When I started to work as a playwright, I wouldn't even know the theme of my plays. I knew that *Rocket to the Moon* was going to take place in a dentist's office and that there was going to be a little dental secretary there, a little nurse who was going to take him over, take him away from his wife. But I didn't know what that play would be, so to speak, about love in America, about the search for love, and all the things it turned out to be about.
>
> [Clurman] finally got to think I was kind of like a cow who dropped a calf and didn't know anything about it. Because this is what happened in the Group Theatre, and I was very resentful of it. I dropped this calf and some people would rush up and grab it, wipe it off and take it away, and I would be left there bellowing. And while they were hustling this calf around, you'd think I had no relationship to it. I let them, too. I would let them do it but with a great deal of resentment. I never would have let any private producer do anything of this sort. (Quoted in Brenman-Gibson, 515)

During the rehearsals of *Rocket to the Moon*, Odets was in a dreadful state—"lonely, confused, wrathful, repressed, nervous, tense and unhappy." With so many things going awry in his life—his failed marriage, his rejection of the trash Hollywood wanted him to work on, his writing blocks, and his despair over the brutal *Kristallnacht* attack on German Jews—what had been fruitful collaboration now seemed to him appropriation of his creative work. The full force of Odets's growing dissatisfaction with Clurman as a director was not directly discharged until just over a year later when *Night Music*, their final collaboration, was a painful failure.

The period between the production of *Rocket to the Moon* and *Night Music*, from November 1938 to February 1940, won the Group great approbation at the very time the members seemed to be losing heart. The company was very busy with two full-length shows and several experimental projects running on Broadway. They introduced the work of Irwin Shaw and William Saroyan, staged a second Robert Ardrey drama, successfully revived *Awake and Sing!*, and even made a start on their first classic, Chekhov's *The Three Sisters*. They held their largest, most elaborate, most comfortable summer retreat at Smithtown on Long Island. Bobby Lewis directed his first Group show, and Kazan polished his skills with two more productions. Broadway saluted the Group as having "won its battle on Broadway very much on the original terms laid down on its grim-visaged manifesto when the Depression was first taking permanent hold in the country. Founded on an acting company, able, persistent and wisely managed, it is the foremost acting theatre in this country."

What outsiders did not see was that in the course of achieving this victory the Group Theatre was falling apart. Severe internal dissension, lack of appropriate plays, ongoing financial disaster, and the dark clouds of fascism and world war were destroying the dreams announced at the beginning of the Depression decade. The mood was anything but celebratory. Their conflicted feelings about the oncoming war in Europe were closely matched by their conflicted feelings about the oncoming season for the Group. Agitated discussions during their summer retreat at Smithtown in 1939 revealed their situation in the theater to be as uncertain as the world around them.

Yet, in this tumultuous summer they tried to realize a long-held dream—a production of *The Three Sisters*. In Clurman's interpretation, the play was about the lot of the Group Theatre. Its small-town atmosphere seemed very American to him, and he found a "real thesis" applicable to the people and the place in the summer of 1939. His three sisters were not languid, depressed Slavs, but "full-bodied, energetic…wonderful, healthy people whose health and fullness is not given a full opportunity to expand in the world in which they live" (original source not found; quoted by W. Smith, 383). Clurman felt he had grasped the torch that Chekhov had lit. The central image that he hoped to develop in concrete theatrical form was embodied in his phrase, "The three sisters are the light that shines in the darkness" (quoted in W. Smith, 385). The spine for the play was their own—"to find a full life in a world that has no opportunity" (383). From this "delicate" but "strong" play, the Group could take heart and learn "to accept life," to "understand and not merely to preach." Performing Chekov's drama of youth would be "an exercise in spiritual and technical achievement."

It was not to be. The company was acting out of desperation. They had once again rejected as inappropriate to the times Odets's labor saga, *The Silent Partner*, and Irwin Shaw's *The Golden Years* was turned down as not ready for rehearsal. It was not a propitious moment for their first classic play, despite an excellent cast and a new acting version by Odets. Clurman, who asked Stella to codirect with him, confessed that his work "became halting, indecisive." He thought perhaps the play was too delicate for his "rather violent approach," and he felt a general "loss of heart due to a foreboding about the future" (*FY*, 257). Hitler and Stalin had signed a nonaggression pact and shortly England and France declared war on Germany. But, it was Clurman's inability to control a war between Stella and Carnovsky over the acting style appropriate for Chekhov that destroyed the promise of *The Three Sisters*.

Then, too, the members were losing the unified will to keep going. Some succumbed to what Odets called "the incubus of success"; others were tempted, confused, or simply exhausted in the effort to keep their Group alive in the hostile Broadway environment. As the head of the theater, Clurman felt with great pain what he called the "falling off of aspirational force," and desperately tried to revive the old Group passion while putting its operations on a sounder commercial footing. Odets, on whose plays everything seemed to depend, was going through his own personal and professional crisis and demanded a larger general role for himself in recreating the Group.

Thus, beneath the generally cordial atmosphere that prevailed during the development and staging of Odets's *Night Music*, there was a strong sense that these were
"last days," as Clurman put it. Odets worked on his "Two Monkeys" play (an early
title for *Night Music*) in Mexico, where he was hiding out during a long separation
from his wife and recuperating from a serious automobile accident. He considered
this new project "unlike anything he had done before," and was determined "not
to be rushed" and not to give Clurman an "incomplete script" that he could "spoil"
with his revisions. Clurman jocularly agreed "to spoil plays only by directing them."
Initially very enthusiastic that this would be a "smash hit... movie sale and all... yet
interesting, moving, a good play," Odets became increasingly frustrated that he could
not shape what he called his "gently serious, essentially plotless play" to express all
that he had in mind. Like his hero he was "sore as hell"—at Hollywood, which turns
artists into trained monkeys, at the war that had started in Europe, at the failure
of his marriage, at narrow, petty, middle-class lives, at unemployment and poverty.
But Odets, eager to cure himself, wanted his fable to show that "anger must bear
children," that is, be used in a positive way to create real, meaningful American life.
By the fall, he was again under pressure; the company needed the play for the current season since Robert Ardrey's *Thunder Rock* had quickly closed and Irwin Shaw's
The Golden Years had been turned down by Clurman. Unhappy to be once more
writing a play "tailored to the urgent production needs of the Group," he, nevertheless, increased his nocturnal labors on the script, but was not confident about his
accomplishment. And, it didn't help his self-esteem that Clurman could not raise
the backing for a new Odets play. Reluctantly, Odets had to commit himself to write
the screenplay of *Night Music* in return for a substantial investment in the Broadway
production and contributed the remaining financing himself.

Odets and Clurman bickered about which Broadway theater should house the
show. Clurman thought the intimate Lyceum would be right for a play that he
considered "like a conversation," but Odets rejected the older theater for the newer,
larger, more fashionable Broadhurst, where he had told them to charge the very high
price $4.40 for opening-night tickets. (*FY*, 263) He was aiming for a hit. They also
had differences over casting the female lead—and no wonder. Eleanor Lynn was at
first given the role of the heroine Fay Tucker, which resembled her very successful
Cleo Singer in *Rocket to the Moon*, but about a week into rehearsals, Odets decided
she was "way off type" (*Time Is Ripe*, 6). He and Clurman abruptly fired her, telling
her someone more womanly, more mature, was needed. Around the Group office,
however, the boys put Lynn's problem more directly: "No tits." Odets, still eager to
"dejewish" his work, also preferred a "shiksa" for the part. He had given Clurman
money to scour the Hollywood studios for a starlet. They tried to negotiate for
Margaret Sullavan, who was eager but tied up at her studio. Clurman suggested
Sylvia Sidney; she was wrapped up in her new baby and family life with husband
Luther Adler. Odets headed off what he suspected would be a hint from Carnovsky
that they try Phoebe Brand, who turned down one of the lesser parts in irritation at what was going on. Finally, they hit on blond, cool Jane Wyatt, the Nordic
type Odets confessed he always "went for." The male leads—the volatile, angry,
frustrated Steve Takis, and the protective guardian angel of young lovers, detective
Abraham Lincoln Rosenberg—were written for and promised to Elia Kazan and

Morris Carnovsky. The many minor, colorful New York types were played by established Group actors—Meisner, Bohnen, Nelson, Smith, Coy—and recent additions, among them Virginia Stevens, Harry Bratsburg (later Morgan), Lou Polan, David Opatoshu, Fred Stewart, Bert Conway, Nick Conte, Philip Loeb, Katherine Allen (pseudonym of Pearl Adler, niece of Stella), Florence Odets (sister of Clifford), and Bette Grayson, who was to become Odets's second wife and mother of his two children. Gorelik's sets were planned to capture in a highly theatrical and entertaining way the fractured world of the play, and Hanns Eisler, the distinguished refugée composer, would be writing incidental music to cover transitions between the many episodes and scenic shifts. With this "ideal" cast and excellent creative team, plus a script the director and the company all liked, they started rehearsals in good form.

From his first reading of *Night Music*, a musical fable about the New York misadventures of a young fellow sent from a Hollywood studio to bring back two trained monkeys for a film, Clurman had noted most of all the "constant sense of impermanence and insecurity in the people and in the town." He was struck by the fact that the characters seem to have no other possessions except those they "carry in their little suitcases."

Clurman's initial impressions were borne out in his close analysis of the topical play. In style, he considered *Night Music* an "ambling lyric improvisation." Odets himself called it "a song cycle on a given theme," which Clurman identified as "homelessness." (*FY*, 261) Young Steve Takis's adventure takes him through the "brilliant and dismal circus" of New York City. The opening scene finds him at the police station, where his frisky monkeys have landed him, penniless and in trouble. There his life is gradually transformed by the avuncular detective and the sweet young actress, who falls in love with him. The three of them move from the stage door of a theater on closing night to the seedy Hotel Algiers with its troubled transients, to Central Park, a restaurant, the great World's Fair, and the airport in their search for some place to belong—a home. Its entertaining form conveyed a serious, topical meaning—the frightening stasis or "stagnation" before the impending war. "Everyone seemed to be waiting," Clurman wrote. "Everything was in question, and all the old answers rang a little false beside the darkening reality. The tone of the play was gentle and melancholy, as if the clarinet the play's hero tooted was his only weapon to combat the featureless chaos of 1940" (*FY*, 262).

Steve Takis, whom Clurman saw as an "angry Pierrot, tender and quarrelsome, immature and profound," was a comic version of the Odets hero and also typical of all who are "struggling, loving, aspiring" (*FY*, 261). The production aimed to go beyond the poetic realism of the earlier Odets plays to a more total theatrical realization of the bittersweet, rather absurdist mood of the script. Gorelik designed comic projections—cartoon figures on a musical staff—to be thrown on the curtain during transitions from one New York City locale to another, accompanied by Hanns Eisler's modernist music. The sets themselves were "vignettes on small platforms" against a backdrop done in phosphorescent paint to appear as if projected in neon light.

Although Clurman later wondered if he could be accused of "putting my own words into Mr. Odets's mouth," he felt he was accurately translating Odets's message into effective stage terms. "Everything proceeded smoothly and Odets seemed extraordinarily pleased with every aspect of our work" (*FY*, 262). Kazan, playing the lead, confirmed that "everything was harmonious" during rehearsals. The three enjoyed the best food and wines together and would relax "in self-satisfaction with our Boch panatellas" (*A Life*, 182–83). Even the usual chore of cutting a half hour from the script went off well. The only serious difference Clurman recalled having with Odets concerned Kazan's playing of "Suitcase Steve." Clurman was trying to tone down what he felt to be "raucous, complaining, unsympathetic" qualities in the character, but Odets insisted that the "element of cockiness and sharp impertinence" was essential. The audience, he believed, ought to "dislike the boy during the whole first act," a mistake, he would later confess, since the usual theatergoer wants someone to root for. (*FY*, 262–63) During their grim out-of-town opening in a Boston snowstorm, Odets began to complain that Clurman "was not doing enough to improve the production." Clurman, on the other hand, refused to follow Odets's remedy to make further cuts, fearing to destroy the fragile dramatic structure. By the time of the New York opening on February 22, 1940, Clurman recalled that Odets said: "Harold, I think this is the best play and the finest production in New York." To which Clurman quipped in reply, "Yes, that's what worries me" (*FY*, 263).

Had Clurman known what Odets was really thinking, he would have been devastated. Odets's Journal for 1940, published as *The Time Is Ripe* in 1988, covers the rehearsal period of *Night Music*, revealing Odets's agitated assessment of his friend's direction almost from the beginning. It is fascinating to follow the trajectory of his volatile responses. Once they had settled the casting of the female lead, Odets's initial reaction to the early rehearsals when Clurman was still discussing the script, was positive. "The whole shape of the play is already there, for the script is an easy-playing one—it almost mounts itself. What actors need, from what I can see, are a few more playwrights like Odets and directors like Clurman" (*The Time Is Ripe*, 10). As Clurman started to put the show on "its feet," Odets described him as "still indecisive and shaky about actual physical staging, but as splendid as ever about explaining the character's psychology to the actor." Although Clurman's vaunted patience and the warm festive atmosphere of his rehearsals relaxed the players and freed their creativity, Odets saw them also as ploys by which Clurman made a virtue of his weakness as a director. By the middle of the rehearsal period, Odets found the rehearsals "dull," but remained "boldly unobtrusive," anxious, yet "timid about stepping on the toes of the director or actors" (*The Time Is Ripe*, 16).

Odets and Clurman had such an intense, symbiotic relationship that they had difficulty confronting each another in a critical way. In his Journal Odets confessed, "Harold C and I never face each other when I have to criticize some of his work." Struggling together over the years in the maelstrom of the Group life involved a great deal more for these two than just getting the show up. "Writing a play," Odets believed, "is the only way I can explain and interpret myself to myself." He needed Clurman's keen, sensitive, analytic mind because, as he put it, "when he discusses, interprets, or directs a play of mine," he "abstracts my painful experience for me." In the Journal, he explained, "this constant uncovering of the self is one of the prime impulses in the creative mechanism, it and the constant effort to relate the self to persons...outside of the self." The "search for reality," which he called "the common activity of all my characters," was his personal activity as well.

On this search, Clurman was the ideal creative companion for Odets. Despite Odets's complaints that "Harold's character" had made the company "bungle" not only *Night Music* and also *Rocket to the Moon*, Odets was still able to understand and appreciate Clurman's "genius." It was what he called "the Russian temperament" as found especially in the characters of Dostoyevsky.

> They are men of moods, not of action; they are deeply intuitive, "irrational"...they bathe in their impressions, they stammer...and yet their inner climate is one of intense spirituality and truthfulness; they are mostly completely the opposite of the average American male—inefficient, inept, clumsy, never impatient of results, never "complete," trusting an inner "instinct"...lacking clarity...general instead of concrete...in short, the Russian soul!!! (*The Time Is Ripe*, 41–42)

This was an insightful description of Clurman, who couldn't open a can or boil an egg or talk into the right side of the telephone, let alone run an office or negotiate the chicanery of show business; yet, his head and spirit scaled the heights. Odets saw himself in Clurman, saying, "I share...some of these 'faults'" (42). In taking Clurman to task, he was excoriating himself. Even his assessment of Clurman's directing process could easily apply to Odets's playwriting. "He is able...to set a whole microcosm spinning, but is unable, after that, to control any of its actions" (*The Time Is Ripe*, 42).

When the predominantly negative reviews of *Night Music* appeared, the only counter-attack the Group mounted was a literary one. Clurman published his interpretation of the play in the *New York Times*, and Odets penned a satirical sketch for the *World Telegram* about "morose Mr. Morgan, the critic." In his Journal, Odets wrote bitterly,

> So, friend, this is the American theatre, before, now and in the future. This is where you live and this is what it is—this is the nature of the beast. Here is how the work and delight and pain of many months end up in one single night. This is murder, to be exact, the murder of loveliness, of talent, of aspiration, of sincerity, the brutal imperception and indifference to one of the few projects which promised to keep the theatre alive. (*The Time Is Ripe*, 49)

When *Night Music* closed after 22 performances, a few of those murderous critics wrote columns recognizing that the departure of *Night Music* marked the failure of American theater where the baby is often thrown out with the bath water.

If Odets and Clurman had been able to get past the critical brickbats, they might have taken heart from a few reviews that recognized *Night Music* as part of a new point of view and a new style for the new decade. Rosamond Gilder, writing in *Theatre Arts*, described how the sets and music combine with staging to make the very real Group actors seem—just for a moment—"like marionettes not yet brought into the action by the hand of the invisible puppeteer." She identified Clurman's directorial innovation as the wedding of the Group's "technique of detailed and introspective performance, so admirably tuned to Mr. Odets' style" to innovative "pictorial stylization" (*Theatre Arts*, April 1946; quoted in Weales, 139).

Clurman, however, had to deal with something even more painful than critical and popular rejection—an attack by Odets. The destructive reviews would finally precipitate the explosive release of those feelings Odets had been confiding to his Journal about Clurman's directing, Kazan's acting, even Gorelik's sets. After the opening, Odets wrote:

> The pain of the past week has been a double one for me. On one side are the reviews and the really irresponsible men who wrote them; and on the other side is my profound dissatisfaction with Harold's direction of the play and the general condition of the Group at present. Harold must lessen the gap between his first-rate critical perceptions and the production intentions with a play of mine, and what he finally produces on the stage. There is something positively weird and understandable about his inability to work into a production the brilliant ideas with which he starts rehearsals. (*The Time Is Ripe*, 50)

According to his notes, it took Odets several weeks to bring himself to tell Clurman off. (He does not record Clurman's reaction.) For his part, Clurman recalled that he never did respond directly to what he claimed were Odets's repeated attacks on him. That was not his way. Odets's "refined analysis," as Clurman dubbed what he considered the recurrent onslaught against him, left him disoriented. "I had very little idea of what I had done or failed to do. I simply felt a dull ache" (*FY*, 266). He knew he would not direct Odets's next play. Indeed, he never directed a play by Odets again. Being analytical, he sought to understand the "deep-seated disorder" that had brought them to this very sad end. What he came up with was a characteristic Clurman social-psychological interpretation. The problem, as he saw it, was "the desire for this-and-that" that afflicted the whole Group, but was particularly evident in Odets, its most famous member. "He wanted to be the great revolutionary playwright of our day and the white-haired boy of Broadway. He wanted the devotion of the man in the cellar and the congratulations of the boys at '21.' He wanted the praise of the philosophers and the votes of *Variety's* box-score" (*FY*, 266).

There was even more to the Odets's quandary than the contradictions Clurman's insight contained, perceptive as it was. "Even the discerning Clurman," wrote Margaret Brenman-Gibson, "did not comprehend the complexities of the profound characterological and creative struggle within him." Odets believed that Clurman's view of him was "as honest as it can be from one man's point of view." Each man seemed to see in the other a reflection of some of his own deep inner struggles. Together they reflected the dilemma of making the kind of theater they wanted at the end of their decade of collective endeavor. (See Brenman-Gibson's extensive analysis of Odets and Clurman)

After anguishing about the tension between his feelings for Clurman and his dedication to his own development as an artist, Odets determined to rid himself of the Group actors, whom he called "minor Parsifals," and by implication of Clurman. (*FY*, 247) Clurman responded with a long letter that assessed the interconnection of Odets and the Group that contained his credo for creative collaboration:

> [T]he Group, for all its faults, had helped create him just as he had helped create it, and that a denial within himself of his past would be injurious to his spirit and thought in the

future...If he wanted to cut himself off from the old Group, it became deeply necessary for him to attach himself to a new one. This was more than a personal matter: it was his all-round human and artistic problem. As man and artist he would grow no more unless he found people, a cause, an idea, or an ideal to which he could now make the gift of his love (that is, his talent) to replace his old enthusiasms, loyalties, fervor. Such men as he could not live and mature alone. Such as he must be forever attached to a body of people and a body of belief greater than themselves. They alone could offer nurture to his spirit, serve as the recipient of his passion, the counterweight of his ego. (*FY*, 275)

Clifford Odets was never to forge another sustaining creative connection for the four additional plays he would write. *Clash by Night* (1941), which was produced out of the Group office by Billy Rose, was directed by Lee Strasberg. *The Big Knife* (1949) was also directed by Strasberg, who was one of the producers along with Odets and Dwight Deere Wiman. Odets directed his last two plays himself—*The Country Girl* (1950) and *The Flowering Peach* (1954). For Clurman, too, there would never again be such an intimate collaboration. Indeed, it is difficult to find a comparable creative relationship in the history of the American theater. Together, the dramatist and the director, supported by the Group ensemble and the Group Idea, constructed unique theater events that linked the individual and the group, the intensely personal and the large social crises of the time.

Odets's parables of American lower-middle-class life were psychic dramas projected from the deep unconscious, as Dr. Brenman-Gibson has amply demonstrated. But they were also self-reflexive in another sense. The Group actors and the Group experience so deeply penetrated his consciousness that, like his intimate personal life, they became raw material for his creative imagination. They were not only colorful content, but also became the form of his drama. Odets not only wrote for the Group acting company, he wrote about them as versions or "masks" of his own "personal gallery." Their individual quirks—even the revelations of their handwriting—brought out something in him just as the characters he created brought out the actors' gifts and collective ideals. Collaboratively, they gave life to a cast of new American characters—urban, ethnic, aspiring, alienated, abrasive, tense, sexy, romantic. Together, they made a special kind of theater poetry out of the shared concerns of their own lives, the loneliness, frustration, and degradation of the Depression years, the conflicts of choice between commercial success and artistic and personal integrity, and the deeply emotional aspiration that only people working together for a common aim can make the world a true home for men and women.

In the difficult birth of five Odets productions, Clurman was the acknowledged "obstetrician" (Odets, *Six Plays*, x). He would never again so fully realize his all-encompassing idea of the director, but Clurman was able to reach out to other writers, directors, and actors, and students of theater with those personal gifts and large ideals that had inspired his staging of the plays of Clifford Odets.

Figure 1 The founding directors of the Group Theatre (left to right), Harold Clurman, Cheryl Crawford, and Lee Strasberg, at Dover Furnace, Connecticut, 1932. Photograph by Ralph Steiner, courtesy of the Steiner Estate. Billy Rose Theatre Division, The New York Public Library for the Performing Arts, Astor, Lenox, and Tilden Foundations.

Figure 2 The Group Theatre Company at an afternoon talk by Harold Clurman, Brookfield Center, Connecticut, summer 1931. Clurman (extreme left) gestures with a stick; Clifford Odets is wearing shorts (lower left with back to the camera); Stella Adler (right) is seated in the rocking chair; Franchot Tone (extreme right) is looking down. Photograph by Ralph Steiner, courtesy of the Steiner Estate. Billy Rose Theatre Division, The New York Public Library for the Performing Arts, Astor, Lenox, and Tilden Foundations.

Figure 3   Clifford Odets's *Waiting for Lefty* on Broadway, 1935, with Elia Kazan with fists clenched (center) in juxtaposition to the three capitalists (right). Photo by Vandamm Studio and used by permission. Billy Rose Theatre Division, The New York Public Library for the Performing Arts, Astor, Lenox, and Tilden Foundations.

Figure 4 Following reorganization in 1937, this group of members met with Morris Carnovsky (seated left) to discuss changes. Next to Carnovsky (left to right), Elia Kazan, Kermit Bloomgarden, Harold Clurman, Roman Bohnen, and Luther Adler. Photo by Alfredo Valente and used by permission. Billy Rose Theatre Division, The New York Public Library for the Performing Arts, Astor, Lenox, and Tilden Foundations.

Figure 5 *Golden Boy* by Clifford Odets, Belasco Theatre, 1937. (Left to right) Phoebe Brand, Morris Carnovsky, Roman Bohnen, and Frances Farmer. Photo by Alfredo Valente and used by permission. Billy Rose Theatre Division, The New York Public Library for the Performing Arts, Astor, Lenox, and Tilden Foundations.

Figure 6 Group Theatre Company, *ca.* 1938. (Left to right, back row) Art Smith, Walter Fried, Sanford Meisner, Ruth Nelson, Lee J. Cobb, Leif Erickson, Roman Bohnen, Morris Carnovsky, and Kermit Bloomgarden. (Middle row of three) Luther Adler, Phoebe Brand, and Harold Clurman. (Front row) Irwin Shaw, Eleanor Lynn, Frances Farmer, Robert Lewis, and Elia Kazan. Photo by Alfredo Valente and used by permission. Billy Rose Theatre Division, The New York Public Library for the Performing Arts, Astor, Lenox, and Tilden Foundations.

Part III   Politics

10. Art That Shoots Bullets ⟡

In his later years Harold Clurman was always distressed when people dismissed the Group as a theater of the left. He would shout in his inimitable way, "Left, right, middle, a lot of meaningless words!" What was important was the Group's determination to address the spiritual as well as physical hunger and dislocation of the Depression. Yet, for the young people of those years, as Clurman acknowledged, "the demands of the spirit...could only be satisfied by action that in some way became social and political." Inevitably, he and most of the others in the Group found themselves in the maelstrom of left-wing theories and activities all during the 1930s. As they tried to clarify what they wanted their theater to be, the left's utopian vision, its Marxist analysis, powerful rhetoric, and disciplined, dedicated activism modified and extended the Group Idea.

But radical politics did not come first—not in time and only occasionally in importance. While others in the 1930s came to art through their social consciousness, the members of the Group, Clurman would later explain, came to social consciousness through their art. Politics per se were hardly mentioned in Clurman's initial 1930–31 talks, but in his April 1931 article in *The Drama* he developed a "first statement of principles" about the nature of theater art that carried political implications, which was not purely aesthetic. He explained that "[t]heatre was a cultural unit," and that in terms of a cultural unit, "America has as yet no Theatre," just some of the separate elements for making a theater. Only where "there is a community of desire, interest and understanding" between artists, audience, and the larger group to which they both belonged could there be a Theater. (essay reproduced in Clurman, *Collected Works*) Initially, he emphasized to the actors spiritual exhortation in the manner of Edward Gordon Craig who believed: "After we reform the art of the theatre, we must remake the life of the theatre" (see *Reunion*, 485). He tried to build among his audience a shared conviction that theater must "grow in relation to society, from significant and authentic life experience." He remained dedicated to the view that true art only grows out of what he called the "subsoil" of the personal, but for him the personal was imbedded in the complex context of the total life experience. In the next few years, as economic upheaval and political activism shook the lives of Clurman and the Group members, the rather theoretical understanding of theater as a public art, a "cultural unit," took on contemporary radical, ideological meaning.

There is no doubt that during the Depression, communist ideas, communist-influenced causes, and even Communist Party membership activated many members of the Group. Not all, by any means. Some members were rather apolitical even as they flowed along with the radical current. A few were even what Sandy Meisner years later called "out and out reactionaries." Meisner himself initially wanted the

Group to be just a "regular theatre," but, like others, became more radical. The theories and strategies these young artists absorbed seemed to cover everything, not only how to fight against the social and economic havoc of the Depression and the rising threat of war and fascism, but also how to make a true theater. Communism offered them a worldview; some felt it was a religion. However defined or distorted and whether accepted totally, partially, or even not at all, the communist ethos of the 1930s was much talked about, intensely felt, and contributed to the special fervor of the Group's life and work.

Fitting theater practice and radical ideas and ideals together often led to divisive day-to-day struggles; every decision could have a political as well as an artistic or financial dimension. Political commitment also caught them in many contradictions. Dedicated above all else to American art, experience, and tradition, they were vulnerable to the accusation of foreign influence and control; comprised mainly of middle-class participants, they were exhorted to stage plays for and about the proletariat; intensely individualistic, they tried to commit themselves to a collective way. But like so many others in the 1930s, the members of the Group endured all the unsettling tensions or tried to work them out because of their profoundly American hope.

The widespread radicalism, or the Movement, as it was called, was part of the positive response many Americans made to the convulsions of the Depression. In the Group, Marx and Stalin were tossed together with Emerson and Whitman in a kind of home-made synthesis. Many of the members confronted the despair of the Depression armed with the hard-to-understand and mostly unread economics of *Das Kapital*, the socialist experiment in distant Russia, and what they considered the best aspects of the individualistic American tradition. Odets's throwaway joke in *Awake and Sing!* captures the spirit of the Group's political mix: "Who's Marx?" sneers the self-satisfied businessman Morty as his idealistic father Jacob lectures him on the virtues of Soviet communism. "An outfielder for the Yanks," quips the sardonic boarder Moe. (*Six Plays*, 73)

Well before the founding of the Group, the three directors and others in the company were predisposed to embrace a radical critique of capitalism. Clurman espoused a mystical humanism that he had learned from his Russian-born father, whom he characterized as "something of a Marxist." Crawford's midwestern childhood dream of becoming a missionary attached itself to the social-religious vision of theater she gained from Professor Samuel Eliot at Smith College before she adopted the religion of the Group. Strasberg learned about Marx and Lenin from his older brother and was exposed to the socialist organizations in their Lower East Side neighborhood. The experienced Franchot Tone had played leads during the late 1920s in the bohemian but radical New Playwright's Theatre whose leaders, Mike Gold, John Howard Lawson, and John Dos Passos, proclaimed a "revolt on Fifty-Second Street." Novices Bobby Lewis and Sandy Meisner had acted in what has been called the "strongest drama of social protest in the nineteen twenties," Maxwell Anderson's *Gods of the Lightning*, about the Sacco and Vanzetti case. In the 1930s these young people accepted the general "left" consensus, which the critic John Gassner described as "the banner under which one fought *against* fascism and Nazism and *for* human decency and social reforms...without the commitment to the overthrow of capitalism and the establishment of a 'dictatorship of the proletariat.'" Believing what has been called the myth of the end of the capitalist world, they admired the remote Soviet experiment as the ideal workers' fatherland of the future and used their casual familiarity with Marxist theory as a rough map for social change.

It was not these abstract ideas so much as the work in their theater that became the truly radicalizing experience for the Group. At Brookfield, their first summer, the members were immediately immersed in what one enthusiastic reviewer of *The House of Connelly* dubbed "artistic communism," a good term for what they were trying to do. They organized themselves as a collective of sorts—no stars, no top billing, no solo curtain calls. Everyone pitched in to help run the operation—from sweeping floors to sending out publicity. Salaries, while not equal —except when there was no money to pay anyone more than a pittance—were nevertheless governed somewhat by the Marxist dictum "From each according to his abilities, to each according to his needs." Phoebe Brand recalled that people with families would get a little more money. Communal living during a number of summers and much shared life during the winters served their economic necessity and their collectivist notions. Most of all, the craft they were learning required disciplined exploration of the relationship of the self to the ensemble and the social circumstances of the text, as well as sacrifice of individual ambitions for the good of the whole. Although Sylvia Feningston, one of the more political members whose boyfriend was a Communist Party functionary, scolded them at Brookfield for not paying more attention to the terrible events in the world outside of their isolated artistic Eden, the fact is that the daily activities—the training, the rehearsals, the classes, the lectures, and even the upbeat ending they tacked on to Paul Green's play—were themselves significant political gestures.

Very quickly, however, the Group discovered the difficulties of adjusting the often competing claims of Broadway and their social idealism. For the Siftons' *1931–*, the company's second play, the ensemble used their craft to demonstrate with powerful immediacy the reality of the Depression they were living though. But this political parable alienated the typical Broadway patron. Only the gallery gods responded positively to their radical fervor. On closing night, according to Clurman, "there was something of a demonstration in the theatre, like the response of a mass meeting to a particularly eloquent speaker" (*FY*, 72). Although critics on the left, in the *Daily Worker*, the *New Masses*, and socialist *New Leader*, some taking note of the Group Theatre for the first time, chastised the authors for not being ideological enough and for not providing an explicit communist resolution, they also found much to praise. This Group production made "a chain of connection with the demonstrations of the Communist workers in the streets." Robert Sisk of the *New Leader* commended the Group for realizing the truly revolutionary principles that had brought them together, namely, that actors were capable of thinking and that plays demonstrating the relationship of the individual and society were the most exciting. The varied and violent reactions in the theater and in the mainstream press made it clear that a redefinition of theater would be necessary if performers, audiences, and critics were to know what to make of a play like *1931–*, one that called on them to "do something," not just sit back to be entertained.

A redefinition of theater was indeed taking place in the early 1930s. It was shaped by the new workers' theaters springing up below Fourteenth Street and in part by the Group working on and off Broadway. A month before *1931–* opened, Hallie Flanagan Davis, director of the Vassar Experimental Theatre and later head of the Federal Theatre Project, was already proclaiming in the pages of the prestigious *Theatre Arts Magazine* that out of the burgeoning workers' troupes "a theatre was being born" (November 1931). It had the potential of becoming what theater had been at "certain great moments of its history, a place where an idea is so ardently enacted that it becomes the belief of actors and audience alike." A kind of poetics of politics was being pieced together by the avowedly communist theaters downtown and the Group uptown. Often working in tandem, they carried out a radical reconsideration of art. It may not have changed the world as intended but it did change what theater meant for the participants and for many who came after.

Just about the time the Group company was being gathered in 1930, the Workers Laboratory Theatre was taking shape in response to the Depression. The actors were mostly amateurs who used crude, didactic shows to convey Communist Party dogma to workers in their union halls or on their neighborhood street corners. Although the Lab's objectives, membership, and style differed sharply from the vaguer social-humanist aesthetic of the professional Group, from the beginning there were links between the two theaters. Two of the more experienced founding members of the Lab, brothers Jack and Hyam Shapiro, had worked with Strasberg at the Chrystie Street Settlement House where they claimed they had been instrumental in making him their director. Al Saxe, who was to direct the Lab's most famous agit-prop production, *Newsboy*, also knew many of the Group actors from whom he picked up techniques to use in classes for the Lab.

While the Group was staging its repertory of formal dramas performed by trained professionals in regular Broadway theaters, the amateurs of the Lab were touring around town, rejecting the luxurious materialist accouterments of Broadway stages and at first turning their backs on the whole heritage of formal Western theater and drama. Mass chants, brief scenes of confrontation, colloquial, stylized talks, jazz rhythms, vaudeville routines, gymnastics, simplified, stock characterizations, and energetic calls to action addressed directly to the audience communicated their Marxist analysis of the inevitable conflict between bosses and workers and the role of the Communist Party in bringing victory to the proletariat.

The Lab members were able to bring life, art, and politics together in a very direct way, especially through the Lab's Shock Troupe, modeled on the Soviet Union's "Blue Blouse" companies that in the 1920s combined indoctrination and entertainment for Russian workers and peasants. Each member was provided with very meager food and lodging; 12 of them lived in a five-room East Side tenement flat with 13 cents a day allotted for each person's food. It was their job to perform wherever and whenever they were needed. In this way the Lab projected unambiguous Communist Party dogma of the so-called Third Period, during which, according to the 1929 Comintern fiat, capitalism would collapse after the 1920s boom. Since life in the United States at the beginning of the Depression seemed to be following the Comintern scenario, the abstract, stylized confrontations the Lab staged between the capitalist with big cigar and fat belly and the exploited workers led by the heroic communists seemed to capture the reality of the day.

They knew what they wanted to say. The problem was how best to do it. It wasn't long before actors, directors, and even party officials became dissatisfied with the rough agit-prop sketches, which, they complained, only required "shouting a few slogans." "There has been much discussion pro and con about form in the workers' theatre. Which is the real revolutionary form? Is it satire, realism, symbolism? Must we laugh in the revolutionary theatre or shall solemnity rule the day?" queried Al Saxe in a preface to *Newsboy* (quoted in Taylor, 52 ff.). Again and again in manifestoes and festivals, they addressed the problem of form, style, entertainment, and art in relation to their message. Searching for answers, the Lab not surprisingly looked to the Group, which was about to open its second season in the fall of 1932. In the *Worker's Theatre* magazine that the Lab had initiated, the Group was hailed as "the only sign of life in the present moribund drama." The Group was "still shy of making any political alignment," but given the failed economy of the nation and its impact on theater, they believed that the Group was "nevertheless being pushed step by step toward political clarification, and toward at least a theoretic acquaintance with Marxism."

As the Depression deepened, the Group did experience an inexorable pull to the left. Many of the members turned to Marxism and the Soviet Union for answers. Of the interest in Russia and Communism, Eunice Stoddard recalled, "Of course, everybody was interested, because this was something new. If you wanted to know about the world, you wanted to know about communism. You didn't necessarily embrace it, but you followed it closely to see what it was doing." Clurman found himself reading more about politics, history, and society and discovered that Strasberg was doing so too. As they gathered at Dover Furnace that summer, Strasberg urged his listeners to pay attention to the world around them, an injunction Odets dutifully noted in his Diary. Among the many visitors who passed through their summer compound were various political activists, and discussion became more heated than ever as unfamiliar words were bandied about—"right deviationist," "Trotskyism," "social fascist," "undistributed middle class."

Increasing social violence moved many of the members from aesthetic communism to active commitment. "If you had lived in those days," Phoebe Brand explained years later, "you would know that almost everybody felt that there was no way out...of the horrible morass the country was in at that time. No way out except socialism." In his Diary Odets recorded his horror at the brutality of Federal troops gunning down the men of the Veteran's Bonus March on July 28, 1932. But he drew a hopeful conclusion from the event. "I soon realized that it was a valuable portent and helps to hasten the day when the people will make a just government" (quoted in Brenman-Gibson, 233). This romantic radical optimism was widely shared even though few, including Odets, had yet to embrace the Communist Party. Everywhere leftists saw signs of imminent revolution: a protest in Union Square or a riot of Midwestern farmers would lead them to cry out, "It's begun."

In this expectant mood the Group looked beyond the inspiring model of Stanislavsky's Moscow Art Theatre to the innovations of his disciples Vakhtangov and Meyerhold, who had made theater serve the revolution and the new Soviet

society. The company listened entranced to Russian-born Mark Schmidt's transla-
tions of recent Soviet theater publications Strasberg had acquired. The often abstruse
essays exhorting the theater to become "an ideologically cemented collective" were
validated for them by the extraordinary accomplishments of Soviet theater. Here
was the relationship of art and society they were dreaming of. Russian communism
"was connected with the idea of the theatre," recalled Kazan, "that it would be a collective thing where art would be supported. And the great art in the theatre at that
time was Russian art. We respected the country, because they produced these plays
and we saw the films they did. They were remarkable" (a version in *A Life*, 105).

The intense political current that shot through the Group's encampment that
summer of 1932 was fed by the plays being rehearsed. Although they were hardly
agit-props, the shows were implicitly political. Dawn Powell's *Big Night* was a bitter,
albeit somewhat comic, attack on the desperate competition for success that drives a
small-time advertising hopeful to offer his wife to a client to sweeten up a lucrative
deal. John Howard Lawson's *Success Story*, which was to open their season, was no
casual entertainment but a sort of Marxist morality drama drawn from Lawson's
own life, which was torn between the art theater in New York and movie commercialism in Hollywood. As the Group waited for him to work out an appropriate ideological ending for the play, they argued heatedly among themselves. A few rejected
Clurman's psychological interpretation in favor of a class analysis. The ideological
tug-of-war within the Group was already under way.

On returning to New York, needy members decided to live communally in the city
in that up-town version of the Lab's even poorer flat on east 12th Street. Many in
the Group had hit bottom. Phoebe Brand remembered that she "didn't have any
money at all . . . I used to walk twenty blocks to get to the theatre and walk back. We
scrounged" (*Reunion*, 514). Odets later claimed he was living on ten cents a day, and
Clurman's father had lost all his money in the crash. In these dire circumstances
about half the company pooled their meager resources to rent a ten-room, cold water
flat far west on 57th Street near the railroad tracks. Three days after leaving Dover
Furnace, Odets complained in his Diary: "The Groupstroy is an apartment for a
dozen of us who have no money and no nothing. We have beds here and food in the
icebox and we are back in New York, I with an empty feeling."

Although it was necessity that threw them together in what Clurman called the
Group's poorhouse, the collective solution was part of the "experiment in living"
that was so important to their "experiment in theatre." It was Meisner, still living at
home in the Bronx with his parents, who dubbed their run-down flat Groupstroy,
wryly identifying it with the heroic effort involved in building the much-talked
about Russian hydroelectric plant, Dnieperstroy. Seven dollars a week from each
person ran their commune. Out of that sum they paid the rent, which was about
50 dollars, hired a cleaning woman, and provided food for everyone. There was no
central heating; the candle coal they burned in the many fireplaces filled the house
with smoke and coal dust. Tony Kraber shared the front room with Alan Baxter
and Philip Robinson; his fiancée Willi Barton, an apprentice at Dover Furnace, was
in a tiny bedroom down the hall; Carnovsky and Philip Barber were in the next
room; further down the hall Strasberg and Paula were together, and Odets had a

tiny room at the back of the flat. Bobby Lewis, Grover Burgess, Lewis Leverett, and Art Smith were part of the curious household. Kazan later found a spot for himself in the flat. (Stella was a block away in her usual, more comfortable surroundings.) Group members who were better off helped out: Beany Barker gave them the checks her father sent her, and Dorothy Patten brought food from her parent's townhouse. The women did the shopping, and they all took turns cooking various specialties. Kazan said he made an Anatolian concoction of bulgar with lambkidney bits and vegetables. He recalled that Paula boiled chicken as requested by Strasberg, who mostly kept to his room reading, "like a man in exile." Odets would appear from his minuscule bedroom to make stuffed cabbage, potato pancakes, or hot chocolate and read them sections from the appropriately named *I Got The Blues*. The others remember him typing day and night, balancing the machine on his lap in his tiny cold room as he labored over what would become *Awake and Sing!*

Kazan thought that "the atmosphere of the apartment was saturated with disappointment," perhaps because he hated group living, and Crawford, who always found their communal housing during the summers difficult, remarked on the "uncomfortable abrasion" of the relationships she found when she came to visit. Others, however, treasured it as a difficult but memorable time. A few were still acting in *Success Story*; others did anything they could to keep the theater going. Kraber, for example, talked to various organizations around the city in an effort to build audiences. "The atmosphere was jollier than one would expect," Clurman remembered. Meisner liked to visit because he found it cheerful in the way that poverty is cheerful for young people. It was romantic to be making it against the odds, an adventure. There were the fun and games and sexual adventures of young artists squeezed together in their decaying flat. The straightlaced morality of the period engendered rumors of free-love and orgies among the wild-eyed radicals. For most of them, however, Groupstroy happily combined economic necessity, collective struggle, communal intimacy, and youthful creativity.

By the beginning of 1933, it looked as if the whole Group Theatre experiment might come to a sudden end. Groupstroy had to be vacated because they could not keep up with their collective rent. In a January 29 *New York Times* piece, Clurman analyzed their dire situation, explaining that the Group Theatre "refuses to strain along lines that do not advance or clarify its aims, but that, on the contrary, impede and falsify them" (see also Clurman, *Collected Works*, 4). Among themselves they discussed just what would "advance or clarify" their aims. Attacking Clurman's dedication to high literary standards, Strasberg urged that instead of waiting for American literary masterpieces to be written for them, they should consider revivals, indeed, anything that would be "good theatre."

But good theater hardly seemed an appropriate aim for the socially minded Group during the worst winter of the Depression. "So deep was the crisis at this time," Clurman was to remember, "that virtually every conscious person was attempting to find some basic answer to society's jitters, and for the moment they were willing to consider any idea that promised a solution, no matter how extreme or unpopular." After all, in the 1932 election campaign that brought Franklin D. Roosevelt to the White House, more than 50 leading artists and intellectuals—among them Sherwood Anderson, John Dos Passos, Waldo Frank, Sidney Hook, Lincoln Steffens, and Edmund Wilson—came out in support of William Z. Foster, the Communist Party candidate for president. In the Group some certainly considered joining the party, and a few may already have done so. The members began to press for a far more radical theater than the directors had anticipated. What *Workers' Theatre* had said about the Group's political tensions at the beginning of the 1932 season seemed to be coming true. The magazine had doubted that the Group could continue to "straddle" Broadway and Marxism.

That is what began to happen. Mary Virginia Farmer, condemning the leadership's failure to put on plays of a "revolutionary nature," put her energies into founding the more radical Theatre Collective along with Max Gorelik and Jack and Hyam Shapiro of the Lab. About the same time the new Theatre Union, a professional company that attracted a working-class audience by charging low-admission and dramatizing proletarian subjects, also attracted various people from the Group—Molly Kazan, Sylvia Feningston, and Clifford Odets. Both companies wanted to combine the Group's professional skills with plays of more explicit political content.

The Group itself, despite the terrible winter they had experienced, had come to life again on Broadway in the fall of 1933 with their first hit, *Men in White*. Although defended by Sidney Kingsley and by Strasberg as "idealistic," *Men in White* was not what many of the members thought their theater ought to be producing. Friends accused the company of giving up the hard tasks of forging a socially conscious theater in favor of making money. What was even more painful, Clurman later wrote, was that while the Group was succeeding with a "play that to our more intimate critics was on the level of a *Saturday Evening Post* story" (*FY*, 129), the newly founded Theatre Union was hitting hard at the inevitable relationship of capitalism and war in *Peace on Earth* and planning a strong statement on the Negro problem in *Stevedore*. But the Group's success on capitalist Broadway had its unexpected consequences. Perhaps bored in a long run, or guilty about earning steady wages, or newly converted to activism, or irritated with their directors' unwillingness to take a stand on the issues of the day, many members rushed downtown to work with the workers' theaters during the run of their hit show.

During the next two years, a kind of symbiotic dance developed between the Group and the various workers' theaters. Group members moved toward political commitment just as the left-wing troupes started testing longer scripts using individual characterization and less dogmatic themes. Each partner offered the other what it needed. From the left came disciplined activism and unity of life and art in accordance with Marxist praxis. From the Group ensemble came professional training for actors and directors, a collective definition of theater art, and a style of organic realism for staging social, even revolutionary dramas. Their lively interaction, it is interesting to point out, began before the Comintern issued its formal directive in 1935 for the workers' theater to exchange ideological agit-props for a mid-decade Popular Front peoples' theater. Thus, when the American Communist Party abandoned its sectarianism to embrace all fighters against the rising tide of war and fascism, the Group and the left theaters were given official sanction to do what they had been doing for some time.

What is most striking is the extent to which the leading members of the Group Theatre, including the three directors, participated in the left theater activities. Some seven or eight gave classes for the Worker's Laboratory Theatre, but teaching the Stanislavsky system as interpreted by Strasberg was more than just a technical exercise. Talks Strasberg gave to the Lab on affective memory "stirred things up" and led to requests for articles by him from Ben Blake, the editor of *Workers' Theatre Magazine,* who believed that the workers theaters had "reached a state of development where this would help them a great deal." Strasberg replied that he would try to find the time to "prepare an article on the subject of affective memory, especially as I am at the moment going over the whole field from the standpoint of dialectic materialism." Just as Stanislavsky's system had been attacked as appropriate only to the world before the 1917 Revolution, Strasberg's method was considered by some on the left as middle-class subjectivism. Molly Kazan, for example, derided the Group's emphasis on individual psychology at a time when an objective, materialistic perspective was needed. But Strasberg himself was obviously eager to bring his method into line with radical thought. In this he may have modeled himself on his idol Vakhtangov, who adapted Stanislavsky's system for the emerging socialist society. Among the Russian theater documents he had translated for the Group was a Marxian analysis of the Stanislavsky system by V. Zakhava, director of the Vakhtangov Theatre. It was quickly printed in *New Theatre Magazine* in a version edited by Molly Kazan, then assisting the magazine's new energetic editor, Herbert Kline.

Many in the Group contributed to this increasingly professional and less sectarian periodical that had grown out of the rough-textured *Workers' Theatre.* Along with Bromberg and Kazan, Strasberg pushed aside the furniture in their editorial offices to teach classes. Luther Adler, enthusiastic about the magazine, offered his business acumen and wit to keep it solvent. Bobby Lewis published a three-part series titled "Five-Finger Exercises for the Actor" based on his classes for the Theatre of Action, as the Workers Laboratory Theatre was newly named. These very practical exercises on concentration, relaxation, and sense memory made the Group's method widely available to the young actors in the several hundred little theater groups on the left. Clurman and Strasberg published articles on acting and directing and about their recent Russian trips. Clurman wrote critiques of the theater season, even commenting on the Group's own productions under the pseudonym Harold Edgar, which he also used in writing theater columns for the *Daily Worker.* Strasberg and Clurman also contributed articles to *Theatre Workshop,* the more theoretical left journal where some of the Russian theater documents that had been translated for the Group were published. From these varied activities came the New Theatre League School, where a staff made up of Group teachers would train hundreds of young people through the end of the decade.

Strasberg's course on directing at the Theatre Collective school had considerable impact. Filmmakers Ralph Steiner and Leo T. Hurwitz discovered a new approach to films when Strasberg showed them how to find the basic idea of a script, realize it through sets and backgrounds, work creatively with actors, and engage audiences emotionally concerning socially important themes. With these techniques they felt they could make films communicating their "revolutionary viewpoint to an increasingly receptive audience." At one of the Group's own business meetings the members pleaded with Strasberg to teach such a course for them, but were reassured that they had heard it all in their own classes.

Participants in the various workers' theaters, especially those in the Theatre of Action, felt themselves "the unofficial children" of the Group, actor/stage manager Perry Bruskin recalled. "We felt it was like our father organization. And a number of our better actors graduated into the Group."

Downtown the Group actors not only spread the word about their method but also had opportunities as teachers and directors they might not have had uptown. The experience of Kazan and Odets is instructive. Kazan had been radicalized the terrible winter of 1932–33. All he could earn was ten dollars a week; when his father's rug business failed, he wrote in his notebook, "I know the source of his sickness. The capitalist system." The summer of 1933 at Green Mansions he spent his mealtimes by himself studying Lenin. "It was a time of doubt and self-questioning for many middle-class intellectuals...To let everyone know where I stood, I wore a 'working-class cap,' with a rabbit's foot tucked under the brim" (*A Life*, 106). He wrote a play about a bread strike. Then he and Art Smith wrote and performed with actors from the cast of *Men in White* an anti-Nazi agit-prop about the Reichstag fire. Kazan frequently spoke from soap-boxes in Harlem and acted skits on street-corners and at union meetings. Proselytizing in this way, he and others would, in his words, "go forth from the Group Theatre like the apostles of Jesus, teaching, instead of brotherly love and the Ten Commandments, the art of Stanislavsky as filtered through Strasberg." His destination was the Theatre of Action, which became, he later wrote, "my personal acting company, and I became, for a time, their hero" (*A Life*, 106–107). Kazan was fascinated by this troupe of intense, street-wise young Jews, as he described them, because "they went all the way with their idea—collective living, collective rule, collective bankroll." The actors, in turn, admired him for his talent and for being "a down-to-earth guy," unlike some others in the Group, who seemed to Al Saxe to have a "holier than thou" attitude. (*A Life*, 107)

With the Theatre of Action, Kazan had a chance to codirect a full-scale production with Al Saxe. Since *The Young Go First*, an attack on the Civilian Conservation Corps, had no complete third act, Kazan guided the actors in group improvisations to flesh out the script. It wasn't hard since the structure followed the left-wing ideological pattern, which Kazan described as "a ritual, as unvarying as the Catholic mass." His job was to make the action come alive.

Down at the Theatre Union in the fall of 1933, Odets, still only playing bit parts in the Group, was being hailed "as the best damn acting teacher that ever lived." Often deeply troubled himself, Odets was drawn to the impoverished, the downtrodden, the abused, the many who had fallen by the way. He and Clurman, who had become his closest friend, a sort of older brother, had wandered the desolate city streets the previous winter, being "strangely attracted to people and places that might be described as hangdog, ratty, and low." They haunted dismal burlesque houses and concocted meals from cafeteria condiments. (See Clurman's version, *FY*, 114–15) For a time Odets satisfied his need to "share his destiny with the lowliest workers, with those who really stood in the midst of life" by working with young actors in the Theatre Union's Studio, which was initiated to improve the rather lackluster acting in their productions. Theatre Union's objectives struck Odets as "more daring than those of the fence-sitting, hair-splitting Group."

Although the Theatre Union leaders did not think much of Odets as an actor and were concerned that his psychologizing Group method might weaken their Marxist orientation, the young actors loved him. For them, Odets tried to be both Strasberg and Clurman. He taught them Strasberg's version of Stanislavsky with care and dedication, but applied it to proletarian material, which the company felt gave it new meaning. Like Clurman, he harangued the actors about a large vision of theater, but one with a definite Marxist twist. Frequently invoking the Communist Manifesto and the Soviet Union, he exhorted the class "to present a Marxian interpretation of our present society in precise theatrical terms." His students were so carried away by his revolutionary analysis that they urged him to leave the Group and become the director of a new permanent acting company. By 1934, however, Odets felt too preoccupied with his playwriting to take up their proposal. (See Brenman-Gibson, 276 ff.)

Busy dickering for a production of *I Got the Blues* and writing away on *Paradise Lost*, Odets was concerned for what he called the "new coming world." Activism and aesthetics came together for him and his cronies with *Waiting for Lefty*, the most famous theatrical realization of 1930s' radicalism. Everyone who was around had a version of how the script was put together and claimed to have some input. *Waiting for Lefty* probably started as a modest project during the disappointing Boston run of *Men in White*, *Success Story*, and the premiere of *Gold Eagle Guy* in the fall of 1934. The company was having a rough time even though the actors were feted by socialites and college professors sponsoring their tour. Odets and others activated by the Marxist imperative to bring down the doomed capitalist economy were drawn to historic Faneuil Hall to hear radical agitators. Here, a fiery labor leader appealed to Odets for a workers' play to take around to union meetings and benefits in the Boston area. Odets called on some of his special cronies in the Group to form a writers' unit dubbed "SKKOB," the last initials of Art Smith, Elia Kazan, Alexander Kirkland, Clifford Odets, and Roman Bohnen. The idea was to work collectively, with each one writing a scene to be fitted into Odets's dramatic framework. He kept at it when the five grew tired of the "trifling" agit-prop piece and went around to the dressing rooms in the basement of Boston's Majestic Theatre asking certain actors to be in the project. "Yes, of course, Clifford, delighted," was Ruth Nelson's response. Odets observed of his writing *Waiting for Lefty* in four days for a Boston benefit that "urgency creates its own art level" (Brenman-Gibson, 303).

Nevertheless, the Boston benefit never came off. In a not unusual ploy to keep radical groups from gathering, the fire department claimed the Boston meeting hall was hazardous, and the hurriedly prepared show was put aside. It was not until the company was back in New York at the end of the year that Odets's "workers' play about a strike," as they called it, was scheduled for a New Theatre Sunday night benefit and premiered on January 6, 1935, at the old Civic Repertory Theatre on 14th Street. Molly Kazan brought the script from Boston to New York to be entered at the last minute in the *New Theatre* magazine's one-act play contest. It was so far superior to anything else submitted that the editor Herbert Kline said it was a "no contest win for Odets." *Waiting for Lefty* was originally scheduled to be sandwiched between an excerpt from Philip Stevenson's *God's in His Heaven* performed by

Theatre Union actors and a group of dances by Anna Sokolow. At the Group actors' insistence, *Waiting for Lefty* was saved for last, a lucky shift that made history.

In writing the 40-minute agit-prop, Odets drew on what he had learned about the violent New York taxi-strike early in 1934. His recent commitment to the Communist Party provided the ideological underpinning. Each of the six brief episodes dramatized evils in contemporary capitalist society—poverty destroying family life and the hopes of young lovers, secret chemical warfare research, anti-Semitism, class bias, commercialized culture, stool pigeons, and corrupt unions. Like the agit-props of the workers' theaters, Odets's mise-en-scène was simple. On stage in a semicircle of chairs sat a committee of angry taxi drivers waiting for their leader Lefty to lead them in a strike vote. With actors planted in their midst, the audience became the waiting rank and file union members. A gunman lolled against the proscenium while the corrupt union boss Harry Fatt, blowing smoke from his cigar, warned the drivers on stage and in the audience not to strike. His ominous presence remained in silhouette as each driver stepped into the spotlight to relive a moment of traumatic transformation. The audience watched the moving vignettes in which the cabbies, a young doctor, scientist, industrialist, a labor spy, and young lovers reenacted the personal crises precipitating the need for strike action. Actors in the audience charged onto the stage to expose a stool pigeon and to shout the terrible words, "They found Lefty—behind the car barns with a bullet in his head."

In the white heat of creation Odets made use of the different kinds of theater he had experienced—from the emotional resonance of the Group's acting methods to the structure of popular minstrel shows that his audience had enjoyed on the vaude-ville subway circuit. Including the audience in the action was something he had tried years earlier when on tour with Mae Desmond's company; it was also widely used in the agit-props. The rhythmic structure of the Lab's very successful *Newsboy*, with its free movement through time and space and juxtaposition of mass action and individual emotion, was probably also in his imagination. And, of course, he drew on the compulsory final call to action of the agit-props. Full of echoes and influences, the show, nevertheless, introduced an original dramatist who could create vibrant characters with a few bold strokes and let them speak in the very fresh, punchy-poetic voice and vision of Clifford Odets.

Waiting for Lefty was more than Odets's personal accomplishment, however; it was also the triumph of collective endeavor by the Group actors. Odets wrote the script and codirected it with his fellow actor, Sandy Meisner. Perhaps his very positive experience directing with the Theatre Union emboldened him, although Meisner remembered that "there didn't seem to be anything special about it" (*Reunion*, 504). Each brief two or three character episode was rehearsed separately in the actors' dressing rooms. The parts were written with the specific actors in mind, and, as Kazan recalled, "over the years, in our acting classes, we'd all done scores of scenes like the ones Clifford had written" (*A Life*, 112). Extending the improvisational process used in Group rehearsals, Odets said he deliberately "left room for the connection between the scenes, collective discussion to decide what the boys wanted to do in the way of production ideas...No, do what you want, boys, change, cut, add. I said to myself—this is SOME thing" (quoted in Brenman-Gibson, 305).

Just as Odets brought to the action of the taxi strike the anguish of some of his personal traumas, especially the psychic combat with his father detailed in Brenman-Gibson's biography, so the other actors also enlarged their performance with personal content. Ruth Nelson, caring, concerned, self-sacrificing, and disappointed at the bits she had mostly played in previous shows, had a chance as Edna, the wife who turns her husband Joe into a militant, to cry out in her deep, moving voice, "My God, Joe—the world is supposed to be for all of us." Julie Garfield, the former juvenile delinquent, brought authentic street sounds and street smarts to the young lover in the Sid and Florie scene, but the role also revealed his sweetness and sincerity. In a scene later deleted from the script, Paula Miller as a secretary in a producer's office was her usual mothering self, nurturing a hungry, unemployed actor with the Communist Manifesto. Bobby Lewis used an intimate emotional memory—being caught in flagrante delicto—to blush deeply in shame and fright when identified as an informer by his own brother. Kazan projected his working-class loyalty as the devoted unionist who exposes his brother as a company spy. In subsequent productions he took over from Joe Bromberg the role of the agitator Agate who gives the red salute, "the good old upper cut to the chin" as he rouses the cast and audience with the final frenzied cries: "HELLO AMERICA. HELLO. WE'RE STORMBIRDS OF THE WORKING-CLASS, WORKERS OF THE WORLD...STRIKE! STRIKE! STRIKE!!!" (*Six Plays of Clifford Odets*, 31).

In every way *Waiting for Lefty* was the actors' show; officially, the Group Theatre and its directors had nothing to do with it. It was what the radicals among them wanted; a theater that spoke of their deepest needs, beliefs, and the issues of the day to receptive audiences. They were as desperately hard up as the taxi drivers they incarnated; minutes of Group meetings reveal that by the last performances of *Gold Eagle Guy* the actors were not even drawing the minimum wage of 32 dollars a week they had set for themselves. Like the strikers, the actors were fighting their leaders, who seemed resigned to closing for the season. Led by Stella, whom Bobby Lewis dubbed their very own La Passionaria, the actors insisted that the Group commit itself to staging at once Odets's *Awake and Sing!* Rehearsing *Waiting for Lefty* the actors felt "relaxed and happy," working on their own without the intimidating presence of Strasberg. His reaction when he saw one of their final rehearsals had merely been a shrug of his shoulders and a confidential, "Let 'em fall and break their necks" (Brenman-Gibson, 313).

But they would not fall or fail. For *Waiting for Lefty*, "[t]he emotions were those in our hearts," recalled Kazan, "anger at what existed, demand for a change, and confidence that the change—you know which—would come... Which is how we felt: that artistic problems could be confronted and solved by group action, by us together" (*A Life*, 113). The audience, responding to these emotions, turned *Waiting for Lefty* into a triumphant celebration. Actors and audiences transformed the danger and despair of the Depression into hope and aspiration. Odets, overcome by the extraordinary reception, dubbed it theater "at its most primitive...its grandest and most meaningful...the audience became the actors on the stage and the actors on the stage the audience, the identification was so at one that you saw for the first time theatre as a cultural force...I forgot I wrote the play, forgot I was in the play...The proscenium arch disappeared" (quoted by Arthur Wagner in Brenman-Gibson, 316).

For Ruth Nelson it was "a night to remember all the days of your life":

> The audience was so with this play...it was the essence of why the Group Theatre was formed...It all came into flower...The audience was so enamored that they played the play with us from scene to scene and moment to moment. The response was extraordinary. I'll never forget we stood on the stage with tears rolling down our face...and...you couldn't believe...that this was happening. And I felt, oh...the balcony's going to come down, because the audience was stomping their feet. They couldn't applaud any more so they stomped their feet...It was an extraordinary night.

The ovation lasted almost 45 minutes. Kazan, remembering and rereading the play for his 1988 memoir, "was thrilled to the verge of tears," even though he had turned "violently anti-Communist." (*A Life*, 115)

Clurman captured the significance of the opening night of *Waiting for Lefty* in these often-quoted words:

> It was the birth cry of the thirties. Our youth had found its voice. It was a call to join the good fight for a greater measure of life in a world free of economic fear, falsehood, and craven servitude to stupidity and greed. "Strike!" was *Lefty*'s lyric message, not alone for a few extra pennies of wages or for shorter hours of work, strike for greater dignity, strike for a bolder humanity, strike for the full stature of man. (*FY*, 148)

Waiting for Lefty was quickly repeated at various theaters as a benefit for "The Group Theatre Sinking Fund for Experimentation." At the Fifth Avenue Theatre, they performed *Waiting for Lefty* for the taxi drivers union on a program with *Dimitroff*. Tony Kraber as the young Lab Assistant was so carried away by his true emotions that in "busting" the Industrialist played by Carnovsky he broke the handsome actor's nose. The text was immediately printed in the February issue of *New Theatre*, which was inundated with requests for copies. Three hundred groups paid royalties in advance. Although there was some carping from doctrinaire left-wingers, Herbert Kline praised the "comrades" of the Group for "breaking ground for revolutionary theatres to follow." No more would Kline have to make up "lame excuses" for the Group; Odets's unique agit-prop was the best example of the power of "theatre as a weapon." The Group could no longer be dubbed the "Grope Theatre," for *Waiting for Lefty* had achieved "absolute audience identification" for its message, Kline wrote in *New Theatre*.

Performed at strikes and meetings as well as on college campuses—it won the George Pierce Baker Cup in New Haven—and became a lively political gesture against the ruling class, which often used its oppressive power against the performers. The play was banned in Boston, with actors arrested there, and in Newark, where along with supportive audience members, they were held without bail. When the Broadway critics finally saw the production, most succumbed to its rousing spirit and theatrical skill, but for them it was just a show by a playwright with "an intuitive sense of stagecraft." "Despite being lumpy with propaganda," the play was admired for being "alive with familiar speech," for its "dramatic force," and "humor." Odets's communism was even commended as the inspiration for his vigorous art. Serving activism and entertainment, the play became one of the most widely played short plays in the country and in the world.

After the opening of *Awake and Sing!* in which the range of Odets's talent and themes were applauded, *Waiting for Lefty* was given an official Group Theatre production. Clurman asked Odets, as the radical playwright of the hour, to write another short play for the evening's program. It took Odets only five days to put together the script of *Till the Day I Die*—another feat of intense creativity. The play filled out the bill, providing parts for those not cast in *Waiting for Lefty* or *Awake and Sing!*

Based on a letter published in *The New Masses*, this anti-Nazi melodrama made a strong, topical statement that was hailed as a potent contribution to the fight against fascism. Only a few other plays about the Nazis had been produced on Broadway, but they had not communicated the horror of their depravity as vividly as Odets. Six months earlier, when Elmer Rice had staged *Judgment Day*, removing the 1933 trial of the revolutionary Dimitroff for the Reichstag fire to a mythic Balkan country, he had found that audiences "pooh-poohed" him as "exaggerated and alarmist." But Odets was heralded as a "thunderbolt" writing "iron fisted and exciting stuff" using "a machine gun instead of a pen." He dramatized the arrest and brutal torture of the sensitive, idealistic violinist Ernst Tausig, a member of the communist underground struggling against the Nazis. Blacklisted by his comrades, including his brother and his sweetheart who fear the Nazis have turned him into an informer, he takes his own life in order not to betray their cause.

Till the Day I Die, like *Waiting for Lefty*, became a staple of the workers' theaters, winning praise from many critics for attacking an important theme and in turn being violently attacked, notably in Hollywood where Will Geer was savagely beaten for directing a production by "Friends of New Germany." On Broadway there were reservations about the show: the treatment lacked subtlety, it was more propaganda than play, it was removed from the writer's experiences. That *Till the Day I Die* was not as successful as *Waiting for Lefty* is not surprising. Calling the play "a hasty job," Odets explained that he had not been able to structure the borrowed materials from articles in *New Masses* and *Fatherland* by Karl Billinger to make as effective a creation as *Waiting for Lefty*.

Yet, the play had many recognizable Odets touches, especially in the occasionally vibrant American colloquialism and in psychological details intended to render the Nazi torturers and the communists underground more complex. Odets's biographer found the play full of the playwright's "unconscious fantasies" about himself, his father, Harold Clurman, Hollywood, and the Group. These personal obsessions hardly helped to make the melodrama seem believably German, but they are interesting in themselves, especially the furtive scenes of the German underground at work, which seem loosely drawn on the model of the American Party Units. The German comrades surreptitiously mineograph leaflets, hold meetings, report on theater-of-action groups, worry about the police and informers, debate what action to take. Odets introduces the name of Overgaard, the functionary who recruited some Group members into the party and who knew all about covert activity. Fear of informers was felt even in the Group circle where some of the stage hands and even one of the actors were suspected of being FBI informants. He includes a touching scene of their wounded leader, "one of our leading theoreticians," just returned a broken man from the detention camp and unable to guide their difficult decision. The character is called Stieglitz (recalling the famous photographer-guru) and was acted by Lee Strasberg (listed as Lee Martin in the program), the only role their leader played with the company.

As the focus of the play shifts from the theme of Nazi brutality to the complicated issues of dedication to the cause and communist discipline, it reflects more directly the tensions of Odets and his Group comrades. The German Communists secretly debate blacklisting Ernst Tausig to protect the other comrades and their "proletarian cause." Against the background of Odets's favorite Mozart and Beethoven sonatas, Ernst's brother Carl voices the revolutionary credo: "Is there time for music today? What are we fighting for? I need not answer the question. Yes, it is brother against brother. Many a comrade has found with deep realization that he had no home, no brother—even no mothers or fathers!... There is no brother, no family, no deeper mother than the working class" (*Six Plays by Clifford Odets*, 146). But unlike his source in *New Masses*, Odets does not allow Carl to shoot his brother for the cause. Rather the brutally tortured Ernst gains a kind of immortality by taking his own life. The concluding scenes reverberate with Odets's ambivalence about sacrifice of the self for the collective good, the issue that their current success made troubling for him and his Group colleagues.

The actors were carrying out their own version of revolutionary sacrifice as they raced from one theater to another, acting in the three plays of Odets running simultaneously on Broadway. Kazan, for example, stage-managed *Awake and Sing!* at the Belasco and then raced in a cab to the Longacre to play comrade Baum in *Till the Day I Die*, then, as Agate, rouse the audience in the final moment of *Waiting for Lefty*. With the Broadway triumph of radical plays by their own playwright, the Group members had made it in show business at the same time that they were no longer outsiders in the now widely recognized left theater. "They were part of the main current, which to an extent they had helped create," wrote Clurman. People wanted to join the Group Theatre as if they were a cult.

The members were busy off stage as well as on. They gave lectures, classes, and benefit performances. They were in demand everywhere, especially Odets. He churned out two short pieces: *Remember*, about the degradation of public welfare, for the Negro People's Theatre, and *I Can't Sleep* for Carnovsky to perform at a Mecca Temple labor rally, where Odets himself entertained with an improvisation to a Beethoven symphony. The latter, an emotional memory "monodrama," full of Odets's personal ambivalence and guilt, dramatized an alienated, lonely, middle-class Jew who rediscovers his need for solidarity with the poor and dispossessed. Odets also judged play contests, wrote articles on revolutionary theater, and volunteered free advice to rehearsals of "valuable plays." He had become the Golden Boy of the left-wing theater.

Nevertheless, miraculous as 1935 was for the political activism of Odets and the Group, that year marked an end as well as a beginning. Only *Waiting for Lefty*, *Till the Day I Die*, and to a certain extent *Awake and Sing!*, all playing simultaneously, contain more or less explicit political appeals and can be said to satisfy

Odets's own injunction that "new art works should shoot bullets." The plays that immediately followed—*Paradise Lost*, Odets's middle-class tone poem; *Weep for the Virgins*, Nellise Child's neglected woman's play; and *The Case of Clyde Griffiths*, Erwin Piscator's epic version of Dreiser's *An American Tragedy*—did not succeed in rallying audiences or pleasing the critics of either the left or right. The times were changing. The Popular Front program sanctioned by the Comintern in 1935 brought the communists out of their sectarian isolation and into new political alignments with Roosevelt's New Deal. Earl Browder's catchy slogan that "Communism is Twentieth-Century Americanism," while it opened up new possibilities, also weakened the solidarity engendered by the old left ideology and caused confusion. In a similar way, the very successes of the Group also destroyed its ability to project a collective radical voice. Along with the adulation of the left came overnight celebrity, bringing with it entry to the Stork Club, to Hollywood, to the whole American dream that still had a strong hold on the largely middle-class Group egos. The members balanced conflicting values. Traveling to Moscow to a Soviet Theatre Festival was considered in the same breath as going to pick up contracts in Hollywood; driving around in his new Cadillac, Odets was writing his strongest labor play, *The Silent Partner*. The new opportunities forced members to reconsider the fragile unity of life and art they had briefly achieved.

Although the leftward turn in the years up to the end of 1935 had released both individual and collective creative energies, it had also entangled the Group in controversies that were sometimes acrimonious. An estimated three-quarters of the Group were left-wing, yet they had diverse notions about how to realize their vague utopian aspirations in the actual work of the company. It was turning out to be very difficult to agree on how to be politically correct, have the "right line," choose appropriate plays, be effective theatrically, make art, reach Broadway audiences, develop individual careers, adjust the power relationships of actors and the directors, and remain solvent. Among their many thorny problems was the existence of a secret Communist Party Unit in their midst. Publicly revealed in the 1950s House Committee on Un-American Activities hearings, it became the most notorious aspect of the Group Theatre's politics.

11. Pro-Unit Is Pro-Group ❧

On April 10, 1952, Elia Kazan appeared in Executive Session before the House Committee on Un-American Activities. He had come to Washington at his own initiative "to amend the testimony" he had given about three months earlier when first subpoenaed by the Committee. The dignified Black man who had discretely delivered him the "pink slip" ordering him to Washington on January 14, 1952, had confided sotto voce: "This will be a secret session. You don't tell anyone, we don't tell anyone. We expect you to be a cooperative witness" (*A Life*, 443). That Executive Session was not made public, but shortly after, a gossip column in the *Hollywood Reporter* carried a lead story that Kazan had confessed to "Commie membership," but that he had refused to talk about any of his "old pals from the Group Theatre days." That was the position he had intended to take, Kazan recalled in *A Life*, the autobiography in which he revealed his version of these traumatic happenings—from a distance of 35 years.

As his unwillingness to be a "cooperative witness" leaked out, however, Kazan felt "in the clutch of a dilemma" (*A Life*, 449). The Committee had indicated it would recall him, his Hollywood career seemed in jeopardy, his marriage to Molly Day Thacher was on the rocks, and his classic film *A Streetcar Named Desire* had just lost the Academy Award that seemed destined for it. Suddenly, what he described as his long-worn mask as a "progressive sympathizer" fell from his face. After consulting others like Arthur Miller and Lillian Hellman who were also preparing to face HUAC inquisitions, as well as Clifford Odets and Paula Miller Strasberg whom he would have to name, Kazan made what he called his "difficult decision." He asked for an Executive Session of the Committee at which he presented a written statement that spelled it all out. He detailed his own membership in the Communist Party for a year and a half, from 1934 to 1936, the operation of a secret Communist Party Unit in the Group Theatre, its tasks, and its membership: Lewis Leverett, J. Edward Bromberg, Phoebe Brand, Morris Carnovsky, Tony Kraber, Paula Miller, Clifford Odets, and Art Smith. The story released by the Committee, including all the names and other details about the Group Theatre, appeared in the *New York Times* on April 12. On a previous page, in the theater section, appeared a startling two-column advertisement of self-justification placed by Kazan. He claimed that he made known the facts of his communist activities of 16 years ago in order to help America "protect" itself from a "dangerous and alien conspiracy." He issued a call to others: "Secrecy serves the Communists...Liberals must speak out."

With this action Kazan changed his destiny and that of many of his old friends in the Group. He became identified as "the epitome of a betrayer," as Victor Navasky suggests in *Naming Names*, forever shadowed by the image of the informer. Some of his intimate Group collaborators became victims of the vicious blacklist, and what remained of the unique Group spirit was shattered. In addition, the red label was from then on publicly stamped on the whole Group Theatre despite Kazan's own attempted disclaimers. The issue of Communist Party involvement exposed by Kazan became part of the complex legacy of the company, became, for some, a handy tag to attach to the whole Group experience.

Important as the consequences of these hearings and revelations were, they do not provide a very solid basis for understanding radical politics in the Group. There was much more to the story than whether or not a member was willing to answer the famous question—"Are you now or have you ever been a member of the Communist Party?" Yes, there was a Communist Unit in the Group. Kazan's testimony was generally corroborated by Clifford Odets in his 1952 HUAC appearance and also by contemporary documents and later interviews. His list of members was probably accurate as well. And some of the activities he attributed to the Unit were probably carried out by Party members. But just what did the existence and activities of a Party Unit, revealed in the early 1950s during the height of the Korean War, the McCarthy Senate Hearings, and the jailing of Communist Party leaders, mean for the Group in the 1930s during the Depression, the Roosevelt New Deal, and the Popular Front?

Exploring radical activism in the Group is no easy task. In *The Fervent Years* Clurman suggested that the company moved left during the decade of its existence, but he never dealt directly with its heavy involvement in many so-called front groups and with the Communist Party itself. Issued in 1945 at the end of the war, Clurman's manuscript was substantially cut, he said, because of the paper shortage. There is good reason to believe, however, that he also censored his original manuscript, which he claimed later was lost [the deletions are in the Butler Library at Columbia University], because he felt intimidated by the early anticommunist investigations already undertaken by the Tenney Committee in California and the Dies Committee in Washington. Herbert Kline, his close associate in the 1930s as editor of *New Theatre Magazine*, reported that shortly after publication, Clurman invited him to the Russian Tea Room, his home away from his nearby apartment on West 57th Street. According to Kline, Clurman wanted to "apologize" to him for the way he "chickened out about *New Theatre*." Kline quoted Clurman as saying:

> I realize how you must feel about my avoiding mention of the role of the magazine, the New Theatre League, and all of your cooperation with Lee, Cheryl, and myself in the Group Theatre. But my publishers insisted that I should avoid being open to 'red-baiting.' With my consent they cut an entire chapter about you, your brother Mark [Marvin], Molly [Kazan], [Elia] Kazan, and even my participation with Clifford and you in the early *Lefty* days.

Kline went on that Clurman explained "congressional committee terrorizing of writers and theatre and film leftists had frightened him as it had his publishers." The story rings true. In the "Epilogue/ 1945–55" to the 1957 edition of *The Fervent Years*, Clurman acknowledges the "political constriction" that led to a "political hush," without directly connecting the subsequent "cessation of all serious discussion" to the lacunae in his book. (*FY*, 305–306)

That Clurman muted and eliminated references to the Group's radical political and theatrical activity is not surprising. Even in the 1930s, the so-called Red Decade, membership in or close association with the Communist Party carried with it potentially serious hazards; one's job, career, even one's life might be in jeopardy. It was a violent time; striking mill workers in the south confronted the deadly assaults of the National Guard, pickets at Orbach's Department store in New York City were beaten by cops and hired goons, Jews shuddered at the rising tide of native anti-Semitism fostered by demagogues like Father Charles Coughlin, and protesters of all sorts faced nightsticks and jail. Actors who staged *Waiting for Lefty* and *Till the Day I Die* confronted refusal of permits to perform, censorship, arrests, and beatings. Odets dramatized the fatal price of activism in these plays and later in his unproduced union play, *The Silent Partner.*

But the crises of the times called for action. Despite possible danger, becoming a communist became an acceptable activist gesture. It was not enough to write plays that "shoot bullets," one had to take a stand on all the issues of the day. In the workers' theaters many had found the way to link aesthetic experimentation and radical content in productions with personal commitment to struggle for socioeconomic change. To make life and art one, they joined the Communist Party. "Thousands of people went into the Party every year," Harvey Klehr pointed out in *The Heyday of American Communism: The Depression Decade.* It was not hard to do; Party functionaries were always on the scene at the workers' theaters. They were also around the Group urging people to sign up. "The fruits of being socially involved in society had a certain logic which led you eventually to joining a party if you wanted to," Carnovsky explained.

In the fall of 1934 when Odets joined the Party, it certainly seemed like the logical next step—although his pal Clurman cautioned him against such a move. "What does Marx know about playwriting?" he objected. But people were grasping for new ideas. There was lots of talk, Odets later explained, "about amelioration of conditions, about how should one live, what values should one work for," and a "great deal of talk about Marxist values." He joined the Party, as he told HUAC, "in the honest and real belief that this was some way out of the dilemma in which we found ourselves." He identified J. Edward Bromberg as the colleague in the Group who recruited him.

Odets showed off his membership card to select friends, and, of course, he was not alone. Kazan had joined the party in the summer of 1934; he testified that he had been recruited by Tony Kraber, his roommate in the Group, and by Sid Benson, a stage-struck Party organizer who became a close friend of many in the company. In turn Kazan said that he brought Phoebe Brand into the Party. It was usual Party practice to link all those who joined up as a "Unit" in their workplace. For the Group it meant a Unit in their theater. Kazan identified J. Edward Bromberg and Lewis Leverett as the co-leaders, and Morris Carnovsky, Art Smith, and Paula Miller Strasberg as additional members in the Group Theatre's Unit.

The Party Units often carried out their tasks in revolutionary secrecy, a heritage from the early 1920s when the Palmer Raids forced the recently organized Communist Party to go underground. Like other Party "fractions" in noncommunist organizations, the Unit in the Group no doubt tried to keep a low profile. That was surely not easy if they were meeting, as they are reported to have done in the winter of 1935, once a week in Joe Bromberg's dressing room after their performance on the stage of the Belasco Theatre. Despite the intimacy of their life together and the cramped backstage spaces, their meetings seem to have gone mostly unnoticed. Kazan, whose exposure of the Unit at his HUAC testimony in 1952 made its efforts seem conspiratorial, confessed in *A Life*: "I was astonished years later, when I read Cheryl Crawford's account of her life, that she had no suspicion there were weekly meetings of the CP cell in the Belasco Theatre" (Kazan, 121). Although Crawford continued to reiterate her ignorance of the Unit and Clurman did not confront it in the original edition of *The Fervent Years*, others have confirmed some vague knowledge of it. Strasberg probably knew of its existence since his wife Paula was a member and their home the place of some of the Unit's important meetings. Paula said years later that she never told her husband about "assignments" she had from the Unit to influence his decisions in the Group. Such secrecy between them was perhaps not too surprising since Strasberg, his nose in his books, reputedly hardly communicated with his wife at home except to upbraid her. In a 1966 interview with Margaret Brenman-Gibson, Strasberg implied that he and Clurman knew of covert activities but observed that they were not aware of the "amount of Communist Party activity" and the degree to which discussions with Unit members involved "foregone conclusions."

Although it is difficult to document the work of the Unit or to verify with certainty the membership, the range of activity associated with the Unit does emerge. Throughout the decade people in the Group joined the Party and like thousands of others, left it. Stella Adler quipped that one never knew who was in and who was out. "There was a certain amount of dabbling in the matter of joining up" was the way Carnovsky put it. To outsiders they may have been Broadway's theater of the left; among themselves the relationship between Party member and fellow traveler must have been a constantly changing one as it was in many organizations during the 1930s. Being a communist or participating in communist-inspired activities was not the big issue it was to become. There was a kind of continuum that ran from liberals to fellow travelers to Communist Party membership. Although important, the differences among them were not clearly marked. "The lines of leftism, liberalism, in all of their shades and degrees, are constantly crossing like a jangled chord on a piano" was how Odets put it when questioned by HUAC interrogators in 1952. (Quoted in Miller, *Clifford Odets*, 200) The young people felt good about living in a free country where they could say what they liked and join what they wanted to.

The four main tasks of the Communist Unit spelled out by Elia Kazan in his HUAC testimony form a framework for examining both the pervasive activism in the Group and the little that is known of the Party directives. The first objective for the members, Kazan testified, was to "educate" themselves in Marxism and Communist Party doctrine. Classes were the thing in the 1930s—for information, for recruiting, and for indoctrination. That's where one bought those "penny and two-cent and five-cent pamphlets" that led Odets to join the Party. "You read some pamphlets, you listened to someone talk, and finally a person would ask you if you didn't want to join the Communist Party," Odets said. "In my case, it happened:

'No, I don't. When I am ready, I will.' I was not ready that month. I was ready a month or two later." Once in the Party, he confessed he didn't do much studying by himself or with others "because it was a little beyond me, and my interest was going toward writing plays." Bobby Lewis, who contemplated but did not take the big step of joining up, also tried classes on Marxism and dialectical materialism. For him, one was enough; "It was so damn boring." Yet Bobby had many serious discussions with Andrew Overgaard, the Party recruiter, about the Soviet Union, especially about various questions concerning civil liberties that troubled him. He was never satisfied with the official line that bread came before human rights. Had the Party offered better answers to his questions, he said, he too might have joined. (*S&A*, 74)

Education in leftist ideas was nothing new to people in the Group. Carnovsky recalled that Strasberg would push books at the actors, and not just on theater. He would say: "Read this, read that, and become educated in this matter." At Dover Furnace, during the hard summer of 1932, Strasberg brought his brother Arthur to lecture to them on Marxist economics and history. "Get wise" was Strasberg's doctrine. Beany Barker remembered people turning up to translate bits from Karl Marx for the Group; some tired actors fell asleep but others were turned into activists. She herself attended classes as well as meetings at the John Reed Club, the radical cultural organization, and possibly some Unit meetings. Although she confessed that she never became very knowledgeable about Marxism or the Communist Party, she felt that as a member of the middle class she would be "squashed" between the proletariat and the capitalist. For Stella the classes she took in Marxism at the Workers' School early in the 1930s to prepare for her role in the never produced *Man with the Portfolio* informed her thinking the rest of her life. Billy Kirkland went to classes, he said, to find out what it was all about. When he challenged the teachers on tenets like the end justifies the means, he was thrown out.

The second task Kazan listed for those in the Unit was helping the Party gain a "foothold" in the Actors' Equity Association. In theater union strife, as in the widespread labor organizing that marked the decade, it is hard to separate the Party members from other activists. For Tony Kraber, for example, it was the struggle of the actors in Actors' Equity that served to radicalize him. On the other hand, Bobby Lewis, not a Party member, said he "spearheaded" the fight in Equity for the cast of *Sailor, Beware!*, an action that initiated the movement for change in the actors' union. The actors of this hit comedy resisted the decision of the producer to cut wages when attendance fell off slightly in the spring of 1934. They called on Actors' Equity for support against what they believed were unjustified cuts and the firing of actors who led their protest, but their union refused to become involved in their cause. The cast then appealed to fellow actors playing on Broadway. Lewis and other members of the Group's *Men in White* helped them win reinstatement of the fired actors and some restrictions on the producer's freedom to cut salaries. They became part of "the younger element," as the activists in Equity were at first called, determined to force the ruling Council and the longtime president of Equity, Frank Gillmore, to serve the needs of the membership and grant them fuller participation in making the decisions that affected their lives. In angry meetings the militants were attacked as un-American Reds, but in 1935 they organized themselves as an activist caucus, the Actors' Forum, in which Group actors participated. It didn't last long, but as a result of the insurrection, important reforms were made by Equity—providing greater membership participation, rehearsal pay, cut boards, reduced minimum pay differentials between junior and senior actors, and other necessary improvements. The activists revived the spirit of revolt that had originally brought Actors' Equity into being in 1919 as one of the first unions for professionals. (See *S&A*, 74)

Kazan testified before HUAC that the action in Equity was a "tactic" to "gain prestige for individual Communists and sympathizers who hoped the party would then run the union." To be sure, communists were active in the confrontations in Equity, and Andrew Overgaard, one of the Party's trade union experts, gave the actors advice on how to deal with the Equity leaders. An unpublished autobiographical sketch by Overgaard captures the spirit of the time. He wrote that very late one night, when he was already in bed after a heavy meeting with the Furriers Union, a boy came to the rooming house where he lived. He asked Overgaard to come at once to a meeting on 72nd Street with the actors of *Sailor, Beware!* and their friends from the Group Theatre, who had sent for him. "I was sleepy," recalled Overgaard, and responded, "What do I have to do with actors and what do I know about their problems?" His landlady, a very "sincere comrade," convinced him he had to go. He spent, he noted, several hours with about 40 actors, helping them to come up with a plan to settle the strike so that the actors were able to go back to work the next day. In the early hours of the morning, Overgaard and Joe Bromberg, whom he described as "always interested in left-wing activities," walked from 72nd Street to 4th Street. "A wholesome association with the Group Theatre resulted," he wrote. The actors liked this sandy-haired, red-cheeked, robust agitator. Kazan recalled that of all the "leading comrades" he met in his Party days, he liked Overgaard best; he was independent, "up-front about his Party membership," and "proud to be what he was." (Overgaard paid the price for this openness in the hysteria of the 1950s when he was deported to Denmark.) The Group invited Overgaard to visit for a few days at Ellenville during the rehearsals of *Gold Eagle Guy*. Asked to speak to the company about the labor movement, he discussed the current taxi strike and the organization of bus and subway men. Odets was there and later asked him: "What would I have to do if I joined the Communist Party?" He replied: "What would you like to do?" Odets said: "Write a play." "Write a good one" was Overgaard's answer.

Although the Party could be doctrinaire, intensely critical and controlling in its dealings with so-called cultural workers, they did moderate the political chores they imposed on artists, who like the intellectuals were often troublesome for the Party. Especially in the middle of the decade, when they were building the Popular Front, CP leader Earl Browder took a position that echoed Overgaard's words to Odets. At the founding of the American Writers' Congress in May 1935, Browder proclaimed that the "first demand of the Party upon its writer-members is that they shall be good writers, constantly better writers so they can really serve the Party. We do not want to take good writers and make bad strike leaders of them."

Support for various organizations considered Party fronts was next on Kazan's list. He asserted that "providing 'entertainment' for the meetings and rallies of front organizations and unions" occupied most of the time of Unit members, and that

what they did was "strictly propaganda." Much of their so-called propaganda entertainment was drawn from those experimental exercises done especially in the summer of 1932 at Dover Furnace. Carnovsky and Bromberg performed their gibberish
conversation between General Sherman and General "Useless" S. Grant to popular
acclaim. "Red" Hamlet, renderings of Walt Whitman's "I Sing the Body Electric,"
and Browning's "Pipa Passes" done as a parody of Herbert Hoover were Bobby
Lewis's hit numbers for progressive audiences. Sometimes he appeared twice a night
after he had finished playing in the current Group show, even doing a benefit in
Harlem for the Scottsboro Boys.

Many in the Group marched along in the exciting May Day Parades, which were
considered Party events. One year the Group concocted a float made of a large red
cloth with holes cut to reveal the heads of the actors wearing the hats of various
workers trades. Everyone came along. Stella graced the parade with her glamorous
presence as if at an English tea party. Impatient for the huge march to get under way,
she evidently dashed off by taxi to Jay Thorpe's Department Store. Beany Barker
would have joined the marchers, but she had a matinee, and art came before politics
for her. She felt herself practically an outcast for not participating; on the other
hand, she thought it hypocritical of her friend Dorothy Patten to march, given her
lifestyle. Patten, the Group's southern belle, once brought her maid along to the
parade, according to Lewis. "Whether to convert her, or in the event the 'honorary
proletarian' needed some sustenance on the long march down Eighth Avenue, wasn't
clear" was how he put it. (*S&A*, 72)

The enthusiastic left-wing consensus and the casual relationships with Party
functionaries still leave open the question of the precise impact of the Party Unit on
the complex decision-making process and the overall direction of the Group—the
most troubling issue about Party politics in the Group. In his testimony before
HUAC, Kazan charged that last among the "fourfold" assignments of the CP
Unit was the injunction "to capture the Group Theatre and make it a Communist
mouthpiece." Despite gaining some influence, collecting some money, and taking
up time at meetings, the Unit, he stated emphatically, failed in its takeover attempts:
"[T]he control of the Group stayed firmly in the hands of the three non-Communist
directors" (*A Life*, 446). Yet for Beany Barker and others the struggle over politics
was what "insidiously destroyed the Group." Details about left politics culled from
personal and organizational records substantiate Clurman's observation, deleted
from *The Fervent Years*, that "politics or an interest in social problems did indeed
contribute a vocabulary, an issue, and an image for the basic questions involved."

Nowhere is the truth of his remark more evident than in the 41-page paper (appar-
ently nonextant) he read for over an hour to the company on April 5, 1934, in an
effort to "analyze the whole subject of the Group's discontent." To quell incipient
rebellion among the increasingly radicalized members, Clurman set out what he
called a "party line" for the Group, which while not the line of the Communist
Party, was his attempt to analyze the Group's ideology in terms of Marxist terminology and thinking. In responding to a request from Mike Gold, the communist
cultural guru, to define the Group's position in Marxian terms, Clurman said "the
Group is a lower middle-class theatre with revolutionary tendencies." The political

readings done by Clurman and Strasberg in 1932 revealed to them that the Marxian approach to society was the most scientific statement of the ideology, more mystically expressed by the directors in their early exposition of the Group's ideas. The philosophy of Marx-Engels-Lenin, they realized, explained much that they had been groping to say about the theater in relation to life; it helped to simplify, clarify, extend, and complete their whole artistic approach. It taught them the crucial importance of classes in the formation of societies. The directors understood, in a word, that they had been unconscious Marxists, but that a more conscious Marxism might be a distinct aid in the building of a correct technique for the Group Theatre.

Looking back at his earliest statements to the Theatre Guild and at his initial talks, Clurman now interpreted them "in philosophical, historical and political terms...analogous to communism in the broadest sense, and it was this feeling interpreted as a technique for the theatre which gave the quality of a 'social-religious' experience to many of those who attended." This ideology turned them away from what they now considered "the debris of bourgeois-capitalist civilization" and stimulated the search for truth in acting and direction, in plays about American history and current social struggles, and in relationship with audience. The work of creating such a Theatre, in which every play will be a truly revolutionary play, will prepare the way for the social changes to come and will contribute to American life after it has been transformed.

Against the background of these values, Clurman rejected as rather crude sloganeering the pressure some actors kept bringing on the Group to "clarify" its ideology and become more like the workers' theater. He itemized the many activities of the Group in the founding and training of the left theaters, in writing for the *Daily Worker*, in entertaining at communist gatherings, in providing speakers for events under "so-called revolutionary auspices." The members must "understand that each person is a true revolutionary in so far as the work he does best is dedicated to some phase of the struggle." Clurman's discussion of organizational tensions and plays, to be explored in the following chapters, details the many problems confronted in trying to operate their theater in terms of Marxist tenets so at odds not only with the world around them but with their own middle-class background.

During 1935 and 1936, the heyday of the radical movement, the company as a whole was extensively involved with left-wing activism. As a theater they advertised their shows regularly in *New Masses* and the *Daily Worker*, along with the *New York Times*. Committees were appointed to handle collections for various causes and to schedule the deluge of requests for benefit performances of *Waiting for Lefty*. The arrests of actors trying to perform *Lefty*, and numerous attempts across the country to suppress productions, roused vigorous protests from the company. A conference to advise "all the theatres who want to collectivize" was considered. The communist-oriented groups wanted the Group to perform not only as fund raisers but also as instruments to "politicize" unenlightened workers. When Herbert Kline appeared at one of their meetings with cries of help for *New Theatre*, the whole organization came immediately and warmly to his aid.

In company minutes as well as in letters, a changing ethos appears in the developing Popular Front period. Ironically their most radical productions—the Odets plays—had brought them acceptance on the left as well as popular acclaim and some measure of conventional success. Performing for causes began to give way to earning money for the Group. The members had all endured five years of sacrifice for their collective existence; now they saw the possibility of reaping some individual rewards and living normal American lives. Julie Garfield captured the mood in a letter to Odets early in 1937: "Mind you I don't want to starve or live a cushy life," he wrote. He wanted work that "has sense and meaning," but he also wanted "a car and a baby and a nice home." Success and the changing political climate meant that they could look beyond left sympathizers for audiences. Broadway itself was giving them some competition with social plays such as *The Petrified Forest*, *The Little Foxes*, and *Of Mice and Men*. And between 1935 and 1939 there were the Federal Theatre productions—*It Can't Happen Here*, *Dead End*, *One-Third of a Nation*, and other Living Newspapers; the Orson Welles–John Houseman voodoo *Macbeth*, and Mark Blitzstein's labor musical *The Cradle Will Rock*. *Pins and Needles*, the 1937 hit musical of the International Ladies' Garment Workers Union, had thousands singing a "song of social significance." The Group began to worry that some of their old leftist skits might offend new Popular Front spectators. They were labeled a "red theatre"; only "Moscow gold," someone charged, could account for the success of their revolutionary plays. The members argued about whether they should continue to stage plays of radical content or take advantage of their new acclaim by doing more Broadway-oriented shows.

Clurman, with his subtle and undogmatic sensibility, was always hard pressed to make clear where he stood on politics and art. Although he tried again and again to explicate just what he thought ought to be the Group's unique perspective, he was pulled in different directions over the years. Shortly before the founding of the Group, he and Gorelik were visiting the important dramatist Sidney Howard, who asked: "Is your theatre going to be Marxist?" Clurman replied: "We are not going to be constricted by Marxism." Howard observed: "Marxism is a roomy philosophy," a truth Clurman was to discover. In the early days of *The House of Connelly* he found himself the odd man out in a symposium on "Revolution and Theatre" to which he had been invited by the left-wing John Reed Club. Introduced as a "middle-of-the-roader" even before he had said his piece, he was attacked as a "liberal," a "social fascist," and a member of the "undistributed middle class" when he argued that "a play didn't have to deal with obvious social themes in order to have social significance." It was on this occasion that he first heard the slogan "The theatre is a weapon." Yet, Clurman's Steinway Hall talks seemed very radical to Lewis Leverett, who said to him, "I hope you're not a Communist." By 1935, when Leverett was leading the Party cadres in the Group, he told Clurman, "We'll make you a Communist."

In the political discussions that filled Clurman's early 1930s letters to his pal Aaron Copland, he was trying to work out his political ideas:

> It is clear to me that people like us are the real revolutionaries in America today and that we are revolutionary in our function as artists and leaders...The Artist's job today is to fight like hell to be an artist which means to find his kindred, to fight for them too and to relate it to as many still living people as possible...and perhaps the Aaron Coplands— because they are as aware of their world as well as their art—are in the final analysis the greater artists as well as the greater revolutionaries.

In a 1980s interview quoted in Copland's autobiography (see Copland), Clurman explained that his "involvement in the Group was more political than Aaron's. I was moving pretty far to the left." By 1933 like so many others, Clurman accepted a communist perspective—still with some caveats. Describing his ideas for a Group magazine that he dreamed of starting, he wrote to photographer Paul Strand that it would have "a really creative, critical seeking, profoundly and solidly communist and revolutionary point of view (without narrow communist sectarianism and dogmatism and without liberal vagueness or meaningless tolerance)." Frustrated in his career, he even considered going to the Soviet Union, but decided to expend his energies and talent on a theater column for the *Daily Worker* during the 1933–34 season. The challenge engaged his considerable literary ability in this year before he directed his first production. It also allowed him to articulate a critical stance that put his theatrical sensibility at the service of his politics, taking positions that made sense to him personally and yet were usually acceptable to the Communist Party organ. Writing under the pseudonym of Harold Edgar allowed him to speak his mind free of the Group connection and also protected from the ill effects of identification with the communist cause. (See *Complete Works* for *DW essays*)

Clurman's second column linked Broadway and the Soviet Theatre, which he confessed he had not himself yet experienced. (*DW,* September 25, 1933) The Soviets provided a model for the workers' theaters, but also offered a "school of theatre craftsmanship" capable of transforming practice within the "orbit of the professional bourgeois stage in America." He took as his standard the Soviet concept of a theater "vibrant with emotion, movement, color, music" expressing "some specific and unified idea." For him the Russian ideas, which American critics dismissed as communist "propaganda," were integral to the exciting theatrical craft that the world admired. In subsequent articles he examined current Broadway hits, condemning almost all.

In contrast to his disappointment with popular Broadway shows Clurman celebrated the "sense of joy," "fresh enthusiasm," and "confidence" of the collective, committed radical theaters. Their work could only be seen intermittently at various programs and festivals, where he sometimes served as judge. He admired their "zest and verve" and their "clarity and directness...within modest limits of sincere revolutionary sentiment with hardly any hangover of shabby theatricalism." At the same time he offered judicious suggestions for making cuts and avoiding slogans or caricatures. He warned that inept comic intrusions could rob a work of the "tone of earnest reality" without which the play would be "'theatre' in the conventional sense of the word." Taking the short pieces seriously, he pointed out in detail what improvements were needed since the productions often "suffered either from faulty presentation or from inappropriateness of form." He even took his friend Bobby Lewis to task for what seemed to him artistically incomplete in his often performed, agit-prop take-off of Hamlet's soliloquy. His serious, close analysis of the left theater got him into hot water when he criticized *The Third Parade,* a drama about the Bonus March produced by the Jewish workers' group, known as Artef. While admiring this unique Jewish workers' permanent company for its contributions to revolutionary theater, he found the actors unconvincing as American World War I veterans in the play. He suggested that until their acting skill was more highly developed, these performers should stick to their usual plays about Jewish workers, which they were able to carry off with conviction and authenticity. Nathaniel Buchwald, also writing in the *Daily Worker*, quickly attacked Clurman for "laying down the law for revolutionary and workers' theatres" in ways that demeaned working-class actors, confining them to their ethnic backgrounds rather than allowing them to deal with "revolutionary plays of the world's struggle." Clurman vigorously defended his careful comments, protesting as well the attempt to shelter radical theaters from criticism. But he concluded the series of heated exchanges saying in yet another column that the controversy was good because it reflected the left's "cultural vitality and interest" in contrast to the usual fear that "derogatory criticism will damage commercial chances." When more professional American revolutionary theater began to emerge from the early agit-props, Clurman hailed its accomplishments in the positive, powerful drama of Black working-class revolt of Paul Peters and George Sklar's *Stevedore*, produced by Theatre Union, and in John Wexley's docudrama based on the Scottsboro case, *They Shall Not Die*, staged for the rather conservative audience of the Theatre Guild. The perceptive insights that would make him one of American's best critics in later years are present in these lively, early columns.

Clurman even managed to place the Group in the context of workers' theater in his *Daily Worker* critique of *Men in White*. He identified the Group's uniqueness as the only professional theater organized as a collective and assimilating the Stanislavsky-Vakhtangov System for American actors, but hoped they would leave behind the Broadway success their technique has earned them in this popular play in order to stage the "drama of a classless society" and devote their "superb technique to the Revolution." For him finding a "political equivalent" for their theater ideals was essential. In the Group discussions, too, he would reassure the members that "we will do more revolutionary plays by the time we are through than any other organization in America." Yet, just as he had tried to steer Odets away from joining the Communist Party, so he also tried to steer the Group away from radical commitments that might limit their acting opportunities and the possibilities for success or at least making ends meet as a theater.

The rejection of Maxwell Anderson's *Winterset* strikingly illustrates how art and politics figured in their play decisions. Anderson's unique modern verse drama, inspired by the Sacco and Vanzetti case, would seem the perfect Group play, yet there were all sorts of problems. Anderson wanted Burgess Meredith to play his doomed hero Mio, but although close to the Group, he was not self-sacrificing enough to meet their demands for membership. Clurman found *Winterset* "cold" and disliked its "atmosphere of an 'Elizabethan' East Side." Although Strasberg thought the play had "distinction," most of the members were even more negative than Clurman when the play was read to them. Most important, there was pressure from the Communist Party Unit. According to Paula Strasberg, the Unit had been "instructed" by the Party that *Winterset* "should not be done." It fell to her to go to Clurman's home to give him the Party "line." No doubt the objection was to Anderson's rather sympathetic portrait of the old judge who sent the anarchists to their death. In the Unit both she and Clifford Odets thought *Winterset* should be done despite the orders to reject it, she later claimed. The combination of Party pressure and the legitimate critical evaluation of powerful members like Stella, who "walked out of the room when it was read because she thought it a bad play," killed its chances with the Group. When *Winterset* became a huge success and won the Pulitzer Prize, there was ambivalence, regret, and anger within the Group.

Clurman was accustomed to efforts to convince him to take positions congenial to the Communist Party. Over the years the Group welcomed many Party functionaries from Mother Bloor, the communist's grand old lady union organizer whom Crawford befriended, to Andrew Overgaard, Sidney Benson, and V. J. Jerome. As the Party's cultural boss, Jerome discussed plays with left theater workers before they were staged and gave or withheld approval. Theatre Union and Theatre of Action had their plays checked out. "Without the 'imprimatur of the CP' theatres could face difficulties," confessed Michael Blankford in later years after he rejected his early associations with the Workers Laboratory Theatre and Theatre Union. "It meant reviews in *The Daily Worker* and *New Masses* would be unfavorable, that satellite organizations and unions would not subscribe for theater parties, and that sympathizers in the producing group would be under constant criticism until the play was either revised or canceled." Pressure of this sort was applied in a subtle way to Strasberg when he was directing Ernest Hemingway's *The Fifth Column* for Broadway after he broke with the Group. Alvah Bessie, a writer who was to become one of the "Hollywood Ten" jailed for defying HUAC, wrote to Strasberg suggesting ways to make Hemingway's play about the Spanish Civil War more "politically correct." If the production was "impeccable in its presentation of historical events," he promised that it would have the "unqualified support" of all the organizations working for the Loyalists. In the Group Strasberg, so concentrated on his actor training and directing, was perhaps less often targeted for such pressure than Clurman. All three directors were, however, deeply involved in the struggle with the actors over the control and direction of the company, a clash in which the CP Unit, it is claimed, played an important role.

A big blow-up, ignited by Max Gorelik, suggests how confusing the issues could be. Although never a Party member—it seems his first wife was—Gorelik was a political and artistic radical. His agitation for formal Group membership that would allow him more input not only in production but also in financial and organizational planning, for which his business experience qualified him, was first granted and then retracted. Pertinent to the issue of Party influence is the fact that the directors seemed to be consulting and even perhaps taking orders on what to do about Gorelik from Overgaard, the Communist Party emissary. They wrote to Gorelik that they were waiting to hear from Overgaard in order "to arrive at and be confirmed in a decision that has become increasingly necessary for us to make." This seemed ironic to Gorelik. As a communist union expert, Overgaard was usually called upon to advise the workers not the bosses—and Gorelik considered the three directors bosses. At a Group meeting the directors were questioned about Overgaard's involvement in the decision. Strasberg explained that the directors felt the need for a union specialist in taking their action of retracting membership from Gorelik. Overgaard remained in contact with the directors, urging, for example, that they hire Gorelik to design their next show, *Awake and Sing!* Many years later Kazan told Gorelik that the directors had "softened up" Overgaard by having him as a guest at Ellenville where they treated him with "deference" and introduced him to Wall Street big shots. These reported machinations suggest that the Unit was a force to be reckoned with and that there was easy interaction between the Group and Party functionaries.

Clurman had told the members in his long 1934 talk that the directors "completely approve" of their desire to "share the workers' struggle," but want them to realize that making every play—classic or contemporary—"a truly revolutionary play" is the Marxian task that confronts the directors and actors; this work is part of and not apart from the struggle against war and fascism. Let the radical actors not "threaten to walk out on the Group at the least sign of tension, difficulty, inconvenience, disappointment or failure," he urged. Self-discipline and restraint are called for so that essential meetings are not befogged with complaints about one another, the directors, and the capitalist system. "Let us talk less of revolution for a while and attend to our specific daily job."

The harsh Actors' Committee Report (a copy is in the Luther Adler Collection, NYPL, Lincoln Center) on *Johnny Johnson* that led to the resignation of Crawford and Strasberg and the collapse of the Group as they had all known it came to be viewed as "part of a political stratagem instigated by a secret Communist cell to gain influence over the organization." Kazan testified to HUAC that he "was instructed by the Communist unit to demand that the group be run 'democratically.'" Since, he explained, the communists had "no chance of controlling the directors," they thought that if actors had the "authority," they would be able to call the shots through what he called "the usual tricks of behind-the-scenes caucuses, block voting, and confusion of issues." In an interview with Michel Ciment in 1974 Kazan expanded on the "issue" that caused him to leave the Communist Party. He said it was his "refusal to follow instructions that we should strike in the Group Theatre and insist that the membership have control of its organization" that got him into trouble. He claimed that he told the Party functionaries that the Group was "an artistic organization," and he "backed up Clurman and Strasberg who were not Communists." In *A Life*, he elaborated the story, writing that it was the actors' success in *Lefty* that had set the stage for the radicals to take over the Group Theatre. At least that is what he was told when he was honored by an invitation from V. J. Jerome. Kazan wrote, "It was my task to deliver Comrade Jerome's instructions (suggestions? no, instructions) to the cell." His message to the comrades at their regular Tuesday meeting was that "our cell should immediately work to transform the Group into a collective, a theatre run by its actors" (128). He recalled his surprise at the Unit members' prompt agreement with this directive; he alone opposed the move, an action that led a short time later, after a bitter Unit meeting, to his resignation from the Party.

Kazan's communist plot scenario seems a rather simplified version of the complex tangle of interests at work in the Actors' Committee Report. He himself hesitated as to whether V. J. Jerome gave "suggestions" or "instructions" to be relayed to the Unit. It was no secret that the leftists thought the Group had to stop sitting on the fence. That the Unit tried to influence policy in the Group over the years and did this in consultation with Andrew Overgaard, and occasionally on orders from V. J. Jerome, is corroborated by notes of a Group Unit discussion. Undated but probably from mid-summer 1935, these notes suggest what the view was from inside the Unit. Instead of naive actors uncritically carrying out orders from the Communist Party headquarters, there seems to have been animated debate with strong differences of opinion. What was at issue in these particular discussions was a paper by Clurman, probably written after his return from his second visit to the Soviet Union in May 1935. His five-week tour there with Crawford seeing 35 plays in as many days had sharpened his sense of what role politics should play in theater. He felt that although in the Russian theaters there was usually a clear political line, it was not organic to the creative work. Indeed the Russian audience, he discovered, preferred musicals to ideological shows. The Group's unique approach, he believed, would lead to political consciousness that was organic. But he felt this high aim could only be achieved if the Group exercised the kind of artistic and personal discipline that he admired in the Soviet artists. After he read to the Group from his Soviet Diary, he warned them against the brash overconfidence and sectarianism that was making them "not only the pests of Broadway but very bad workers in our own domain." He called for serious self-criticism in order to raise standards to the highest and become a true, popular American theater.

Among themselves the Unit members argued about their "prime task," coming up with the conclusion that "Pro Group is Pro Party and Pro Party is Pro Group." In this context one member considered Clurman's warnings as an attempt to restrict the activities of the Party members, and following the suggestion of V. J. Jerome, urged the Unit to "disassociate" itself from Clurman's words. The speaker, defending Clurman's paper, claimed that he and other Unit members helped Clurman draft the remarks, which were informed by the Unit's conversations with Overgaard. It was Overgaard who helped them formulate the Unit's overall purpose, which, in the jargon of the period, was "to neutralize the Petty Bourgeoisie." The Unit recognized that the Group was not and never would become a workers' theater. The Group's task, as they analyzed it, was to stage shows of interest to everyone, something they alone could accomplish. Such popular performance would help the Party lead a "true people's front," although it would require some reorientation for the Unit members. A "precise Marxist analysis" of the Popular Front approach would also help them rediscover the true nature and aims of the Group, which Clurman was urging the whole company to do. Instead of being anti-Party, this rethinking would gain new Party members, raise the political level of their sympathizers, and most important, demonstrate to the Party leaders what the Group is really about.

One of the crucial questions raised is why the Group directors, who are "such close sympathizers," do not join the Communist Party? The Party "bureau" had suggested the directors be invited to this Unit meeting, but faced the problems that the directors "do not trust the cultural leadership of the Party." Any direct interference by the Party would "lead to an explosion and resignation of some of the directors." Rejecting the notion that Clurman's paper constituted a kind of "yellow dog contract," restraining both the communists and everyone else, the speaker believed it should be accepted as "our self-imposed discipline." Their improved craft would become the weapon to create a "true people's front." The speaker argued that it was not their theater work that branded them as Reds, but rather the "peripheral dribbles—our third-rate speech making and 4th rate organizing."

The "peripheral dribbles" of the Unit members and others in the Group were obviously a source of tension. At one of the regular Group meetings in the spring of 1936, Lewis Leverett, identified by Kazan as one of the coleaders of the Unit, took up the issue saying that "during the last few years there have been occasions when it was strongly intimated that certain people were giving too much emphasis to political work." This complaint, he added, "was directed to Communists." He wanted to make clear that although "it is not necessary that everybody in the Group be Communists," he believed that "out of what some people are, has come good artistic work." And he defended his "right to do political work" as part of what was necessary for him and his art in the Group. In *The Fervent Years* Clurman recalled the excitement of some of their "political work"—Phoebe Brand and Frances Farmer featured in newspapers wearing lisle instead of Japanese silk in support of China, Sunday night benefits to raise money for Loyalist Spain, protests defending the Federal Theatre against commercial producers and investigative committees. "None of this was strictly Group business, since it was all carried out on the individual initiative of the actors themselves; but as the Group was the center from which these people proceeded, it was, in a manner of speaking, all Group work" (*FY*, 219).

The Group's new fame and the politics of the Popular Front intensified activism in the company. Odets, of course, was wanted everywhere; his HUAC file documents his wide-ranging participation. But when a political expedition to Cuba in June 1935 ended badly, it probably led to his resignation from the Party. It was Jack Lawson who suggested to him that he head up a committee organized by the recently formed League of American Writers to look into the abuses of the dictatorial Mendieta-Batista regime in Cuba. Odets would have a salutary sea voyage and at the same time take a stand against the rising tide of fascism. What Odets didn't know until they were about to disembark in Havana was that the committee itself was to be thrown in jail immediately on arrival. This dramatic gesture was part of an elaborate plan only imparted to him and some of the others on the high seas by the real head of the junket, whom he assumed to be a communist. On arrival in Cuba Odets and the others were hustled off to jail for 24 hours and then shipped back to New York. Their incarceration became a cause célèbre. A dockside rally in New York had been widely advertised by *The Daily Worker*. There were formal protests, cables, mass meetings, and news and magazine stories, several written by Odets, who especially condemned what he saw as the collusion of the American Embassy with Cuba's dictatorship. He also made notes for what he called *The Cuban Play*, which was never produced.

Behind these public consequences was the private anger Odets felt at being manipulated into a dangerous and somewhat ludicrous adventure. He himself described the committee members tearing up letters they were carrying as the Cuban police boarded the ship as "like a scene from a Charlie Chaplin movie." The trip had been deemed too dangerous by the Communist Party to allow Mother Bloor, the Party organizer originally intended to head it, to participate. The comrades, it seemed, had taken advantage of him. It was not long afterward that he probably resigned from his brief Party membership (see Brenman-Gibson, 362 ff.).

In his HUAC testimony Odets also attributed his departure to Party attempts to control his creative work. It is clear that Party interference drove many from the ranks of the cultural front. Kazan's departure from the Party, for example, was precipitated by the "conspiratorial behavior" of the Unit members and the complex issues of the actors' rights versus the directors' control. He admitted, however, that what really got to him was being put on the carpet by his Group Unit. A "Leading Comrade," a Detroit Automobile Workers Union organizer, was brought in to lead the attack on him. The "Man from Detroit," as Kazan dubbed him in a long note he made of the traumatic event, attacked him for being a "foreman type" who wanted to "curry favor with the bosses." At the conclusion of the meeting there was what Kazan called "the classic holding-the-door-open-for-the-return-of-the-transgressor" ploy. But Gadge Kazan would not humble himself to accept the Party line on the Group; he would not "walk back" on his knees, he wrote. He admitted his very strong personal reaction. "I was very angry, humiliated, and disturbed—furious, I guess—at the way they booted me out of the Party." His comrades voted against him; he went home and sent off a letter of resignation. (*A Life*, 130–31)

Those who opted out of the Party were obviously freed from its instructions and discipline as well as the contradictions that often resulted. Yet leaving the Party did not really make a great deal of difference. They were all still part of the large movement that had thrust them into the Party originally. Odets continued to be as active as before. When in 1952 the HUAC investigators questioned his ongoing involvement with communist-front organizations after leaving the Party, he answered that "the Communists have picked up some of our most solemn and sacred American tunes and they sing them. If I as an American liberal must sometimes speak out the same tune, I must sometimes find myself on platforms, so to speak, with strange bedfellows" (quoted in G. Miller, 200).

For Kazan, too, resignation from the Party did not change his kinship with his "old comrades," as he noted in his autobiography. He even kept the "respect" and "devotion" of the actors in the more directly Party controlled Theatre of Action. Some of them may have been secretly sympathetic to him. They were not happy having to clear their theater work with V. J. Jerome. Kazan put his relationship to the Party and its activities after his resignation this way : "I was glad to be *out* and glad to still be *in*" (*A Life*, 131).

This "out but in" ambiguity marks much of the Group's involvement with the communist movement. When the reorganized Group came to life under Clurman's sole leadership in 1937, he said that there would be "no ideologic and moral whipping in this theatre." Despite all the changes in personnel, organizational structure, and play choices, the Group still seemed to be struggling with left-wing politics. Only now they had new adjustments to make. Clurman, for example, justified his rejection of Odets's *The Silent Partner* not only because this strike play might again raise the cry that they were a "Red Theatre," or because of its artistic difficulties. He turned it down for Group production because staging it "at this time would be socially detrimental... It is not a united-front play." He explained to the company in 1939 that "plays are not of protest now. They are plays of affirmation." With plays like *Rocket to the Moon*, *The Gentle People*, and *Night Music*, the Group seemed to be in tune with the new line; radical protest had given way to personal dramas with upbeat endings.

Just what they were affirming, however, was sometimes unclear. The company was at Smithtown when the Nazi-Soviet Pact was signed in August 22, 1939. No one knew what to make of this sudden rapprochement. Odets figured out it must be a smart political ploy by the Russians, and others rationalized an action they could not really understand or defend with the sad words used by Frances Farmer: "Stalin must know what he is doing." The company was about to stage Robert Ardrey's *Thunder Rock*. Ardrey recalled that the Pact occasioned "painful disarray in the more Marxist-tending ranks," but he helped to adjust the play to the communist position of nonintervention in the "phony war," as the struggle of England and France against the Nazis was dubbed that summer. Audrey's hero called on America not to go to war. "America's . . . got a bigger job than war. Peace. Peace in the face of war, that's the job, and she can do it" (quoted in *Thunder Rock* in *Plays of Three Decades*).

That last summer together at Smithtown in 1939, the Group, like the whole world around them, seemed on the brink of dissolution. Struggling with the many inconsistencies, the members felt the fabric of their life together being torn apart. Emotions ran higher than ever. Clurman was at it again, talking till he was blue in the face, trying to revive the spirit that had first brought them together. Politics had been absent then; now, however, along with many other troubling issues, Clurman had to confront the political tensions and animosities that had grown over the decade. As always, in what he himself called his "prolix" remarks, he talked around the subject, starting with the need to recognize and preserve the contradictory, the chaotic, the inconsistent as the "usable subsoil" of art. He decried didacticism in art because it ignores experience for generalization. The artist must have freedom so that he can create "a world in which we will want to live." For Clurman the "social aspect of art" was not "differentiated from the art aspect" just as the individual's self-realization was not isolated from society. Accept yourselves as artists, he told his avid but troubled listeners, and reach out to your audience showing them their wishes and their strength. Fight fascism—the cry of the hour—as artists. Don't fool yourself with "didactic results," or restrict what is done to the "latest strike or the recent actuality." While urging them to work toward a new society, he also finally said it outright: "No political theatre can exist at all in the American theatre today as a professional theatre."

Clurman's rhetoric captured the Group's unique, contradictory position. The Group was not primarily a political theater and was never under the control of the Communist Party. But the Group was also not apolitical, nor was it wholly out of the Party's range of influence. They were "in and out." The very American dream that animated them was, like so much in the 1930s, tinted red. There were those in the company who jumped up to sing the "Internationale" whenever their side won out. Some felt that the "enormous political dissension" led to the breakup of the theater. Many were fellow travelers who believed in the radical ideal but sometimes objected to Party pressure and interference. Among those who became Party members, a few, some original Group members and others latecomers, remained committed; some made a hasty exit, but did not necessarily cut themselves off from their former ties. Several years after he left the Party, Odets made frequent, extended notes about his political thinking and feeling in his *1940 Journal*. Two passages reflect a continuing ambivalence that was not his alone. On January 23, a day after Earl Browder was arrested for passport violation, he wrote:

> Communism needs to be Americanized before it will have any effect in America. My personal feeling about social change is this. I have one opinion as a private citizen. But in the world of the theatre, in relation to my plays and audiences for them, leftism as understood by the Communists is impossible. Any excessive partisanship in a play defeats the very purpose of the play itself. To be socially useful in the theatre, one can not be more left than, for instance, [Fiorello] LaGuardia. Unless one is writing pamphets or agitational cartoons, only clear but broad generalizations are possible. But one must make sure to write from a firm core even through, in my opinion, an attempt to reach as broad an audience as possible should always be taken into consideration. I thought once that it would be enough to play in a small cellar, but I soon saw that those who would come to the cellar were not the ones in need of what I could say. (*The Time Is Ripe*, 15)

On April 9, however, Odets revealed his personal assessments of his radical core.

> Today there is Marx and a party which had been arousing in American intellectuals (workers less, I think,) a new sense of how a living world can be made. Despised and scorned on all sides, this party has yet had deep and extraordinary influence on every aspect of cultural life in this country. It has even been the dynamo for organizations and new patterns of thought many times removed from its radical core. It has given writers like myself a reason and a way of life. Of course this party has had behind it the enormous prestige of Russia and the profound philosophical system of Marx, Engels, and Lenin, a load they have not always carried with ease and distinction. And yet, because of it, new inroads have been made into American life, paths that will not be given back to the wilderness. (*The Time Is Ripe*, 109)

Although the HUAC investigations thrust the Group Theatre and its members onto the public stage in the 1950s, the crude scenario the committee and its "friendly" witnesses offered was not intended to and could not do justice to these complex interrelationships of people, performance, and politics. Kazan's 1952 testimony served to transform the rich but contradictory Group experiences of the 1930s into the bitter legacy of the 1950s blacklist. In his 1988 autobiography, however, along with his anticommunist rancor, he recorded a moving "emotional memory" that captured the original impulse of himself and many of the others to turn left. As he reread *Waiting for Lefty*, he felt again the "yearning for meaning, for dignity, for security in life." He confessed: "The Communists got their influence and their power by speaking up for these universal human desires...and by being militant before the rest of society knew it should be. Something in me reenlisted" (*A Life*, 115).

12. Premature Feminists and the Boys ❧

S ince the distribution in 1983 of the film *Frances* about the beautiful but ill-fated Frances Farmer, the contradiction between the Group's avowed collectivist aesthetic and social ideals and the evident sexism of some of the members' actions have been projected in lurid colors for all to see. In one of the film's most distasteful scenes, Harold Clurman, played as a crude, cigar-smoking vulgarian without feeling, dismisses Frances from the London production of Odets's *Golden Boy*, the play in which she had made a striking hit in New York. In an earlier scene in the film she was in a similar manner brutally rejected by the exploitative and equally vulgar Clifford Odets, who loved her and then abruptly left her when his wife Luise Rainer returned from Europe. Although some critics have protested—and with justice—this reduction of two important creative figures in American theater to crude stereotypes pictured in incidents of uncertain accuracy, the whole question of the attitude of the men to the women cannot be overlooked. Although the few surviving members of the Group, well on in years, have often been reluctant to rake up old personal tales, what seems clear is that despite the seemingly equal creative and social environment of the Group, as the women saw it, they were, nevertheless, "second class citizens."

Like the much more visible men in the company, the women were dedicated to the Group Idea as well as animated by the general radical fervor. They shared with the men the trials and triumphs of the performance process and the optimism and disappointments of radical activism. Yet, in the day-to-day actuality of the Group's experiment in theater and living, the women experienced ambiguities and paradoxes when they were relegated to conventional 1930s gender roles off stage and on. Looking back years later at their troubled lives in a company that has been called "aggressively masculine," the talented Margaret Barker and Ruth Nelson contemplated writing the Group story from the women's point of view—a task that was too emotionally charged to undertake. How the women negotiated between the many conflicting values all the members felt—middle-class upbringing, bohemian artist's life, the Depression, Marxism, the Stanislavsky system, individual careers, collective messages, and the pervasive sexism—is a neglected dynamic in the Group story.

If we can assign gender to decades, the 1930s was a male decade. In contrast to the 1920s, which we think of as the period of the "flapper" and the "new sexuality," the 1930s was the period of what President Roosevelt called "the forgotten man" and the "new deal." Confronted by the worst economic disaster in our history, the nation turned away from issues such as women's rights, which was "thrust into the back seat." Women themselves were thrust into the backseat. "Don't steal a job from a man," they were admonished as they were dismissed from factories, banks, and schools. "Women belong at home" was the refrain. Despite legislation to restrict the employment of women, their proportion in the labor force actually increased, especially in the low-paying jobs usually open to them, while their numbers in professions and businesses fell. As the unemployed men lost the traditional authority and power that had accrued to them as breadwinners in a patriarchal society, the women carried out women's work as well as men's. The Depression became a time of confusion and anger as men and women tried to sort out their gender roles.

In the Group 13 women filled out the full complement of the original "Chosen Ones." Included were the two Jewish women who would marry Clurman and Strasberg—the elegant, highly professional, and dramatic Stella Adler and the outgoing, earthy bit player, Paula Miller; two society girls from Chattanooga and New York—Dorothy Patten and Eunice Stoddard; the Bryn Mawr College educated, rising young star Margaret Barker; the theater-trained Ruth Nelson and Phoebe Brand, one from the west coast and the other from the east; the experienced performers Mary Morris and Mary Virginia Farmer; novices Sylvia Fenningston, Alixe Walker, and Gertrude Maynard; and, of course, Cheryl Crawford from Akron, Ohio, Smith College, and the staff of the Theatre Guild. Later, there were other interesting women: Molly Day Thacher, the Group's playreader who was the wife of Elia Kazan, Helen Deutsch and Helen Thompson, publicity and audience development experts—the first Helen became a film writer and founded the New York Drama Critics Circle, the second, an expert in group sales, later founded the Play of the Month Club. By the second half of the decade, some of these women had dropped out; several young Hollywood players—Frances Farmer, Eleanor Lynn, Sylvia Sidney, and Jane Wyatt—were cast in later productions.

For these "girls," as they were called in the 1930s, and especially for some of their families, it was important that they were participating in a theater that was noncommercial, artistic, social, or even socialistic rather than displaying themselves in show business. Despite the increasing number of young "ladies" who had become actresses since the turn of the century, theater continued to be looked upon by many substantial citizens as a demeaning occupation, especially for women. Through most of the nineteenth century actresses were often equated with harlots in a theater that was seen as the haunt of Satan. The high-minded art and little theater movement of the teens and 1920s, in which women producers, directors, and playwrights played a vital role, was seen as more congenial venue. It was here that most of the Group women began their careers. Stoddard explained: "To me, from my background, this is what theatre should be. Ensemble. Moscow Art Theatre stuff. The Stanislavsky kind of thing...it's very natural for me to gravitate toward this hope" (a similar Stoddard comment is in W. Smith, 428).

Some were able to permit themselves the luxury of art and of social commitment because they were fairly free of money and career pressures. They were looking for opportunities for personal growth and development, which they did not find in the commercial theater. Patten had been disillusioned and disappointed with her first few years in theater. "I had always dreamed of the theatre as an exciting but above all, a creative place for experience for actor and audience...enjoyable, informative, inspiring." She found, however, that there was "little sense of the theatre as more than the 'box office' or the 'star'... There was no permanency so that the actor might constantly study and improve his knowledge and his craft" (Wilson, 31).

In the difficult Depression days the Group offered both women and men a bit of economic security along with continuity, stability, innovation, and collective idealism when everywhere else there was unemployment and alienation. Clurman liked to quip that during the Depression the young people who founded the Group were not depressed. On the contrary, he would insist. "We were saying, 'We don't have to be depressed. We're poor. We have no money, but we have seen the things that we have just expressed, the things in life worth living for, our enthusiasm, our fervor, our love, our hate, our anger, our joys'—all the things that we felt as young people" (*Reunion*, 475). The Group would manage to be on Broadway, an attraction for young professionals, yet somehow not of Broadway. The company was both in and out of the mainstream just as it was in and out of the radical movement. And the women epitomized the liminality of the company; they were in the Group, but not always fully of it.

Another important enticement for some of these young women must not be neglected. When asked what had originally brought her to the Group, Brand pointed to Carnovsky, her husband for over 50 years, and said, "I went to hear the talks Harold gave initially because I was interested in Morris" (*Reunion*, 514). Stella, too, came to the Group not only to work on the craft of acting but also to follow Clurman, who had fallen in love with her. He invited her to come to the meetings while she was working in Maurice Schwartz's Yiddish Art Theatre. "I was hooked. He was everything I thought that a theatre man at that time should be. He said: 'You're lost here. You won't be able to find your way alone. Please follow me,' and I had the tendency to follow a man, and so I followed Harold Clurman into the Group Theatre." She described him as "a kind of Jesus Christ with a sense of mission... I was... attracted to the fanaticism... I belong by instinct to a theatre which had a program... and Clurman was inspiring as he talked of the program" (*Reunion*, 507). Clurman reminisced, "I promised her some magnificent release that I hardly understood myself." Their romance over the ten years of the life of the Group—they did not marry until in 1943 and were divorced in 1960—had more drama in it than many of the plays they staged.

The "magnificent release" that Clurman promised in some degree to all of the young women started out with a sense of shock. From the moment of their departure for Brookfield, they confronted different sensibilities and different codes of behavior. Dorothy Patten wrote that she'd never forget that first day:

> They were driving up to Connecticut. It was raining like fury and I was in the front seat with a girl [Stella Adler] who had just come from three months' tour of one-night stands in which she played a tart, with hair blonded in streaks. The third person in the front seat with us was a dark-complexioned boy [Harold Clurman] who had been in charge of the summer's preparations, and hadn't been to bed the night before. He had hollow eyes and quite a stubble of beard. It just happened that these two were very much in love, and hadn't seen each other for several months, so-o-o. Well, anyway, all the way up in the car, I was wondering WHAT kind of people was I having to spend the summer with??? (A version of this story is found in Wilson, 35)

Barker remembered her amusement as a round Bobby Lewis squeezed into her rumble seat with his cello as well as her fascination at the whole "business." "I had had a protected and generous background, although I had been abroad and all that, and I had an older brother. I came from Baltimore and had two years at Bryn Mawr College. I thought I was terribly sophisticated in the ways of the world, but I was really pretty much of an innocent then" (*Reunion*, 521). Even seeing the hairy bare chests of the young men as they wandered about shirtless was hard to take. Indeed, she recalled that "the whole Group experience of living together was a kind of a shocker."

Unprepared for the freewheeling, somewhat bohemian, adult summer-camp atmosphere at Brookfield, the young women from the Brearley School, Bryn Mawr, and Chattanooga kept themselves a bit apart from the more experienced theater types. Among other things, they may have been intimidated by some casual sex there, although Crawford couldn't remember much going on the first summer. Later summer retreats were more erotically venturesome. A gossipy biography of Lee Strasberg quotes, without identifying sources, observations like these: Clifford Odets "would make you if he could"; Luther Adler "was a grabber" who confessed that the men all had a "lech" for blond, cute Phoebe Brand. Lesbian and homosexual relationships were part of this sexual game. (Adams, 130–31)

Yet, the young women felt it to be a "mad but exciting time." They were studying the new technique of acting with Strasberg, whose subjective probing must have been even more challenging for the women than it was for the men. Working especially on emotional memory, they were encouraged to turn themselves inside out, making their most private moments the source of their public art. Brought up to conceal the secret-self behind accepted gender behavior, the young women struggled to expose and use hidden emotions and to become self-identified. The unique combination of psychic and social exploration needed for their art was thus as shocking as the unconventional personal and organizational way of life. Barker, with a drinking problem and confusions over her sexual identity, felt "clobbered." Nelson asked to be excused from Strasberg's classes. "We wanted to learn to be good actors, to be good workers, to be good artists," she reminisced, "but we argued and had those dreadful things called meetings" (*Reunion*, 531).

At those "dreadful" meetings, the women joined in the contentious discussions about, among other things, play choices, opening and closing shows, and political activity. Virginia Farmer and Molly Day Thacher became critical of the failures of the largely male leadership to take more radical action. They decided to give much of their energies to the new workers' theaters. Brand and Paula Miller went further in joining with the men in the Communist Party Unit. Others like Stella were dedicated activists in and out of the Group; she particularly recalled giving out leaflets in front of the Public Library at 42nd Street to help the cause of Republican Spain against Franco's fascist army. Brand and Frances Farmer were written up in the press because they wore lisle stockings instead of silk ones to protest Japan's invasion of China.

"You have to have lived in the thirties to realize that everybody was interested in the political situation," Stoddard suggested. "It was a time of enormous hope, because Mr. Roosevelt had come in, because of the New Deal." Since the Group "functioned to serve society," Nelson believed that "it was quite in the natural course of events that as a result of this, theatre should go very left in later years...It worked right into a political aspect of life" (*Reunion*, 530). In response to questions about her political activities, Brand explained that one had to relate what people did to their personal background and the economic conditions. "I don't think anybody started out to be politically minded. It sort of grew from a certain situation." Of his wife Paula's involvement in the Party, Strasberg is quoted as saying: "She thought this was child's play. She did not understand the nature of the professional revolutionary movement in which rules are given and you must obey." She was certainly no thinker; in joining the Party, "she was obviously doing what many others were doing" (Adams, 173).

The women were also active in the ongoing effort to adjust power and authority in their theater between the directors and the ensemble. Although they would not have said so in the 1930s, the issue of democratization, of full participation, can be viewed from their perspective as a feminist as well as a leftist, equalitarian political gesture. In the Group as in other radical organizations of the decade, women were in a contradictory position. They were freer politically, creatively, and even sexually than in the larger society, but the basic questions of women's liberation from sexist oppression tended to be subsumed in the larger socialist agenda that was to bring liberation to all. Indeed, on the left, feminism came to be viewed as a middle-class ideology inimical to their commitment to destroy capitalism. Communist women's organizations, for example, argued against the Equal Rights Amendment, which was first advocated in the 1920s, fearing it would rob working women of the limited legal protections they had. The Communist Party refused to publish Mary Inman's *In Woman's Defense*, the one major American theoretical study that brought Marxism and feminism together in the 1930s. Part of their objection was that in linking working-class and middle-class women, feminism destroyed the class basis of their ideology. Preoccupied with adjusting their bourgeois background to the working-class struggle against capitalism, the women in the Group tended to put aside thoughts of personal liberation, accepting, however reluctantly, the male chauvinism of the left, which did not differ much from that of the right. Thus, it is not surprising that when asked in the 1980s, the decade of feminist consciousness raising, what it was like to be a woman in the Group, some of the women aired complaints about how the men treated them that they had rarely expressed openly before.

A few of the somewhat older and more experienced women like Virginia Farmer and Mary Morris complained from the beginning of the paternalistic attitudes of Clurman and Strasberg who "spoke to everybody as to pupils who had to be instructed, sinners who had to be saved, mental babies who had to be whipped into growing up." To Barker, the male domination seemed "a certain kind of European thing...perhaps a Jewish thing." Brand remembered that over the years all the women "felt that we did not get the kind of fair shake the men did...that we were being overlooked." She went on,

> Well, Frances Farmer, Ruth Nelson and I would very often feel, "Oh, those guys are off there again...Not thinking about us." For example, when everybody was invited to go to Hollywood, the men had a meeting one night and didn't invite Ruth and me. We were pretty sore about that since they were settling our future without asking us. (*Reunion*, 514–15)

At one of the confessional sessions on individual acting problems at Smithtown, Brand, Nelson, and Frances Farmer expressed concerns about their creative development that suggested that the women's needs in performance differed from those of the men. Brand explained that she gained from her studies with Strasberg an awareness of herself as a "sensitive instrument," but later rebelled against his constant probing. This led to her wanting to be left alone for a time; she felt she had improved by exploring the craft on her own. Hoping to move on to a next stage at Smithtown, she confessed that she also "wanted to be handled with kid gloves," to be "coddled." She resisted taking Clurman's direction yet felt she needed it. Clurman commented that her confession suggested anxiety, feelings of inferiority, and lack of confidence. Nelson recognized the tendency she had to think too generally, not being specific enough in tackling the stage tasks. She felt able to discover "an original truth in relation to a character," but found herself falling back on "conventional attitudes" that obscured her rich perceptions. She needed help, but also believed she had to find her own way.

There was always the question of enough roles for the women. In discussing Odets's 1937 *The Silent Partner* at Smithtown, Clurman confessed that "obviously the women's parts are not as good as the men's. We have a woman problem and I don't snicker in any way at this problem. The women are important to the Group and to me certainly." Clurman became very defensive when producer Joseph Verner Reed complained to him that the Group failed to "develop any outstanding actresses to equal the men." He replied that

> it was to be noted that for some reason most of our plays had much better roles for men— our actresses certainly noted it!—and that because of the nature of a small permanent company an actress like Stella Adler was called on to play parts as varied as Geraldine (*The House of Connelly*), Sarah Glassman (*Success Story*), Gwyn Ballantine (*Gentlewoman*), and Bessie Berger (*Awake and Sing!*). If some of Broadway's women stars tried to cover an equivalent range of roles, their limitations might be exposed and their glamour diminished. (*FY*, 192)

In an interview over 30 years after Clurman recalled this exchange in *The Fervent Years*, Stella observed: "Repertory involved a lot of risks. You can either be developed in repertory or used up like an old rag. I suffered a great deal in the Group being a tall woman. When I left I was asked to play a countess and a queen. When I was in the Group I was asked to play a Jewish mother" (*Reunion*, 509). She felt betrayed by the man to whom she had entrusted herself in the accepted romantic manner of the time. When she joined the Group, she was sure her lover was kidding when he said, "In our first production you will play a maid who bobs on and off the stage" (*FY*, 85). By making her play the role of the padded, grey-haired Jewish matron Bessie Berger in *Awake and Sing!*, Clurman had ruined her career, she insisted. She acknowledged the contradiction between her glamorous appearance and taste and her intellectual and emotional commitment to a radical, proletarian theater. It was ironic for her that the wished-for collapse of capitalism would result in her playing "peasants." Bobby Lewis remembered that she would "proudly proclaim that she could live in any communist country as long as she were the queen." But since the Group was a "serious theatre," she confessed: "I finally buckled down to being a serious actress, and said I had to do it. I had to be a character actress there" (*Reunion*, 506–12). The other roles mentioned by Clurman gave Stella's regal beauty more of a chance to be seen, and she even played the scandalous, sexy actress Adah Isaacs Menken in Melvin Levy's unsuccessful costume drama *Gold Eagle Guy*. Early on, she was widely heralded for her performance as the idealistic secretary Sarah Glassman in *Success Story*; Joseph Wood Krutch admired her "splendid performance, emotional and true...." (Reviews, September 27, 1932) But, in this play, as in so much of the Group repertory, it was the scenes "between the men that command attention," as another critic noted. (Reviews, November 13, 1934)

Off stage, the relationships among the men in the Group were emotionally powerful while their relationships with the women were ambivalent or exploitive. Some of the gender—as well as class and ethnic—tension that made life difficult for the women can be suggested from the diaries and letters of Clifford Odets. In the early days Odets confided that he felt love-hate relationships with what he repeatedly called the "Nordic" non-Jewish women in the company. (See Brenman-Gibson, 582) Their first summer, he was attracted to Barker and Stoddard, whose "white skin" stirred his "Hebraic blood." He dreamed of conquering these "Nordics, blond, cool, well-mannered, finishing school . . . having most everything that we Jews wished we had." Violent phantasies overcame him when he felt denied of the "nurturance" he needed from these women. Of one ladylike "Nordic," he wrote that he dreamed of sinking

> my fist into her belly. It would go right through with a squash and hit her backbone which would collapse and make the head fall down off the top and roll away in the grass like a pumpkin. Then I'd kick the pumpkin head and it would squash juicily, the mouth saying at the same time, "MY DEAR young man, what in the WORLD are you DOING?" (Brenman-Gibson, 235–36)

Women were either powerful and nurturant or pupil-disciples, according to Brenman-Gibson's analysis of his complex attitudes in her biography of the playwright.

The voracious sexual appetite of Odets as well as of his friend Elia Kazan has been set out in detail in books by and about them. In a period of lonely depression during the rehearsals of *The Case of Clyde Griffiths* Clurman, writing to Odets, revealed the casual sexism.

> A new element at these rehearsals is the presence of a number of quite pretty girls in small parts. I'd like to have some of them but I haven't the energy to engage in those preliminary gestures and efforts needed for a "respectable" affair! Anyhow it must be nice for the men in the company to have the stimulus of some new faces and new bodies.

In a rather unenthusiastic letter congratulating Odets's decision to marry Luise Rainer, Clurman contrasts being a "free man" who is "innovative because it means playing a game in which one makes all the rules oneself," with the "responsibility," "compromises," and "giving up of oneself" in marriage. But since marriage "engages one with life," Clurman considered it good for Odets, who has "never written women's parts as good as Gus, Myron, Sam [Feinschreiber], Uncle Morty." (The major repository of Clurman letters is in the Billy Rose Theatre Collection, NYPL, Lincoln Center; see Note on Sources.)

Among themselves the men competed for conquests. Odets, Franchot Tone, and Luther Adler were energetic contestants, and Odets "always had a special interest in Clurman's women." The rivalry seemed to intensify the powerful sense of "bruder-schaft," of male bonding, in their creative endeavor. For Odets, Clurman was not only "obstetrician to his plays," and "his favorite character outside of fiction," but also "the primary witness" of his life. Odets also had a special relationship with Kazan, whom he called a "Greek from Turkey who seemed like a Jew." Group members noted the "tenderness, almost a physical charge between these two men." Those who did not know them well linked Odets with both Clurman and Kazan as lovers.

For these men so emotionally, creatively, and intellectually intertwined, the woman they loved above all others was the Group. Passion for their aesthetic ideal was more than a recurrent metaphor. The women in their lives literally looked on the Group as the "other woman." Luise Rainer, for example, said that the Group was "Clifford's whole life, he was like a man with two wives, only I feel that his first love was his greatest" (Louella Parsons quoted by Brenman-Gibson, 510). Stella, too, was distressed to have to share Clurman with his Group cronies; he was always inviting his special pals to share lodgings with them or to come along on romantic outings, like a trip to Paris. Some claimed Stella took famous lovers in revenge. When Odets brought Luise Rainer to New York, Clurman looked upon her as a threat, and, in turn, Odets complained that in pursuing Stella, Clurman jeopardized "the Group's future because of the vanity and caprice of a powerful woman" (Brenman-Gibson, 509).

In this charged atmosphere, the women's complaints are readily understood. Stella was most vocal in her insistence that the Group "was really a man's theatre. It was male dominated. The theatre was aimed at plays for men. They understood men…The women were ruined, absolutely neglected. Any actress that stayed was an idiot" (*Reunion*, 509). In her view the men were not "great lovers, not romantic. They were boys. Clifford was a boy. He didn't write for women. He wasn't really a man yet. It was very frustrating being in a theatre like that" (*Reunion*, 509). The other women resigned themselves to the inequities, but not Stella. From her privileged position as Clurman's girlfriend, she clamored again and again for better roles for herself. The suppliant suitor Clurman appealed again and again to Lawson and Odets, among others, to write a play with a good part for Stella.

This tall elegant beauty did not fit any of the gender stereotypes. She was neither Eve nor Mary; emotional but also thoughtful, involved with love, but hardly passive, she was a leading lady in a decade that did not feature female protagonists. Brought up in great luxury in her famous father's home, she had been taught to be independent, smart, and hardworking from her earliest days on the stage. On her own after an unsuccessful, very youthful marriage, she often had to carry the heavy responsibilities of supporting her daughter and her aged mother as well as making a career for herself. She was venturesome in her professional activities and in her personal life. She once announced to Clurman, "I feel the need to sin, and you make me feel I have no right to"; sin meant money, Hollywood, and also men. (*FY*, 170) Yet, like many women in this confusing time, Stella clung to conventional gender notions. She wanted her man to be a success, make money to support her and her daughter, and provide the elegant lifestyle she was accustomed to. Despite her three marriages, however, she felt that she never really understood what marriage was. "I would say that I married three people, artists, and none of them asked me to understand marriage, and I don't. I have lived a life and I was married, but I don't know anything about it."

In the Group she was admired by her circle as performer, teacher, director, raconteur. She alone succeeded in challenging the artistic domination of Strasberg after her tutorial with Stanislavsky, and often served as spokesperson for the actors against the directors. Others blamed her for failures in the Group because her sometimes cruel treatment disabled Clurman as a leader. As early as the first summer at Brookfield, Clurman wrote to Paul Strand that Stella "in her confusion, in her impulsiveness toward good and evil, kindness and destruction, positive and negative, clarity and chaos represents to me all these things in the whole group—that is—in the whole world" (Clurman's letters to Strand, Paul Strand Archives, Center for Creative Photography, University of Arizona). After the collapse of the Group, she and Clurman married and were later divorced, although they remained connected personally and professionally. When the Harold Clurman Theatre was opened on 42nd Street in 1979, Stella did not appear to share in the celebration, saying she was annoyed at the seating arrangements, involving Clurman's second ex-wife, his current companion, and herself. A *New York Times* story on the occasion concluded with a telling comment by Clurman: "I can handle Stanislavsky, I can handle criticism. I can handle the Group Theatre, but I can't handle my women."

* * *

Stella was not the only woman who was difficult for the men "to handle." Cheryl Crawford, the other preeminent woman in the Group, often felt herself to be a mere appendage to her difficult codirectors. "They might not ever have stayed together without my mediation," she believed. Their "furious conflagrations" often brought tears to her eyes, but she recalled that she wasn't sure that she cried because "I was carried away by their exaltation or jealous that I could not verbalize my beliefs with anything approaching their vehemence and endurance" (Crawford, 91). Her contributions to fund raising, administration, and play development were never fully acknowledged by her associates because the general view seemed to be that a woman was not "capable of doing what the men were doing." In 1937, the White Paper of the Actors Committee evaluated Crawford as the director who has had "six years of dirty jobs. We appreciate this, but she strikes us as a disappointed artist" (*FY*, 195). In later years Crawford insisted that she had never had artistic ambitions, but early stories suggest otherwise. She had directed lively productions at Smith, had been assistant director to Winifred Lenihan, head of the Theatre Guild school she attended, and began to direct a play by Philip Barber intended to follow *Red Rust* in the Guild's Studio when the whole venture was called off by the Guild board. But as a woman she had had difficulty even landing a job as a stage-manager. "Females were actresses or nothing."

She did manage to talk the sympathetic Theresa Helburn into letting her be "third assistant stage manager" as well as casting secretary at the Guild. (Crawford, 31–32)

With this experience it was not inappropriate for her to become codirector with Lee Strasberg on the Group's first show, *The House of Connelly*, which she acquired for the company from the Guild. By the middle of the summer at Brookfield, she told Clurman that she wanted to withdraw from being codirector because "her contribution was small, and she felt herself more of an appendage to the production than Strasberg's colleague" (*FY*, 51). In truth, Clurman had not given her the job from any high assessment of her creative abilities but because he thought she would be the best person to work with the two Black actresses. He listened sympathetically, but convinced her not to quit. "What was suffering was her ego," Clurman remembered telling her, "and that hurt was trivial compared to what she would contribute and learn, by sticking to her job" (*FY*, 51). In the Brookfield Day Book she confessed that his criticism of her "was just and true," but very painful. She took herself off in her car to the countryside where she came to terms with her "injured pride," and "resentment went away." Yet, over the years there was always a sense of pique; despite her essential contributions to the Group, she remained the "shiska" to her two Hebrew prophets. (Crawford, 52; see Barranger's coverage of the Group)

Although her codirectors did not think much of her as a director, it fell to her lot to direct the two plays by women playwrights the Group produced. Unlike most of their repertory, these plays both centered on women's lives, and like the Group women themselves, both plays suffered neglect during the production process. Looking for a last minute substitute in 1933, Harold Clurman remembered Dawn Powell's *The Big Night*, a script he had read in his days as a playreader for the Theatre Guild. Powell, a Greenwich Village satirist, exposed the male world of advertising "four-flushers, sycophants and go-getters" who are willing to exploit their wives in order to make business deals. Ed Bonney in the play pressures his wife to make a play for the rich "cloak and suiter" Jonesie so he can capture another account for his advertising company. Clurman had been "skeptical of the play's success because audiences might find it unpleasant." Yet, he bought it for the Group, attracted by its "tough…talented and witty" quality. (*FY*, 84) Since he did not feel ready to direct and Strasberg did not like the script, Crawford undertook the assignment.

Women directors on Broadway were rare, and a show with a woman director, a woman playwright, and a woman stage-manager (Alixe Walker) was worth a story. Building up interest before the opening Ruth Seinfel (Goode), writing a feature for the *New York Post*, touched on the novelty of *The Big Night* having a "girl playwright, girl director, and girl stage-manager." Will these theater "girls" manage to "keep from tearing each other's hair?" she asked, invoking the usual clichés. "Unfortunately, they have nothing but good words for each other" (*NY Post*, January 1933).

The rehearsal process was not as smooth as the publicity hype suggests. Crawford recalled: "I cut my professional directing teeth on *Big Night*. 'Cut' is not quite accurate as it eventually turned out. It was more like an extraction" (58). She could not transfer what was in her mind to the actors, and became exasperated. Moreover, the production developed casting problems. Franchot Tone rehearsed the lead role of Ed Bonney but then left abruptly for Hollywood; his replacement did not work out and had to be replaced, a rare occurrence for the Group. Lewis Leverett who, according to the author, was the only good-looking guy they had around, ended up playing the part opposite Stella as the beautiful, sensitive, exploited Myra Bonney. Clurman wrote that the actors became critical of Crawford's direction. He claimed he took over the last weeks of rehearsal, something Crawford does not mention in her recollections. (*FY,* 107) On the opening night, Crawford wrote in her diary: "[M]y first directorial job. People won't like it" (60). *Big Night* closed after nine performances.

What neither one of them mentions is that in the course of their very extended rehearsal process—Powell says they were at it for eight months—the script acquired a burden of heavily underlined meaning. Intended as a satire on lower-class businessmen, "it should have been done in four swift weeks" (*FY,* 107). At least that was the view of Dawn Powell. First, the character of Jones, intended by Powell to be a "lumbering, good-natured, hearty Chicago type," was turned into a "real Jewish type" named Schwartz. (See W. Smith, 116) When his wife Myra, played by Stella, having found her marriage a disaster, leaves her husband at the end, the play veered from Marx Brothers comedy in a drunken party scene into the complaints of the ex-model Myra who has found that her husband belittles her brains and her ideals. She cries out repeatedly that he is never going to understand her. Bobby Lewis remembered that Stella gave the lines and the role strong personal emotion, reflecting her own ambivalence and frustrations with the Group's men.

Dawn Powell's bitter comedy was seen by audiences as an "insult to the American way" and critics declared the play unpalatable, sordid, and "realistically tiresome" (*NY Herald Tribune, NY Evening Journal,* January 8, 1933). Within the company, the total failure of the show was memorialized in one of the famous Group jokes. Whenever Clurman was in an "enthusiastic state of mind," the members would repeat Stella's jibe to him: "Harold has a great idea. He's going to revive *Big Night*" (*FY,* 106).

In the years between *The Big Night* and Nellise Child's *Weep for the Virgins,* Crawford was elected to direct Odets's *Till the Day I Die,* which seems to have been staged by the actors themselves. The script for *Weep for the Virgins* was attractive to the Group as a rare play about what Clurman called "the backward elements of our working-class." All the people in it want to escape their "sordid surroundings," especially the mother and her three daughters who dream of Hollywood as the promised-land for a pretty girl (*FY,* 164). Child had come to New York by freight from California, where her work in a fish cannery had given her the subject for her play. (The playwright's name, by the way, was Lillian Gerard, but in a gesture of female solidarity with her mother, she called herself Nelly's Child, thus, Nellise Child.)

The play became "a kind of Group stepchild" (*FY,* 164). Strasberg refused to direct it; Crawford took it on, although already hurt by her previous directorial failures. It was done without the usual careful preparation and no one polished the talented but disorganized script. Despite John Garfield in the lead, Ruth Nelson, Paula Miller, and Phoebe Brand as the hapless virgins, and a Boris Aronson set, it too ran only nine performances. The playwright found the experience with the Group so painful that years later she would not be interviewed about the production. The preopening publicity about her suggests a lively, but scattered young woman who called herself an industrial unionist who hated the communists who she accused of "having contempt for the people they are trying to manipulate" (see *FY*, 164).

Child's play, an impossible mess in plot, dialogue, and theme, captured something of the cultural confusions of working-class girls, for whom her play weeps. They are unable to be content with the monotony of working in factories like the cannery, where the girls understand one another and feel they are doing something worthwhile. They are misled into thinking that they can do something else with their lives by way of "the fabled path of Hollywood" (*FY*, 164). Her themes, like those of Dawn Powell, touch in their different ways on women's issues not found in most Group plays.

Some young Group actresses, who realized the Hollywood dream, quickly turned from the glamor and gold it promised to the creative and personal riches of the Group Theatre. The beautiful, intelligent, rather high-strung Frances Farmer thought of the Group as the artistic and ethical "elite." She had caused a furor in her hometown of Seattle when she won first prize in a National Scholastic high school contest with an essay entitled "God Dies." In the Drama Department at the University of Washington she had learned about Stanislavky and socialism from Sophie Rosenstein, an instructor who would become a coach of film actors in Los Angeles. Having found herself politically and artistically, Farmer again inadvertently shocked the community and her domineering mother when she won a trip to the Soviet Union for selling the most subscriptions to the city's communist newspaper. (Since she was becoming known as the star of the Drama Club, she didn't sell them herself, but allowed some radical friends to do so using her name.) The trip to Moscow was a transformative experience for the bright 20-year-old who had never been away from home. A few weeks after returning to New York, where she hoped to act in an artistic theater like the Group, she was given a screen test and very quickly a Hollywood contract. Although she had extraordinary success in Hollywood, she hated the movie world and its values. Returning east to appear in summer stock, she was seen by Clurman who brought her into the Group to play Lorna in *Golden Boy*.

Despite her initial enthusiasm for the Group and her success in *Golden Boy* as the tramp from Newark who knows all the tricks, Farmer was very troubled by the attitude toward women in the company. She raised the issue of women's roles and needs. Phoebe Brand recalled an evening when Farmer tried to challenge the men. In her "violent and passionate way," said Brand, "Frances cried out, 'Why don't you ask me what I want to do?'" (*Reunion*, 515). Clurman, who is reputed to have had an affair with Farmer, later asked Brand, "Do you have any idea what she was talking about?" Thinking back to Farmer's protests and questions, Brand considered her in many ways a "premature feminist." (*Reunion*, 515)

Farmer later had a violent emotional crack-up, was institutionalized for seven years in mental hospitals, and may even have illegally been subjected to a lobotomy. In her painful and no doubt distorted autobiography, *Will There Really Be a Morning?*, she blamed the Group for the beginning of her problems with despair leading to her drinking and smash-up. She was stricken by what seemed to her "the bottomless sense of work-futility, even what she called a 'prostitution' of her talent," which had begun with the Group. "My artistic id was clobbered to shreds," she later reported, "and the emotional trauma that climaxed the relationship with Odets finished the job" (Farmer, 192–93; cited in Brenman-Gibson, 578–79).

Like Frances Farmer, Eleanor Lynn came from Hollywood to New York to play the female lead in *Rocket to the Moon*; she, too, faced disappointments after her initial success. She had just completed a year under contract to Metro-Goldwyn-Mayer and was recommended to Harold Clurman by John Garfield and Joe Bromberg with whom she had played in a satirical Hollywood show put on by the left-wing Theatre Arts Committee. This fragile, five-foot-two-inch, lively youngster proved just right for the role of Cleo Singer, who has been called Odets's "most appealing female character, and one of the most attractive and forceful characters ever created by an American dramatist" (G. Miller, 100–102). The competition for this unusually good woman's role seems to have been considerable; even the star Luise Rainer, Odets's wife, wanted to play it. Lynn said she had much in common with Cleo who, like herself, was young, eager for life. To her the Group seemed to promise "fantastic," "undreamed of" creativity. Her outstanding success in *Rocket to the Moon*, however, did not guarantee her future with the Group. She was cast as the young woman to play opposite Elia Kazan in Odets's *Night Music* and then fired after rehearsals started. It was rumored that she was not considered sexy enough, "no tits," is how it was supposed to have been crudely put among the men. Although this blow did not end her career, her early promise was never realized in part because her confidence and idealism were undermined by this episode.

Even a star like Sylvia Sidney did not fare very well in the Group. Married to Luther Adler in London during the run of *Golden Boy* there, Sidney was not at all happy playing the female lead in *The Gentle People* in 1939. Like the others, she looked to the Group for an opportunity to extend and enrich her skill as a performer in serious stage work. She had attended the short-lived Theatre Guild school in the 1920s along with Sandy Meisner and then spent years playing the working-class ingénue with great success. Now married to Luther Adler, she found herself listening to Clurman, who urged her to join the Group, where she would learn her craft and develop as an actress. Disappointed that she was excluded from Clurman's private acting rehearsals held for the others, she confronted him one day: "Look, I am not doing anything with this part. I've been playing this kind of part in films, for which I get an awful lot of money, and what the hell am I doing here, playing this part for a hundred and fifty dollars a week?" Clurman told her to relax, explaining "all we want is the Sylvia Sidney personality projected in the movies." She resented being used as a box-office draw. Although she admired the acting of leading players, she became bitter about the Group's leaders and found the men destructive to talented, intelligent artists like Frances Farmer. (See W. Smith, 349)

Again and again, the high hopes of women in the Group ended in disappointment. The Group was by no means worse than other theater companies in the treatment of women; indeed, the Group women believed their organization was probably much better than others. Yet, they felt frustrated. Some realized that in going on the stage, even the Group stage, they would have to fit the popular notion of the actress—pretty, flighty, sexy. Although the Group succeeded in changing the very idea of the male actor—from gentlemen and matinee idols to rough, volatile, passionate men—the women remained to a large extent trapped by female stereotypes. The absence of more women in the company with conventionally glamorous, sexy, star power was said to contribute to the failure of some of their productions. For example, critics and members believed the Group did not have anyone to play the sexy, "material girl" in *Success Story*. Dorothy Patten, despite all the effort made to transform her, did not project the image, and was considered a factor in the failure of Lawson's play. Young movie stars or starlets like Frances Farmer, Eleanor Lynn, Sylvia Sidney, and Jane Wyatt were cast in leading female roles in most of the later productions, much to the distress of the original women members, who one by one disappeared into minor parts.

Dedicated to reflecting the life of their time, the Group plays also reflected, usually without conscious intention to do so, the conflicts concerning gender roles that developed within society at large during the Depression. The characterization of women, the locales in which they are found, and the language used about women and their relationship to men suggest the world of threatened, traditional male values seeking to keep women in their place. The dramatic parts for women tended to be smaller than those for men, even in the context of the Group's ensemble approach. Most of the women characters were fixed in the domestic scene, where their job was to maintain the conventional middle-class family unit. Clara Gordon's repeated "Have a piece of fruit" in *Paradise Lost* epitomizes women's nuturant action. For many of the women portrayed in the plays the revolutionary gesture is to have babies or inspire and support their men. Those who try to take charge become agents of disaster while the men are seen as victims of the social chaos of the Depression. The mature women who fulfill their tasks are called "darling, dear, wife, momma, and beautiful," and the young ones, the prize of love, are "referred to as queenie, daughter, child, beautiful, young, and naive." Nonsupportive females are given titles such as "tart, nag, she-devil, hussy, hens, spinsters, and creature." Without reducing the complexity of felt life in the Group plays to these isolated elements, feminist analysis can reveal the values encoded in the basic building blocks of drama—action, character, setting, language. The gender confusions of the decade are richly articulated in *Awake and Sing!*—the passive Myron Berger and his forceful wife Bessie, whose action precipitates the play's ending.

> Here I'm not only the mother, but also the father. The first two years I worked in a stocking factory for six dollars while Myron Berger went to law school. If I didn't worry about the family who would? On the calendar it's a different place, but here without a dollar you don't look the world in the eye. Talk from now to next year—this is life in America. (Odets, *Six Plays*, 95)

Just as Odets's words project more than women's confused status in the 1930s, so, in the memories of most of the women, the power of the Group idea seemed ultimately more important than the difficulties. Whatever the frustrations off stage and whatever the disappointments about how their careers developed, most of the women felt that in large measure they did gain that "magnificent release" that Clurman had spoken of. They became most truly themselves by being part of a meaningful collective creation. For Cheryl Crawford, it was "the sense of being part of something bigger than ourselves held together by a common purpose" that made the Group more than an "occupation. It was our life." When it ended, she wrote that without these bonds, she became "that naked individual I had tried to avoid" (a version found in Crawford, ix, 101).

The roles assigned to the women in the best-known plays produced by the Group were frequently small and often limited to nurturing and supporting the men in the plays rather than directly expressing female aspiration or action. They are rarely the main movers in the plot or the single center of dramatic interest. But in the ensemble structure of most of their plays, the women do convey important themes. As created by the Group actresses through their organic creative process, their characters often seem to express best what it was that the Group as a whole and the women individually wanted to say. In lyric phrases, especially in the plays written for the company by their own Clifford Odets, the women did offer moments combining sustaining, passionate love and rousing political activism.

During an interview for *Reunion*, Ruth Nelson, whose career with the Group spanned the beginning and ending of the company, summarized the contradictory experiences of the Group's premature feminists. As she reflected on those years, she concluded that the Group was "sort of a disaster" in terms of her career but "a great life experience that I think all of us will treasure." She played more roles than any of the other woman in the Group, but described them as "mostly little bits and pieces here and there through the years"—with the exception of the major role of Edna in *Waiting for Lefty*. Looking back 35 years later, Ruth Nelson concluded: "Working together with a group of like-minded people, working for a common goal outside of ourselves, going together, suffering, and having joy together: it was a life experience that was very deepening and enriching. Nothing can compare with it. Nothing" (*Reunion*, 526, 531).

13. Organization, "Angels," and Audiences ❧

"The Group is a Theatre—and as such is a collective," Clurman declared in the early days. He and Strasberg had learned from Boleslavsky that true theater is an ensemble of players with a leader who, like the coxswain of a rowing team, makes it possible for them to work collectively. In the performance process, the two directors, guided by this version of the collectivist ideal, created a unique, even if imperfect, interdependence between them and their ensemble, involving their actors to an extent not found elsewhere in professional theater. For them individual self-realization could only be achieved through identification with the group they had created. But collectivism, considered a "key word" in the vocabulary of the 1930s, had many meanings. Clurman himself concluded that the issue of collectivism engendered "misunderstandings that beclouded the Group's relation with the world and its relationship with itself." The ongoing struggles over the needs and obligations of the individual versus the claims of the directors or the company or society raised the basic question: Is the Group as an organization a collective? (parts I & II of *FY* also focus on many of the issues in this chapter)

No one gave much thought in the beginning to how the Group's inspiring but complex vision would translate into an organizational structure and the complex financial plans needed to support it. At Brookfield they thought of themselves as a family and of their theater as their home. They never relinquished this initial sense of intimate relationship, valuing the intense, albeit often contradictory, emotions engendered by the shifting allegiances in their long association. Yet, when the company returned to New York at the end of the first summer, the directors, somewhat reluctantly, fell in line with another model, that of Broadway show business. After the opening of *The House of Connelly*, they legally incorporated as the Group Theatre. The three directors were transformed into the officers and owners of their property; stock was issued and a few shares were even sold. Looking back at this action, Clurman identified the strikingly different attitudes of the three directors. He noted that only the business-like Crawford "knew the meaning of our gestures." Strasberg, then, as on many later occasions, remained "unconcerned," the aloof artist. And Clurman, always ambivalent about having to serve art, society, and Mammon, "was anxious to get [it]...over with as a perhaps necessary evil." Incorporation did not immediately affect their dealings with their family of actors, although Clurman recalled that in one tense exchange in which he refused to fire a stage manager the actors found difficult, he did not hesitate to tell them that the Group was the directors' theater to do with as they thought best.

Although artistically in revolt against the Theatre Guild, the directors, nevertheless, mirrored aspects of the parent theater, which was helping them out with money and scripts. The Guild Directors considered their process of production a collective one, and in the 1930s, when Russian terms were popular, they were even dubbed a "soviet," but creative and business control rested in the hands of its high-powered board of directors—the "terrifying six," as they were called—who each contributed to running the theater. In a similar way Crawford, Clurman, and Strasberg designated themselves the directors of their company and apportioned the work according to their skills: Strasberg directed, Clurman taught and talked, Crawford looked for scripts, took care of the finances, and "calmed" the fiery tempers of her two codirectors. But unlike the Guild, which never succeeded in establishing a permanent company despite an effort to do so with the Lunts, the Group had started out with 27 actors whom the directors themselves had inspired with collective creative and social values. Without contracts, without promises of particular casting, without any discussion of the power or authority of the leaders or the role of the governed, the actors had committed themselves to work exclusively with the directors. From the first they felt themselves to be collaborators in the experiment they had undertaken, members of the same family.

In the early days the actors accepted the trio in charge. In turn, the directors began to meet with the actors to deal with decisions that concerned them all. They voted to release Bill Challee, for example, to take a role for $150 a week in a Jed Harris production instead of being an extra at $40 a week in *The House of Connelly*. Later in their first season, the actors voted against the decision of the directors and Maxwell Anderson to close *Night Over Taos* after only a few performances. Stella, coming from her secure background in the Yiddish family theater, insisted that "actors never close a play when there is the slightest possibility of keeping it running." The ensemble was willing to accept whatever pay was possible. A week later the show ended with the actors each getting only ten dollars, but they had had their say.

Clurman interpreted the interaction between the participants and the leaders as a symbiotic relationship. He saw them as one, a unified group, but like a healthy family open to arguments and disagreements and unable to have a good argument without all having the same premises.

Although restrained by family feeling and by mutual respect for one another's unique qualities, the "peculiarities" of the three directors led very quickly to many disagreements among the odd trio. Crawford saw herself as the practical one, mediating between her two "immoderate" boys who were given to violent explosions (52–53). The men had encouraged Crawford to join with them because, as Clurman put it to her, they needed "someone who believes in our approach and who knows how to get things done." They were respectful, grateful, and patronizing toward her. Early on Clurman, for example, refused to consider complaints against her and protests urging she be removed from the Group. It was his policy not to act on any of the recurrent charges made by various members—in part out of laziness and in part out of his sense that such crises were endemic in an intimate group and that they would work themselves out.

Much to Strasberg's irritation, Clurman assumed the role of presiding director in early company meetings. Involved as he was in his torturous love affair with Stella and frustrated as well by his failure to direct or find fully rewarding outlets for his varied talents, he was often utterly unable to carry out programs. The Group suffered, Crawford claimed, from his suffering. Yet he believed that his impassioned interaction with people allowed him to push them toward what he called an ideal state of being. Clurman thought that Strasberg's alternately withdrawn and hysterical responses to people, his self-repressions and aloneness, and his sense of "superiority...which is never altogether tainted by exposure to the world," kept him from assuming the often difficult responsibilities of decision-making. Strasberg liked to enunciate the high principles that he believed should animate their organizational activities, but tended to cave in quickly when challenged, especially by outsiders, and he shied away from the nitty-gritty of management. These tasks fell on Crawford, who carried the burden but always felt frustrated and put-upon. The three, for all their varied talents, were not stalwart pillars for an increasingly complex organization.

The actors worried about the solidarity of the triumvirate, which would, indeed, collapse in 1937 with the resignation of Strasberg and Crawford. Most often in their dealings with the actors, however, the directors, despite their acknowledged internal struggles, presented a united front. On one thing the three readily agreed. Despite the collective aesthetic and social ideal, the Group as an organization had to be in some sense a dictatorship. Clurman would explain that this was so "not only by virtue of its initial organization through the three directors but by virtue of the directors' belief that a theatre can only function properly as a theatre under a dictatorship, a dictatorship acknowledged and desired by the actors themselves."

Responsive to dynamic changes within the Group and in the larger world of the 1930s around them, the actors came to see things differently. They never wholly rejected the importance of the leaders, the nurturance of Crawford, and especially the creative and intellectual preeminence of both Strasberg and Clurman, but the argumentative company, undoubtedly at times prodded by the Communist Party Unit and its fellow travelers, asserted the needs and rights of the company in grievances, petitions, documents, constitutions, committees, and endless confrontational meetings. Their objectives were both selfish and selfless—to achieve better roles, salaries, outside opportunities for each individual and also to live, work, and grow creatively as an "ideologically cemented collective."

Ironically, it was the leaders who had introduced the company to this socialist concept of theater found in the writings of Vakhtangov just as it was they who had initially radicalized the members through their work process and through lectures and readings on theater and society. Now, they were caught up in what Clurman called the "excitement and glamor of political controversy." But, in notes for a possible chapter on the ideal of a collective in *The Fervent Years*, Clurman tried to distinguish between a collective theater in the Soviet Union, inspired by socialist ideology, and one in capitalist America. For the Group, the collective idea, although colored by the successes of the Russian experience, especially in theater, had to be understood in a different sense. Inspirational and a bit vague as always, Clurman's interpretation did not anticipate the wide-ranging implications of collectivism for their theater.

There was the daunting problem of finances. For this theater whose theme came to be Odets's "Life should not be printed on dollar bills," the Group's preoccupation with money was an ironic demonstration of Marxian economic determinism. The "cash nexus" often undercut their family ties and collective artistic efforts. Unlike the budget for commercial shows, theirs had to include support for a permanent company of close to 30, commitment to the actors' artistic development, encouragement of new American playwrights as well as the usual items of professional play production on Broadway. After a promising start at Brookfield, for which the Theatre Guild gave them $1,000, which was supplemented with encouraging gifts from friends and associates, their expectation that the Guild would fully finance *The House of Connelly* was shattered. When the Group rejected the board's orders to restore Green's original ending and make some casting changes, the Guild provided only half the required money, about $5,000. Eugene O'Neill, coming across an unhappy Crawford in the Guild office and probably remembering his days with the Provincetown Players, wrote her a check for $1,000; Samuel French, Paul Green's publisher, made up the additional $5,000 required to open the show.

Despite their differences, the Guild supported the Group's efforts by contributing $5,000 toward the production of *1931–*. An additional $10,000 was collected from the enthusiastic Franchot Tone, interested friends, a stranger from the Yale Drama School, and the Elmhurst Foundation. But this sort of scrounging for funds for each show was not what the directors had in mind. After the warm reception of *The House of Connelly*, the Group issued its first declaration of intentions, urging the public to support the company as a permanent theater institution. "The Group...still rests on a makeshift foundation," Clurman wrote.

> Of course it would not be impossible—though difficult and wearing—to go on from production to production in this way. But whatever the nature of our productions or the success they might win, this would not be establishing the Group Theatre so that it could carry out the real object it has set itself. To do this it needs an endowment of $100,000.

The Group would repeat this appeal for sustaining funds all through the decade, but to no avail. The directors broke from the Guild early in 1932; as arrogant rather than humble suppliants, they could not convince their benefactors that their artistic mission was unique. Suddenly they were thrown on their own. "I realized with a shock," Clurman recalled, "that we were now financially on the same competitive status as any commercial management. This was precisely what I had not wanted. We were not a commercial theatre."

The disappointing reception of *Success Story* in the fall forced the directors to renege on their original commitment to pay salaries to all members, whether cast or not, as long as the Group had a show in production. Only 18 of the 30 members were to be on salary for the 1932–33 season; the rest were told they were free to take jobs in other shows but would remain Group actors, always a difficult status to define. This significant retreat from their original ideal was defended as a practical necessity by Crawford and Clurman, who, in retrospect, also felt the directors had undertaken to support too many people, including a few who were not working out. Strasberg, taking the high-road, opposed the cutback, believing the action meant the Group was turning into a stock company. In January 1933, with the closing of *Big Night* after only seven performances and with no other script in sight, the directors met with the company to announce they were ending the season. Clurman concluded that "pursuing the ordinary course of theatre production becomes folly" when your objectives are "fundamentally different from those of Broadway."

The Group would not have a show on the boards again until the fall of 1933. In retrospect Clurman thought the theater should have quit as early as 1932 when they failed to gain the Theatre Guild's sustaining support, the public endowment for which they appealed, or the patronage of millionaire Otto Kahn, who confessed he could not help them as he had helped many artists in the 1920s because even for him "the capitalist system was not working very well."

The actors, huddled miserably together in Groupstroy in the terrible winter of 1932–33, blamed the three directors in part for their suffering and disappointment. In the activist spirit of the Depression, they clamored to participate more fully with the directors in running their theater. Among themselves the directors argued the issue of responsible leadership for their community. Clurman suggested a single director, himself, aided by the other two, but was quickly turned down. A major confrontation in the spring of 1933 reveals how linked collectivist commitments to equality and questions of money were. (*FY*, 123–24) Strasberg responded on behalf of the directors in a paper that Clurman thought was an admirable "summary of our inner history up to this point."

Strasberg couched his analysis in appropriate Marxist terms, pointing out that the Group came into being to free the actor from becoming a "commodity" in an impersonal system that offered no possibilities for technical or artistic development but rather packaged his individuality as a type and left him "frightened by his economic insecurity." In place of these destructive patterns, the Group boasted a "collective form of organization—to combat individual exploitation." But since the Group was constrained by economic realities, it was "Utopian" and "naive" to think that the directors could resolve the problems "on the basis of some ideal equality." Referring to the dictum "From each according to his ability—to each according to his need," Strasberg insisted that people in the Group were paid "in relation to their importance to the Group." Strasberg attacked the recurrent tension between rhetoric and reality, claiming that the initial collective dedication had turned into "rifts, splits, cliques, bureaucratic alignments, based on personal interest masquerading as Group needs."

He countered the actors' demands for democracy with his basic artistic credo: "In the theatre, the director with complete authority is an absolute necessity. You cannot decide anything in the theatre by majority vote." Unlike the actors' concerns, the "directors' personal interests are identical with . . . the purpose for which the Group was founded." Defending the business office and rejecting proposals for a business manager, Strasberg placed his hopes on organizing audiences from unions and clubs, including playwrights in the company, and stimulating the writing of new plays.

A few actors were "bored" and "embarrassed" by this administrative talk, some were reassured by Strasberg, but most were deeply "troubled." "The directors were fine people," Clurman recalled from the discussion, but "it was clear that they were not business people." Strasberg, who had started out coolly analytical, ended by screaming at the actors, "I don't care what you say." Odets, still shy about speaking out, echoed back, "And I don't care what *you* say." In one of his abrupt temper shifts,

Strasberg quietly agreed, "I know." Like the many meetings that were to follow over the years, this one was both combative and inconclusive, although in the next few months young Philip Adler was hired as business manager and Vassar Experimental Theatre alum Helen Thompson was given the task of audience development. Most important the actors succeeded in establishing an Actors' Committee.

Strasberg's defense of the directors' business dealings was not totally misplaced. At the time of this 1933 blow-up, the company with its modest means and its rather inept business negotiations had managed to stage five new plays that attracted considerable critical attention. But their financial record suggests why the actors were unhappy with their lot. *Night Over Taos*, for example, was paid for by Maxwell Anderson, Franchot Tone, and Dorothy Patten's father. This costume drama with its much-admired set by Robert Edmond Jones cost $5,078: $1,000 going to Jones for his design, another $1,000 for costumes rented and purchased, a bit over $1,500 for set construction and painting, about another $1,000 for rehearsal and publicity, the rest for props, lighting equipment, and miscellaneous. The $1,500 director's fee, which the three directors were to divide among themselves was not paid. The actors' salaries for one week of regular pay ran from $150 for Franchot Tone and $125 for Carnovsky, a substantial reduction from the original $300 a week they were to receive to replace their Theatre Guild salary, to as low as $15. Strasberg and Clurman received $25 and $20, while Bobby Lewis earned $20 for his Indian bit part that stole the show. Crawford did not take any payment; she recalled that she managed to live on her savings from her well-paid Guild job. That the Group was able to produce this show at all after the box-office failure of both *1931—* and of the short tour of *The House of Connelly* was something of a triumph.

Even more impressive, Crawford, with her commercial know-how, had managed to convince Lee Shubert to finance and provide a theater for their fall 1932 production, *Success Story*, which cost only $6,500 and had a relatively small cast. Although not the success they hoped for, it ran for 128 performances, their longest thus far. Shubert retrieved his investment by taking "first money" for the operating expenses of the Maxine Elliott Theatre. To keep the production on the boards during its last five weeks, the directors were not paid their weekly salary and all the actors went on half-pay. Struggling together in their Groupstroy poorhouse, the actors did all they could to entice audiences to the show. The company persevered, even managing to open the production of *Big Night* that Crawford directed in January 1933. It cost $4,500, but the Group was hard put to raise even this small sum. In her diary Crawford, having a very difficult time as director of *Big Night*, was simultaneously worrying about the financing. "Hard to work with that pressing on me all the time. Don't think I'm a really good businesswoman. Must get the money or we're washed up. Nerves jangly. We're trying to run a business like a philanthropy (60)."

The most egregious financial blunder was made by the very unbusinesslike Strasberg that winter when the company was ensconced at Groupstroy. The story goes that Bess Eitingon, who had been part of the Provincetown Theatre circle, told Sandy Meisner that she wanted to give the Group $50,000, the money a wedding gift from her new husband, Motty Eitingon, an immigrant who became a highly successful furrier. Meisner alerted Strasberg, but with characteristic disdain,

Strasberg did nothing to follow up on this promising largess. Finally the eager, but exasperated donor, who may have hoped to become part of the company, charged up the many flights of steps to their collective pad, a certified check for $50,000 in hand. The reclusive Strasberg simply looked past Eitingon as she repeated her offer. Feeling rejected and terribly embarrassed, she ran from his presence. Eitingon gave the money to Frank Merlin, the producer who would later option Odets's *I've Got the Blues*. Strasberg, ever the artist unconcerned with practical issues, liked to explain that he "honestly couldn't think at the moment what we could use the fifty thousand dollars for." No wonder the radicalized actors exploded with demands for some say in the company's management.

What of the audience and its role in the Group's struggle? The Depression having deprived the company of patrons like Otto Kahn, who might have helped it become a nonprofit theater on the model of a symphony orchestra or a museum, the Group tried to organize a paying audience. The company kicked off a plan for their 1932–33 season at a meeting on March 13 at the Forty-eighth Street Theatre where *Night Over Taos* was having its brief run. For a two-dollar annual fee, one could become part of the Group Audience, with a 20 percent saving on tickets, an invitation to a special show, and get-togethers with the company and distinguished guests. Helen Thompson, who later founded the very successful Play of the Month Club on the basis of her Group experience, organized potential patrons. The Group wanted a responsive membership not a subscription plan like the one with which the Theatre Guild had built up its audience and managed to pay for its shows. Clurman believed that the rigid deadlines required for a subscription series would be uncongenial to the Group's insistence on rehearsing a show until artistically ready to open. Also, the limited size of their permanent company made casting a number of shows in a preset sequence difficult. The announcement of the Group plans created some positive publicity—a nice plug in *Theatre Arts Magazine* and publication in the *New York Times* of the questionnaire the Group sent to famous theater people as part of their search for "new friends and friendly dollars." A Sunday night session with audience members to talk about *Success Story* on October 22, 1932, made the papers. Everyone participated—the directors, actors, John Howard Lawson, and even their electrician Eddie Dolan was dedicated enough to show up. Nevertheless, Clurman considered their overall effort a failure, "partly because we had little time and insufficient funds for such a campaign, but mostly because we were extremely amateurish in the handling of our public relations."

The credo that Clurman reiterated assumed from the beginning that "there is an audience waiting." What he had in mind, in part, was an extension of his personal gregariousness, what he called his "need to be with people, share sentiments with them, feel their presence." In the Program of *1931*– he wrote movingly of the importance of the audience as part of a collective experience.

> A theatre in our country today should aim to create an Audience. Where an audience feels that it is really at one with a theatre; where audience and theatre-people can feel that they are both the answer to one another and that both may act as leaders to one another, there we have Theatre in its truest form. To create such a Theatre is our real purpose. (*FY*, 72)

Reacting against all that was artificial and external in the American theater, however, the company looked to themselves for truthful emotion in the role and in the
ensemble. Ideally, their dreams and passions would resonate for audiences, but their
self-reflexive approach to scripts turned them inward as individual artists and as a
tightly knit group. The long rehearsal periods, often in their isolated self-contained
community, where they shaped scripts to express their collective life, reinforced their
self-absorption. For all the talk about responding to society, they often forgot about
the audience until brought up short by an impending opening night.

In their early theory and publicity the audience was a genial extension of themselves or a high-minded social abstraction. The reality they faced when the curtain
went up was the comfortable, middle-class Broadway theatergoer who, as Clurman
quipped, was usually just passing the time between dinner and bed and who, like
some of the critics, felt ambivalent about the thrust of the Group productions. Not
surprisingly the word went around that the Group was indifferent to the audience.
Although Clurman later confessed that his "attitude toward audiences changed as
soon as I became a producer of plays," he defended his Group against the charge,
explaining that the "casual here-today-gone-tomorrow audience that visits the theatre when there is nothing better to do" was not what the Group had in mind. The
company wanted an "audience sincerely interested in plays that reflect the contemporary human comedy, the passions and problem of our world today."

With their production of *1931–* the Group had discovered in the cheap balcony
seats just such a small but passionate audience for a show that addressed contemporary problems. The affluent orchestra patrons, whom they needed to keep the
show running, left in terror or shied away from their message. Watching the final
riot of the workers with distaste, these Broadway patrons nevertheless concluded,
"[F]ortunately, it won't do any harm, because the bums will never see it."

The perceptive, radical Max Gorelik, who had put the grim, harsh reality of the
Depression so strikingly on the stage for *1931–*, urged the Group to turn its back
on Broadway in order to interact fully with the new audience that would include
working-class "bums" as well as enlightened middle-class activists. In *New Theatres
for Old* he would later elaborate a theory of modern theater as a "tribunal" involving the active, collective participation of the audience. But the Group directors paid
little attention to the observations of their designer, whom they considered "impatient" and "extremist." (*FY*, 72)

Soon, the very hard times the Group was having in New York made the company
consider quite seriously the possibility of relocating in Boston or Chicago where they
might develop regional community support. Maybe the Group should be "playing
off the main street, and in smaller theatres," Clurman wondered. But Strasberg
chastised him, insisting that it was their job to go after the big audience. The world
beyond New York was in their highly professional eyes the territory of stock companies and road tours just as venues below Times Square bespoke radical amateurs.
Unlike the later rebels of the 1960s and 1970s who decentralized American theater,
leaving for Off and Off Off Broadway, the Group hoped it would be possible to
transform commercial theater into true theater. Their Depression-bred optimism,
tinged with some very traditional American dreams of success, encouraged them
to think they could bring "some spiritual order" to the "lurid anarchy" of show

business. They were Broadway's Dreamers. "Damn it all," Clurman wrote to Paul Strand when proposals were made to move out of the city, "if we had $60,000 (which managers often drop on one show) we could start a fine repertory season in New York, *order* plays, revive plays like *Processional* and *Hairy Ape*, carry out the *real* program of the Group Theatre" (Strand letters are in the Strand Archives at the University of Arizona). Ignoring the contradictions inherent in trying to realize their true theater on Broadway, especially during the depths of the Depression, they determined to push ahead. Strasberg, recovering his spirit after the disappointments of *Success Story* and *Big Night*, urged Clurman, "Let's chance it for another season."

Following their long hiatus, the production of *Men in White* in the fall of 1933 thrust the Group Theatre much more into the mainstream of Broadway audiences and financing despite their essentially noncommercial values. The Group continued to raise funds from generous individual donors, but more often depended on Broadway coproducers and Hollywood backing—either directly from studios or from Group members who were making it on the West coast. For the Kingsley script Crawford had put together a deal with the new managerial team of Sidney Harmon and James Ullman, who had optioned the play, and the Shuberts, who would serve as a silent partner if the Group staged the play and put up half of the $12,000 budget. Unable to interest a film company, Crawford raised the Group portion indirectly from Hollywood. Doris Warner, daughter of one of the Warner brothers, covered their $6,000 share. Her father evidently thought the experience would cure her interest in theater, but the show ran for 311 performances and the script was sold to Metro-Goldwyn-Mayer. Although the boon was not as great as it would have been if the Group had owned more than 22.5 percent of the show, the directors were able to take their $1,500 fee as well as $50 each a week; the whole company was supported, starting with top salaries of $200 for a few down to modest sums for those at the bottom. No salary cuts this time!

Important as money was to the very existence of the company, it was not financial distress alone that stirred the increasingly radicalized actors to action. During the long run of their hit play, the actors, troubled that they were not using their new fame and fortune to achieve important creative and organizational objectives, submitted an appeal to the directors signed by " 'The Group,' with a small dissenting minority." The tone of the document was conciliatory, offering the "thinking" and "planning" of some members who have been meeting together "in the assurance that it will be read and accepted, thought about and answered, in the same simplicity of desire and thought in which it was formulated." Instead of complaints, they made suggestions that went beyond hard-time grievances to solutions of basic problems—special matinees of experimental productions to use earnings from *Men in White* in ways that would also "fire us again with the enthusiasm which we are losing"; actor participation in acquiring plays from home and abroad for future productions; frequent short meetings for reports about plays being considered, the company's financial status, earnings, movie rights, and so on; a more specialized business department to replace Crawford and Alixe Walker, who were not primarily business people; the establishment of the repertory scheme about which the directors had long talked.

Although the ensemble was being hailed in the press, the actors questioned what the directors meant when they talked about a member's "value to the Group" as the basis for salaries? How can the real value of a person as actor and Group member be balanced with the value of the actor's opportunities to use his gifts? "What do rewards of salary and work mean to a Group actor as differentiated from what they usually mean in the commercial theatre?" They proposed casting related to individual growth and development rather than "the partially opportunistic" approach being used, and more alternate casting, especially to relieve the monotony for those in the *Men in White* long run.

Professional disappointment and ideological disaffection grew so intense in this period of success that plans for "some kind of breakaway to form a more vital theatre" were considered. Outside of the Group in the burgeoning workers' theaters, where many were becoming active, they saw other ways of structuring theater work and building a responsive audience. The Workers' Laboratory Theatre, a permanent collective of amateurs, lived and worked together, more or less sharing money and decisions, as long as the members kept within the ideological limits of their Communist Party comrades. They sought their audience on street corners, on picket lines, and at Party functions. The Theatre Union, on the other hand, was in the control of its ecumenical governing board of socialists, communists, and unionists who operated it more or less like a regular professional company, with a strong commitment to paying actors' union wages and generally observing Equity regulations regarding casting calls and rehearsals even though they did use some volunteers who worked for almost nothing. The Theatre Union never managed to bring together a permanent company, although they talked about doing so it did succeed in capturing a new audience of working people and radicals for professional theater by seeking out "the thousands who cannot afford and do not patronize the Broadway Theatre." Keeping prices to a $1.50 top with more than half the seats under $1, The Theatre Union used aggressive trade union tactics to target their special audience—leaflets, posters, speakers, telephone appeals to factories and businesses. Advance sales for benefits organized by sympathetic political, union, and social clubs guaranteed a run of six weeks no matter the critical reception. In this way, for a short time, The Theatre Union managed to triumph over uncongenial reviews and involve an unsophisticated but fresh audience at the Civic Repertory Theatre.

Although willing to learn from these theaters, the Group remained unique among the left theaters as well as on Broadway—a permanent company of experienced professionals who lived together in the summers, worked together in their special way on stage, and off stage helped out by sweeping floors, licking stamps, occasionally making their own costumes, giving talks, interviews, and benefit performances to build an audience. Even Actors' Equity recognized the Group as distinctive, letting the company bypass union regulations concerning wage scales, use of the try-out period for actors, limitations on rehearsal time, even occasionally allowing them to avoid paying the two week actors' bond, because the actors had the security of guaranteed seasonal employment. Little wonder that the most radical members and some of the others as well thought that with a little pushing the Group could become the "ideologically cemented collective" they dreamed about.

Within the company during the run of *Men in White* there was lots of activity—talks, classes, dancing lessons, various experimental projects—but the mood remained restless. Clurman, who was writing reviews for *The Daily Worker* at this point, attributed his own desire to "break away" to "lack of love around me in personal forms and in Group forms." The widely remembered confrontation between Max Gorelik and the directors belongs to this period of painful uncertainty and radical rhetoric. Clurman's rather snide description of the Gorelik episode in *The Fervent Years* captures the mood of the moment. He depicted the designer charging into the Group office, "armed with his wife," to demand a contract for two productions and mocked Gorelik's characterization of the Group directors as "bosses" who were "exploiting" him. Clurman considered the designer so "infatuated" with the class-conscious words that to humor him he agreed, "Yes, we are bosses and exploiters. Now what do you want?" (*FY*, 135) Gorelik insisted that he present his demands to the directors in the presence of his fellow workers, the actors, and an "impartial" witness like his friend Jack Lawson, whose *Gentlewoman* he was designing after fighting with the Group for his minimum union salary. What he wanted was to be made a member of the Group with all the prerequisites of that status.

On the stage of the Broadhurst Theatre after an evening performance of *Men in White* early in 1934, they assembled. According to Gorelik, the actors, "astonished" that anyone would object to him as a member—he had been a Group Associate from the earliest days in addition to designing five of their first seven shows—voted overwhelmingly for him. "Thus certified as a member of an allegedly cooperative enterprise, I asked to see the account books of the Group Theatre," he reported. The already irritated Clurman exploded, "You'll see them over my dead body." Torn between respect and allegiance for their directors and recognition that the feisty Gorelik was expressing some of their own malaise, the actors tried to calm the furious altercation by asserting their democratic prerogatives. Art Smith's exclamation that the Group was so democratic that he could "go over and punch Harold in the nose and not be fired for it" was an expression of faith in the leadership that became one of their favorite quips. (*FY*, 134–35)

All the questions bluntly raised by Gorelik remained unresolved. For the first time some of the actors refused to accept salary cuts to keep the failed *Gentlewoman* playing in the spring of 1934. The success of *Men in White* had brought money quickly for financing *Gentlewoman*. But the actors thought the money had been unwisely managed producing this "confused play," and wanted to have some say on when and how much salaries could be cut. The actors also voiced their unhappiness with the directors' choice for their fall production of *Gold Eagle Guy*, a romantic costume drama that glamorized a capitalist's career, as they saw it. Clurman tended to be dismissive of the actors' agitation, writing to Paul Strand that the "actors grow restive...The Group doesn't please them anymore. 'Rebellion' is in the air." He realized, however, that some response would have to be made.

On April 5, 1934, he read them the 41-page paper that linked the political and organizational problems that agitated the company. After his political analysis he concluded, however, that "concern with ideology is not what causes most of the sore spots that irritate the Group." Turning to the organizational struggle, he took an aggressive stance, rejecting the apologetic, rather guilt-ridden responses the directors had hitherto been making in the endless arguments with the actors. Three main sources of trouble are identified: the actors' eagerness to be cast in better parts, their sense of inequity in the distribution of money, and concern over inadequacy of training to develop in accordance with the Group ideas. Hence, the clamor for an official studio, classes, alternate casting, and careful understudy rehearsals, in a word, for "more work." Come up with a scheme for an "equalitarian" arrangement that will make the Group into a "small Utopia," and I'll consider it, Clurman challenged. He asserted that the directors would eagerly welcome a workable proposal if it comes within a budget that prospective backers will accept, and provides salaries that will keep needed members of the ensemble in the company.

Clurman's long oration ends with a critique of the actors, whose impatience, capitalistic eagerness to "get ahead," and competitive criticism of one another need to be abandoned for constructive self-criticism, better attendance at classes, and common social activities to overcome differences in their heterogeneous membership. He denies the Group has abandoned its early idealism and become a victim of opportunism. The Group "is the most creative and progressive cultural unit in America and will become a model for all cultural collectives of every kind all over the country." But, patience is required. Gordon Craig, the first seer of the modern theater, reminds us that "it takes ten years to build a real theatre" (*FY,* 136).

Clurman believed that his long, hard-hitting paper had defused the explosive tensions. "All is quiet again," he wrote to Paul Strand, to whom he promised to send a copy of this "rare" but very important paper of which he seemed very proud. The actors took seriously Clurman's appeal for self-discipline. Members of the cast of *Men in White* met to take action on Russell Collins's serious drinking problem, which was destroying their careful ensemble playing. The actors also took other practical actions. In May, just before Clurman sailed from New York to join Strasberg and Stella in Russia, the actors proposed granting two-week paid vacations to actors who had been in the cast of *Men in White* since September. When Clurman contended that the company did not have the money to allow such generosity, the actors proposed raising the funds in part by eliminating Stella's two hundred dollar a week salary while she was abroad. Clurman insisted this would penalize her unfairly for not having been cast in *Men in White.* He left for Russia thinking the issue resolved.

Clurman was desperate to get away from the fractious confrontations that he believed had caused the irregular heartbeat his father had discovered in giving him a check-up. He wrote to Crawford from aboard the *Aquitania* how "wearied and worried" he felt after the last meeting with the Group. It was not so much what was said or decided, he noted, but the "evidence of 'pettiness' and 'pride'...a kind of combativeness without point or object." But the actors ignored Clurman's objections. Once he was gone, they managed to have Stella's salary cut by the only director left in town, Cheryl Crawford.

During the summer of 1934 while the actors were running their own workshops—the so-called First Studio—and acting in *Men in White,* Gorelik continued to exchange proposals and counterproposals about his membership. An exasperated letter from Strasberg, dated July 27, 1934, suggests the intensifying tug of war.

Accusing Gorelik of being "mainly interested in getting as much money as you can and at the same time enjoying all the advantages of Group membership," Strasberg underlined the sacrifices by both actors and directors, who could earn high salaries elsewhere, but worked even without pay for the good of the company. He pointed out that membership was granted but could be revoked by the directors and did not of itself confer privileges. "The whole arrangement is one of faith in the general set-up of the Group and in the arbitrary decisions of the Group directors," Strasberg declared while also observing that "the membership is taking more and more a hand in the running of the Group, but beyond a certain point they are ready to trust the Directors implicitly." (Ironically, the actor's implicit trust in Strasberg himself was shattered a little over a week after this letter was written when Stella challenged his acting method in her report at Ellenville on her sessions with Stanislavsky.)

During one of the many late summer meetings at Ellenville, the directors gained the agreement of the actors to rescind Gorelik's membership. Their letter informing Gorelik of this reversal carried the approval of Communist Party union organizer Andrew Overgaard. Gorelik made a final appeal to the Actors' Committee, which he had involved in his conflict, believing that his grievances concerned "the welfare of the Group membership." As members of the committee, Kazan, Art Smith, and Odets seemed powerless to resolve the complex interplay of difficult personalities, chaotic and undefined organizational powers, and behind-the-scenes politics that was now increasingly characterizing the inner government of the Group.

The elaborate production of *Gold Eagle Guy* on which the Group was working at Ellenville cost twice as much as anything the company had produced—$19,855. It did not fare well when tried out in the fall of 1934 as part of the ill-fated Group season in Boston. The expenses had been guaranteed by a committee Crawford and Helen Thompson had organized of Boston Brahmins, including the presidents and faculty members of Harvard, Radcliffe, MIT, Tufts, heads of preparatory schools, chair of the Boston Opera, and various bankers, journalists, and so on. Bud Bohnen, worried that the actors might be asked to take a salary cut, wrote to his wife that he would take a "firm position" against any such effort by the directors, whom he condemns for the chaos backstage resulting from their "postponing decisions at everyone's expense." He could predict "a meeting coming in a few days where the riot act will be read, and where the true nobility of the directors will be duly explained to us, by the directors themselves. They're all right, but they're such kids and they are scared of so many things, but won't admit it" (Bohnen's correspondence is at the NYPL, Lincoln Center).

In New York, *Gold Eagle Guy* survived for 68 performances. When the Group hit bottom again with this disappointing run, it was the actors who developed an equitable scheme for making salary cuts in order to keep the production running and setting limits on how low salaries could go before a show was forced to close. Bohnen and Kraber, both with strong organizational and political interests, concocted a complex graph for proportionate salary reductions based on maintaining minimums of $30 for the lowest paid and $62 for the highest paid. If salaries fell below these cut-off points, a meeting with the directors was to be automatically called to consider closing. The actors' organizational planning was drawn up short by the realization that only the directors could act on the basic problems they were tackling. They voted to form yet another committee to make their scheme acceptable to the directors; it was composed of Odets, Bromberg, Bohnen, Luther Adler, with his sister Stella as chair.

Between the meeting on January 3, 1935, when this committee was formed, and January 13 when the newspapers announced that *Awake and Sing!* would be the Group Theatre's next production, the long-simmering frustration of the actors boiled over. "The actors took the theatre out of the hands of the directors," Odets boasted. With a few hundred dollars the actors staged their independent production of *Waiting for Lefty* for the New Theatre's Sunday Nite Benefit on January 6. In the meantime, the three directors were squabbling among themselves about closing *Gold Eagle Guy* and ending the Group season. Clurman made his usual emotional pitch for persevering, Crawford worried about finding $1,500 for storing the set in Cain's warehouse, and Strasberg kept his cool behind his newspaper. Finally, Strasberg rejected Clurman's latest "breathless professions of faith." He held that a realistic appraisal dictated closing the show, allowing the actors to accept the good offers that were coming their way and the directors to recoup their physical and psychological health before they landed in the hospital or the "psychopathic ward." Defeated by his codirectors, who also rejected his suggestion that they stage Odets's *Awake and Sing!*, Clurman had to tell the actors that the directors planned to close *Gold Eagle Guy* and end the season.

At the famous meeting in the basement of the Belasco Theatre, Stella told the directors that closing was "not what the actors wanted to hear; they wanted to be told that, by hook or crook, we would continue." Despite Strasberg's dismissal when Odets again offered up his play, the playwright asked Luther Adler to persuade his fellow actors to read *Awake and Sing!* or let him read the script to them. His rendition won the day. "This is the play we are going to do!" Luther told the directors. Could it be that the committee that Stella chaired, whose members were all politically left-wing, was acting in concert with the Party Unit, which Kazan claimed had determined that *Awake and Sing!* be staged? Whatever the links may or may not have been, the actors were truly unified on the choice of *Awake and Sing!* (FY, 144–45)

The ascendance of the activist actors and of Clurman, who would now be directing his first production, modified the internal dynamics of the Group. When Clurman and Crawford went off to the Soviet Union for five weeks of intensive theatergoing in the spring of 1935, following the success of *Awake and Sing!* and the double bill of *Waiting for Lefty* and *Till the Day I Die*, Strasberg was ostensibly left in charge. But, it was the Actors' Committee that was "running the business affairs of the Group," according to Bud Bohnen, including trying to "land" the Group on radio and interviewing applicants for membership every Friday afternoon. It took "scads of time," but was rewarding, Bohnen wrote to his father, an artist who always warned Bud against the "frailties" of the Group and the "dangers" of "tying" himself down to a "collective, where your talents were retarded." Given to embellishing the Group image when writing to his father, Bohnen elaborated on the "hundreds" he was interviewing for membership; "former stars...people whose salaries have been up to $2000 a week...all with their tongues hanging out to be taken into this haven." And well they should, Bohnen felt. "The theatre IS a collective craft, and the only way to achieve satisfaction in it is to control the collective conditions."

And this is what the actors ever more energetically tried to do—control the conditions. When the company reconvened in the fall of 1935 after their first vacation apart from one another, the spirit seemed upbeat even though the members were "on the ragged edge financially," as Bohnen put it. Despite the acclaim *Waiting for Lefty* gained for the young Odets, neither he nor Clurman had been able to raise the modest budget of $7,200 for the full-length *Awake and Sing!* Franchot Tone came to the rescue, answering Clurman's call for help without even reading the Odets script. A generous albeit sometimes ambivalent supporter of his old friends, Tone brought money from Hollywood stardom as well as from his independent wealth to the Group. Although he did not contribute the money as a financial investment, Tone did later wonder why, despite its success, he never earned anything from *Awake and Sing!*, which ran for 209 performances.

The Odets-Clurman productions had not been money-makers, but they were morale builders. The company made ambitious plans for the upcoming 1935–36 season—reviving *Awake and Sing!* and *Waiting for Lefty* in New York and on tour in Philadelphia, considering new scripts by Sidney Kingsley and Melvin Levy, Odets's *Paradise Lost* and Lawson's *Marching Song*, as well as a project for a Group Theatre Center with the school, restaurant, and magazine about which Clurman had always talked. Twelve of the leading members, including Odets, Kazan, and Bobby Lewis, eager to make the "Group inspiration a living thing again, and for other practical reasons," proposed "The Development of a Studio" to spur the creative growth of the actors, which was still urgently needed. Actors would be cast in substantial roles in plays—old or new—that they would not have a chance to perform on Broadway. Strasberg was suggested to direct. Despite his failures and the Clurman-Odets successes, he was still the master teacher.

Nevertheless, the actors were determined. Through their Actors' Committee and many ad hoc committees, they kept bringing recommendations to the directors. Meetings were their weapon for radical change. Clurman compared them to those in Dostoyevsky's *The Possessed*, inefficient, intense, anarchic. Tony Kraber recognized that the actors had no training to facilitate self-government; those with organizational skills were "disgusted" with the bunglings of the other members. In the 1950s during his HUAC testimony, Kazan stigmatized the actors' participatory activism as the means the communists would use to take over the Group. Multiple as the intentions among the members may have been, these long, painful meetings were their clumsy, very 1930s, means of developing some of the democratic control they considered essential for their collective life.

Maintaining performance discipline remained a recurrent challenge. In a meeting Kazan called for honor and pride, demanding the best from each actor. But the members voted against punishments, counting on self-discipline rather than bureaucratic rules. Inadequate opportunities to act continued to demoralize the company. Double casting of roles and supervised interchanging of parts were recommended again and again to improve the actors' attitudes. The controversial involvement in outside, frequently political, activities was also seen as a consequence of lack of work. Clurman recalled that actors envied those engaged on the various workers' projects and chastised them for negligence in their performances and carelessness in personal appearance. The contrast between the dedication of the Russian actors he saw on his 1935 trip with Crawford and the recurrent laxity he found in the Group spurred his criticism. He insisted that "unless basic faults are remedied work in the Group will be unbearable."

Odets, no longer just a fellow actor but the playwright of the hour feted by the rich and famous, went beyond Clurman's warning, calling the actors complacent and stuffy. During the fall revivals of *Awake and Sing!* and *Waiting for Lefty*, he wrote a scathing open letter to the acting company. "The discipline in this company stinks! What are we going to do about all the chess games, the idle visitors and their chatter, *Daily Workers*, about the discussion and concentration on anything but the task immediately at hand?" His heavy irony underscores the chaos and marked divisiveness in the company:

> [L]et the directors and a few other fools work out their guts to raise money and find plays and keep the company going. For our part we can check into the theatre fifteen minutes before curtain...sometimes the directors take advantage of us—they had the gall to ask several of us to play small parts and bits in *Lefty*...We have a thing called "the method." This "method" automatically makes us better actors and far more pleasing to an audience than The Lunts, Paul Muni, Ruth Gordon and a host of other popular names.

He concluded his blast with the threatening words: "At present I know at least one playwright who would much rather write plays for Ruth Gordon and the Lunts than for the Group acting company." (See also *FY*, 162–63; Brenman-Gibson, 362, for variants of this event)

The members could be very harsh in their dealings in part because of their intense feelings for one another and their common dedication to the Group. Participants felt secure enough in their bonds not to restrain themselves; indeed, they felt that venting their hostility would strengthen the relationships. And so it was in the Group, although a time would come when the basic structure of relationships would collapse.

Stella's request to be released from playing a bit part in *The Case of Clyde Griffiths* stirred heated controversy. Bud Bohnen speaking for the Actors' Committee and for the directors held that at this stage of the Group's development an experienced actor should not have to play "walk on's." Luther Adler agreed, arguing that Stella was "important in the eyes of the public" and should be released for good theatrical and Group reasons. The exchange turned "very emotional" as cries of "Luther should be censured!" and "Luther is full of shit" pierced the air. Lewis Leverett insisted that the public "wants to see the Group as a collective"; others argued that Stella should present her case before the Group "rank and file." After extended negotiations, Stella's release was approved; instead of acting a small part, she would train actors for the production. Zealous in their dedication to the Group Idea and to their craft, the actors, who were also competitive, had become very critical of one another both on and off the stage. Clurman later observed: "High standards—a basis for destructiveness."

Actors' requests to be released to play in commercial productions or in films were always a tough call for the company, challenging their very existence as a permanent ensemble. Early on, Clurman had reduced Beany Barker to tears when he refused to allow her to take a role in a Marc Connelly play even though she had little to do in either *Success Story* or *Big Night*. He had been "adamant" that their theater would disintegrate if actors took off if they were not cast in lead roles. Yet, about a year later, he led the actors in voting to reinstate Bud Bohnen who had arranged to perform in a try-out for a commercial manager without consulting the Group. It took two five-hour sessions to decide that this very dedicated actor should be allowed back in good standing. Bohnen's financial woes, chronicled in his many letters to his wife Hildur, provide vivid evidence of the struggle to survive in the Group—"nipping" a bit from the rent money, holding the grocer at bay, borrowing from his brother Art, taking advances on his salary. (Bohnen letters, NYPL, Lincoln Center) As late as 1939 at Smithtown, another Bohnen request for release to earn some money precipitated fierce controversy.

Joe Bromberg, another actor with family responsibilities, contracted for a Hollywood stint without requesting a leave, and took off for the Coast in the middle of a production. His coworkers judged this leader of the radical contingent harshly. (*FY*, 173) Clurman recalled that "Carnovsky grew indignant to the point of tears," and Odets, himself already in Hollywood, considered Bromberg an enemy because he badmouthed the Group in Hollywood. Nevertheless, Bromberg justified his abrupt departure; if he had asked permission, he might not have had the heart to leave the company. Indeed, his fellow actors would have met to talk him out of it as they did when Alan Baxter left to play the lead in the Theatre Union's *Black Pit* and perhaps give the movies a try or when Walter Coy decided to part company with the Group. Odets's departure for Hollywood after the disappointing opening of *Paradise Lost* angered the actors. They wanted Clurman to prevent his defection on moral grounds, but they also resented having to stay behind performing his play for as little as 25 dollars a week in freezing New York City while the playwright basked in Hollywood sunshine and glamor.

Despite ambivalence and even anger, the actors also deeply cared for one another. The same meeting that dealt harshly with Stella came to the aid of Russell Collins, whose heavy drinking had reached a crisis point. During a performance of *Paradise Lost* he lost his bearings, unable even to pick up a prompt for his lines. The actors arranged treatment for his alcoholism at a sanatorium outside of New York. Having no money to cover the steep hospital bills, they agreed to barter their talent for Collins's medical care. For six months the actors took themselves out of New York every few weeks to perform for patients at the sanatorium. A very grateful, recovered Russell Collins later rewarded the Group with a moving performance of the title role in *Johnny Johnson*.

The actors' ongoing agitation was compounded by recurrent creative and business mishaps. Hollywood money, this time from Metro-Goldwyn-Mayer, covered the $13,855 required to produce *Paradise Lost*. Despite salary cuts and an elaborate campaign to keep the production on the boards, the show had to close after 73 performances. No longer lionized by Broadway, Odets made the inevitable journey to the

West coast. No one seemed to remember how *Weep for the Virgins* was financed; the most neglected play in the Group's history had only 9 performances. A chaotic tour of *Awake and Sing!* in the spring of 1936 also failed to make money. Desperate to make up for losses, the Group accepted an offer to stage *The Case of Clyde Griffiths* from Milton Shubert. He put up the money, but Crawford found herself fighting with him to wrest what was needed for the elaborate production, which lasted for only 19 performances.

Producing four plays by Odets in 1935 should have marked the Group's coming of age. "Now the Group has put on long pants," Clurman had announced after *Awake and Sing!*, invoking his favorite metaphor of maturation. But things just did not work out. "Something stood in the way," Clurman wrote, although "we were not sure what it was." Bohnen identified part of the problem in the childish and greedy responses of the actors. Although he was so often their representative—he was dubbed a "left-wing compromiser"—they tried his patience. "I get so desperate in these Committee meetings and Group meetings that I'll trade them *all* for the *comparative* sanity of the 3 directors any day in the week with all their faults." But, Bohnen was becoming "fed up being wet nurse to the *democratic impulse*."

While on tour with *Awake and Sing!* in Baltimore, Clurman had a long conversation with Brand and Carnovsky that sharpened his understanding of how the dedicated political members viewed the Group's problems. As if surprised, he wrote to Strasberg that "Phoebe actually spoke of a collision or conflict between the actors and the directors," claiming that the directors "do not respect or love the actors enough." Although Clurman thought her remarks "damned nonsense," he realized that the Group might be destroyed because the actors were confused about the organizational structure and believed the leadership was not accountable.

Clurman now believed that his "way out" was "*the* way out." He was secretly putting together what he called a "new Group constitution or plan whereby the benefits of a certain amount of Group democracy might be combined with a strongly centralized leadership in the person of a single managing director." Not an " 'autocracy' but an intelligent democratic centralism—with ultimate deciding power vested in one man—myself," he wrote in confidence to Odets. It was an idea he had tried out on his codirectors before without success. Now he insisted, "I have to be the managing director and guide the organization," and they agreed to let him take command. While waiting for Clurman's final draft, Strasberg put his thoughts into a letter to his partner in which he characterized the needed changes in the organization as the dangerous but necessary growing up of the Group. The three directors, while best able to lead the Group, must recognize that "collective activity despite its mistakes should not be either belittled or condescended to. If a thing is to be achieved, it can be accomplished only by collective activity utilizing to the full the individual endowments of the people it is composed of." The Group ought to start the next five years with a "new slate" in which all the activities and responsibilities are reconsidered, including the activities of the three directors who ought to do what they are best at—work on plays, training, writing, creating a school, a studio, or institute.

For himself, Strasberg stated categorically that he did not want to be involved in the detailed management of the company.

> ...I am absolutely unwilling to risk my personal sanity in such activity. I think that the three of us have come as near to complete nervous breakdown as I have ever seen people verge on....Personally I do not wish to continue it. This is not the simple emotional reaction—I feel fine now, but I do not wish to *continue* it....Which means that if you decide simply to reclarify the group organization and retain the form of directorial responsibility I will have to receive a leave of absence from performance of those functions for at least a year or two. (Quoted in Crawford, 92–93)

Clurman's "Group Organization," presented to the company at Pine Brook Club Camp the troubled summer of 1936, spelled out a new structure. The authority of the managing director could be modified by his two associate directors and by the Group membership, who would be represented by four elected members of the Actors' Committee. Important tasks could be delegated to this committee, which would meet once a week. The director of each production would have final say in all decisions related to staging his play; the codirectors would serve as dramaturgs, and a production committee would provide feedback and coordinate the requirements of the director and the actors. Votes by the membership would be confined to issues that directly affect everyone, such as salary cuts, summer rehearsal choices, internal discipline. (Clurman typescript in the Luther Adler Collection, NYPL, Lincoln Center; also cited in W. Smith, 270–71) Sensing that bureaucratizing procedures for voting, for hiring and firing, for releasing members, and so on rarely works for intimate groups, Clurman allowed for exceptions: "The Group is a theatre not an army," he stressed. He hoped for efficiency, fewer meetings, and fewer confrontations.

Bobby Lewis quipped, "We don't have to think—we have a constitution." But think they did. At Pine Brook the plan itself became the catalyst for many days of soul searching. The company debated all the issues of their organizational crises. Looking beyond the specific tensions, more radical members like Tony Kraber characteristically wanted to talk about fundamentals—what the Group is, what does it stand for, and what is Harold's plan going to structure? Such questions were legitimate probing, but they irritated the Group's sore spots without providing a cure.

Luther Adler, always eager to improve the Group's image and business dealings, wanted to include larger goals—becoming a national theater or building a school—important objectives that would take sharper business acumen than the directors had shown. Clurman countered that despite all the talk about "lousy" business management, he had been pretty resourceful at raising money." Bud Bohnen admired the plan, but wanted a statement indicating that the managing director's "franchise comes from...a 100% confidence" of the members, something he considered the "beginning of collectivism." Strasberg wasn't so sure about "this marvelous collectivism," but believed the Group had "established for the American theatre a new kind of living, of creating, which will become...the form of American theatre in the future."

Clurman confessed he had "naively" thought his plan a "cure-all," but later admitted that he had probably not done the job of managing director very well. He also came to feel that the various plans "had little bearing on the Group's basic difficulty." Indeed, at Pine Brook as the company struggled with creative and financial challenges to bring the complicated *Johnny Johnson* to the stage, the organizational tensions intensified in part because of the plan, which left unanswered crucial questions. Who can speak and act for the Group; how can delegation of authority for specific tasks be enforced; can the discussions be kept confidential; what items can be voted on by the company; who is a member of the company; and, who owns the Group?

In July 1936, *New Theatre Magazine*'s article "Case of the Group Theatre" echoed their debate. Clurman's joked: "Did you see the end of the article (N.T)— they say all we need is organization—I'm going to write them & say that's just what we're doing now—thank God for *New Theatre Magazine*." By early October the company was in desperate straits. As the ensemble was readying *Johnny Johnson* for its New York opening, Clurman reluctantly broke into the hectic rehearsal period with a special Sunday crisis meeting. He was losing courage. He and Crawford had not been able to raise the money for the production, although he had commissioned the scenery to be built by their stage carpenter, Bill Kellan, who was willing to start without any money. Now Clurman needed to reserve a theater—another very heavy cost. Most painful to him was the financial distress of the actors, who had only received four weeks of half-salary and could only look forward to $25 or $30 of rehearsal money for two or two-and-a-half more weeks—the opening date was undetermined.

Clurman put the challenge directly to the members. If they feel that they are "being strained beyond the breaking point...then all the back-breaking and scrounging around isn't worth it." The financial distress had become harder to bear, what with people now having families and, more important, being "under pressure" because they "are worth more outside now." Aware of the complex mutual obligations of the leader and his followers, he declared, "I am willing to fight, but I don't want ever to feel that 'I held the Group together,' that I am wielding a power over or against you—that I stood in your way to being or becoming this or that. I am the representative of an idea which is as much yours as mine. Maybe this is all gas and I'm again making a big speech about something you all take for granted, but at least let me know that."

Clurman rejected all challenges to his business ability. The cause of the crisis was that the Group was a Group—"30 people being paid in a 9-cast show, continuity of work, etc." He asked for a vote of confidence, which was informally given. "The directors should go on and go more crazy" was how Kazan put it; he had not been released to take a role in a movie and Luther had to turn down a good role in *Stage Door* in order to go on with rehearsals. Russell Collins, playing the lead, offered to give up the role if a name actor would improve chances for financing. Dorothy Patten moved to accept "Russell's thought and give him a vote of confidence," but Eunice Stoddard countered: "No—it's time we cleared that up once and for all." Clurman's answer was a characteristic comeback: "That's right—if we did that it wouldn't be the Group." Without their support and understanding of "what it is to be in a collective, to be creating a collective," he would resign. "I personally want you to know that I need the iron of you to bind me together."

Clurman borrowed $1,500 from film director Lewis Milestone to aid the actors. Odets turned down his request for another $1,500, punishing Clurman for lack of planning. (*FY,* 188) Now, the hunt for funding was desperate. There was no money available from Hollywood where the movie moguls were angered by the new Dramatists' Guild contract that gave playwrights greater control over their plays. (Supporting the Guild had been the occasion for rancorous division between the Group directors and the union-oriented actors.) The generous Bess Eitingon, rejected earlier, now agreed to put up $40,000, which still was not enough for their most expensive production thus far. Milestone put them in touch with millionaire John Hay Whitney. Crawford's honesty and frankness wrested a fair deal from Whitney for his $12,000 investment, but money remained very short for this big production.

After the chaotic rehearsals and the ultimate failure of *Johnny Johnson*, the Actors' Committee issued their brutally frank December 1936 Report—the most painful skirmish in the long, complicated organizational strife. Conceived in secret meetings by committee members Stella, Bohnen, Carnovsky, and Kazan, all activists in and out of the Group, who with the exception of the amiable Bohnen, had no great love for one another, the stated intentions of the report were to make it possible for the Group to go on. But, when exposed publicly in this harsh document, the pressures and frustrations that had been mounting over the years destroyed the bonds that had held them together.

The paper zeroed in on the basic organizational strains in addition to revealing the disasters in their production process and the personality flaws in their three directors. Morale had dropped so low that old idealistic appeals for unity no longer worked. The three directors were now divided into two camps—Clurman versus Strasberg and Crawford. At the same time Clurman's reorganization had cut the actors off from the directors and destroyed the "democratic control" that the members had been evolving in their "old fashioned, longwinded" meetings. Indifference, intimidation, "political intrigue and egotistical ambition," and lack of work had undermined Group relationships and confidence in the company's economics. The paper observed that actors were afraid to raise questions about the ownership of the Group, about the "legal aspect of Group Inc. as compared to the acting collective," or to "urge the adoption of a plan to include them legally." To touch on this "outlawed subject" was thought to be "a sonofabitch at heart."

"Who really is the Group?" is the basic issue raised in the actors' report. We all know that five and [a] half years ago the Group was wrenched out of the American theatre by the sheer force of the directors' will. They, at that time, were indubitably *the Group Theatre*...Now five and a half years have passed—and the picture is different...today the Group is no longer the three directors. It is kept together neither by the domineering paternalism of Lee nor the hysterical faith of Harold...The Group Theatre today is the thirty members (including the individual directors.) Whatever superior talent and wisdom the directors might have today is no longer *the important factor* in holding the theatre together...

If the theatre is to go on it must be built on...love between equals who need each other and derive benefits from each other and thru working with each other. This does not call for artistic equalitarianism. No, we know a theatre, as an army, needs strict and ironclad leadership. But this leadership must not be based on autocratic and unreasoning domineering but on definite projects where the cue for leadership comes from definite plans and abilities...This change of fact about the Group the directors have not adjusted to. They still make the actors feel like stupid and naughty children instead of what is the fact, CO-WORKERS FOR THE SAME IDEA. (Actors Committee Report in Luther Adler Collection, NYPL, Lincoln Center)

The report offers a plan of operation to correct organizational faults and wipe out the "curdled idealism" that had destroyed the spirit of the Group. "Regular, predict-able, sustaining income" must replace the meager existence based on "a gamble for hits"; actors and directors must have "sufficient artistic exercise." Without satisfac-tory creative opportunity, there is no point in making the "tremendous sacrifice" to stay in the Group; both hits and flops deprive a permanent ensemble of work opportunities. The company must "institutionalize" the Group as a theater—ac-quire a theater plant, set up a yearly schedule of production along repertory lines, and develop an organized audience. A theater school is promoted as an immediate way of earning enough money to provide regular salaries while also establishing the Group as the Theatre Center of New York. "Passionate concern for the *Group Idea*," which the committee believes is the "one tattered bond left between us all," demands "IMMEDIATE ACTION" or "DISSOLUTION." WHICH WILL SERVE THE GROUP IDEA BEST? (*FY,* 193–96; Chinoy likely used the committee report in the Luther Adler Collection, NYPL, Lincoln Center)

Read to the members and then with their approval, copies of the report were sent to each of the three directors. Their response was stunning. Despite the tensions among them, at Clurman's suggestion, the three acted in concert. "Since all three of us are under attack, let us resign as a body of directors and along with the actors reconstitute the Group according to the new conditions that may obtain in the future" (*FY,* 196). What that future would be Clurman claimed he was too upset to consider. Shortly he would be leaving for a six-month stay in Hollywood, where Stella, like Odets and some of the others, had gone to try a movie career. Clurman didn't know when he would be back.

The members responded by setting up yet another committee—this one com-posed of the three former directors and Luther Adler, Kazan, and Bohnen repre-senting the actors, but their efforts to plan a new future for the Group produced no results. Clurman was noncommittal; Strasberg, angry and impatient; and Crawford used her bureaucratic skills in an effort to define a role for herself. No commitments for the future could be asked of anyone in these uncertain circumstances. The early days of 1937 were grim as the company postponed *The Silent Partner* rehearsals, cancelled some planned one-act plays, closed *Johnny Johnson*, and called off their season's operations. Before the month was out the actors were taking outside jobs, some went to the Federal Theatre, John Garfield landed his first lead in a Broadway show, *Having a Wonderful Time*, and more than a dozen went to Hollywood, where a Group Theatre deal was made with Walter Wanger for the use of many of its actors. Clurman and Kazan left for Hollywood on January 17 to pick up assign-ments Odets had finagled for them. Their departure from Grand Central Station surrounded by Group cronies, including Lee Strasberg who gave his longtime part-ner a rare edition of Ibsen's letter from his personal library, was the last, rather mournful hurrah of the original Group Theatre.

14. Who Is the Group Theatre? ✑

Now scattered on the East and West Coasts, the members determined to reorganize—a process that turned out to be as painful and as explosive as the Actors' Committee Report. In mid-March 1937, the New York contingent debated whether the Group was capable of being resuscitated or was already dead. Rumors were rife: Crawford insisted no one can use the name of the Group Theatre; she will resign, as will Strasberg. Those on the West Coast have been unresponsive; they remain members of the Group since, as Herbie Ratner remarked, "so far Gadge or Harold haven't started a new group"—a possibility obviously anticipated. Under pressure to determine the destiny of their theater, they also examined various new proposals on financing, salaries, play choices, and a detailed proposal for a Group Theatre School, which had been appended to the Actors' Report as the only immediately practical plan.

A few skeptics were not ready to jump-start the old Group machine. Sandy Meisner insisted a "new spirit" must be sparked first; Billy Kirkland wanted to know what kind of theater the new Group would be before he committed himself. Actor Michael Gordon—with due respect to all of us here, as he put it—wanted to know who will be in the Group? "Without Gadge, without Morris, without Luther, without Bud, without Stella, Harold, Lee and Cheryl, I do not want any longer to be with such a Group." Furthermore, Beany Barker attributed the decay of the Group to Stella's going off to Hollywood, followed by Harold, who can't live without her, and by Gadget, "who doesn't express . . . what he feels," and to other flaws of those in Hollywood. Strasberg wants the Group to go on and is interested in finding his place with them as a director, she reported with enthusiasm. Tony Kraber, regretting the Group never realized the "theoretic ideas for which it was formed," also regretted that Clurman, despite all his wonderful talk, "under stress of life took a wrong road," which led to the Group Theatre wanting to produce hits.

In Hollywood, in the meantime, Clurman had been desperate to get away, not only, as ever, to follow his Stella, who left for Hollywood after doing her stint on the Actors' Committee Report, and, not only to take a flyer working on a movie Odets was writing, but to escape from the painful collisions and failures in the Group. Clurman had encouraged the Actors' Committee to write its report without, he claimed, knowing what would be said. When it was presented, he "discerned a healthy spirit beneath its recriminations." The simultaneous resignation of the three directors in response to the report had been a false united front. A few weeks before the report was presented to them, Clurman and Strasberg had had a serious falling out as they struggled through the disappointments and embarrassments related to *Johnny Johnson*. Despite the tensions between the two men, they had always tried to conceal bitter feelings in order to keep the theater going. Clurman observed that "we respected our main task too much to allow any personal matters to stand in our way." Nevertheless, Strasberg complained violently that Clurman as managing director failed to facilitate his work staging *Johnny Johnson*. When Clurman told him to write his complaints down in an unemotional letter and that in turn Clurman would write out what was bothering him, Strasberg replied in what Clurman considered a very telling, characteristic, but honest reflection of Strasberg's inability to accept criticism, "No, no, that I can't take." When Strasberg and Clurman met to determine what to do after the Actors' Report, the two men were no longer talking to one another. Kazan reported that Clurman told him—in private when they had gone to the "can"—that he would never again work with Cheryl, whom he distrusted, or with Lee, whose personal problems prevented him from realizing his talent. Their long, special relationship had "worn out."

Hollywood provided a perfect refuge for Clurman and other Group members who, while being tested for films, were protesting their loyalty to the Group. They wanted to have the money, prestige, and good life of Hollywood and the artistic and social idealism of the Group. It was Clurman who resisted the pressure to initiate the Group's revival. He even resisted contributing to the assessments the company had voted to help Crawford keep the Group's New York office open. Working in Hollywood was proving interesting; life in movie land was pleasant, especially since he and Stella, ensconced in an elegant house with servants, were happily together. With her new nose and new film-name of Ardler, Stella seemed about to emerge as a star. It was very hard for him to make the choice on which the future of the Group depended.

Elia Kazan's role in this transition period was pivotal and puzzling. He identified himself as the one who wrote most of the Actors' Committee Report, placing the future of the Group in the hands of the actors. That would be consistent with an effort by the radicals to gain control of the organization. But it would seem that Kazan was already on the outs with the Unit and his attitude toward "the people" as potential leaders of the Group was fairly negative. Clurman wrote to Strasberg in the spring of 1936 that "a curious thing is that Gadget whose feeling tends to be what ours is in general can hardly stomach the company of late and avoids them. I asked him why? He answered, 'They are "cynical"; they are full of baloney and they keep on repeating the same clichéd complaints like a record.'"

Kazan kept Odets, then in Hollywood, fully informed about how the three directors responded to the report. The sequence leading to the three founders' resignation almost makes it seem as if he and Clurman had prearranged the scenario in order to put the other two directors on the spot or get them out of the Group. Kazan described Crawford's attitude as showing that "this self-willed little girl wanted to be managing director." He called Strasberg's statement that "it was now impossible for him to work in the Group" a "surly egotistical reply." Yet, Kazan wrote Odets that he had little confidence in what he called "the democratic machinery." He feared that a democratic mandate would empower people he did not respect. He even preferred Strasberg, who at least had important ideas about theater, to other possible leaders. Rumor had it that Kazan wanted to take over himself, something he, of course, later vigorously denied. (Adams, 184) But many remembered that he had said when interviewed by Strasberg in 1932 about becoming an apprentice that his objective was to take over Strasberg's job.

Kazan traveled back and forth between the coasts to see for himself what options the movie business offered and to discover what the Group members at both ends of the country had in mind. Using his backstage skills, he seemed to be organizing the various contenders for the next step. His letters to Odets in Hollywood, crucial to any revival of the Group, pulled the playwright into the struggle. Back in New York, Kazan met with the East Coast people on April 7, 1937, and then filled Odets in about what he had done. Purposely painting a very grim picture for the "true believers" in the East, Kazan penned a very lively, but mean-spirited sketch of the meeting for Odets, writing, for example, that Beany Barker, whose "eyes glowered like a Zealots," complained again and again that Kazan was not an original member and kept heckling him. "I finally reverted to type and shut her up," he said of himself. For Odets's benefit, he lined up those on the East Coast who are "for us and only for us"—notably Mike Gordon, Sandy Meisner, and Bobby Lewis.

In all of this one can see—and the members who remained in New York must have sensed—the new Group of Clurman, Kazan, along with Luther Adler, Bud Bohnen, and, of course, Odets, in the making. What Kazan had in mind for the future becomes clear in an exchange of letters with Strasberg. Kazan was certain that in the fall he would work in a Group, but without the unhealthy relationships of the last year and half. "We need fresh blood; we need to take chances again with new people. Loyalty is no longer enough. The struggle is too fierce." But before any action is taken, they must wait to discover what choice Harold will make—to stay in Hollywood with Stella, whose new nose "is a 'huge success'" and will probably assure a film contract, or return to New York and the Group. When the Group begins again, "it will have Luther, Bud, Jules, Art, Harold, Morris, Ruth, and I think Bobby." Kazan stated frankly that Clurman has not "determined" his relationship to his former codirectors. Since "theatre is a collective art and the working parts have to work or else," it seemed unlikely that Strasberg would be included. Kazan called for leadership, proclaiming "nothing will arise that's good from the will of the majority."

Strasberg, having determined to resign, challenged Kazan in a return letter. "*You are now the Group Theatre*," using "you," he added, generically to include others. What will you do to bring about change besides talk? Had any planning been done before precipitating the collapse of the Group? "If not," Strasberg charged, "your actions were criminally irresponsible...You have destroyed your leadership. You must now find it from your own ranks."

On March 17, 1937, Cheryl Crawford, reacting to the "painful juggernaut" of the Actors' Report and the frustration of trying to keep the Group office in New York going by herself, wrote her letter of resignation to the Council. Affirming belief in a Group theater and regretting her action, she was still convinced that while "the objective or outside situations which have caused us so much strain and difficulty *can* be slowly solved, but the inner situation seems to me incapable of solution at least at this time" (100). She turned down a lucrative job in Hollywood in the hope of producing shows in New York on her own.

Lee Strasberg's letter of resignation followed quickly. He was "no longer willing to wait till Harold and the others rest up sufficiently to make their decision." After biding his time, investigating where he might fit in or lead, he had concluded, as he wrote to his wife Paula in Hollywood, that

> fundamentally the people aren't up to the action...I doubt whether their problems or the relations of the directors (with which Gadge seems to be so concerned) will be helped by the passage of time...I do feel very strongly however that for the people of the Group to have gone ahead and wrecked the Group organization without any immediate and definite plans and assumption of responsibility was a criminal act. It leaves me speechless and breathless to realize that that's what all their talking and complaining came to. (Letter when seen by Chinoy was in Anna Strasberg's possession)

Although Strasberg felt better "personally and physically," after his resignation, he confessed to Paula, "I feel too strongly about the need of a Group Theatre just to throw the whole thing off. The only thing is that for me as a director and student of theatre it is possible to contribute my share to some extent regardless of what I do in the commercial theatre. But that remains to be seen." He had feelers out for movie work and hoped to collaborate with Crawford and others in a pleasant, intelligent producing unit where profits would be shared and the relationship would have "nothing idealistic about it."

The way was clear for a new Group Theatre. On April 2, 1937, Clurman accepted Strasberg's resignation, responding on behalf of the Council, which "is taking over the job of running the Group and will do everything in its power to keep it going and to build it up." Despite all that had gone on, he concluded the letter with a tribute, saying that for himself,

> the years since I have known you personally and "professionally," have really been the years that have made me. I look back at them gratefully and proudly. They were years of wonderful creative collaboration that, we need not doubt, have stamped themselves permanently on the life and thought and activity in the American theatre. Despite the fact that we now "part," I feel sure that, because we represent the maturest thinking and experience in the American theatre, we may still be of invaluable assistance and service to one another in whatever work in the theatre we may undertake from this point on. (Anna Strasberg Collection; now in the Library of Congress)

Over 50 years later, Clurman offered this interesting gloss on the tangled events of this spring. He told Louis Sheaffer, interviewing him, that Crawford and Strasberg were sure that he was not going to return from Hollywood. "They in the meantime...sent me their letters of resignation, but I hadn't resigned. I said, 'I'm taking a leave.' So when I came back I was the sole director, and I think Lee thought I had pulled a fast one by doing that." About this same time Strasberg confided to David Garfield, who was writing *A Player's Place* about The Actors Studio, that "someone who had been involved with the Group's behind-the-scenes political machinations let slip to him that he was not supposed to have resigned when he did. His leaving evidently threw a monkey wrench into the Communist cell's plans to take control of the organization. When pressed for further explanation, Strasberg's interlocutor quickly changed the subject" (*Player's Place*, 37).

The complex machinations leading to the collapse of the original Group organization remain difficult to untangle. As to the relationship of the two men, they never worked together again, although Clurman considered inviting Strasberg to direct for the Group in 1939 and later moderated the Playwrights Unit for The Actors Studio in the mid-1960s. They resisted the many opportunities over the years to launch direct attacks at one another out of continued respect for the Group Idea they had both tried to serve.

Kazan, ever energetic and aggressive, determined to rouse his hero and mentor from his "comatose" state. He appealed in a long letter to Clurman's sense of mission, praised his inspirational force, even showed compassionate understanding combined with realistic appraisal of the complexities of Clurman's debilitating relationship with Stella. Kazan believed that Luther Adler, Bud Bohnen, and he could start on their own, but Clurman was essential. Kazan wrote,

> But I'd rather work with you than with anyone else…I think you and I have the motor, the energy, the fanatical desire and fanatical energy, the brains, the experience, the ruthlessness, the richness, the emotion, the appetite to build the greatest theatre ever built and I think we can do it in America, today. But we can't do it with you split up, un-resolved, hesitating, *un-youthful*.

Kazan and the others started to plan the next stage. By early May, Clurman succumbed to Kazan's moving pleas (to "be his youthful self") and (He) realized that for him "there were no two choices. There was only one course: to begin work again next season with the Group" (*FY*, 206). Even a tearful Stella, who would remain in Hollywood, prodded him one night: "You shouldn't be here. You should be back in New York where your real work is" (from unpublished section of *FY*).

The Group Theatre that came to life again in the fall of 1937 boasted a new organizational structure. As the sole director, Clurman was aided by Odets and a Council composed of Kazan, Bohnen, and Luther Adler; these five were to be the officers of a new nonprofit corporation. Clurman contributed some of his own money to open a new office in the Sardi Building, where with his name on the door, a new secretary, a new business manager, and a new attorney, he set out to run the Group Theatre under new guidelines. His colleagues talked of a new attitude toward box office, big business, and commercial success, and Clurman himself later confessed, "something had changed within me."

Although the shift within the Group was the result of the complex inner dynamics of the company, it was also part of the "retreat from the creative ferment and radical possibilities of the early 1930s" that historians of the era analyze. The success of Roosevelt's New Deal, which ameliorated the worst of the Depression ills, rescuing capitalism rather than revolutionizing America, combined with the need for a United Front to fight against the rising threat of war and fascism brought the radicals in theater closer to the mainstream of American social and economic life. The left-wing theaters had all but disappeared, their radical mission translated into the new United Front rhetoric. The Theatre Union collapsed in 1937; Theatre of Action was absorbed as an experimental unit into the Federal Theatre Project, initiated in 1935. On the Labor Stage that housed *Pins and Needles*, in the political cabaret TAC (Theatre Arts Committee for Democracy), which attacked fascism abroad and reaction at home with spirited sketches and song, and on Broadway itself, lively, hopeful, not too confrontational entertainment replaced the old sectarian messages. Clurman would write that "1937 was the year of hope and confidence among progressives" (*FY,* 214). He would also recognize evitable "traces of cynicism" as he and the others negotiated the contradictions between the ideals that had animated and agitated the old Group, which they would not wholly abandon, and the new organizational practices intended to keep the theater alive on Broadway.

The first thing to go was the permanent, secure collective, which Clurman considered "the fundamental principle" of the Group organization. Clurman stipulated that he "would not guarantee a salary to anyone not employed in actual production work." The sign on his office door that read "Nobody is in the Group Theatre except the cast of *Golden Boy*" set the tone of the unsentimental new management, which would act without the old "religiosity" and without "ideological whipping." His decision devastated those not cast for *Golden Boy*, among them Margaret Barker, who never acted with the Group again, and distressed many of the Group veterans who were among the new "Chosen Ones," including members of the Council, along with Phoebe Brand, Morris Carnovsky, Lee J. Cobb, John Garfield, and Bobby Lewis, who were in *Golden Boy*, as well as Ruth Nelson, Sandy Meisner, and Stella Adler, who served in various production capacities.

After the opening of *Golden Boy* the actors complained that the Council, in league with their new business manager, Kermit Bloomgarden, had become a "clique." Clurman insisted that their suspicion was unfounded, but even Odets later would complain that Clurman, with his "sturdy crutch Kazan," and Bloomgarden "ran everything, had all the fun, all the excitement." Although in earlier years, the actors had advocated a professional business manager, they remained uneasy about Bloomgarden. Some believed that his "hard-nosed" business attitudes contributed to the "slow erosion" of the ensemble values that had distinguished the Group. That Bloomgarden continued to work in the commercial theater, as manager for Herman Shumlin, while functioning part-time in the Group and leaving the many chores to be carried out by the very willing, but inexperienced novice secretary, Ruth Young, was also troubling. The new, pragmatic Clurman put much of the actors' distress down to jealousy, but he also realized it was "another manifestation of the actors' desire to feel that the organization was truly theirs and to participate in every thought process, discussion, decision that affected the Group." He placated the actors with high-sounding words about how he could not function as their leader unless they trusted him.

Clurman, who had not forgotten the past, could not ignore the financial and other constraints in his new reign. Money remained problematic. Clurman had to find "angels" to finance *Golden Boy* despite the fact that he had told his associates that under no circumstances would he any longer raise the backing for shows. The task turned out to be difficult, despite the fact that the play was intended as a "popular success" to jump-start the new Group. In the fall of 1937, with the country in recession, potential backers wanted a return on their investment rather than the satisfaction of supporting an artistic production. The script, ending in the deaths of the Golden Boy and his girl, was judged too gloomy to succeed; stars rather than the Group ensemble would be needed to make it a hit. Clurman found these accepted show business calculations "shameful."

When the company was still without their required budget of $19,000 ten days before the opening, Odets, who had earned $90,000 in Hollywood, and his wife Luise Rainer invested their own money for a 25 percent interest. Other friends from Hollywood, including Walter Wanger, helped out. Most of the remaining Group plays were largely financed in a similar way, directly or indirectly by Hollywood money, but the financial dealings with both outsiders and insiders was always a complicated, frustrating process. Odets, along with his Group cronies, Luther Adler and his wife Sylvia Sidney, and a few small investors from *Golden Boy*, put up most of the backing for *Rocket to the Moon*'s $11,643 budget. Some later claimed the company manipulated the finances to the investors' detriment.

To initiate his last Group production, *Night Music*, Odets reluctantly agreed to write the screenplay and sell the screen rights to the new film company of Al Lewin and David Loew in return for $20,000, to which he added $21,000 of his own money. Odets had felt humiliated when the Group could not raise the money for the expensive production. Clurman admitted that we "hawked it around a bit in the manner customary to a Broadway producer looking for a backer," although Odets thought "that his position as 'America's leading young playwright' absolved his work from the laws of business evaluation" (*FY*, 262). Apart from the Odets plays, Franchot Tone picked up the tab for *The Gentle People*, which did not recoup its production costs. Tone also sustained losses from a scandal at the Belasco's box-office, which robbed the company of some of the advance sale money. Carl Laemmle, Jr., one of several people Clurman had been negotiating with, invested the needed $20,000 for *Retreat to Pleasure*. The Group itself put up money for the experimental shows, *My Heart's in the Highlands* and *Quiet City*, and along with $20,000 from their good friend Dorothy Willard for *Casey Jones*.

Golden Boy's success rewarded everyone. It ran for 284 performances; the Group earned $36,286, plus $15,000 from the $75,000 sale of the film rights. After paying people back, the profits kept the Group going for two seasons. The company was able to guarantee the salaries for 16 members for the 1938–39 season and place designer Max Gorelik under contract for a year. Their good financial standing led Clurman and his council to propose a formal plan for raising the $100,000 subsidy they believed would allow the company to function as a repertory theater. With the advice of lawyers, the Group offered investors 50 percent of profits on four planned plays and subsequent productions. It was the old dream of a theater company being subsidized like an opera house or a symphony orchestra, although Clurman recalled he was afraid to repeat the analogy. When the plan did not find any takers, he concluded that the idea of theater as an institution was dead.

In place of subsidy, the Group counted on the considerable audience support they had developed through benefits and theater parties. The successful sale of tickets at a discount to a variety of organizations—schools, unions, political clubs—in advance of openings guaranteed a run of almost six weeks. For the 1938–39 season, $80,000 worth of benefits were sold. Nevertheless, the benefit audience was obviously not the ideal Group audience.

In answer to some penetrating questions about audiences and play choices from Frances Farmer, Clurman identified the Group's true audience as the small complement of intellectual enthusiasts who came to all of their shows. These devotees were "college students, people who read the *New Masses* and *Nation*, young radicals, school teachers, some lower middle-class and proletariat." They buy the limited number of 50¢ and $1.00 seats in advance for the Odets shows, but their numbers were not great enough to fill the theater even for productions of *Waiting for Lefty*. Reduced ticket prices, he insisted, would not provide money to pay salaries of $100 a week. The company had to compromise its desire for an audience composed of people from difference classes.

For a more complete audience, Odets, buoyed by the success of *Golden Boy*, turned to Hallie Flanagan's Federal Theatre Project. For America's peoples' theater, he considered a plan to offer simultaneous productions across the country of the still incomplete and unproduced *The Silent Partner*—ultimately turned down by Clurman. In a conversation with Helen Hayes, whose husband was the popular playwright Charles MacArthur, Clurman envisioned a theater of the common people—where "we write, direct, stage, and act a play and the audience comes, for everybody in the audience has someone in his life whom he's trying to save or whose common welfare is threatened."

But no such communion materialized with the Group's Broadway audience, which had to be lured by the glamor and entertainment of stars. To ensure that *Golden Boy* would be a hit, Odets wanted the "best cast money could buy." Clurman brought the beautiful, talented Frances Farmer from the West Coast, featuring her along with Luther Adler and Morris Carnovsky, who were gaining movie recognition. The spotlighting of stars—Frances Farmer in *Golden Boy*, Charles Bickford in *Casey Jones*, Franchot Tone, Sylvia Sidney, and Sam Jaffee in *The Gentle People*, even young Eleanor Lynn in *Rocket to the Moon*—was seen in some quarters as conspicuous evidence of the Group's increasing commercialism. It especially troubled the others in the cast who, in addition to being overshadowed, thought the Hollywood players might be earning big salaries. Not so, Clurman insisted, and pointed out his own modest financial position. He claimed no ownership of Group properties or profits, only earned $300 a week and no additional director's fee, and reiterated that he could not offer money as a lure for work in the Group. The actors could expect, he said, "little better than a decent poverty" (*FY*, 238).

In their years in the Group, the actors calculated they had worked 18 weeks per season during the first nine years, with the worst season being 1939–40, followed by the *Johnny Johnson* period. The best were the seasons of *Men in White* and *Golden Boy*. In only three seasons had they been paid the promised salaries; all the rest involved drastic cuts. Distributing the yearly income earned over the 40-week season resulted in an average income of $27 a week; for those at the low end of the scale, the figure was about $19 a week; those toward the top, averaged about $39 a week. The Clurman era, as they called it, was better than the earlier period, but unpredictable.

Clurman himself no longer felt it appropriate to ask the actors to prolong the run of a show such as *Thunder Rock* by taking salary cuts; the play did not justify the sacrifice. When Odets suggested the actors' salary be reduced to keep *Night Music* open, Clurman offered to eliminate his own salary, and that of the business manager and press representative, but not that of the actors. He told Odets, "[M]ost of our actors had earned something like five weeks pay since the preceding spring. To ask them to cut their salaries under such circumstances was mean" (*FY*, 264).

To make up for productions ending in the red and leaving the company without either money or creative work and also to take advantage of their occasional successes, the Group undertook tours with original or alternate Group casts of some of their popular productions—*Golden Boy, Rocket to the Moon,* and the revival of *Awake and Sing!* Philadelphia, Baltimore, Chicago, Boston, and Newark were among cities visited for shorter or longer stops. Some tours made money, gaining the Group a national reputation and wide influence. Others were disappointing, but allowed the company to rehearse new plays while performing.

The road provided ironic experiences. During the successful Chicago tour of *Awake and Sing!,* the stodgy opening-night audience was unresponsive, didn't get the Jewish and New York jokes; some university students, possibly Trotskyites, heckled the actors, whom they may have considered Stalinists and pelted them with oranges. Stella called on the rest of the audience to "protect the actors on your stage." She, Meisner, and Bobby Lewis replacing Joe Bromberg as Uncle Morty, bonded as a disaffected trio whom Clurman dubbed the "Weird Sisters," and a young Arthur Miller sitting in the balcony was inspired to become a playwright. (See *Timebends,* 227 ff.) Taking a show on the road was often considered the best way to fill empty coffers; Luther Adler with his background in the Yiddish theater recommended it highly. But the actors were not willing to keep repeating their more successful productions if it meant giving up work on new scripts and fresh acting challenges, which they considered their primary purpose.

The rising popularity of radio in the 1930s provided opportunity for needed funds. The Group actors performed cuttings of their productions and original pieces on the Kate Smith and Rudy Vallee shows. The company also considered making films in New York and with Walter Wanger in Hollywood. Many of the actors were ambivalent about these money-making projects. They did not mind doing benefits, lectures, teaching in the school that Bobby Lewis set up in 1939, or even licking envelopes for the good of the Group. They considered acting in radio and films as money-making and personal celebrity rather than fulfilling the Group's collective needs.

The Group's unity, to which the company had dedicated itself, disintegrated in the Clurman years. In the final two seasons, desperate efforts were made to patch together an organizational, artistic, and ideological approach that would restore and sustain the Group Theatre—all of this in the face of the fall of the democratically elected government of Spain, of the rising Nazi horror, the Nazi-Soviet pact, and a world hurtling toward war. In extraordinary sessions at Smithtown, on Long Island, in 1939, the company tried to determine just "what a Group member is" and if the Group "could be created afresh, on the basis of mistakes, experiences, and knowledge, acquired in nine years of struggle and accomplishments," as Clurman put it. That so many of the original members still wanted to recapture the impulse that had brought them together and to accommodate it in some way to the changes that had occurred in their lives, the country, and the world, testified to the profound impact the Group Idea had made on them all. Bobby Lewis called it "a miracle."

To outsiders, the very large gathering of performers—Hollywood stars, Group veterans, and eager apprentices—seemed the acme of the Group's ambitions. Newspapers headlined stories, "Group Goes to School." There were classes for movement with Maria Ley (Mrs. Erwin Piscator), speech with Edith Stebbins, acting with Bobby Lewis, scene work with Sandy Meisner and Stella Adler, and script development with Molly Day Kazan. In addition, there were rehearsals of *The Three Sisters* and political talks by their communist labor organizer-friend Sid Benson. The two dormitories at Smithtown were dubbed "Belasco" and "Windsor"; tennis, basketball, and swimming on the hundred-acre grounds of Winwood School provided fun and games. Beneath all the activity, the wild charades, and crazy pranks, there was painful disappointment.

Under the desperate tutelage of Clurman, the members met again and again during the summer in an emotionally charged, urgent search for their roots. What they had started with so much hope at Brookfield was sadly disintegrating at Smithtown. In 1931, they expected to be "untangled" by their technique and their collective life and art. In 1939, they were trying to untangle what it had all meant in sessions that Odets's biographer Margaret Brenman-Gibson suggests foreshadowed the "encounter" sessions of a later decade (565). They examined every professional and personal idea they had tried to live by—collectivism, individualism, socialism, art theater, ensemble acting, subjective probing, commitment to others, self-realization, Russian models, American heritage. They confronted their demons—competition, money, success, sectarianism, jealousy, disrespect, arrogance, domination, lovelessness. They faced one another in harangues, confessions, attacks, and questions—all in the hope of sustaining the Group Idea, which they believed they were in imminent danger of losing or, which, some felt, they had indeed already lost. Captured in a verbatim log of several hundred pages by Elizabeth Gordon, wife of actor Michael Gordon, these sessions, in which they were both students and teachers, comprised the extraordinary last class of the Group. (Copies of transcripts of the log were provided to several members of the Group; excerpts are cited in Smith.)

At the heart of their wide-ranging ruminations were the questions of leadership, internal democracy, individual creative growth, and collective identity. Clurman threw down an initial challenge to the company early in July. Declaring that the old Group was dead, he asked the members if they would give themselves over to his absolute authority for eight months to determine their artistic, professional, and personal destiny. In answer to their negative responses, Clurman struggled to articulate what he was after. He insisted "that a certain type of democracy, a certain way of voting and giving an opinion on everything by raising of hands can't help and can't make you better actors or writers...It's something that has nothing to do with legislation...I say there is a more profound thing" (see Smith for extensive Clurman comments from the Smithtown log).

Groping, vague, loquacious, but also moving, Clurman made an impassioned plea for his leadership as a unifying force. He didn't want to be "Der Fuerhrer," as Bobby Lewis lovingly dubbed this least dictatorial of men. He wanted to be a creator. What Clurman was after had something to do with a willingness to have confidence, faith, respect, and trust in one another and in the Group itself. He quipped that he respected Odets as if he were a dead writer, and that the Group should respect him as he respected Stanislavsky. Arguing for his leadership, Clurman said, "I believe that that is the way we all can really grow...through giving yourselves to me in such a way you would then affirm your personalities, become strong, become individuals and would strengthen yourselves, your power, your influence in the Group." The influence would be reciprocal. He would be their teacher, but also the "pupil of all the people." The process was caught up in what he himself called "Clurman's Mysticism."

In the bedlam that followed his outrageous idea, which was in part intended to spark discussion, the members exposed with considerable bitterness over the contradictions between the creative ideal of mutual interdependence that Clurman advocated and the difficult personal and professional realities with which they had to cope. Bobby Lewis spoke of having to resolve personal problems not through Clurman but on his own in order to make his best contribution to the Group and to Clurman. Uncomfortable in his relationships with his fellow actors and with his own development, Morris Carnovsky decried the lack of discipline and respect for the work and attacked the "Grouplets" that flourished. He sensed the company had reached the end of the impulse that had brought them together. Sandy Meisner complained of the success psychology that had been in evidence since *Golden Boy*, resulting in fine plays such as *Rocket to the Moon* not being produced "in the spirit of the Group."

Bud Bohnen identified a "citizen quotient" needed for their organization. Phoebe Brand wanted more probing craft work, and Ruth Nelson felt she had not developed. Frances Farmer was concerned about the limited opportunities for the women. And from all came complaints about competitiveness, lack of integrity and morality, favoritism in casting, the practical needs that make them unable to work for $40 a week. They wanted a loose rather than a tight membership in which those who wanted to leave for movies or Broadway could still be Group members.

In an effort to clarify his still inchoate notions, Clurman, after hearing the others, posed two alternatives: "[A] Group...standing with their arms around each other's shoulders in a big ring, in which all of us are as grown up men and women really bound together," or, "we can all go back to our own individualities where we will no longer be a Group Theatre and will be impoverished and left to our own isolation."

Clurman's rather confused, pained leadership of his resistant followers was put to the test less than a month later on August 8 when he called the company together at Smithtown to consider whether or not Bud Bohnen should be permitted to leave the Group for five weeks to play the role of Candy in the film of John Steinbeck's *Of Mice and Men*. Not knowing just what he ought to do in these circumstances and wanting the members to assist him in making a new beginning as their leader, Clurman put the burden of decision on them and on Bohnen, who was devoted enough to the Group ethos not to leave without their collective consent. All agreed Bohnen had a desperate financial need for the $1,500 salary; and all agreed that he should go because he would return from Hollywood. People like Jules Garfield and Lee J. Cobb, whose big Packard became an egregious symbol, had become "movie people," lost to the Group.

At issue was the principle on which such decisions were to be made. Should production requirements be paramount? Should only personal needs be considered or should there be flexibility? Others, like Carnovsky and Lewis, who complained that "I should have been with [Alla] Nazimova making money," had pressing financial needs and good stage and film offers, but Clurman, having told them they were needed for the summer, they came to Smithtown. It would be too "ungroupy" to leave, although most of the original plans, like staging Odets's *The Silent Partner* with its very large cast, had been abandoned. Bohnen considered his playing a fine film role "a constructive Group thing," and offered a further "definite Group angle" for his departure. He asked the Group lawyer Arthur Krim and manager Kermit Bloomgarden for advice about requiring director Lewis Milestone to pay a release fee to the Group. He was even willing to do the Hollywood stint for a Group salary.

Kazan, direct and to-the-point as always, warned Clurman that the "general tendency to loosen things" would be very bad for the organization. "Maybe the fabric of our lives in this country will necessitate that. We may all reach crises which will make us go in this direction…But, it is up to you…because this theatre is being run for this theatre not for any individual." Ruth Nelson projected their conflicted feelings. "If I were in a room with Bud and a couple of people, I would say you go, but in a Group meeting I would vote no." Mike Gordon insisted that it was none of his business that people have debts. "Either we have to know that as actors we are going to budget ourselves in a certain way according to the Group needs." Bohnen countered that no problem would exist if they were all involved in productions.

Clurman took it all in, concluding, "I agree with everything that's been said." Although he commended the discussion for being intelligent and mature, others like Bloomgarden considered that Bohnen had been "violently attacked, relentlessly stripped, for even *considering* a Hollywood job." Bohnen left for the West Coast, was not available to be cast in *The Three Sisters*, and the issue came up again and again. Clurman complained that if he were preparing stars for Hollywood he would not have done it by founding the Group Theatre.

Nevertheless, those who remained to be cast in the Chekhov play were not at ease. Casting practices, for example, had been bitterly attacked for inequities and favoritism. Now, Clurman faced immediate problems. There were too many actors and actresses for the available roles, and, although he picked the most experienced, feelings were hurt. "Every piece of casting in the Group is a tragedy," Clurman declared. Worn down by the emotionally fraught summer, Clurman found himself uncertain about how to approach the complex script. He made Stella, more experienced with European plays, his codirector. As always their private battles affected the Group. Clurman one day shouted at the members during one of their many "truth sessions": "It is simply not the Group's business if I've had a fight with Stella. And it's not your business, either, if I want to make up with her." In what he called his "halting, indecisive" frame of mind, he was not able to extinguish intensifying rehearsal flare-ups between Stella and Carnovsky, playing Masha and Vershinin in *The Three Sisters*, or control the secret cabals defending each actor. A frightful family quarrel exploded among the weary and disappointed company. (*FY*, 257) Carnovsky shouted at Stella the worst possible insult: "You are not a truthful actress. I just don't believe you" (quoted in W. Smith, 388). Shortly thereafter, she left the cast and the production had to be abandoned.

At the heart of their tarnished, interpersonal relations remained their inability to define their existence as a collective in a hostile and individualistic capitalist society. "It's simply a word in a book until we find out what kind of collective we are and know each individual's responsibility," Ruth Nelson astutely observed. Kazan felt a distinction between their creative process and their interpersonal and organizational relationships. "I think when we work on a production which turns out well, we have an [artistic] collective...I always feel a rapport in our productions which is almost the highest kind of collective work. Outside of that, I don't know what it is."

Clurman responded to these ruminations with a celebration of the Group as a collective throughout its history. But, he also admitted that he had always been deliberately "elusive" in using concepts such as *collectivism*, preferring the significant values to come through the Group's unique work and life experience rather than in pronouncements. He explained that "Groupism or Clurmanism" derives from his feelings about life, from one of its basic contradictory facts, that of separation and connection. "There is pain and tragic choice in the dialectic of self and other, but maturity comes with adjustment." Clurman queried, "Who is the Group theatre, *they*? It is not they. It is *us*." "The highest self-realization," he argued, "comes through the collective" which each "must serve to become all he is capable of."

At Smithtown, Clurman rarely endowed the Group's collectivism with some of the specific social or political meaning that had been attached to it over the years. He briefly recalled that his Steinway Hall talks had emphasized the need for a theater to "say something," and he acknowledged the socialist context of Vakhtangov's "ideologically cemented collective" had enlarged his understanding. He even remembered rejoicing to discover that his mentor Stanislavsky had founded the Moscow Art Theatre in 1898 not to teach the system but to serve the people. He did not particularly respond, for example, to Art Smith's reminder that "we have followed a general line of fighting for a better life—that Theatre is a weapon to fight with." Nevertheless, Clurman had concluded that political theater could not survive on Broadway and confided that he had always been personally uncomfortable with a heavily didactic approach.

The contradictions and disappointments of the last two years, so painfully aired at Smithtown, had left Clurman debilitated and uncertain. Like so many facing imminent World War at the end of the Depression decade, Clurman emphasized the personal side of the complex dynamic of individual and group. Deeply worried about the possible dissolution of the Group, this "wonderful, miserable organization," he pleaded for a sense of the collective based on the honesty of individuals and a pragmatic communal spirit that says if "something is wrong here, let's fix it, but by joining together with a 'yes' to the Group work."

Ironically, it was the actors rather than Clurman himself who continued to say "yes" to the Group. His characterization of the mood of "intense stagnation" in New York at the end of the decade reflected his own feelings after Smithtown. "History was marking time. Progressive thought and action seemed to stand in shadow, tired and disheartened. Everyone seemed to be waiting. Everything was in question, and all the old answers rang a little false beside the darkening reality." His own answers, he realized, no longer held up. When he summoned up his familiar "professions of faith" in the Group and its mission as "an association of the strongest creative forces in the American theatre," he confessed that he "impressed no one—not even myself." Although he bought plays and planned seasons, he could no longer bring himself to consider fixing the myriad problems of the Group—personal, creative, financial, and organizational.

The actors, frustrated by the unproductive summer at Smithtown, the failure of *Thunder Rock*, and then the many disappointments of *Night Music* in February of 1940, wanted Clurman both to take the blame and provide the remedies they had been advocating for years— democratizing and restructuring the organization. All the problems could be solved if, as Clurman put it, "I would be the leader who carried out the will of the collective—in other words, their will." The actors had begun to move on their own, drawing inspiration from *Waiting for Lefty* and *Awake and Sing!* and the 1936 Actors' Committee Report. In 1939, a committee put together a constitution intended to codify relationships, finances, and authority within the Group. Although their document had no impact at the time, it was modified to become part of the final battle between Clurman and his people in the last year of the Group's life.

At the beginning of 1940, Clurman abandoned the last vestiges of the original Group Idea. No longer would there be any actors on seasonal contracts, as they had managed the previous season. The final blow came when he announced that he would run the Group alone, without the Council or the various committees. Clurman asserted that he would take the advice and collaboration of whomever inside or outside the Group he saw fit to consult, and, echoing the words he used at Smithtown, he claimed that "if the theatre is truly my theatre, you will find that it is yours as well" (*FY*, 268). Shaken by the menacing "family squabble," some actors justified his action as a transition to "smooth functioning. Others accused Clurman of having "established himself as a 'dictator' with the support of Clifford Odets and Elia Kazan." While Clurman told the press that he knew "nothing about dissension," the protesters reiterated that "the Group was originally formed as a collective unit whose policies were to be determined democratically." Molly Day Kazan, who often took it on herself to serve as a Puritan conscience for the Group, resigned. (*FY*, 269)

Despite accusations of collusion with Clurman, Odets initially felt himself outside of the "clash of wills and ego and material needs" that was inevitable in the Group as the "thin varnish of idealism" cracked. During rehearsals of *Night Music*, he noted in his journal that there was a good chance of the Group collapsing; without his play, "there would be no Group Theatre." According to "An Analysis of the Problems" (January 28, 1940) that Odets kept among his papers, if *Night Music* was successful, it might become the catalyst for the transformation of the Group. (*TisR*, 24–25) With consideration of the "inner problems" of the Group yet again, the alternatives that faced the company were unchanged: dissolution, operate as a "semi-artistic, semi-commercial" company, or plan to become the ideal theater the members wanted. A proposed plan offered a somewhat more pragmatic recombination of many earlier strategies, given urgency by the fact that after the "years of 'muddling through,'" the company had to do something. The usual scheme of "major productions reflecting American life more truly than other theatres" carried the warning to make choices "with regard to box-office appeal, not too risky in content or form, yet not too burdened with 'money names' that may destroy the ensemble playing for which audiences come to see the Group." A second line of Sunday night productions could offer classics, Odets's plays, and new writers; continuous classes and studio work to develop the acting to ever higher standards; and integration of new talent in acting and writing. Only such a total program, rather than gambling for hits, would justify the sacrifices the actors would be willing to make as participants in a "vital and living organism" rather than as "employees" in a commercial enterprise. The analysis concluded that the theater that it envisioned would be based on continuity and permanence and "a common world view, a common view of the relation of the theatre to society, and a common acting technique." Given the confusions and differences about basic values exposed at Smithtown, the spirit of compromise and minimal collaboration of the company in decision-making hardly betokened a new beginning.

With the dismal reception of *Night Music*, drastic action was needed to succor the mortally ill Group. Odets, feeling himself deeply wounded, nevertheless took an active role within the company. Planning meetings were called without Clurman, who was attacked for the artistic and organizational collapse. A committee comprised of Bohnen, Carnovsky, James Proctor (their press agent), and Odets met to plan "what an ideal Group should be." Odets confided ambivalent feelings in his journal about making the needed changes but concluded that the four-hour meeting had accomplished little. "The Group Theatre tangle is not going to be controlled or fixed with fine phrases. It will need plenty of hard work, clarity, and discipline and control to make a real Group Theatre on top of what now exists" (3/6/40; *TisR*, 56–57).

The day before this meeting, Odets had finally been able to "have it out" with Clurman about the Group. Odets still had not frankly confronted Clurman about what he felt were the disasters of Clurman's direction of *Night Music*. As to the organization of the theater, Odets explained,

> [W]hat I was looking for...was a Group setup in which *we* made the circumstances as much as possible...I expected and intended to force the New York Theatre to adapt itself to us rather than to continue adapting ourselves to it. This is to be done by real planning and foresight, by hard work, by constant thought and practice. It is no longer...my intention to buck Broadway in terms of *its* values and standards.

According to Clurman, Odets accused him on this occasion not only of giving in to Broadway but also of abandoning dreams of a low-priced, repertory theater. In answer to Clurman's statement that it would take someone over a year just to plan for the kind of theater he wanted, Odets offered to procure $35 a week from the producer Billy Rose for Clurman to undertake the task. This demeaning proposal was made at the very moment when Clurman was preparing to leave for Hollywood to be considered for an important job at MGM.

Odets lashed out at the actors, too. In his journal, he attacked them for having become "VERY flabby!," taking their cue from Clurman's weaknesses, including his inability to plan. "We have all had our Hollywood at home, right here," Odets catalogued the frequently repeated list of sins of which they were all, including himself, guilty, namely, lack of personal and artistic respect and lack of artistic discipline and growth. He accused the actors of "subtle but nevertheless genuine moral and spiritual sabotage," and derided their appeals for greater democracy. Yet, he blamed Clurman for failing in his responsibilities to the "simple souls who essentially are the Group Theatre" (3/13/40, *TisR*, 64–65). Ever critical of his old cronies and complaining of the "great sacrifices" he was being called on to make—he spent thousands of dollars to cover the weekly losses on *Night Music*—Odets met with the planning committee, in which Phoebe Brand seemed to have replaced Proctor. His irritation with Brand for bringing everything "into line according to Communist doctrine," and her disappointment in his retreat from activism added further tension to their deliberations. (6/3/40; *TisR*, 178)

When Odets returned to New York in April after a trip to nurse the wounds of his latest failure, he began to see a good deal of Lee Strasberg, with whom he found himself at ease for the first time in their ten-year relationship. The situation in the Group was obviously among the many things they talked about. Looking to the future rather than the past, Strasberg declared that "the Group was the only place where it would be possible for a theatre worker to function in the theatre" (4/17/40: *TisR*, 120). Odets held Strasberg to be "the most talented theatre director in the English-speaking theatre." "By all means the contradictions of his and Harold Clurman's natures should be resolved into what must necessarily be a higher level of synthesis for the Group" (4/10/40; *TisR*, 111). The return of Strasberg was urged again and again in the Group's final year.

Meeting at the Carnovsky house on May 6, this time with Max Gorelik and Sandy Meisner added, the Committee viewed their Constitution as "in itself a plan of action." Odets confided in his journal: "I was dismayed, disappointed, and angered to find the same old sick and timorous fixation on a 'constitution and democracy.'" He heatedly told the Committee that they had "neglected to chart" all the "practical workings of the theatre." Nevertheless, Odets also noted that despite his irritation, he sided with the actors in "this fight to clarify what is the Group Theatre." Of Clurman, he wrote, "It is my distinct impression, which I shall soon tell him, that he has been trying to fit the Group Theatre into his life which is mostly composed of other elements [namely Stella] that are mostly against the healthy life of a theatre" (5/6/40; *TisR*, 144). In Hollywood, where he seemed unable to get a job and needed money, Clurman wrote to Odets that he "still believes in the theatre," but is "a little sad at the foolishness of the Group actors."

On May 10, the Committee offered all the assembled members their elaborate report, which included a plan for a seasonal method of operation and the Constitution as the basis for the "inner government" of the Group. They considered these plans mature steps for finally carrying out the objectives laid out in the Actors' Report of 1936. After reviewing the economics of the actors' struggles over the years and the hit-or-miss financing of shows in the past, the plan projected a scheme based on renting a theater for a whole season and reducing operating costs; financing five productions as a single project by a collective group of investors; and building on benefit sales to guarantee a six-week-run for each show. The Committee's schedule of activity for 1940 included a dramatization of *Trouble in July* by Erskine Caldwell, which Clurman had already bought; a new Odets play; a classic, possibly *Othello* with Paul Robeson as guest artist; studio presentations of new plays by younger writers; symposia, rehearsals, and long-term training for playing the classics. As to directors for all this activity, they noted: "We are lousy with directors...Harold Clurman, Robert Lewis, Elia Kazan, Lee Strasberg." For all their pages of figures, complex calculations, and definite plans, the $100,000 investment to initiate the plan loomed as the perennial stumbling block along with personal and political clashes that belied the statements about "our unified will and collective judgment."

The Constitution seems an ironic document to cap the long struggle over the inner governance of the Group. Based on a corporate model, it set out in legalistic terms an elaborate scheme based on the authority of the theater being vested in the general membership, who annually elect from among themselves a board of directors, from which officers of the corporation shall be chosen. A certificate of membership would finally identify who was legally a member, with elaborate voting procedures for granting and revoking membership, handling grievances, approving leaves, and employment of nonmembers. The theater would be under no obligation to employ any of its members or to guarantee any salaries, but could do so if desired. Regulations governed meetings, dues, and distribution of income. Crucial appointments by the board were covered: a studio director and a play reader (who must be members of the corporation); a business manager, a promotion manager, a publicity manager, and an office manager, who need not be members; and a play director who need not be a member but must submit a plan of production to the board of directors for approval before being given full charge of the production.

The committee pointed out that this very "conservative" Constitution was "calculated broadly to effect a streamlined democratic centralism." The actors were very proud of what they had put together. A handwritten note in a copy belonging to Gorelik, however, revealed the ongoing tensions. It read, "[S]abotaged by Clifford Odets, Elia Kazan, and Bobby Lewis." Although the report and the Constitution were voted in, the committee members recognized that their Constitution was "a FORM, not a content." Legal structures and elaborate financial calculations could not restore the deep satisfactions of their shared activities, could not make them once again an ensemble seeking to express itself in the collective art of theater or restore their unified community with a shared vision of society and art. The content had come from the people, the Idea, and the times. The early days of the Depression had intensified their need for togetherness and stimulated an activist spirit of social change that made them part of a larger radical movement. Their deliberations in the summer of 1940 were undertaken against the background of the collapse of Western Europe under the heels of Hitler's troops. The uncertainty of which way the Soviet Union would turn agitated the radicals in the Group. Odets's journal alternates notes on the Group's organizational meetings with questions about whether he should sign an antiwar resolution by his communist cronies or reject their notion that "France and England are as bad in this fight as Hitler's Germany." Then, too, which way would America turn? Fragmentation and anxiety, not solidarity and hope, marked the first year of the new decade as the Group was trying to "continue the life line of the organization."

Hitler's troops marched into Paris on June 23, the day Clurman returned from Hollywood, where he had ruined his own chances for a job by screaming boastfully about "ten years of the Group's accomplishments" when it was suggested that he serve a year's "apprenticeship" to the movie business. Clurman wrote that "the outside world in its crack-up appeared to justify the sense of breakdown within me." He may not have been speaking metaphorically; Robert Ardrey wrote of Clurman having a nervous breakdown at the end of 1939, although for reasons more "personal than political." Clurman now rejected the communist line that lumped the Allies with the Nazis as imperialists. It was "wrong even though correct," he told Odets. After destroying Hitler, "the masses, guns in their hands, can turn on their enemies at home." Clurman and Odets both felt that "there was not one thing that you could be for today with certainty that...you would be for tomorrow too." Although their opinions about the geopolitical scene roughly converged, the two men remained far apart on what to do about the Group. All summer, there were discussions over dinners, coffees, and drinks, with Clurman unprepared to do anything and Odets pressing for a total reconsideration. Odets argued that the Group would have to become for them again a "home, a place to work, 'an ideologically cemented collective." If the company can't boldly make this transformation, it's "the movies for us," he declared. (8/19/40; *TisR*, 250–51)

By August, Odets was telling Clurman that he was fed up with the actors, whom he called "minor Parsifals" (*FY*, 274). Both men were retreating from responsibility for the Group to concern with "the truth of myself," as Odets put it. Clurman agreed, hoping that "everyone in the Group would find his or her own TRUE CENTER, for only in that way would a Group Theatre evolve which could be useful to itself and its people and the theatre in general" (7/31/40, *TisR*, 229).

With Odets back in Hollywood working on the screenplay of *Night Music*, Clurman called a company meeting on September 5 to discuss the coming season. He was planning to produce Irwin Shaw's *Retreat to Pleasure* and possibly *Trouble in July* [Victor Wolfson's play based on Erskine Caldwell novel] without necessarily casting Group actors or providing any economic support for them. He was going to work "untrammeled by considerations of duty or ideology." He rejected the Committee's Report and Constitution as a "restatement of what I had hoped to achieve ever since we had come together," but lacking specifics about "time and money to realize its design." He could see no other way but to "carry on at this point as if I were an independent producer" (*FY*, 273).

Clurman's pronouncements came as a "rude jolt" to the actors after their collective efforts to save the Group. Clurman's tendency to reduce the actors' arguments to absurdity rather than deal rationally with them led to angry exchanges. Carnovsky and Meisner protested that the freedom Clurman was offering them was the freedom to be exploited by those who own the theater and the means of production. The Constitution was defended by Gorelik as "protection for the people...against those in positions of delegated authority and power." But, it was Clurman's old pal Sandy

Meisner who asked the crucial question: "How can there be a Group Theatre production without Group actors in it?" Clurman's answer led the actors to a conclusion they could hardly believe. He insisted that any play directed by Harold Clurman was to be considered a Group Theatre production, and, in fact, Clurman considered himself to be the Group Theatre. In a close analysis of Clurman's virtues as well as limitations as a director, Michael Gordon suggested that Clurman did not fully realize how dependent he had been on the Group. "I would like to remind you," he said, "that in every play you've directed, you've had, for the most part, actors who were truly creative artists in their own right; actors who not only had the capacity to be enkindled by your images, but who had the technique to translate these impressions into concrete theatre terms. Not all directors are so fortunate."

Clurman remembered that the meeting grew ugly. His offer to step aside for anyone who could successfully carry on "our common task" was interpreted as yet another mocking affront to the actors, who at the same time complained that he was "abandoning" them in the crisis. "Words flew wildly... I lost self-control, and in my desire to make the basic situation clear my emotion burst forth in a deluge of angry sounds, desperate exaggerations, wild obfuscations. Some of the actors turned from me as from a man lost." Luther Adler summed up the scene by saying sardonically, "Harold wants a divorce" (*FY*, 273).

This was the last official Group Theatre meeting. The marriage was broken; the family torn apart; the form was without content. Clurman carried on in a dispirited manner with *Retreat to Pleasure*, which had no Group actors in any of the major roles, and only Art Smith, Dorothy Patten, and Ruth Nelson in small parts. Odets, looking out for himself, asked Lee Strasberg to direct the "trio" play (renamed *Clash by Night*) he was working on in which he expected Luther Adler and Sylvia Sidney to play the leads. Initially, Odets talked of the Group Theatre as producer, but only, he wrote in his journal, "if we all get together, Lee and Harold particularly, to talk over plans for a new Group organization." After discussion with Clurman, Odets concluded that Clurman himself realized that he was "incompetent to run the Group Theatre." Odets and Strasberg talked of other possible plays to revitalize the Group. Odets wrote in his journal, "FOR LEE STRASBERG IS A WITNESS TO MY LIFE AND WORK! Shall I say the NEW witness?" (11/29/40, *TisR*, 351).

With the failure of *Retreat to Pleasure*, Clurman informed the actors that he would be in Hollywood for the next six months and that "they were free to do what they would or could in regard to the theatre's affairs at home" (*FY*, 278). For the moment, the Group's office was in the hands of Odets and Strasberg for their production of *Clash by Night*. In the fall of 1941, this show was produced by Billy Rose without any participation by the Group.

There was one final call for a meeting with the actors. Bud Bohnen, acting as secretary, asked them to gather on March 19, 1941. Although there doesn't seem to be any record that the actors responded, the rough notes that the warm-hearted Bohnen jotted down in anticipation of the gathering offer a fitting finale to the question of "Who is the Group Theatre?" and the decade-long struggle to define the Group as an American theater collective. He scribbled that "in every past crisis without fail the Group people found their voice through meetings." He identified their reasons now to have a meeting: to disclaim responsibility for company debts, and "to resign officially, to usurp the driver's seat, to find out who wants the yellow devanport to have and to hold." Most important, as Bohnen saw it, the members needed to decide if they wanted "transitional custody or stewardship of the Group name." It was their one important asset and represented all the "intangibles of the Group's great craft tradition created through devotion, discipline, sacrifice and talent." Bohnen concluded,

> I submit this asset has value, not for us all as individuals in a cash sense, but for the eventual carrying forward of the Group Idea in the American theatre, and should be preserved by us in some fashion to be later used, if needed by whatever coalition of brave spirits emerge... to carry on.

Epilogue: The Survival of an Idea ❧

H elen Chinoy left in her archives at Smith College and in her family files in storage a number of versions of how she envisioned her Group Theatre book taking shape. Our effort to record faithfully in these pages that story as she envisioned it has been foremost in our attempt to edit Professor Chinoy's extraordinary work and to proffer it to interested readers.

In her various ideas for a structure for her book, there are indications in each for a fourth part, variously titled "The Survival of an Idea" or "Success Story: The Legacy." In addition she clearly intended to include in part III a chapter titled "Sinning in Hollywood." The contents of part IV would have included several possible chapters on the Group's influence and legacy, including one on subsequent studios, schools, and conservatories that were natural outgrowths of the Group's efforts and one that focused on Group members and their careers from the 1940s forward on Broadway, in film, and on television.

A thorough search of Chinoy's various files and archives failed to reveal any draft for this final part of her book. Some attention, of course, was given to legacy in the "American Masters" documentary on the Group broadcast on National Public Television in 1989 ("Broadway's Dreamers: The Legacy of The Group Theatre"). Serving as the major consultant for that effort, Helen helped to guide the contents (and extensive interviews) to "chronicle the life, times and achievements of the renowned company of the 1930s that introduced 'method' acting, changed the face of American theatre, and has had a lasting impact on films and television."

But, alas, no official concluding written chapter by Chinoy has been found, and our job as editors has not been foolishly to attempt to copy Helen's style, retrace her extensive research, or even make sense of her scribbled notes in her often undecipherable handwriting in order to construct any of these missing chapters or portions of chapters. Nor do we believe this is necessary. The 14 chapters that appear here provide a fulsome and fascinating view of the Group Theatre's dramatic story, told in Chinoy's unique and captivating style with her extraordinary insight. Nothing more is required. However, in her files there is the text for a talk ("The Chosen Ones: The Legacy of the Group Theatre") that was presented at the Pomidou Center, Paris, on November 5, 1988, for a conference on "The Stanislavsky Century." In the talk Chinoy mentions the ending of the Group in 1941 but adds that "it was not really the end. They grouped and regrouped over the years in famous productions, laboratories, schools, conservatories, and studios. They left a legacy that is evident on stage and screen and television, in colleges and universities, in newspapers and magazine criticism."

Her précis for this talk provides a fitting epilogue for her study of the Group Theatre. It is quoted in the next three paragraphs without comment:

> The basic impulse of the Group Theatre was "the impulse to act," but in the summer of 1931 there were many interferences with this simple human desire "to represent fiction with our bodies." There were the clichés inherited from the 1920s when most actors played glamorous ladies and gentlemen while extraordinary theatrical talents were tragically wasted. To this the Crash of 1929 added economic and social devastation not only of theater but of every aspect of American life. Inspired, however, by the famous US tour of the Moscow Art Theatre, the system of Stanislavsky as taught by Boleslavsky and Ouspenskaya, and by a unique American Depression-bred optimism, Harold Clurman, Cheryl Crawford, and Lee Strasberg gathered their lively, young group for an experiment in theater that also became an experiment in living.

> The Group Theatre based everything on the personal truth of its company of professionals; the experience marked the participants for life. They were the chosen ones. They all acquired the "habit of introspective analysis" and were "ruthless" with themselves. It was a painful struggle—finding plays that expressed their activist vision, resisting the lure of Hollywood, taking sides between Strasberg's "emotional memory" and the emphasis on the "given circumstances" that Stella Adler brought back from her work with Stanislavsky, challenging the authority of the founding directors, marching in May Day parades or supporting left-wing causes, battling their individual temperaments, and surviving as a collective on Broadway. It could have been disastrous——the probing of the inner life, the wrangling, the cliques, the apostasies. Yet something uniquely rewarding held them together. Afraid to lie, they created out of their innermost impulses, but the personal was informed by a large idea that was aesthetic, social, and political.

> It was "a great life experience," a "spiritual home," a "close-knit family," "an oasis within the city," a "utopia." No wonder the Group Theatre has been called "the bravest and single most significant experiment in the history of American theatre."

A final editorial comment: For those readers who desire a more explicit review of the Group's legacy, the large collection of books on aspects of the Group (by such participants as Elia Kazan, Stella Adler, Morris Carnovsky, Clifford Odets, Lee Strasberg, Bobby Lewis, Cheryl Crawford, et al.) are readily available and worthy of attention. Wendy Smith's Epilogue provides strong detail of the Group's legacy in her book. And to narrow the assignment considerably, one could not do better than read Harold Clurman's concluding chapters in the 1975 printing of *The Fervent Years*, especially his two epilogues: 1945–55 and 1974.

Note on Sources ᴏ

Helen Chinoy made the decision early in her writing of the Group's story to minimize scholarly apparatus. Her objective was to follow a scheme "that avoid[s] footnotes in the text." Her intention was to have "notes for each chapter take the form of a running commentary which picks up topics and quotes." She then would expect the reader to locate specific sources for all references in the bibliography. Unfortunately, she only left behind one example of this strategy, while from time to time including in her narrative allusions or direct references to sources. Her one full example actually added several pages to the one sample chapter. The length of her manuscript precluded the editors from following this prescription and adding more words to the total or trying to retrace all of Chinoy's more-than-three-decade research efforts in order to locate *all* her sources.

Still, the editors felt that readers of Chinoy's version of the Group Theatre's history needed some suggestion of sources used and the inclusion of signpost references were most helpful in having some grasp of Chinoy's extensive research of both published and archival sources. Our decision is a compromise of Chinoy's wishes. We've tried not to jeopardize or disrupt her narrative, and we've operated on our shared assumption that Helen Chinoy was the major scholarly authority on the Group; over decades, she had assimilated a vast amount of knowledge on all aspects of the Group (as her archival notes confirm). Thus we urge the reader to trust Chinoy's own unique role as a principal authority on this subject—and American theater in general. We have fact-checked when we felt this was needed and have confirmed (or corrected), when possible, quotations from participants in the Group's history. Chinoy did not leave behind a clear sense of sources used for each chapter, therefore our major chore as editors, other than cutting, or otherwise shortening, each chapter in order to adhere to contractual requirements, has been to cite, briefly, selective sources as deemed possible ("redoing" Helen's extensive research was not our objective). Whenever possible we have gone to published and accessible sources, with limited citation of unpublished, archival sources. We are aware that not all significant quotes have sources cited. We welcome corrections and/or additions so that these can be inserted in subsequent editions. In the text the following abbreviations are frequently used: *FY* (Clurman, *The Fervent Years*); *S&A* (Lewis, *Slings and Arrows*); *TisR* (Odets, *The Time Is Ripe*); *NYT* (*The New York Times*); *NYPL* [New York Public Library (for the Performing Arts, Lincoln Center)]. The bibliography that follows reflects in almost all instances sources we know were used by Helen Chinoy.

In regard to the above, we include here some written comments left by Helen, which help to focus the reader on what she felt most important as sources of authority. She states:

> The essential document of the Group Theatre is Harold Clurman's *The Fervent Years*, originally published in 1945 by Alfred Knopf. The basic information about the people, the chronology, and the history of the theatre comes from this invaluable theatrical and cultural history. Central as Clurman's book is to any study, it is one man's view of what was a group endeavor. In my research, I have undertaken to find out what the experience meant in the lives of the other members. *Reunion: A Self-Portrait of the Group Theatre*, a special issue of the *Educational Theatre Journal*, 1976 [now out of print], is a collection of interviews I have published from my researches.

As the major consultant for the 1989 "American Masters" on The Group Theatre on PBS, Chinoy was also centrally involved with interviews, most undertaken by actress/narrator Joanne Woodward, with many of the original members and associates of the Group, and drew on these in her writing.

In Chinoy's version of the Group's history and especially in allowing participants in this endeavor to speak for themselves,

> some of the quotations attributed to Clurman come from *The Fervent Years*...quotations from other participants and many from Clurman are in *Reunion* or come from unpublished interviews and sources [selectively noted in the text]. The main papers of the Group Theatre (including its scrapbooks) are in the Billy Rose Theatre Collection, Library of the Performing Arts, Lincoln Center, New York. The Manuscript Collection at Columbia University Library, New York, has important papers of Clurman and the Columbia Oral History Project Collection has interviews with several Group members.

Since completing her research, the Library of Congress has acquired relevant papers of Lee Strasberg (still in the possession of Anna Strasberg during the years of Chinoy's research) and the Harry Ransom Center, the University of Texas, Austin, has recently added papers of Stella Adler and Harold Clurman to its collection, some seen by Chinoy while still possessed by Adler and Clurman.

In our compiled bibliography, which focuses primarily on published sources used most extensively by Chinoy (and indicated by an asterisk preceding the reference), we include Wendy Smith's *Real Life Drama: The Group Theatre and America, 1931–1940* (1990), an extensive history not used directly by Chinoy but clearly read by her and consulted often to confirm facts, chronology, and the like (her copy of the book with extensive notes survives). But it should be underscored that Chinoy's objective in her history is quite different from that of Smith, who undeniably sought to be as complete as possible, approaching the Group's history as a well-versed outsider. Chinoy, who was born in 1922, lived through the Depression years and admits, as she does in the introduction, that in her late teens she had what some considered radical ideas, especially in her perception of the American theater of the day. Though too young to know the Group intimately, she was aware of it, grew up in nearby Newark, and earned degrees at New York University and Columbia, thus experiencing intimately the theater of the 1930s and 1940s in New York City.

Chinoy's aim was to tell the Group's story as personally and authoritatively as she could, drawing on the words of the participants, providing the reader the context for the decade of the Group's life, offering glimpses of the excitement in the theater of the Group, and finally providing the complex history in broad strokes, warts and all, rather than in a detailed blow-by-blow account, useful though that is. Chinoy's extensive notes, relevant books, and drafts of most chapters can be consulted in her files in the Smith College Archives, Northampton, Massachusetts.

Select Bibliography ❧

An asterisk (*) indicates sources used most extensively by Chinoy; these are from her personal library and include extensive notes inserted plus marginalia. A few titles published since Chinoy's illness in the mid-1990s are cited here, helpful to the editors in various ways.

Aaron, Daniel, and Robert Bendiner. *The Strenuous Decade: A Social and Intellectual Record of the Nineteen-Thirties*. NY: Anchor Books, 1970.

*Adams, Cindy. *Lee Strasberg: The Imperfect Genius of the Actors Studio*. NY: Doubleday, 1980.

Adler, Stella. *The Art of Acting*. NY: Applause Books, 2000.

———. *A Technique of Acting*. NY: Bantam Books, 1988.

Allen, Frederick Lewis. *The Big Change: America Transforms Itself 1900–1950*. NY: Harper & Row, 1952.

———. *Since Yesterday: 1929–1939*. NY: Harper & Row, 1940.

"The American Actor." *Yale/Theatre*. Vol. 9, nos 2&3, spring 1977. Includes essays/interviews with Stella Adler, Sanford Meisner, Lee Strasberg, et al.

Ardrey, Robert. *Plays of Three Decades*. NY: Collins, 1968.

Ashby, Clifford Charles. "Realistic Acting and the Advent of the Group in America: 1889–1922." PhD diss., Stanford University, 1963.

Barranger, Milly S. *A Gambler's Instinct: The Story of Broadway Producer Cheryl Crawford*. Carbondale: Southern Illinois University Press, 2010.

Baxandall, Lee. *Radical Perspective in the Arts*. Harmondworth: Penguin Books, 1972.

Benedetti, Jean. *Stanislavski*. London: Methuen & Co., 1988.

Bentley, Eric. *The Theatre of Commitment*. NY: Atheneum, 1967.

———. *Thirty Years of Treason*. NY: Viking Press, 1978.

Bentley, Joanne. *Hallie Flanagan: A Life in the American Theatre*. NY: Alfred A. Knopf, 1988.

Berkson, Michael A. "Morris Carnovsky: Actor and Theatre." PhD diss., University of Illinois, 1975.

Boleslavsky, Richard. *Acting: The First Six Lessons*. NY: Theatre Arts Books, 1933.

Boris Aronson: From His Theatre Work. Exhibition Catalogue. NY: NYPL at Lincoln Center, 1981.

*Brenman-Gibson, Margaret. *Clifford Odets: American Playwright: The Years from 1906 to 1940*. NY: Atheneum, 1981.

Burke, Kenneth. *A Grammar of Motives*. NY: Prentice-Hall, 1952.

———. *The Philosophy of Literary Form*. Baton Rouge: Louisiana University Press, 1941.

Carnovsky, Morris. *The Actor's Eye*. NY: Performing Arts Journal Publications, 1984

———. *Theatre Arts Magazine* (June–July 1948).

*Carrington, Hardy Michael. "The Theatre Art of Richard Boleslavsky." PhD diss., University of Michigan, 1971.

Chinoy, Helen Krich. "The Impact of the Stage Director on American Plays, Playwrights, and Theatres: 1860–1930." PhD diss., Columbia University, 1963.

*Chinoy, Helen Krich, ed. "The Chosen Ones: The Founding of the Group Theatre." In *Theatrical Touring and Founding in North America*. Edited by L. W. Conolly. Westport, CT: Greenwood Press, 1982. 135–52.

———. "The Poetics of Politics: Some Notes on Style and Craft in the Theatre of the Thirties." *The Theatre Journal*, vol. 35, no. 4 (December 1983): 475–98.

———. *Reunion: A Self-Portrait of the Group Theatre*. Reprinted from the *Educational Theatre Journal*, vol. 28, no. 4 (December 1976): 443–552.

Chinoy, Helen Krich, and Linda Walsh Jenkins. *Women in American Theatre*. 1981. 3d revised ed. NY: Theatre Communications Group, 2005.

Ciment, Michael. *Kazan on Kazan*. NY: Viking Press, 1974.

Clurman, Harold. *All People Are Famous*. NY: Harcourt, Brace, Jovanovich, 1974.

———. *The Collected Works of Harold Clurman*. Ed. Marjorie Loggia and Glenn Young. NY: Applause Books, 1994.

———. "Critique of the American Theatre." *The Drama*, April 1931. Reprinted in *The Collected Works of Harold Clurman*, 1–4.

*———. *The Fervent Years: The Group Theatre and the Thirties*. NY: Alfred Knopf, 1945; NY: Da Capo Press, 1975, with new introduction by Stella Adler (1983).

———. "Group Theatre's Future." *New York Times*. May 18, 1941. Reprinted in *The Collected Works of Harold Clurman*, 37–40.

———. *On Directing*. NY: The Macmillan Company, 1972.

Cole, Toby, compiler, with intro. by Lee Strasberg, *Acting: A Handbook of the Stanislavski Method*. Rev. ed. NY: Crown Publishers, 1955.

Cole, Toby, and Helen Krich Chinoy. *Actors on Acting*. 1949. NY: Crown, 1980.

———. *Directors on Directing*. 1953. NY: Bobbs-Merrill, 1963.

Cooney, Terry A. *Balancing Acts: American Thought and Culture in the 1930s*. NY: Twayne Publishers, 1995.

Copland, Aaron. *Copland: 1900 Through 1942*. NY: St. Martin's, 1984.

Corey, Lewis. *The Crisis of the Middle Class*. NY: Covici-Friede, 1935.

Cosgrove, Stuart. "Prolet Buehne: Agit-prop in America." In *Performance and Politics in Popular Drama*. Ed. by David Bradby, Louis James, and Bernard Sharratt. Cambridge, UK: Cambridge UP, 1980, 201–12.

Cowley, Malcolm. *Exile's Return*. NY: Viking Press, 1951.

———. *Think Back on Us*. Carbondale: Southern Illinois University Press, 1967.

Craig, Edward Gordon. *On the Art of the Theatre*. Chicago: Browne's Bookstore, 1911.

*Crawford, Cheryl. *One Naked Individual*. NY: Bobbs-Merrill, 1977.

Deutsch, Helen, and Stella Hanau. *The Provincetown: A Story of the Theatre*. NY: Russell and Russell, 1931.

The Drama Review: The Group Theatre Issue, vol. 28, no. 4 (Winter 1984): 1–72.

Engel, Lehman. *This Bright Day: An Autobiography*. NY: Macmillan, 1974.

Evans, Alice. "A Theatre of Action." *New Theatre* (May 1934): 11–12, 33.

Farmer, Frances. *Will There Really Be a Morning?* NY: G.P. Putnam's Sons, 1972.

Fearnow, Mark. *The American Stage and the Great Depression, A Cultural History of the Grotesque*. Cambridge, UK: Cambridge University Press, 1997.

Filippov, Boris. *Actors without Make-up*. Moscow: Progress Publishers, 1977.

Flanagan, Hallie. "A Theatre Is Born." *Theatre Arts Magazine* (November 1931): 909.

Fletcher, Anne. *Rediscovering Mordecai Gorelik: Scene Design and the American Theatre*. Carbondale: Southern Illinois University Press, 2009.

The Flying Grouse. Group Theatre magazine. Two issues published: February and June 1936.

Garfield, David. *A Player's Place: The Story of the Actors Studio*. NY: Macmillan, 1980.

Gasper, Raymond D. "A Study of the Group Theatre and Its Contributions to Theatrical Production in America." PhD diss., Ohio State University, 1955.

*Gassner, John. *Producing the Play*. NY: The Dryden Press, 1941. Included are essays by Clurman, Lewis, and Gorelik, each closely studied by Chinoy.

Gold, Michael. "A Bourgeois Hamlet for our Times." *New Masses*, April 10, 1934.

Goldstein, Malcolm. *The Political Stage*. NY: Oxford University Press, 1974.

Gorchakov, Nikolai. *The Vakhtangov School of Stage Art*. Moscow: Foreign Languages Publishing House, n.d.

Gorelik, Mordecai. *New Theatres for Old*. NY: Samuel French, 1940.

Gornick, Vivian. *The Romance of American Communism*. NY: Basic Books, 1977.

*Hethmon, Robert H., ed. *Strasberg at the Studio*. NY: Viking, 1975.

*Himelstein, Morgan Y. *Drama Was a Weapon*. New Brunswick, NJ: Rutgers University Press, 1963.

*Hirsch, Foster. *Kurt Weill on Stage: From Berlin to Broadway*. NY: Knopf, 2002.

———. *A Method to Their Madness: The History of the Actors Studio*. NY: Norton, 1984.

Houghton, Norris. *But Not Forgotten*. NY: William Sloan Publishers, 1951.

———. *Entrances and Exits: A Life In and Out of the Theatre*. NY: Limelight Editions, 1991.

Houseman, John. *Runthrough*. NY: Simon & Schuster, 1972.

Kaplan, Alan, and Thomas Klein. *Harold Clurman: A Life of Theatre*. PBS Documentary, July 3, 1989.

*Kazan, Elia. *A Life*. NY: Alfred A. Knopf, 1988.

Kazin, Alfred. *On Native Grounds* (1942). NY: Anchor Books, 1956.

———. *Starting Out in the Thirties*. Boston: Atlantic–Little, Brown, 1965.

Klehr, Harvey. *The Heyday of American Communism: The Depression Decade*. NY: Basic Books, 1984.

Kreymborg, Alfred. "America, America!" In *Proletarian Literature in the United States*. Ed. Granville Hicks and others. International Publishers, 1935.

Krutch, Joseph Wood. *The American Drama Since 1918*. NY: Random House, 1939.

Lahr, John. Review of *Awake and Sing!* revival. *New Yorker*. October 26, 1992.

Langner, Lawrence. *The Magic Curtain*. NY: E.P. Dutton & Co., 1951.

Lawson, John Howard. *Processional!* NY: Thomas Seltzer, 1925.

*Lewis, Robert. *Advice to the Players*. NY: Harper and Row, 1980.

———. *Method or Madness?* NY: Samuel French, 1958.

*———. *Slings and Arrows: Theater in My Life*. NY: Stein and Day, 1984.

Lyon, James K. *Bertolt Brecht in America*. Princeton, NJ: Princeton University Press, 1980.

Macgowan, Kenneth, and Robert Edmond Jones. *Continental Stagecraft*. 1922. Reprint. NY: Benj. Blom, 1964.

MacLeish, Archibald. "The Hope for Poetry in the Theatre." *New Theatre* (December 1935): 9.

Malague, Rosemary. *An Actress Prepares: Women and "The Method."* NY: Routledge, 2012.

Malden, Karl. *When Do I Start?: A Memoir*. NY: Simon & Schuster, 1997.

McConachie, Bruce A. *Melodramatic Formations: American Theatre and Society, 1820–1870*. Iowa City: University of Iowa Press, 1992.

McDermott, Douglas. "The Theatre Nobody Knows: Workers Theatre in America, 1926–1942." *Theatre Survey* (May 1965): 65 ff.

Meisner, Sanford, and Dennis Longwell. *Sanford Meisner On Acting*. NY: Random House /Vintage Books, 1987.

Miller, Arthur. *Timebends*. NY: Grove Press, 1987.

Miller, Gabriel. *Clifford Odets*. NY: Continuum, 1989.

Mordden, Ethan. *The American Theatre.* NY: Oxford University Press, 1981.

Munk, Erica. "A Theater in Search of a Politics." *Village Voice.* June 15, 1982.

Murray, Edward. *Clifford Odets: The Thirties and After.* NY: Frederic Ungar, 1969.

Navasky, Victor. *Naming Names.* NY: Viking Press, 1980.

*Odets, Clifford. *Six Plays of Clifford Odets.* NY: The Modern Library [*ca.* 1935] 1963.

*———. *The Time Is Ripe: The 1940 Journal of Clifford Odets.* NY: Grove Press, 1988.

Pack, Richard. "Shock Troupe in Action." *New Theatre* (November 1934): 33.

Paris, Barry, ed. *Stella Adler on America's Master Playwrights.* NY: Knopf, 2012.

Paxton, John. "The Fabulous Fanatics." *Stage.* December 1938.

Pells, Richard H. *Radical Visions & American Dreams: Culture and Social Thought in the Depression Years.* NY: Harper & Row, 1973.

Rabkin, Gerald. *Drama and Commitment.* Bloomington: Indiana University Press, 1964.

Reinelt, Janelle. *Crucible of Crisis: Performing Social Change.* Ann Arbor: University of Michigan Press, 1996 (see especially introduction, 1–12).

*Reynolds, Steven Clarence. "The Theatre Art of Robert Lewis: An Analysis and Evaluation." PhD diss., University of Michigan, 1981.

Rich, Frank, and Lisa Aronson. *The Theatre Art of Boris Aronson.* NY: Alfred Knopf, 1987.

Rosenfeld, Lulla. *Bright Star of Exile: Jacob Adler and the Yiddish Theater.* NY: Thomas Y. Crowell, 1977.

Sadkin, Davis. "Emblem of an Era: A Critical History of the Group Theatre in Its Times." PhD diss., Kansas State University, 1970.

*Salvi, Delia Nora. "The History of the Actors' Laboratory, Inc., 1941–1950." PhD diss., UCLA, 1969.

Sarlós, Robert Károly. *Jig Cook and the Provincetown Players.* Amherst: University of Massachusetts Press, 1982.

*Scharfenberg, Jean. "Lee Strasberg: Teacher." PhD diss., University of Wisconsin, 1963.

Shank, Theodore. "Political Theatre, Actors and Audiences: Some Principles and Techniques." *Theater* 10 (Spring 1979).

Sheaffer, Louis. *O'Neill: Son and Artist.* Boston: Little, Brown, 1973.

Sheehy, Helen. *Eva Le Gallienne: A Biography.* NY: Knopf, 1996.

Shnayerson, Michael. *Irwin Shaw: A Biography.* NY: G.P. Putnam's Sons, 1989.

Smiley, Sam. *The Drama of Attack.* Columbia: University of Missouri Press, 1972.

Smith, Julia. *Aaron Copland.* NY: E.P. Dutton, 1953.

*Smith, Wendy. *Real Life Drama: The Group Theatre and America, 1931–1940.* NY: Knopf, 1990.

Steiner, Ralph. *A Point of View.* Middletown, CT: Wesleyan University Press, 1978.

Stevens, Norman. "Case of the Group Theatre." *New Theatre* (July 1936): 26.

Strasberg, John. *Accidentally on Purpose.* New York: Applause, 1996.

*Strasberg, Lee. *A Dream of Passion: The Development of the Method.* Boston: Little, Brown and Co., 1987.

———. "The Magic of Meyerhold." *New Theatre* (September 1934): 14–15, 30.

———. "Moscow Rehearsals." *New Theatre* (May 1936): 19–20, 33.

———. "Russian Notebook." *The Drama Review,* vol. 17, no. 57 (March 1973): 106–21. Also excerpt from Strasberg's "Diary on Visit to Russian, 1934." 110–12.

Strasberg, Susan. *Bitter Sweet.* NY: G.P. Putnam's, 1980.

Taylor, Karen Malpede. *People's Theatre in Amerika.* NY: Drama Book Specialists/Publishers, 1972.

Terkel, Studs. *Hard Times.* NY: Pantheon Books, 1970.

Wagner, Arthur. Interview of Odets, October 9, 1961, for doctoral dissertation. Excerpts published in *Harper's,* September 1966.

Wainscott, Ronald H. *The Emergence of the Modern American Theatre, 1914–1929.* New Haven: Yale University Press, 1997.

Watkins, T. H. *The Great Depression: America in the 1930s.* Boston: Little, Brown and Co., 1993.

Weales, Gerald. *Clifford Odets.* (1971). Paperback ed. NY and London: Methuen, 1985.

Williams, Jay. *Stage Left.* NY: Scribner's, 1974.

Willis, Ronald A. "The American Laboratory Theatre, 1922–1930." PhD diss., University of Iowa, 1968.

Wilmeth, Don B., and Christopher Bigsby, eds. *The Cambridge History of American Theatre. Volume II, 1870–1945.* Cambridge and NY: Cambridge University Press, 1999.

Wilmeth, Don B., with Tice L. Miller, eds. *Cambridge Guide to American Theatre.* Paperback edition. Cambridge: Cambridge University Press, 1996.

Wilson, John. *The Dorothy Patten Story: From Chattanooga to Broadway.* Chattanooga, TN: Chattanooga News-Free Press, 1986. Pp. 31–55 on Group Theatre experience.

Wolfe, Donald Howard. "The Significance of the Group Theatre." PhD diss., Cornell University, 1969.

Zuker, Joel Stewart. *Ralph Steiner: Filmmaker and Still photographer.* NY: Arno Press, 1978.

Index ❧